Canoa

Canoa

TAINO INDIGENOUS DREAM RIVER JOURNEY

MIGUEL A. SAGUÉ-MACHIRAN

CANOA
TAINO INDIGENOUS DREAM RIVER JOURNEY

The people, events and places portrayed in this story as actual people,
places and events are real. Some names of persons and places have been
altered or changed to preserve privacy, but this is all real.

The vast majority of these factual events can be independently corroborated
since the author has led a very public life and much of his activity has been
witnessed, or in some way documented (in some cases by the press).

People, places and events portrayed in this story as features of dreams or visons are just that,
features of dreams and visions. The author represents hereby that these dreams and visions
were really experienced when he says they were experienced as far as he can remember them.

iUniverse books may be ordered through booksellers or by contacting:

iUniverse
1663 Liberty Drive
Bloomington, IN 47403
www.iuniverse.com
1-800-Authors (1-800-288-4677)

ISBN: 978-1-4917-8896-7 (sc)
ISBN: 978-1-4917-8895-0 (e)

Library of Congress Control Number: 2016903198

Print information available on the last page.

iUniverse rev. date: 03/15/2016

CHAPTER I

SHOOTING STAR

1. THE FIFTH SUN

The heat from the small treeless area below created the necessary thermals. All the large bird had to do was apply her graceful streamlined silhouette to these warm updrafts to keep her aloft and even rising. As she spiraled upward the broad panorama beneath her opened ever wider. Huge expanses of green lay there criss-crossed only by an occasional road or two. To the north and west lay the wide silver ribbon of the swollen river as it arched southward toward the reservoir. On the far side of the stream lay the Allegheny Indian Reservation.

The hawk scanned the field below for the slightest sign of movement. Near the New York State Park service buildings on the edge of the clearing there stood several garbage cans, which often times attracted rodents. The bird had learned to watch those spots for possible meals.

To the East and South the formidable verdant carpet of the Allegheny Forest stretched as far as the air-borne eye could see, crossing the invisible state line into Pennsylvania. Each graceful circular sweep of the handsome flying predator brought it over the east bank of the river. As the bird flew over the edge of the water the reflection of the hot August sun caught her squarely in the eye and made her blink involuntarily. She opened her eyes just in time to see a long slender object beneath her, knifing its way down the middle of the stream. Down there, bathed in sweat, two men strained against their canoe paddles trying to cover as much distance as they could before nightfall.

I sat in the back of that canoe and tried my best to maintain the rhythm of my paddling in perfect synchronization with that of my partner. He turned to smile at me. "How are you doing back there?" I had to catch my breath to answer him. "Just fine!" I panted. He grinned through his thick red beard then turned back around to face the front.

Sven and I had been friends for about three years. An artist like myself, he also shared my love for the outdoors and my interests in tribal culture and ancient wisdom from all over the world. Now surrounded as we were by the breathless beauty of the northeastern forest we found ourselves sharing an adventure which I had yearned for and planned for years.

We were navigating the whole length of the Allegheny River practically from its origin at the New York State, Pennsylvania border to its confluence with the Monongahela, 250 miles south at Pittsburgh. We were expecting to spend two weeks on the trip.

The monotonous repetitive action of paddling the canoe in silence, mile after mile had a sort of trance-inducing effect on me. As I kept up the rhythm, my mind drifted. I began to sense a kind of hum, a strange vibration. I can hear it even now as I write this. I sense it best when I close my eyes. It is a kind of dream-noise, a mysterious personal recollection of a primal memory. Every time I've experienced this sensation it has manifested itself as a slow murmur that flows evenly over the darkness. It is a smooth linen sheet sliding up the globular surface of a distended pregnant belly. And so, as I paddled forward, this singular abdominal murmur grew, as it always grows when I dream it. My paddling became automatic, my consciousness of that murmur, overwhelming.

Many times in my dreams I have heard echoes of such a murmur, a kind of primordial contraction. The murmur was silent. It was a quiet murmur in a quiet womb. It was a quiet contraction. It was followed by another and another still, because that is the nature of maternity labor. It is cyclical and repetitive like the smooth strokes of my paddle in the water. And that's just what this murmur was, the echo of a maternity delivery, a birth. Here in the midst of the Allegheny National Forest I was again experiencing that peculiar sensation that had haunted me for years. The unique experience of a cosmic birth; a birth expressed in murmurs. The murmur came in waves, waves that crashed with singular force upon the face of a steadfast will, like the ocean against a sea-cliff. They were quiet contractions which grew and intensified and crashed upon the steadfast sea cliff-will of a determined primogenitress.

I stared at the back of my friend's head as I strove to keep in rhythm with his paddling but I was only partially conscious now of his presence in the canoe. I was entering a kind of trance state and in that trance state I was witnessing a timeless moment of maternal determination. I looked down at the river water all around our canoe. The circular ripples created by the paddle formed into facial features on the surface of the water. They were the features of a female face, straining forcefully as she heaved and pushed, as she bore down on the process of creation. Amid contractions of awesome proportions, in the darkness that no one saw (or failed to see) the sun spirit's head "crowned" in the dilated cervix of his mother's uterus. Our sun was born, and no one witnessed its birth. It traveled the dark tunnel of the galactic birth canal which the Maya ancients called the "Black Road" and emerged unseen into existence. And yet that's precisely the event that I witnessed in my daydream in August of 1982. In waves, with rhythm, in song, in prayer, it was born. We were all born. The new cycle began, amid a spray of stars, planets and asteroids, of future meteors. In the darkness that no one saw, a moan reached no ear. Yet I hear it. I dream it. I see it. I saw it on that placid August afternoon on the Allegheny River in 1982, and I still see it now, sitting here writing these words over 30 years later. I see the primal act of creation and I am present when the first morning dawns. I am witness to the cosmic birth. We are all witnesses to this birth. In our most intimate dreams we witness the ultimate act of creative expression, and the end result of that great primal effort was a wondrous work of art wrought by the ultimate creator spirit, the ultimate artist, the Cosmic Mother. That work of art that we all did or did not witness, which occurred as the end result of that long arduous day of maternity labor was non other than the birth of the Sun itself.

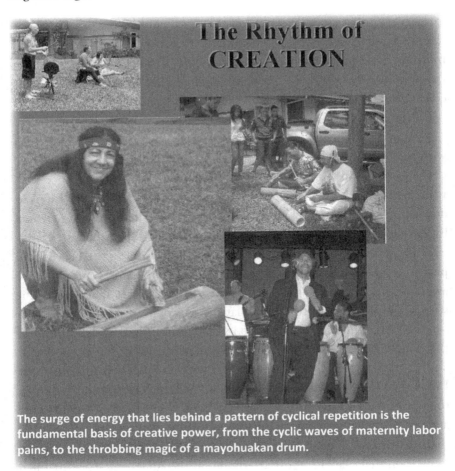

The surge of energy that lies behind a pattern of cyclical repetition is the fundamental basis of creative power, from the cyclic waves of maternity labor pains, to the throbbing magic of a mayohuakan drum.

Today I am a sixty-four-year-old Cuban-American retired school teacher. I am writing this in the year 2015. The subject I taught during the last twenty years of my professional teaching career before I retired was Art. I was an Art teacher. I helped children become conceiving progenitors in their own right by providing them the opportunity to be as creative as the Cosmic Mother was on the day of the sun spirit's birth. They birthed their creations just as she did.

As I sat in the back seat of that canoe I ruminated over the years during which I have become convinced that art is a unique language, a medium of expression which revolutionized my species as early as 260 centuries ago, and maybe earlier still. It was essential for us humans to evolve into artistic beings because to effectively communicate the language of the soul we needed to become creative creatures like the Cosmic Mother, and art is the ultimate expression of creativity. The emergence of Art among humans way back then in the Ice Age was almost like the birth of a great celestial light. It was a kind of solar genesis, the birth of a sun, that illuminated humankind. And so, in a way, at that point when humans discovered art, we can say that a new sun was born also. So, the sun was, indeed, born billions of years ago as the astro-physicists claim, but, in a manner of speaking, it was also born 260 centuries ago, in the IceAge, with the creation of Art. And now, 260 centuries after that birth, it is time for it to be reborn again, because like the repetitive waves of maternity labor, divine births also happen in cycles.

It takes roughly 260 days, in other words, nine months, for a human fetus to come to full term and for the birth of a baby to take place. And likewise, it can be said that it takes 260 sacred units of time for a sun spirit to be born, for anyone to witness its birth. As I said before, I witnessed that birth. When I witnessed that birth I existed in the form of a conscious, etherial, spiritual entity of potentiality, just like you, just like all the rest of humanity. In that form, we all waited patiently those 260 sacred units of time as the cosmic belly grew round and full, and then we watched that cosmic mother give birth to the sun. In that ethereal spiritual form we watched it be born billions of years ago and we also watched it be born 260 centuries ago during the Ice Age when Art was born.

Some of the ancient Indians of what is now Latin America (the region of my origin) called this bright heavenly body "The Fifth Sun" in reference to their belief that this sun was but one in a series of suns which had previously been birthed and then passed on cyclicly, one after the other. So the sun that shone in the sky on that August day when my companion and I paddled down the river in our canoe was, in fact, the Fifth Sun. I believe that the entrepreneurial Maya traders of the Yucatan visited my natal homeland, Cuba, many times over the years on trading journeys, before the coming of the Europeans, and shared some of the secrets of the mystical and symbolic solar birth event with my Taino Indian ancestors. The ancient Tainos, in turn, added the wisdom of those Mesoamerican sages to the wisdom of their own medicine men and dreamers and thus arrived at their own unique poetic interpretation of the primordial birth. The ancient Tainos used the poetic language of their mythic narrative to express the solar birth. They related that the sun, which they called "Guey", travelled down the dark vaginal tunnel of the Cosmic Mother, Ata-Bei, who manifests her body in the form of the bulk of planet Earth, and emerged into the cosmos via a primordial terrestrial cave called "Iguanaboina".

Could it be possible that it was this event, this birth, the birth of the Fifth Sun, that I was experiencing at that moment as I sat in that canoe back in 1982? Could this murmur, this echo of ancient cosmic contractions be the birth of Guey? I wondered silently as I paddled, watching the ripples on the water form themselves into a mother's face. I daydreamed of births. I daydreamed of my own birth. I was born in 1951. And then in 1979, my son was born. Upon that event I was reborn also. My son's birth was a difficult labor. The contractions washed over his mother, my wife, time after time, each one crashing upon her steadfast will. And before this onslaught her will clung tenaciously like the face of a sea-cliff. She was, at that moment, the primordial Cosmic Matriarch incarnated as a human woman.

My son was born on August 10, 1979 via a Caesarean section delivery like the character Deminan of Taino legend. On that day I saw a dark graceful figure rise into the sky, with wings outspread it circled and soared ever upward; the bright flash of rusty red fanning out behind it. I still preserve in my memory that image, to this day. I see there the flight of the red-tailed hawk. In its shrill cry I hear the sacred chant, in its flight the sacred dance, in its eye the sacred art. The majestic bird grants me the gifts of creative hope, compassion, and firm determination, the tools of the artist, the mighty weapons in the timeless battle.

2. SVEN

"Hey Sven, remember when we met?" I called out casually after a long silence. I paddled as I spoke.

Sven kept paddling also as he spoke. "Sure, Miguel...It was an informational demonstration that was part of an in-service workshop at your school. I came in with Betty and the others."

I nodded with a smile. He was correct. He worked for a unique agency called "The Imaginarium". It was headed by a remarkable eccentric named Betty. The organization was, in fact, a performance troupe, dancers, artists, musicians, and of course, "Squeegee", which was Betty's clown persona.

As Squeegee, Betty became transformed. She was a whirlwind of fun and general merrymaking. But it was not just the fact that Squeegee entertained that made her unique. It was the fact that she drew the children wholly into the program. The Imaginarium performance engulfed its mesmerized audience. The children did not just sit and watch. They were drawn physically into the fun, dancing, singing, hopping, and whirling to the rhythm of the talented musicians who always accompanied the magical clown, and creating. The children created large crayon and paint images on enormous sheets of white paper. They co-operated in the creation of bizarre shapes when they were helped bodily into colorful strechy sacks within which they could move and twist and contort, and make themselves into otherworldly forms. Garishly decorated in the colors of Betty's hired face-painters, the children skipped into Squeegee's magical world of art and movement bedecked in colorful corrugated cardboard crowns and crepe paper streamers of their own creation.

Squeegee and the Imaginarium

The Imaginarium was contracted by the educational director of the preschool program where I was working in 1980. They were to put on a demonstration of their organized mayhem to teach us teachers some innovative ways to draw creative behavior out of children. It was a demonstration that changed my whole outlook on childhood. That is how I met Sven. He was multitalented. He could construct all sorts of useful items out of metal or wood, or fix things that had gone wrong under the hood of the Imaginarium's brightly painted old van. He could also play a mean conga drum! Sven was something of a renegade, kind of a black sheep of the family. Something of a hippie, interested in Eastern meditational traditions, the I-Ching of China, and surprisingly, Santeria! Santeria is a ritualistic subculture of Cuba which combines certain aspects of traditional Catholic beliefs and a smattering of Ancient Taino Indian spirituality, with a generous helping of African ceremonial belief from Nigeria. Sven had been introduced to Santeria by an equally talented musician and storyteller who had also done a stint in the Imaginarium. Temugin Ekunfeo, a lifetime resident of the city's predominantly African-American neighborhood of Homewood, had taught Sven about Santeria. Thousands of Cubans migrating into the country throughout the sixties and seventies had established this uniquely New World version of ancient African tradition in the United States and many U.S. African-Americans such as Temugin had embraced it as their own. Sven wasn't black, but that was of no consequence to him. He was fascinated by Santeria. He loved the drumbeats, the chants, the rituals.

"I'm quitting the Imaginarium, Miguel." Sven continued as he paddled on.

"Oh really? that's too bad you're so good." I responded.

He turned around and glanced at me for a minute. "Too much hard work, man! I sprained my wrist two weeks ago lifting some of Betty's heavy boxes!"

He turned back to look forward again and resumed paddling.

"You got another gig lined up?" I asked.

"Well, there is a new outfit starting up next year up on the North Side called the "Pittsburgh Children's Museum". I've already been interviewed. I've got a good chance of being part of the staff when they open."

"Good luck" I told him.

We paddled on in silence for about half an hour then I said: "Hey Sven, which Santeria Spirit do you like best?"

"Oh...let me see." He mumbled. "There is Shango, the spirit of the thunder... too fierce! And then there is Yemaya, and Obatala...but I think my favorite is Ochun...Yea, Ochun the spirit of the river."

He reached down into the water and splashed his face with the cool liquid. Then he scooped up another handful and turning around to face me, his beard still dripping, he extended the little puddle of water in his hand toward me. He smiled and said: "Ochun!"

I was familiar with all the African spirits he had mentioned. These were names I had grown up with. They were part of Cuban culture. African slaves were brought to my native country hundreds of years ago by the Spanish conquerors after the enslaved Native population decreased dramatically. They were brought in to work in the mines and in the tobacco and sugar plantations. These African people brought their culture with them. Each one of their ancient gods became identified with a Catholic saint under the compelling inducement to conversion of the Spanish Catholic monks and priests of that time. Sven had taken the time to inform himself on the facts surrounding all these sacred entities.

"It always fascinates me" he commented "how each of these African spirits became associated with a character from Christian tradition, Yemaya became one of the many manifestations of the Virgin Mary, 'Our lady of Regla'. Babalu is Lazarus, a character from the gospels. The beautiful Ochun, bride of Shango, assumed the persona of that miraculous little statue housed in the chapel that sits on top of the old copper mines in the eastern Cuban Oriente region."

"You know Sven..." I interjected. "That particular statue is said to have been found by two Indian boys and one black boy floating in the waters of Nipe Bay on the north coast of the island. That's why when you see her depicted in religious cards she is always shown in the company of a boat with three men in it. Those three boys fished her out of the water and put her into their boat. Later in the retelling, the legend was changed to include a white boy in the boat. Replicas of the little statue have always been easy to find in stores anywhere along Bergenline Avenue in the Little Havana section of Bergen county, New Jersey and in the Little Havana neighborhood of Miami, Florida for years.

We Cubans call this icon 'Our Lady of Charity of El Cobre'. 'El Cobre' is the name of that old copper mining district in Oriente region. Hundreds of Taino Indians and African blacks had died during the 1500's working as slave miners in the ore-rich hellholes beneath those hills. Now, that hill still stands, all somber but still active. On top of that hill there's a chapel built to house the icon and there it stands to this day. In a way that chapel is a kind of peaceful memorial to the vanquished races, who have somehow survived five centuries of oppression. And it is also a kind of testament to the power of reconciliation between races."

"Yea…" Sven added. "And Temujin's Cuban friends told me that the way the legend goes, the statue itself chose the location of its final enshrinement-place. The peasants of Indian and African descent in the area, whose men worked and died in those mines, tell that when the statue was found by those three boys in the water up north it was brought to shore and it originally was stored up there near the large bay. But soon it began to behave in pretty peculiar ways. Some say that it disappeared from there and reappeared down south in El Cobre. What I heard was that the peasants swear that this happened several times until the local ecclesiastical authorities finally conceded to building her the chapel over that old mine.

"Exactly!" I agreed. "It was as if that melancholy little icon insisted on keeping a perpetual vigil over the graves of her native children who were buried in death right there were they had toiled in life."

Then Sven concluded: "The interesting thing about those popular legends is that her behavior seems to mimic the behavior of ancient Taino sacred images as it was recorded by the Spanish. The colonial records confirm that according to Native informants, ancient Taino sacred images sometimes would dissappear from places that did not suit them and would re-appear in other places where they preferred to be." I was amused at how well-informed my Anglo-American friend was about all those obscure elements of Cuban culture.

Popular legend aside, documented historical records from the previous century which I myself had discovered in the book "Cuba, Economia Y Sociedad" by the Cuban researcher Levy-Marrero confirm the arrival on the southern coast of Cuba of a shipwrecked crew headed by a Spaniard named Ojeda at a time when the island was still unexplored by Europeans. Ojeda was a pious Catholic, deeply devoted to the Virgin Mary. He carried with him a small figure of this saint to which he prayed periodically throughout his difficult travail in the mangrove swamps near the shore. He prayed, asking the Virgin Mary to deliver his group in that desperate hour of need. Ultimately he pledged to give the statue in gratitude to the first people who came to his aid.

Ojeda and his men were finally rescued by a group of Taino Indians from the village of Cueiba. True to his pledge he gave them the statue, just as he had sworn. To his surprise, the Indians welcomed the gift as if they had always been expecting it. They enshrined it in a native temple and adorned it with beautiful native cloths. Then they sang chants to it and performed dances normally reserved for their mother spirit Ata-Bei.

Three years later, the Spanish missionary/historian, Bartolome De Las Casas, visited that region and witnessed a great areito feast dedicated to the little Catholic icon by the local Tainos. Eventually the little statue vanished from the historical record during the bloody conquest of Cuba by the Spanish that took place soon after Las Casas' visit. I had read about this incident in Cuban history and I was convinced that it was this same statue that made her miraculous reappearance almost a century later in the waters of Nipe Bay. How ironic it is that, after one hundred years in hiding the little statue should reveal herself to a group of simple peasants, one black and the other two, Indians.

As they fished the miraculous statue out of the water they noticed it was sitting on a wooden board which bore the following inscription: "I am the Virgin of Charity."

These thoughts danced around in my head as I continued to paddle.

"Hey, Sven..." I finally called out.

"Uh-huh" He answered absently.

"Did you ever hear the old Afro-Cuban legend of Ochun and Babalu?" I offered.

Sven shifted in his seat. "No. I don't think I've ever heard that one." His curiousity was aroused.

"Well," I began using my best story-telling voice, learned from my santero friend Temujin. "It seems that the chief sky spirit Olofin got very angry at Babalu for some serious infraction that the latter had committed. Olofin cursed Babalu and made him sick. Soon Babalu's body was covered with sores. In a couple of days he died.

11

The river spirit Ochun felt that the punishment Olofin had meted out to Babalu was too severe. She came to Olofin and begged him to restore Babalu to life. Olofin was unmoved by her entreaties. He refused to grant her this wish..."

"That's why I like Ochun..." Sven interrupted. "She's nice!"

I agreed with him. In keeping with her identification with a so-called "Lady of Charity" Ochun appears charitable and kind-hearted in this legend. And yet as I continued the story, I realized that the river-goddess also exhibited a wily, imaginative inventiveness which ultimately proved her the winner in her contest of wills with the supreme Yoruba deity.

"Ochun approached Orumbila, the confidant of the spirit Olofin. In secret she asked him to help her cast a spell on Olofin. Orumbila consented, so Ochun handed him a container of magic honey and asked him to sprinkle it all over Olofin's palace. The sweet aromatic charm of the magic nectar overwhelmed the powerful spirit so that he longed for more.

'Who has anointed the rooms of my house with this fragrant substance?' He demanded. 'I must have more...Orumbila, Come here tell me how I can have more of this stuff.'

Orumbila, who was in on the trick, answered him: 'Master, I can not provide what you ask for. Only a woman can bestow this gift upon you.'

Olofin was desperate. He seemed addicted. 'I must have more!' He cried out. 'What woman has anointed my house?' He went from room to room questioning every female in the palace. Finally he approached Ochun. 'Was it you that spread this delicious stuff all over my home?' He asked her.

'Yes.' She answered triumphantly. 'And I can get you as much as you want. But first you must bring Babalu to life!'

Olofin was helpless. The delicate young river goddess had overcome the powerful old sky god. Olofin brought Babalu back to life and Babalu became an important devotional personality in the Afro-Cuban spiritual pantheon."

Charitable compassion and creative inventiveness verging on craftiness, as well as all manner of love magic clung to every interpretation of the El Cobre icon like a mantle. It seemed that the interracial triangle of hope was quite complete in this remarkable little statue. The white conqueror, Ojeda saw in her kind compassionate face the hope for immediate salvation for him and his crew in their moment of desperation. The African Yorubas saw Ochun, wily and creative in the way she exercised her charity. The Indians saw in her Ata Bei, the mother of the waters, the Earth spirit, mistress of creativity and creation, nurturing, kind, sustainer of all life. And yet at the bottom of all her interpretations the little icon contains one focal aspect of symbolism which encompasses all the rest; it is <u>Loving Compassion</u>.

These were my thoughts about Ochun as I paddled along in the back of the canoe that sunny August afternoon. The sun arched across the sky overhead as we paddled in unison all day, and before we knew it night fell. We were forced to drag the canoe up onto the river bank and search for a campsite. We climbed up the steep side of a hill in the dark, our path Illuminated by flashlights in our search.

A little after midnight during the dark early hours of the new day on August 10, 1982, a large chunk of extraterrestrial matter entered the earth's atmosphere. This happened in the very earliest hours of the morning on my son's third birthday while the sky was still pitch black. During that night, a large chunk of rock from outer space died. It died after traveling billions of miles across the solar system, it died quietly, but as it died it created a brilliant display across the clear star-studded sky over the hills of Northwestern Pennsylvania. It burned spectacularly, painting a streak of light overhead, and then it disintegrated in a white flash of hot friction as it entered the earth's atmosphere. Its death did not go unnoticed in the night. I saw it die. It died quickly. At that moment I did not view its death as something negative. I perceived it as something beautiful. When I saw it I called it a "shooting star." In my mind's eye it seemed to be born suddenly out in the corner of the sky. It seemed to travel from right to left and to fade gradually, leaving a glowing streak behind itself. It is a wonder to me that I should perceive the death of a rock as the birth of a star. Was that event good? Was it evil? Was it a birth? Was it a death? No human being on earth would ever have found out about that rock's existence had it not died so spectacularly.

I was very tired that night. My travelling companion and I needed that beautiful spectacle to make us forget our fatigue. It was pretty! The pleasure was better because we could share it with each other, so we did, as we stood high on a wooded ridge in the Allegheny National Forest of northwestern Pennsylvania. We perceived it as a good omen. We gazed upon the catastrophic demise of an ancient entity. We witnessed the end of something that was probably born on the same day as the sun and that had probably traveled down the "Black Road" and emerged out of the vaginal cave, Iguanaboina, with it. We watched it. Then we calmly set up our camp, pitched the tent amid the trees and fell asleep just a few hours before sunrise on the morning of August 10, 1982, the morning of my son's birthday, the morning of the sun's birthday.

3. THE FIRST DREAM

It was the third night of our journey and we had made relatively good time in spite of some minor set-backs. I dozed gradually, comfortably wrapped in my bedroll in the tent. In the background the loud hiss of the water as it rushed over the nearby dam into the river below created a kind of noisy lullaby upon which I was carried almost magically into the realm of sleep. Then, in front of me, dream images began to materialize. I began to see. My eyes struggled to focus in the darkness of sleep. The dream picture sharpened. It became gradually clearer. I began to discern the muted panorama of a tropical forest at midnight.

The deep shadows of the foliage waved and quivered upon the nighttime breeze, a small clearing bathed in brilliant moonlight.

I looked up. Beyond the crowns of the jungle trees, overhead the black sky sparkled with a billion twinkling diamonds; then the sudden flash of a falling star, streaking quietly but splendidly across the stygian dome above.

I heard a sound in the underbrush, a whisper, and then a girlish laugh. Then three slim figures burst out of the thick foliage. I saw the three young girls race out of the bushes and cover the short distance across the clearing in the blink of an eye. They were like three little falling stars, their clean white cotton cloth gowns gleaming brightly in the moonlight against the brooding darkness of the surrounding jungle.

At the riverbank the three girls quickly stripped, shedding their homespun garments. In the moonlight their tanned skin glowed radiant, their smooth long hair shined black as the sky overhead.

Leaving their clothes on the grass at the river's edge the girls splashed into the water, their laughter mingling with the night sounds of the jungle.

14

The cool liquid felt good, a relief from the oppressive heat of the tropical summer night. They splashed water at each other, then with a whoop the oldest, a girl about thirteen years old jumped up and grabbed one of the other two. The other girl fell back laughing as her friend submerged her head playfully in the water.

The splashing, the chasing, the squeals and laughter lasted for about half an hour. It probably would have gone on for another hour. But it didn't. Suddenly the carefree play stopped. The younger girl surfaced and shook her head. She rubbed her eyes and looked at the other two. The other girls stood stock-still in the water. Their chests heaving, their wet hair hung in black cascades around their shoulders.

They stared hard at a clump of trees and bushes just beyond the spot where their clothes lay. At first there was nothing, no sound, no movement. Then there it was again. It was a slight shiver of the branches, a sudden subtle rustle of the leaves. Three sets of large frightened brown eyes stood riveted on the spot. The branches parted and disgorged one figure, a man, running, dashing madly toward the girls in the water.

There was a high pitched scream of terror. The youngest girl barely eleven years old darted sideways, splashing desperately away from the man's path as he approached the river's edge.

The other two girls remained paralyzed where they stood, the cool river water swirling around their hips.

The man looked to his left at the youngest girl when he reached the water. She emerged from the river about eight yards downstream from him. She covered her nakedness as best she could with her hands and padded away on bare feet. She ran through the grass of the clearing disappearing finally into the jungle.

He kept staring hard at the spot where the girl vanished into the foliage. There was an awkward sway to his body as he stood there, the unsteady wobble of inebriation.

He turned his gaze at the two remaining girls. His eyes were glazed and dull. The girls stared back at him, wide-eyed with fear.

Finally he moved. He strode forward into the water. The cool liquid splashed up on his tall leather boots and on the ample stuffed material of his satin pantaloons. As he strode into the stream he glowered and began to mumble: "How many times have I told you not to hang around with this filthy riff-raff..." His speech, sixteenth-century Castillian with a slight Catalan accent, was badly slurred, almost unintelligible. As he moved into the deeper water his hands were tightly balled into fists. "Just because your mother was a heathen savage doesn't mean you have the license to run with these animals. They are nasty, evil-smelling creatures of hell and I won't stand for it!" He was addressing the oldest girl. He approached her in the hip-high water. Her skin was slightly lighter in color than that of her companion betraying her mixed racial ancestry.

"Just look at you...!" He continued. "Here you are standing naked next to this monkey!" He nodded viciously in the direction of the other girl, a much younger child, a shy full-blood Indian. She lowered her face and began to sob.

The Spanish nobleman turned his face back to the light-complected half-breed. She was different. She was older and used to his rantings so she didn't cry. She stood her ground and glared defiantly back at him. The bearded Spaniard stared hard at the young girl.

"Yes..." He continued, taking a step forward in the water. "Yes, I think you have forgotten that my noble blood also runs in your veins. You don't seem to remember that it was I who blessed your heathen mother's womb with my noble seed. You, my dusky little jewel..." Unsteadily he drew nearer to her. "You are, in fact, my offspring, an honor you don't deserve... Yes you are mine. You belong to me, not to these savages..."

The young girl pulled back slightly as she felt the strong smell of wine in the Spaniard's breath. He lifted his hand and made a grand sweeping gesture, which almost caused him to topple into the water. "Well actually this all belongs to me, including unfortunately all these lazy brown Indian apes you love to hang around with so much. But you... you my little jewel, you are special. You are more mine because I begot you... I gave you life!"

With this last word he drew his face very close to the girl. She grimaced in disgust at the smell of alcohol and pulled away. "Oh... You find me repulsive, eh?" He leaned back with a smile. Then he looked over at the full-blood Indian girl standing in the water to his right sobbing and staring at him with a terrified look on her face. "What are you staring at, monkey?" The girl looked down quickly.

The man sighed and looked around him. "I'm so sick and tired of this infernal place, this jungle, these lazy brown monkeys, and the heat, the damned ungodly heat!" He looked back at his daughter. "I would give my whole fortune right now for a month in the cool northern highlands of Catalunia, a week in Barcelona, Ah! A month in the snow-capped Pyrenees..."

The nobleman closed his eyes. Slowly in the blur of his drunken haze he reviewed the story of his personal struggle to rise through the ranks of the army of the Catholic Spanish monarchs from the position of a humble Catalan man-at arms to the position of knighted don. He tried hard to imagine himself back in his cool northern Spanish homeland, but the sound of the full-blood Indian girl's sobbing brought him back to reality. "Shut up!" He screamed turning to glare at her. The girl put her hands up to her mouth and struggled not to make any noise. Again the Spaniard turned back to his daughter. "You draw back away from me... well, I'm drunk. I'm repulsive to you. No matter. Hell! I'm repulsive to my own kin. Look at Roberto, He thinks I'm disgusting too. Ah! yes, big brother... what would I do without him? I would be lost! He manages all my money because I can't do it myself; I'm not good at that sort of thing. Why should I be? I am a gentleman; my skill is in the art of war. I am a warrior. I rode with the great conquistador, Diego Velasquez. I win the treasure. I bring home the spoils of conquest. Let others manage it. That task is beneath me. It is a job for Jews, that's what they do best....well, except for Roberto, he's probably a better money manager than any Jew." The Spaniard tilted his head back and laughed. "Maybe he is a Jew!" He let out another peal of laughter. "Maybe the whole family is Jewish and we had no knowledge of it..." the Spaniard stared hard at his half-breed daughter the smile fading from his face. "You're a member of the family, do you feel Jewish?"

The girl only stared back at him. "No, I don't think so, not you, you are no Jewess. You have the unmistakable mark of these savage heathens stamped on your countenance! You are indeed your mother's daughter. Ah! Now there was a grand heathen for sure!" The man licked his lips as he remembered the girl's mother. "It's a pity she's gone now. Before the smallpox disfigured her face she was by far the most beautiful bitch this heathen race had the courtesy to produce. What a plum that woman was! What a fuck! What a marvelous, black-haired, brown-faced, cassava-eating roll-in-the-hay she was! I had a grand time making you!

Yes my offspring, when I lost your mother to the pox I lost the only thing that made life in this hellhole worth living. And now you are all I have left of her!"

There was a sullen melancholy ring to the Spaniard's last words. "Oh, yes, you find me repulsive... yes of course, I am repulsive..."

He reached out and grabbed the girl's shoulder roughly. She winced and whimpered softly. "Yes, yes I am repugnant. But look at yourself here..." The Spaniard pulled at the girl's shoulder again, and again she winced grimacing. "Just look at you, girl! You are here with these animals up to your bare ass in a forest river, naked...frolicking in the goddamn wilderness like a goddamn savage and naked, naked for Christ's sake!"

The Spaniard lurched forward in the water and grabbed the young girl by both shoulders hard. His rough fingertips dug painfully into her flesh. "You are no better than these beasts..." He ranted, bringing his face up close to hers. The girl yelped with pain and shook away from him with a loud gasp. "Get back here!" He yelled stumbling forward toward her. He latched his strong hands on her shoulders again. The girl brought her hands up and pulled at his fingers digging into her flesh.

She managed to dislodge one of his hands from her aching shoulder then wriggled away from him. But he screamed diabolically and lunged at her. They both fell into the water together.

The man regained his feet first. He stood there wiping the water from his face as the girl got up. He glared at her with a hard mean look in his eyes. "Here you are, like an animal, my own flesh and blood... look at you, and so naked!" He stared hard at her. The girl turned her body away from him and tried to cover herself with her hands.

The man continued to mumble: "Yes, here you are... so wild, so naked, so wild... you are too wild, too wild! You need to be tamed..." He kept staring at her up and down. "Yes, you need to be tamed like a wild animal! I tamed your wild naked mother, and by God I will tame you also!"

With that the man made one last ferocious lunge at the frightened girl and wrapped his arms around her waist. The girl screamed and punched at his face with all her might. The other young woman screamed also and without thinking stepped toward the two struggling figures as they splashed about in the shallow water.

The man pulled away briefly and put a finger on his bleeding lower lip. "You little bitch... you've struck me!" Both girls were sobbing uncontrollably.

The Spaniard's daughter panted, backing away from him. She wiped water from her face, turned and started wading around the man and toward the shore.

"Where are you going?" He yelled and lunged at her again. She screamed. He grabbed her by the hair and jerked her head back. The girl struggled and kept screaming until her voice was choked off as he locked his lips over hers. She stumbled backward gagging into his mouth.

At that point the other girl jumped at him. She splashed on top of him knocking him away from his daughter and began to shower him with punches and kicks.

The Spaniard regained his balance and shoved the Indian girl away from him. Then he stood up and turned to face her. He swiftly drew a long dagger from a scabbard at his belt.

"I'm going to send you back to your heathen gods, you she-ape!" He screamed, and charged at the dark-skinned girl. The terrified child stepped back with a desperate shriek. The Spaniard's daughter brought her hands up to her mouth, her eyes wide. "No!" She yelled. "Don't kill her...!" But the Spaniard reached out grabbed the full blood girl by the wrist and holding her tight, plunged the blade repeatedly into her chest and side. The girl grimaced horribly. Then slowly she slumped into the water.

A huge cloud of blood stained the water all around her as she floated before him face up. The other girl shrieked, then she shrieked again. She covered her eyes with her hands and shook her head desperately. She continued to scream at the top of her lungs.

The man covered his ears with his hands and yelled: "Callate! (Shut up!)" He watched the dead child float away and dropped the dagger. It splashed into the water next to him and sank to the muddy river bottom. His daughter's scream continued to reverberate through the moonlit stillness of the tropical night.

"Shut up, shut up, shut up...." He closed his eyes and tried to clear his head. Then he splashed forward toward her, grabbed her by the wrist and pulled her screaming toward the shore.

The girl began to struggle again but the man stopped suddenly and swung a vicious punch at her jaw. The world grew hazy for her. Her knees buckled in a slowly dimming whirl of pain and she only barely sensed as her attacker hauled her out of the water and unto the riverbank.

She lay on the grass and looked up at him moaning softly as he stood over her and pulled off his breeches.

At this point in my nightmare I began to wake up. I was jolted back to consciousness with the image of the Spaniard violently raping his daughter upon the grass on the bank of the stream.

I woke with such a start that Sven's sleep was also interrupted. "Hey, what happened...?" He mumbled shifting in his bedroll. I rubbed the sleep out of my eyes panting and gasping for air. I was sweating. "It was nothing..." I answered him. "It was nothing, just a bad dream. I just had a bad dream." Sven chuckled and rolled over next to me. Soon he was fast asleep again.

I stayed awake. I stared into the darkness inside our tent. "What the hell was that all about?" I asked myself. I had never had a dream like that before in my life. It was so real, so vivid. Who were those people participating in this violent little drama dressed in what looked like Elizabethan period costumes like actors in a Shakespeare play? And yet whoever they were, I knew they were not acting. The images I saw in my dream had a haunting realism to them, as if in sleep I had peeked into an event in another realm.

I lay there shaken and sweaty. My heart behaved like a machine gun. This was not an auspicious way to spend the early morning hours of my son's third birthday, two hundred miles away from him in the middle of the forest and up to my ass in nightmares.

It was only the third night of my river adventure and I was already having misgivings about it. I decided to go back over the details of the dream but found that it was quickly vanishing from my memory. The more I tried to remember the bloody sequence of events the less I was retaining.

When I realized that analyzing the dream was going to be impossible I turned my mind to other matters, perhaps in an attempt to calm down the rate of my heartbeat or my heavy panting; or perhaps just to keep myself awake for fear that renewed sleep would take me back to the frightening dream. Maybe it was better that I was forgetting it!

I started to think about the beginning of our canoe adventure. The pleasant thoughts of our preparations for this journey and the initial three days we had already spent on it began to calm me and speeded the process by which I was forgetting the dream.

4. THE COLD SPRING LONGHOUSE

Our journey had indeed begun three nights before. In the darkness of the early morning hours on August 8, we arrived by car at the Allegheny Indian Reservation in the westernmost portion of upstate New York. I had called ahead from a gas station telephone booth in Union City, Pa. As we rested just off route 6 our prospective hosts on the reservation had answered my telephone call with their usual warm-hearted hospitality. "Don't look for any pay-campsites" Fidelia laughed amiably over the phone line. "We'll put you up here. You can camp out on our front lawn overnight. Just don't wake us up if you get here real late in the night." The motherly tone of her voice was reassuring. I thanked her and told her we would be very quiet when we arrived to pitch our tents on her grass.

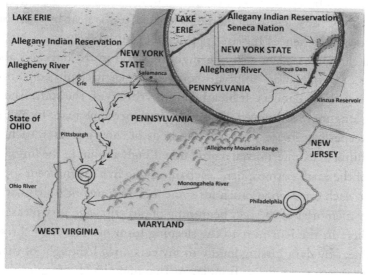

Pennsylvania and parts of neighboring states

We arrived at the Steamburg Resettlement Area of the reservation at 2:00 in the morning. It took us a while to find Fidelia and Avery's home because they had purposely built it back away from the main road where their privacy would be assured. Their little homestead had maize and tomatoes as well as sacred tobacco growing in the yard and an outhouse in the back.

Sven and I put up our tents that night in the front lawn of that one-room cabin up away from the reservation's West Bank Perimeter road. Not far from us on the gravel driveway the old 1976 V.W. van belonging to Rick, our driver, stood quietly, parked for the night.

Rick, a long-time friend and roommate of Sven's had volunteered to drive us here from Pittsburgh for gas money. He had brought his girlfriend Joanie along for the scenic ride. Now, inside their van, the young man and woman nestled into each other's arms drifting off into pleasant sleep. Atop his van, lashed securely to the roof of the vehicle, lay the "Peapod", our twenty-year-old Canadian-built wood and canvas canoe. The Peapod was in mint condition with the original woven cane seats and a brand new coat of green paint, which made it look for all the world like a giant green bean.

In our tent Sven and I slept wrapped in our sleeping bags. We slept with sacred tobacco growing not far from us to our left, tobacco destined, I assumed, for the solemn ceremonies celebrated at the near-by Cold-Spring Longhouse, the Seneca Indian Traditional Spiritual Center.

The longhouse slept also that night. It stood in the darkness about a quarter of a mile away, empty, echoing the ancient chants, dreaming of False Face mask dancers. It breathed in rhythm with the stars. The Cold Spring longhouse journeyed like an initiated medicine man, like a Seneca "faithkeeper", in its sleep. It saw hundreds of shooting stars, each one a large chunk of extraterrestrial matter unwillingly caught in the unforgiving grasp of the earth's atmosphere, each one dying in a magnificent spectacle of light, each one a good omen for someone, on someone's birthday.

My memories of the very beginning of our trip were very pleasant. As I lay there in the tent next to the sleeping form of Sven with the sound of the near-by dam hissing loudly in my ears now, I thought of that first night on Avery and Fidelia's front lawn. That night had been quiet and still, unlike the rugged noisy riverbank we were camping on tonight here, next to the dam. I had dreamed on that night also but, oh boy, those dreams had been so different! I thought about the dreams I had on the first night. It was curious that I could remember clearly the dreams from three nights before but by now couldn't bring up the vaguest image from the nightmare I had just had an hour ago!

Anyway, on that first night there on Avery and Fidelia's front lawn I fell asleep quickly and soon I began to dream. I dreamed of a human shooting star. This human shooting star had lived long ago around the beginning of the nineteenth century. His name was Handsome Lake. He was a Seneca Indian from Pennsylvania. I had learned the story of Handsome Lake in the late nineteen seventies while I was doing scholarly research as part of my job duties working for Pittsburgh's Council of Three Rivers American Indian Center. At that time I was compiling information about the history and culture of North American Indians for our center's cultural curriculum project.

In the course of my research I learned much about this remarkable man. I discovered that during most of his lifetime he had lived the life of a typical Seneca tribesman. He grew up in the wild forests of Western Pennsylvania and New York. He was nursed from childhood on the traditions of the people of the Iroquois Confederacy, a confederacy to which his own Seneca nation belonged, along with five other related tribes.

Like anyone living in any culture, he knew joy and he knew sadness. He knew victory and ultimately he learned the acid taste of utter and unconditional defeat. His people were conquered by the encroaching white civilization. He lived to see his people defeated and dishonored. He saw his people's lands shrink from great territories encompassing all of what is now Pennsylvania, almost all of New York and most of Ohio and Ontario, to tiny dots upon the map of a powerful new nation called the United States of America. The ancient confederacy, which had once bound the Seneca Indians to the other Iroquois nations, was dealt a mortal blow. Handsome Lake saw despair all about him. His people had degraded from living in the traditional beautifully-crafted longhouse dwellings, built of elm-bark, and housing whole extended families, to living in miserable individual cabins built of logs like the ones used by the white settlers. As time went by they continued clustering in loose little villages, surrounded by the traditional cultivated fields of maize, squash and beans. But soon the people began to abandon the fields. Despair bred hunger. Many took to drinking the white man's whiskey and in the furor of inebriation, lawlessness and murder began to become part of village life.

Through my research work at the University of Pittsburgh library's extensive Native American collection I learned that by the beginning of the eighteen hundreds the ancient pride was gone from the "Haudenonsionii", the league of the Iroquois. Handsome Lake himself became a drunk.

He drank until he was a death's door. He became like an extraterrestrial rock caught in the grip of certain destruction. And in that situation of hopelessness this great meteor made a momentous decision. He decided to shine! And what a glow he emitted! He marked a bright path across the dark starless sky of a dying people. By the time he had burnt up they knew their shooting star was indeed a good omen.

One day upon waking from a drunken coma that nearly took his life, Handsome Lake arose a new man. Up there on the banks of the Allegheny River, in the beautiful wilderness of Northwestern Pennsylvania's Allegheny Forest, he gathered the people and began teaching them a message of hope. He called it "GAIWIO"; The Good News. His teachings revived half-forgotten ancient ceremonies. It condemned the new vices. It organized the people around a common faith. The old dances began again to be performed. The old chants were again intoned. The sound of the turtle shell rattle rose into the night sky and mingled with the rhythm of the echo of the solar system's birth. The water drum throbbed in time with the people's heartbeat, like some mystical pacemaker correcting a huge communal fibrillation.

The beat of those drums had come to Handsome Lake in a vision during his coma and now it set all the hearts of his followers to the same rhythm as they had once been. Handsome Lake healed a great sickness, a mortal ill, an ailment that would have effectively put an end to the Seneca Indian people. When this shooting star finally burned up he left a living thing behind. This newly revived entity, which he devised to breathe life into the ancient spirituality, revolved around a special building, a sort of temple which became the focus of his followers' veneration. Although it did not resemble, in any way, the old traditional multi-family bark dwellings, which had once gone by the name "longhouse", this new temple was granted that title. Even to this day the large plain building which modern Seneca Indians use as their ritual meeting house is still called "Longhouse".

Eventually several of these "Longhouses" cropped up all over throughout Iroquois country from Buffalo, across the Finger Lakes, all the way to the Adirondacks, in each reservation. But the very first one was built along the banks of the Allegheny River, where I now was, and came to be known as the "The Cold Spring Longhouse." I've visited the Cold Spring longhouse. I was invited there by Avery and Fidelia back in the 1970's. I've watched the sacred False Face Mask society dancers during Midwinter festival performing their healing ceremonies. That was back in the old days, before the Senecas closed these ceremonies off to outsiders. The Cold Spring longhouse had become a friend, a teacher and a symbol to me.

As I lay on Avery's and Fidelia's lawn on that warm August evening, I dreamed of the Cold Spring Longhouse. In those dreams I saw Handsome Lake himself. I saw him as a creator. He was a kind of artist, and as an artist he became a birth-maker. He birthed something. He brought life back to something that was near death. He looked at me with eyes full of firm determination. In those eyes I sensed a burning urgency. In my own heart those eyes kindled a similar urgency of determination, and in my hands I sensed the genesis of a new modern-day longhouse. I knew the time had come for the building of this new temple. It would be called "CANEY." This is a word used by my ancestors, the Taino Indians of the Caribbean. It denoted a special building which not only served as a home for the chief of a Taino Indian village, but also as the repository of the most important sacred objects and a center for certain rituals and ceremonies. In the ancient times the Iroquois longhouse was a dwelling where people lived, and also a place for indoor ceremony, now it is a kind of temple. In effect, the Taino caney of old was also a dwelling, but it too is something of a temple much like the Cold Spring Longhouse.

The "Caney" that materialized in my consciousness at that point was not so much an actual physical building as it was an unclear philosophical concept, a spiritual construct. My conceptualization of this new spiritual entity was very vague at that moment. A year earlier I had gathered with a number of other people who were interested in the Indigenous spiritual tradition of Central America and the Caribbean. We had organized formally and met sporadically, and prayed and chanted Taino sacred songs together, but we did not have a very clear idea of where we were going with our efforts. Now, a year later, as I dreamed in my sleeping bag up there on Avery and Fidelia's lawn I had no more than an inkling of what this Caney was going to be, beyond the idea of a prayer-and-meditation group. New inspirations were forming in my heart that had not been there before. I was not clear what exactly my role was going to be in this endeavor. A number of years of training under the guidance of Indigenous elders from my own culture, and childhood experiences within the traditions of my people had prepared me to an extent, but at that point in time I still was not completely ready. What I needed at that moment was the intervention of spirit forces. This intervention would make itself dramatically evident during this trip and catapult me into the next phases of the work I was destined to do. I had not known it that night but soon I was to launch myself on a magical journey of discovery and vision. Powers far beyond my control would utilize my love for art and music to help create a wholly new and novel spiritual version of the CANEY. The group of people who had joined together in 1981 would evolve and mature. We would name our group "The Caney Circle" and we would grow. Of course, much of that evolution was in the future and not at all clear in my mind that night as I lay on Avery and Fidelia's lawn. It would take the experiences of this down-river pilgrimage to solidify the real purpose of the new Caney group effort.

In 1492 Christopher Columbus arrived in the Caribbean. The colonization process that he initiated there put to a violent end the culture of the Tainos. And not only that one but eventually all of the ancient Indian traditions which had flourished for eons in all parts of the Americas from the Caribbean to the Yucatan, to the banks of the Allegheny River and far, far beyond.

Now, with the specter of Handsome Lake gazing down at me I realized that some day soon the new Caney would again ring with the chorus of the old chants, just like the Cold Spring Longhouse. I just wasn't sure how it was going to happen.

CHAPTER II

BIRD, FISH AND CRICKET

1. SHARK

I smiled in the darkness of the tent at our campsite next to the dam as my memories of the first night at Avery and Fidelia's home soothed away the last vestiges of uneasiness left in me by my nightmare. My mind turned over the details of my first night's dreams of Handsome Lake, and then I began to go over the events of the following day. I recalled waking up on Fidelia's and Avery's front yard that next day. It was the morning of August 8, 1982. We had awakened to a delicious cup of coffee in the one room of Avery and Fidelia's one-room home. Avery Jimmerson was a famed mask-carver. He had been featured in anthropological books and magazine articles about the Seneca Indian culture. His carving skills were as widely appreciated as his ability for singing the old Seneca songs. The walls of the cabin were graced with a number of traditional Seneca False Face masks.

We chatted good-naturedly for a while and even sat mezmerized as Avery pulled out a cow-horn rattle and performed three beautifully excecuted songs from his people's tradition. Then, thanking our hosts for their hospitality, we departed the Steamburg Resettlement Area in the old V. W. van. We travelled the length of the reservation, along route 17 with the Peapod strapped to the roof of the van. We reached Salamanca, a largely non-Indian town located at the other end of the reservation, at around 10:00 in the morning. After bidding goodbye to Sven's friends and thanking them for the ride, we put the canoe into the river where it flowed through the town of Salamanca, New York and began our two-week odyssey.

As we made our way down the first half-mile of the river, which was quite shallow here so near its source, a little kingfisher flew ahead of us. It dipped into the water and darted back out again with a minnow in its beak. The bird flitted away so fast that I didn't have a chance to get a good look at the living creature whose life it was about to snuff out. I had wondered briefly about that little fish that day when I saw it lose its life. Now as I lay in my bedroll in the darkness of night, going over the events of that bright summer morning, my thoughts on that little creature returned to me. I remembered that as I helped Sven paddle the canoe past the spot where the kingfisher had made his catch I contemplated the fate of that little fish. Then I began to think about larger fish, carp and blueguill, which fall prey in these very waters to birds much larger and powerful than the kingfisher. These waters are the home of ospreys, hawk-like aerial predators, which can swoop from a considerable height and snatch unwary fish out of the water with lightning speed. The frightening thought of being carried away in the sharp talons of a hawk floated before my mind's eye for a moment then faded before an even more terrifying image. The waters outside Santiago Bay in Cuba, where I was born, are inhabited by fish much bigger than the little minnow whose death I had just witnessed, quite a bit bigger still than the carp and blueguill which the Allegheny forest ospreys find so tasty. Those fish tend to be ten feet long. No victims to any other animal's predatory instinct, those fish are themselves fearsome predators, at the top of the food chain. Those fish can snuff out the life of a human being as easily as the kingfisher snuffs out the life of a minnow. The Taino Indians, who were the Indigenous inhabitants of Cuba 500 years ago, called these fish "KA-HA-IA." Today, in the English language they are called "sharks." Of course these huge toothy-grinned creatures don't really care what anyone calls them. Actually they are not aware that we call them anything at all. They function on a level of awareness, which is completely alien to us. It is a level of awareness that does not deal with the concept of justice or injustice, good or evil, fairness or unfairness. They simply are. They simply kill.

I looked down at the river water around me as I paddled the canoe and I imagined the water full of sharks. I tried to imagine the horror of finding myself on the high seas in a flimsy craft like the Peapod canoe surrounded by those creatures. My shark musings brought to mind an unforgettable childhood memory of my first terrifying experience with the presence of a shark in Cuba. The curious thing about the experience is that I never actually saw the shark. The terror was created as a result of my coming face-to-face with the aftermath of a shark attack. It was the experience that established my life-long phobia of sharks. I was about eight years old. It was a time of endless carefree summer days at the beach, my sister Consuelo and I happily splashing in and out of the ocean surf. We stomped over the frothy sand on feet shod with protective tennis shoes against the eventuality of an unfortunate encounter with a prickly sea urchin or a poisonous jellyfish. Sometimes we tossed a big colorful beach ball between us.

One particularly sunny afternoon as the temperature of the sand rose to egg-frying levels our beach-ball game was interrupted by a disturbance some distance down the beach. I stood frozen with the ball in my hands. Somehow, intuitively I knew something had gone frighteningly wrong down there where the small knot of people near the edge of the water was quickly growing into a crowd. I saw my uncle get up from the big beach towel he bad been lying on and start walking down the beach toward the ever-expanding crowd. "Stay here" He called out to us as he walked away. But I dropped the beach ball and followed, timidly at first, then more confidently. Consuelo did not join me.

My uncle was not aware that I was following behind him. He arrived at the site of the commotion, and I right at his back. There was a deafening din of screams and excited voices emanating from the center of the curious crowd. My uncle stood in front of me in his sandaled feet struggling to see over the heads and shoulders of the mob. I dropped down on hands and knees and tried to peer through the forest of legs. I caught glimpses of a human form sprawled on the sand in the middle of the ring of gawking curiosity seekers. Blood was spattered and smeared all over him and on the sand around him. Over the clamor of the crowd I could discern the anguished tones of a man's screams and groans.

I struggled to get a better view. A woman seemed to be hunched over the prone form of the stricken man aiding him in some way. Then

I caught sight of his face. It was a brief, fleeting glance. For a second our eyes met through the maze of shifting legs. It was a face I would never forget, contorted beyond recognition, his eyes wide with pain. His moustache arched dramatically over his distended lips. His teeth gritted in a frightening grimace.

I looked away quickly and stood there staring at the sand beneath me. My heart pounded in my chest. The air seemed to literally ring with screams and groans. Then I heard somebody say: "It must have been a big shark; look at the size of his wounds. I covered my ears and ran away from the scene. As I ran I contemplated the nature of this terrifying animal which could reduce a grown man to a writhing moaning heap on the ground. It must be a powerful creature indeed!

In the days and months following that incident I thought a lot about sharks, what a frightening creature! In my child's mind it took on an aura of omnipotence. I began to visualize this menacing, man-destroying being, capable of somehow lumbering out of the water and prowling through the city streets devouring people at will. This petrifying vision of utter evil ruled my imagination for years and often kept me up at night.

Obsessed from early childhood with the topic of Indigenous culture, the author at the age of eight attempts to kindle a flame using traditional fire drill technique while on a beach outing with his sister.

One of the most dramatic memories I retain of my uneasy childhood relationship with the imagery of sharks is that of a warm evening in the summer of 1958. That night my mother and father had made a trip together to the house of a relative living in the town of La Maya. They had left us kids back in Santiago at the home of my grandmother Maria, my mother's mom. My uncle Onesimo had already loosed the big lion-like Tibetan mastiff guard dog, Reti, into the main portion of the inside enclosed patio that most of the older houses in Santiago feature. This patio had no roof, was open to the sky, but was surrounded by the rooms of the house on two sides, and by partition walls on the other two sides. During the day the fearsome, vociferous Reti spent most of his time trapped in the deepest portion of my grandmother's patio, completely fenced in, surrounded by tall decorative palm fronds, and tropical fruit trees like a real lion in a jungle. He spent his days back there separated from, but barking ferociously across the fence at the many grandchildren who milled about in the flower and foliage-garlanded main portion of the indoor yard. His bark sounded more like a roar. We were all terrified of Reti. But in the evening things changed when we kids were all supposed to be absconded snugly in the safety of our beds. There was a kind of uneasy thrill in the act of getting up out from under our sheets, when we knew that Uncle Onesimo was letting the big dog free in the patio for the night. There was a kind of exhilarating excitement in the act of peeping out the wrought-iron barred windows of the many bedrooms that surrounded the patio, and watching old Reti from behind the safety of the masonry house walls. He was like a wild jungle animal in a zoo, finally freed for the night, moving his enormous mass up and down the tiled patio floor chasing after lizards and sniffing in the flower pots.

That particular night as I watched Reti through the bars of the grated window, sleepiness finally caught up with me and I tiptoed quietly away, leaving the old dog to his own devices. I climbed into the big bed and wrapped myself up in the covers. I lay there with my eyes closed, listening to Reti snuffling in my grandmother's dieffenbachia in the patio outside. As I lay there I could still hear him sometimes making quiet doggie whimpering sounds, other times clattering up the

31

patio on his enormous padded paws, clicking his big claws on the tiles as he chased lizards.

The soft background noises of the dog roaming around outside my window began to blend into the tapestry of my drowsiness and I began to dream as I entered that strange region of pre-sleep that precedes true slumber. In that half-awake state Reti's noises were transformed from canine to fish and back again. I began to image a giant hybrid monster creature, half-dog, half-shark roaming around outside, trying to find a way to get in at me. The sniffing, the quick clicking of the claws on the tiles, and the low dog growls, all blended into a menacing semi-reality. My heart began to beat loudly just like the day of the shark-attack on the beach. I felt the paralysis of terror control my whole body and the overwhelming horror of impending doom as the noises outside began to penetrate the wall more and more ominously. I just knew a big terrible dog-faced shark-thing had finally waded out of the harbor and found its way to my grandmother's house, and was here for ME!

Then something extraordinary happened. A song came to my rescue! At first the melody arrived gradually and almost imperceptibly. There was a sweet voice of a woman and then there was a chorus, and then footsteps, like a bunch of people marching about to the rhythm of the song. The melody built up and lengthened and grew in intensity and the footsteps gathered momentum and turned into rhythmic stomping until I started to return from deep sleep. The singing roused me from my dog-shark nightmare. I sat up, very quietly and still in my bed, rubbing my eyes and listening. Reti's sniffing and the clicking of his paws continued outside but there was no longer fear, just the deep beautiful harmony of voices making its way from the house next door and over the partition wall into my grandmother's patio. The shark was very far away now, and had no power over me. I listened to the singing for a long time. I knew that it was the singing that had made the shark dreams go away. I lay down again and eventually drifted pleasantly off to sleep. The lovely chant became woven into my dreams.

The next day I heard my grandmother comment on the songs that had emanated from the neighbor's house that evening. I remember the word "los espiritistas" (the spiritists). Many years later I would learn that next door to my grandmother's house there lived a woman who followed the tradition of Cuban spiritism called "El Cordon". As part of their ceremonies these people sing and dance ecstatically in a circle just like the ancient Tainos did centuries ago. That was the sound that rescued me on that warm summer night in 1958.

After that evening I had many, many other opportunities to listen to the beautiful chants of the Cordon tradition on other nights when I stayed at my grandmother's house, and when the neighbors celebrated their ceremonies. Those melodies became the first sacred blessing that my ancestral Taino tradition bestowed on me and I did not even know that it was of Indigenous origin. I simply thought that it was just a bunch of people singing beautifully. It would take many years before the Native origins of that tradition would be revealed to me. I came to associate those beautiful sounds with the magic that saved me from the demonic shark entity of my childhood. Eventually I came to adopt one of those old melodies that had been burned in my memory as the chant for our Caney Circle guanara sweatlodge ceremony.

On the morning of our first day down the river, as I paddled, I still imagined a school of sharks swimming menacingly alongside the canoe. I shifted onto a more comfortable position in the canoe seat as I remembered those remote childhood fears. I realized how those early symbols of negativity had become the archetypes of negativity in the sacred mythology, which had been revealed to me over the following years.

Of course, I know now as an adult, that sharks are, in fact, relatively vulnerable creatures. In fact for every human that is killed by a shark, hundreds of sharks are slaughtered by people for commercial purposes every year. Furthermore, "Kahaya" is the mythic totem animal representing the Taino spirit of harsh teaching trials, Guakar. As such, the shark presents itself in our culture more as a tough teacher and guide than an enemy.

**The shark is the totem creature of the spirit of
trials and challenges in Life**

And yet at times the image of this ocean-going predator becomes for me personally, more than just that of a marine organism or a totemic emblem. I am sometimes compelled to perceive it as a destructive trickster spirit, the patient one who waits, the being who looks for the proper opportunity, the moment of weakness and then attacks!

I looked down into the water and continued to imagine sharks swimming around the canoe. In fact I spent that whole afternoon mulling over my personal shark phobia and its origins as I paddled in silence behind Sven.

Well, this particular shark-infested memory of my first afternoon down the Allegheny River was proving almost as uncomfortable as the nightmare I had just awakened from!

I rolled over in the tent trying not awaken Sven again with my motions. I reached for a canteen that lay next to my bedroll and drank. "What a quirky mind I have." I thought to myself as I recalled my grisly shark musings of two days earlier.

I lay back down on my soft bedroll, the sound of the water going over the dam in the darkness still ringing in my ears. What in the hell had possessed me to start thinking about sharks back there on the river on such a beautiful summer afternoon? I kept bringing up memories of that pretty day as I lay there in the blackness of the night. That day had been very bright and eventually even the imaginary sharks had disappeared from around the canoe leaving me in the calm peace of the great forest and the liquid repetitive swish, swish of the two paddles. Above us a solitary hawk circled over the river. We continued paddling leisurely down stream, watching the kingfishers exhibit the amazing skills for which they were named. As we neared the spot where the Allegheny River flows beneath the Route 17 bridge we spotted the Seneca Nation of Indians tribal wildlife refuge. The Indians have created tall nests sites for the benefit of endangered bird species in the vicinity. We saw several large hawks soaring gracefully overhead and perched or landing on the very tips of dead trees.

"Is it an eagle?" Sven exclaimed excitedly, lifting his paddle out of the water and using it to point to a large bird, which had winged away from a nearby treetop as we approached. "I'm not sure." I answered. "It looked more like an osprey." "It was so big!" he retorted.

We paddled in silence for something like five minutes then he spoke again. "You know, we're a little behind on our schedule." "What do you mean?" I asked surprised. "I thought we were making pretty good time?"

"Well..." he insisted, "We are paddling into a pretty stiff wind and the river has gotten much wider."

In fact, the stream had more than doubled in width during the last few hours of our journey. I began to feel a sense of urgency and frustration. "I wish we had given ourselves more time for this adventure." I remarked with a sigh, thinking that I had requested a very limited amount of time off from my job at the Indian Center in Pittsburgh. "Oh we'll be alright Miguel" he answered. "We'll probably catch up down by the dam if we portage around at night." The thought of trying to do anything in the stygian forest darkness made me laugh.

"Are you kidding me? We can't see anything out there at night!" I retorted. "Well, I'll tell you this; if we make it to the dam tonight we can certainly use our flashlights to scout out a portage around it. I'm pretty sure the only portage area we will find is going to be on the restricted side of the river so it's better that we do our scouting under the cover of darkness anyway."

He was right. The unrestricted side of the big dam was too steep to attempt a portage of our heavy canoe. We would have to do it on the restricted side, which had a gentler slope. It was one of the many times I wished I had brought a lighter fiberglass canoe. I began to ponder the origins of our little craft. As I mentioned before, it was a fine old wood and canvas model built in Peterboro, Canada. It was built along the design lines of the traditional Indians river crafts of North American Eastern woodlands tribes, and yet the name by which this kind of boat is identified is not of North American Indian origin.

The woodland Indians of North America, who built these kinds of boats hundreds of years ago, had a different name for them. The Ojibway people who excelled at creating the original birch bark canoes called their crafts "wigwasi jeemon". The word "canoe" comes from someplace else, another Indian tribe far to the south. It is derived from the word "canoa", a word used by my Taino Indian ancestors living on the Islands off the coast of Central America. It was a word used to denote a much different sort of craft, a wooden dugout fashioned out of a single large tree-trunk. It was on those islands where Columbus heard the word "canoa" for the first time in 1492 and from whence that word spread north with the European conquerors. They gave the name "canoe" to any Indian boat they found anywhere in North America, even if the Indians there had a different name for their boats.

As a native of Cuba, one of the Caribbean islands, I knew the history of the word "canoa", the word from which the name "canoe" is derived. I smiled as I leaned into my paddle. By doing so I helped propel my "canoa" towards its destination.

2. TWO MARTYRS

It must have been three or four in the morning. I was as wide-awake as ever. My mind continued to go over the events of the sunny afternoon two days before, all the thoughts and daydreams I had experienced as I paddled along behind Sven in our "canoa."

That afternoon had begun to turn into evening and I felt the shadow of the Route 17 bridge glide over us as we approached the New York/Pennsylvania border. We had a long way to go before we reached the dam. I wondered if we would make it by sunset.

Because of the tightness of our schedule, the fact that I knew that I had to get back to Pittsburgh on a specific date so I could return to work on time, I felt chased, hunted by time itself, like the darkness of the night was a pursuer whom we needed to elude. The feeling of being a kind of hunted fugitive chased by Time itself, made me think of famous fugitives of the past. In particular it made me think of a specific fugitive, a man whos story I had learned as a school boy in my history class back in my old elementary school in Cuba.

He lived over five hundred years ago. He too fled before the onset of impending darkness. In 1511, that man abandoned his home. He didn't want to leave, but he felt compelled to do so because he was sure that to remain would mean certain destruction for him and his people.

The home he was reluctantly abandoning was the region at the western portion of Haiti. This nation, which has seen so much suffering and injustice since those early times, is located on approximately one third of a small island in the Caribbean called "Hispaniola." In pre-Columbus times Haiti had the same name it bears today, "Haiti." it was the name given to it by its Taino Indian inhabitants. Next to Haiti, on the other side of the island of Hispaniola, was the land that the Indians called "Kis-ke-ia (usually spelled Quisqueya). When they came with Columbus in 1492, the Spanish renamed this land calling it "Santo Domingo." The word Domingo means Sunday in Spanish. Sunday was a very holy day for the Spanish colonizers who quickly conquered the island during the sixteenth century. Each Sunday the Spanish would refrain from regular activities and gather together with their religious leaders to celebrate an elaborate ceremony known as "Holy Mass." During that ceremony they commemorated the selfless sacrifice of a very holy man who, they told the Indians, had died to redeem all human beings. During the hundred or so years that it took to completely despoil the Caribbean Indians of their lands and their way of life, the Spanish would occasionally take brief rests from their work of conquest to teach their victims about that very holy man. They taught the hapless Indians, that the holy man's name was Jesus.

They told the Indians that Jesus had always preached brotherhood, justice and peace.

The man who left his home in 1511 against his will was a Taino Indian chief called Hatuei. He had never been very clear on the whole concept of "holy mass" or its association with the religious creed of brotherhood and peace. All he knew was that some unimaginably violent people, strong beyond belief, armed with diabolical weapons and mounted on hellish four-legged beasts that trampled the people underfoot had invaded his country. From his point of view, all he knew was that these fiends took great pleasure in killing, and in taking that which did not belong to them. Hatuei had a lot of difficulty understanding what was so "holy" about any of these activities. He had witnessed the violent rape of women in his family. He had endured cruel and unrelenting servitude under the power of insatiable men who forced his people to work without rest growing food for their voracious appetites and panning for gold in streams in the vain hope that eventually it would make them rich. He had seen children impaled with sharp steel-tipped lances from horseback or beheaded where they stood with one mighty sweep of a broadsword.

Hatuei perceived these people as demons from another world. He observed that they had a peculiar habit of always shouting a special word just before launching one of their typically ferocious attacks. This word was their war cry. He did not realize it then, but this word happened to be the name of one of Jesus' apostles. The word was "Santiago." It means "St. James." The Spanish believed that the apostle James had personally traveled to Spain in the years after the crucifixion of Jesus during the era when all of Europe and much of the Middle East from Spain to the Fertile Crescent was part of the Roman Empire. They believed that James had brought the religion of Jesus to their pagan Roman, Iberian and Celtic ancestors, thereby converting them to Christianity. They even believed that a portion of the body of St. James still remains in Spain. The place where this relic was reputed to rest carried the name "Santiago De Compostela." A great church was built there and the place became a pilgrimage center throughout the Middle Ages. They believed that in the 1400's the spirit of Saint James had led the Catholic monarchs on their victorious conquests against the Muslims who had controlled Spain for centuries.

Hatuei, the Taino Indian leader who left his home and fled to an unknown future in 1511, did not associate the word "Santiago" with Christian victory, peace or compassion. He associated it with unimaginable violence and merciless brutality. He associated it with ruthless slavery. So he picked up his belongings and loaded down some canoes, back there in Haiti, just like Sven and I loaded down our canoe, at Salamanca. He had several dozen followers with him when he left.

This little fleet of Indian canoes crossed the narrow stretch of sea separating the western tip of Haiti from a larger Island to the west. They landed on this larger Island, which is called "Cuba." Here they proposed to make a new home for themselves. The sixteenth century Taino inhabitants of Cuba posed no objection to the arrival of Haitian Taino immigrants. They made the refugees comfortable and listened with sympathy to their stories of Spanish atrocities back in Haiti. In 1511 Spanish conquest had not yet reached the Island of Cuba!

In Cuba today Hatuei is recognized as the country's first hero martyr. Hatuei had no intention of becoming Cuba's first martyr. He was in Cuba precisely to avoid martyrdom, but martyrdom was his fate. It followed him from one island to another. It held him fast like the grasp of the earth's gravity upon some piece of extraterrestrial rock. So he decided to shine for his people, just like the meteor Sven and I saw on the morning of August 10, just like Handsome Lake would do two hundred years later. His opportunity to shine came when later that same year a man signed away the lives and freedom of thousands of human beings living at that time in Cuba. His name was Diego Columbus, Christopher Columbus' son. Diego Columbus had been made governor of Hispaniola. As governor under Spanish imperial law, he had the authority to order an expedition of conquest across the straits separating Hispaniola (where he resided) and the as-yet unexplored Island of Cuba. He did make that order. So in the name of the monarchs of Spain, King Ferdinand and Queen Isabela and in the name of Jesus Christ, three hundred armed Spaniards with swords, horses, guns and armor crossed the narrow sea gap, which separates the two islands. These veterans of wars against the Moslems in Europe, were led by a particularly cruel commander, a barbarian named Diego Velasquez-Cuellar. Hatuei knew that he had been followed by Velasquez. He gathered the Indian people together one afternoon and spoke to them of the scourge that was about to befall them. In the great congregation there were many Taino Indians who had followed him on his flight from Haiti to Cuba. They knew and understood what he said when he spoke of the incredible horror of Spanish domination. There were many other Taino Indians in the crowd who were natives of Cuba. Not having experienced yet what Hatuei was saying about the Spaniards in the neighboring island, they found it difficult to believe the things Hatuei related. They couldn't believe that anybody could be so cruel, so vicious and so greedy.

Hatuei organized a resistance. The Indians armed themselves with stone manaya hatchets, and wooden makana clubs. They wielded their baira bows and arrows, painted themselves with red war paint of the biha plant. They would fight for freedom. They would fight for their families, their children, their homes, their country and their lives. They fought for four years. In the end many had died and their bodies and souls returned to the nurturing womb of Ata-bei, their earth mother. Eventually Chief Hatuei was captured by Velasquez in 1514. To make an example of him, Velasquez ordered Hatuei to be bound hand and foot to a tall stake and burned to death. The Taino Indians of Cuba had never seen anyone purposely burn a human being to death.

Before the match was set to the pile of wood at Hatuei's feet a Christian priest elevated a crucifix attached to a long stick and brought it close to the victim's face. The priest told Hatuei to confess his sins and kiss the crucifix so that his soul may go to the Christian heaven. Hatuei was not aware of the fact that the man represented upon that crucifix was also reputed to have died under torture as a result of his concern for the welfare of others. Hatuei asked if the souls of the Spaniards went to heaven. The priest said that the good Spaniards went there. Hatuei answered that he did not want to go to a place where such cruel people existed. "The best of the Spaniards are vicious and greedy," he cried out as the executioner set the match. He died tied to a piece of wood just like Christ. They were both martyrs. Hatuei died listening to the gurgle of his own body as it roasted slowly. He died smelling his own burnt flesh. He died because he wished his people to live. Hatuei became a human shooting star. He added the brilliant glow of his own sacrifice to the sum total of the cosmic glow.

Precisely the same year of Hatuei's death, the Spaniards founded a city in the southeastern shore of Cuba. They named the city in honor of the man whom they credited for bringing to their heathen ancestors Christ's religion of peace and compassion. They named the city "Santiago," after Saint James. That city is now the second largest in Cuba. I was born there.

Hatuei was captured

As it turned out Sven and I never did reach the dam that day. I chuckled to myself in the darkness of the tent as I lay there on my bedroll and remembered just how wrong we had been about the location of the dam. In fact, as a result of a navigating miscalculation, we soon realized we were still a good two days away.

We found a campsite opposite the Onoville marina on the evening of August 8, 1982, set up our tent and ate dinner before retiring. That was the conclusion of our first day on the river as I remembered it that night lying there in my sleeping bag near Kinzua Dam. I turned over and drifted off to sleep.

3. JENUSHEDAGO

I wasn't asleep for long. It was proving to be a restless night. Soon I woke up again. I wondered what time it was. I knew it must be almost four in the morning but for some reason I could not get back to sleep. It sure wasn't like the night before. I had slept very well that night. The following day had found me refreshed and well rested. Now as I lay in my bedroll in the tent next to the dam I recalled that beautiful second morning of our trip near Onoville. I woke up about 8:00 in the morning that Sunday August 9. We launched the canoe and proceeded with our trip from Onoville.

Sometime later that day our canoe finally crossed the New York state border into Pennsylvania. Not long afterwards we reached the site where the Seneca Indian village of Jenushedago had once stood. Jenushedago was something of a small reservation along the shores of the Allegheny River, which had remained a viable Indian community in Pennsylvania till well into the twentieth century. It had once been the home of Handsome Lake. Back in its heyday, the leader of the village of Jenushedago was a man called Cornplanter. Cornplanter was not a full-blood Indian. During my research on North American Native history I discovered that his father had been a Dutchman by the name of Johannes Abeel. I am not a full-blood Indian myself. In my veins flow the bloods of Indians, Africans and Spaniards. I too am a mixed-blood hybrid man.

I, a mixed-blood hybrid man came to visit Jenushedago the site of an eighteenth century village led by a mixed-blood hybrid man. The village was no longer there. Although the land where Jenushedago once stood had been promised back in the 1700's by the U.S. government and George Washington himself to Cornplanter's descendants in perpetuity, most of the area was involuntarily evacuated of Indians and purposely flooded by the Army Corps of engineers in the mid 1960's. This action was carried out over the vigorous protests of Seneca Indians, descendants of Chief Cornplanter's people, who lived in the general area at that time. This intentional flooding was part of a Corps of Engineer project called "Kinzua Dam." The dam created a large man-made lake or "reservoir" which placed under water large amounts of Seneca land, and forced the relocation of scores of tribespeople in the 1960's. One of the most humiliating episodes of the battle between the Kinzua Dam project versus the Seneca Nation was the day when members of the Seneca tribe were obliged to dismantle the Cold Spring Longhouse and move it in pieces to higher ground to save it from the rising waters of Kinzua reservoir. An even more traumatic event was the day they had to dig up the remains of Chief Cornplanter so that his grave would not be swallowed up by the new man-made lake. This historical event was later immortalized in the words of a song called "Now That The Buffalo's Gone" by the Native Canadian singer Buffy Saint-Marie. The lyrics to that song go like this "A treaty forever George Washington signed. He did dear lady. He did dear man. That treaty's been broken by Kinzua Dam, and what have you done for these ones?"

I walked on the narrow strip of shoreline that remains above water in what had once been Jenushedago. As I trudged along the banks of the river I sensed my kinship with that other half-breed and I sensed more. Cornplanter died over a hundred years before I first stood on the site of his village. While he was alive he was both a war leader and a peace leader. He fought to defend his homeland, the woodlands along the Allegheny River. In doing this he unwittingly followed in the tradition established two hundred years before him by Hatuei, the Taino Indian leader of Cuba who had also taken a stand against the European invasion.

Like Hatuei, Cornplanter was defeated. He was not burned at the stake as Hatuei had, but his people were penned in within the boundaries of reservations in New York and Pennsylvania. After his defeat Cornplanter decided that the most effective means for assuring the survival of his people was to establish tolerable peace between the conqueror and the conquered. Within that peace he strove to improve the lot of his people. He was not very successful. Hunger and demoralization followed and only the great spiritual revival brought about by Handsome Lake's religious reform, a movement supported by Cornplanter, was capable of saving the Seneca people from utter oblivion.

When I read the story of Cornplanter in the 1970's I learned to admire what he tried to do and what he stood for. That is why I wanted to walk on the land where he walked so many years earlier. I continued to stroll along the shores of the Allegheny River here. My thoughts drifted away from Cornplanter and Handsome Lake. Curiously I suddenly felt distant from them. I no longer felt the presence of such great shapers of history, the great leaders or the great chiefs. Instead, I looked into the water of the Allegheny River. It rippled placidly here at this point on the stream where the flood of the Kinzua reservoir was already evident. It seemed to whisper names and echo voices, not the voices of orators delivering historical speeches easily found in history books. These were voices of children. They were the giggles of little girls and boys running naked in the clear splash and spray of river water. They were the voices of women exchanging neighborhood gossip as they rhythmically pounded corn into meal, in the tall waist-high mortars with their heavy wooden pestles.

I heard the little every day worries and concerns of people who didn't know and didn't care about their place in the scheme of history. I felt that I knew them. I knew their joys and their sadness. I cried when they cried. I was certain that I had laughed when they laughed. I had tasted the sweetness of their food and shared the coolness of their shade. I had even known the tenderness of their love-bed, shared in the ecstasy of its climax. They were the millions of anonymous ghosts who haunt that little strip of land. They were the legitimate inhabitants of the forest, from whom the land will never be stolen. If these phantoms still live on the banks of the Allegheny at Jenushedago, they live just as vividly in the chants and dances of the Cold Spring Longhouse, the Seneca temple back upstream. Then, suddenly the image of other ghosts and of other voices popped into my mind. In my mind other specters, Taino specters, awakened, brought back to life by the songs of the Cordon dance wafting in the air above the palm-thatched roofs of rural Cuba, and within the sacred confines of a new temple forming itself at that moment in my mind and heart, the Native temple called "Caney."

We continued our journey after a brief stop at the ancient site of Jenushedago. That evening, after navigating the length of Kinzua reservoir, we finally reached the dam itself. We spent hours that night, the evening of August 9, scouting the best portage route around the huge dam. As we had predicted, the scouting had to be done under the cover of darkness because the area we were wandering around in was restricted and posted with "No Trespassing" signs. As we topped a high ridge next to the dam Sven and I spotted the beautiful shooting star which I mentioned at the very beginning of my story. It flashed across the sky just after midnight on the morning of August 10.

We portaged around the big dam in the dark and camped on its downstream side near a fish hatchery. In the water, young fry swam around drowsily, oblivious to the fact that many of them would some day end up on a kingfisher's menu. We set up our tent and went to sleep. That's when I had the nightmare. Now I lay awake in my bedroll, unable to sleep, the hiss of the water falling over the Kinzua dam spillway ringing steadily in my ears.

I tried to give that old nightmare another try. What the heck I might as well try to remember it. What could it hurt? But I couldn't. Try as I did I could not bring back one image of the horrifying dream. It was as if someone had erased it completely from my memory.

In fact I was destined not to remember my dream for years to come, not till long after my two-week river adventure had been concluded. Actually that violent nightmare by the Kinzua dam would be only the first in a series of strange dreams which would haunt many of my nights on the river, for the rest of the journey! The odd thing is that as the two weeks of our adventure wore on I would awaken from each dream only to forget it. No matter how much I tried on the following days I had no better luck recalling any of the subsequent dreams than I had recalling that first one! And none of the dreams ever came back to me for years afterward.

4. ESCAPE

I was feeling a little drowsy now. About time! It must have been four thirty in the morning. I needed some sleep. I felt myself drifting off to sleep. Soon I began to dream again. The very first thing I saw in my dream was a young man. The young man moved stealthily in the night. His birth name was Sagua but he was a slave of the Spanish, nothing more than a simple human cog in the great "encomienda" forced-labor system that had been imposed upon his people a few years before he was born. The Spanish frowned upon his pagan name and had baptized him with the Christian name, "Diego". The name was a variant of the more ancient "Tiago", the name of Spain's revered patron saint, San Tiago or San Diego, Saint James. The hacienda where he lived was located about seventy kilometers east of the Spanish town also named after that saint, Santiago De Cuba.

Sagua peered into a dark building through an open window. With some trepidation he scratched gently on the peeling blue paint of the jamb.

He expected an answer, but none was forthcoming. Sagua scratched again. He heard some stirring inside so he spun quickly around against the side of the building pressing his back tightly upon the whitewashed plaster wall. Sagua's heart was pounding so loudly that he could almost hear it in the stillness of the sleeping hacienda. Heavy drops of sweat trickled from his forehead, but he was reluctant to move even to wipe the stinging salty liquid from his eyes.

Finally he heard a voice. It was a whisper, at first barely audible. "Diego...Diego, where are you?" It was a girl's voice. She was calling him by his Christian name as she talked to him in Spanish. "Here I am!" he whispered hoarsely back in the Taino Indian language. "Are you ready?" "Si" she answered simply.

Sagua swung back around to face the open window. He could hear the rustle in the darkness as Ana fussed with her bundle. Further in the depths of the darkened house he could make out the faint sawing of the master's heavy snore.

He heard the master's snore

"Are they all asleep in there?" he asked as he grabed the bundle handed to him through the window. "He is the only one here, the others are in Baracoa". She answered. Sagua watched as one slender leg slid out of the rectangular opening in the white wall. Then the pretty half-breed girl appeared framed in the windowsill. He helped her down and they ran together in the direction of the jungle. As they passed the servants' quarters a yellow glow suddenly appeared at the door. Ana pulled violently on Sagua's arm. They both flattened against the wooden wall of the tool shed. They watched nervously as a semi-silhouetted figure wearing only a pair of white cotton trousers stumbled out into the courtyard holding his lamp.

He moved toward the stable. Near the stables with their sleeping horses he laid the lamp on the ground and began to fumble with his pants. In the distance Sagua could not make out what he is doing. "What is that old man up to?" asked Ana. "I can't tell!" answered the boy straining to see the dark figure in the muted moonlight. Suddenly they both heard the unmistakable splashing sound as the old man relieved himself on the dust before the stable. "It's Pedro, the old horse-groom, I think he's pissing!" whispered Sagua turning to the girl. "I figured that out by myself, Diego!" Ana answered sarcastically. "Hush, girl!" Sagua glared at the girl. "He'll hear us!"

"This is what I think of you!" They heard the old Indian mumble quietly as he finished. "You filthy, no-good, dung-eating, four-legged beasts!" Sagua and Ana giggled softly as the old man rambled on in the Taino language with his angry diatribe to the sleeping horses.

"The master thinks you are so wonderful, so fine. He thinks you are so beautiful, so I have to spend my old age brushing you and feeding you. He treats you like children. You eat better than I do!" Ana and Sagua slipped quietly from behind the tool shed and tip-toed around the servant's quarters. They disappeared into the brush as the old man finished his monologue to the horses. A snort and a soft whinny wafted out the window of the stable. "If you are so wonderful why can't you take care of yourselves like other animals?" Sagua and Ana were half way to the river by the time the old groom finally trudged back through the open door of servant's quarters. He took the edge off his bitterness by downing a swig of nasty cheap liquor before returning to his humble cot.

The two youngsters had been planning this escape for weeks. They knew most of the master's family would be visiting relatives in Baracoa, about sixty kilometers away on the eastern coast of the island that night.

Ana had scouted the best escape route on her last trip to the river. She studied all the possible crossing places on the river while she was there to wash the master's clothes. When they reached the stream she pointed out a stony stretch on the riverbank where they would not leave any footprints. They picked their way along the large slippery stone slabs till they reached the crossing place. "This is where the river is the shallowest." Ana whispered in Taino. Sagua studied the fast moving water. "I don't know, Ana. That water is flowing pretty fast here. If we lose our balance the current could drag us under and drown us!' Ana nodded. "I know, but we have no other choice. The next closest fording is half a day's walk up river. That's in the opposite direction to where we intend to go." Sagua's face drooped in consternation. "If we do that we won't be far enough away by daybreak. The dogs will run us down right away." "Our only chance is the crossing right here." Ana answered.

Sagua reached into his bundle and drew out a rope. He tied a loop around his own waist then wrapped another turn around Ana's. He led the way into the cool rush of water. The refreshing liquid was a relief from the heat of the summer night as they both stepped gingerly trying to keep their balance while the force of the stream surged about their thighs. The coolness of the water on her skin brought an ugly memory into Ana's mind. She fought to drive the images from her consciousness as she concentrated on the work at hand. They struggled along until they reached the deepest place. Here they had to lean heavily against the current swirling up to their hips. Several times they slipped and almost stumbled on the slimy pebbles upon which they treaded. The water began to get shallower as they fought on past the stream's mid point.

Suddenly Sagua felt a painful thump on his thigh. His right arm became ensnared in the tangle of branches bristling on a floating piece of driftwood. He spun violently out of control as he struggled to free his arm. Ana felt the tug on her end of the rope and gasped. Then she was swept off her feet. Sagua freed his arm from the branch and pushed it away from himself. He still managed to keep his bundle above water with his other arm, but could feel himself being dragged as his toes clung desperately to the river's bottom. Ana was already under water when the big branch floated past her. She bobbed up and took a deep breath then struggled to

48

touch bottom. Her legs flailed about wildly, but she could not reach the river floor with her feet.

Sagua somehow managed to keep from losing his tenuous toehold on the underwater stones. He succeeded in stopping himself from getting dragged along. He then steadied himself upright. Taking a firm hold of the rope with both hands he lunged at the current and wrestled against the pull of the struggling girl.

Ana finally managed to feel the slippery surface of a large stone slab with her left foot. She hooked her toes around the edge of the submerged rock and paddled desperately with her hands until she succeeded in positioning herself directly above it. Then she pushed herself up and leaned against the current with all her might allowing Sagua to relax his grasp on the rope.

The two youths slowly dragged themselves out of the water at the other bank. They lay panting heavily on the pebbles for a while as the babble of the water rang in their ears.

After a long breathless silence Ana gasped; "We can't stay here long." Sagua continued to breathe heavily and did not answer. Ana raised herself up on her haunches and ran her fingers through the dripping black locks of his hair.

"You look like a drowned dog, Don Diego!" She exclaimed. Sagua shifted himself on one elbow and looked up into the girl's face. Her winsome smile warmed him. "If you call me by that stinking Spanish name again I'll be forced to throw you back in the river!" He hissed up at her in mock anger. "Is that so?" she giggled a defiant retort rising to her feet. Sagua followed her up with his eyes. He was beginning to feel a little dryer now. Suddenly the girl shook her head violently over him spraying him with a shower of cold river water from her hair. That accomplished, she bounded off into the woods with a squeal. "You are going swimming again!" shouted Sagua wiping the water from his face as he jumped up to follow her. They ran playfully along an old forest trail, which led into the mountains. As the rise of the trail became steeper Ana began to slow down. Eventually the boy caught up with her. She let out a high pitched squeak as they both went rolling upon the forest floor.

Liying in the moonlight shafts which filtered through the tropical foliage they kissed. It was a long hungry kiss, the kind of kiss that good missionary monks frowned upon.

"Don't call me 'Diego' anymore." The boy whispered when their lips parted. "Don't call me 'Ana'," she retorted. "My name is 'Caoba', Mahogany." The girl shifted unto her back on the leaf littered ground and brought her hands up behind her head. "That word, 'Caoba'; it is the name of a magic wood." She continued. "People say that an agreement arrived at while standing on a mahogany floor will be based on friendship and trust.

"Fair enough..." Sagua agreed. "I'll call you by your Indian name 'Caoba' you call me by my Indian name, 'Sagua'. No more Ana and Diego!" He gazed into her gentle round face. She smiled, then she pushed herself to a sitting position. "Come on, silly we are still wet and we need to cover a lot of ground!"

She was just about to stand, when Sagua said "Caoba, let's get rid of these clothes, they are wet and smelly." Caoba stopped and looked at him in shock. "What will we wear?" she said. "Nothing!" he answered. "Oh yeah?" Caoba smiled. "Yes Caoba, I'm serious." Caoba stared sternly into his eyes. "Sagua you want to go naked like the old-time heathens?" Sagua frowned at her. "The old-time heathens were our parents!" There was an accusing look on his face. "All right, yes! I know that, but no one walks about naked anymore!" She complained. "Why?" He countered rising to his feet. Caoba stared up at him with a lost look on her face. "Why?" He insisted. "Well...because...because...it's not right! It's not moral! And anyway, the master won't allow it. He says it's an old pagan custom and sinful!" she stammered in Spanish rising also. "The master! The master!...A curse on the master, a curse on his law and a curse on what he may think is sin!" raged the boy. "And don't talk to me in Spanish anymore, we shall speak the tongue of our ancestors or say nothing at all!" Sagua turned away from Caoba and strode a few paces off. Then he spun to face her again. "I am no longer afraid of the master." He said coldly staring at her with a fixed gaze.

He reached around himself and pulled off his dripping rough spun blouse. His chest muscles rippled like copper knots. Then he began to pull off his trousers. Caoba looked on in shock as he finished stripping. He stood before her a little sheepishly at first. Then he threw his chest out

"Old man Caimoni taught me about the old ways!" He hissed. "He told me how it was before there were white men here on our island. I know about these things! I am not an ignorant idiot!" "Darling, I know you are no idiot." Caoba replied, her voice pleading for forgiveness.

"I am not an idiot!" He continued obliviously. "Old man Caimoni taught me well. He told me all about our land before the white men."

Suddenly the concept of a land without Spaniards struck the girl and she leaned back again upon the tree. She looked up pensively into the branches and abandoning her efforts at placating her lover, she echoed his words; "Our land before the white men!" The idea of a land with no white men, with no masters was so remote that it seemed like a fantasy.

"Yes, yes!" Sagua continued excitedly, forgetting his anger. "There was a time not long ago when there were no white people here!" "That was before we were born." Caoba mumbled still looking into the tangle of branches overhead.

"Not that long before we were born." Sagua countered. "No white men, no whips, no war dogs...only our ancestors living peacefully, tilling the soil, harvesting cassava roots from the yuca plant, growing corn, tomatoes, squash, pumpkins, avocados and sweet guavas!" He smiled turning to face her.

"Our people were free then, Caoba. Our people lived here.

Only our people walked this country!" "Only our people!" she echoed dreamily turning to face him. "Yes, yes, yes, only our people lived here, performing ancient ceremonies, which should have never been allowed to die!"

Caoba's eyes were fixed on his face, all flushed with excitement, but she was looking right through him, beyond to a remote time, which properly belonged to people long dead, a time into which Sagua's words were now transporting her.

"My mother told me about the old ceremonies before she got sick and died." she said. "My mother told me they were beautiful. She told me the people stood hundreds at a time in a great circle around the fire. Men and women locked arms and danced to the rhythm of the maiowakan drum. They danced and danced and sang the old pagan songs..."

"The sacred songs!" Interrupted the boy. "Yes, yes of course, the sacred songs. The songs of life and death." "That's it Caoba. Now you know what I am talking about." "The songs of life and death!" She repeated reverently. "Yes, Caoba, the song of freedom. We must sing that song again!" Remarked the boy.

Caoba looked back up into the branches above them and smiled. Then she began to hum sweetly. She hummed an old Taino song her mother had lulled her to sleep with as a child. Sagua smiled also. He laid his head on her shoulder and dozed off. Soon she was also asleep. They dreamed forbidden dreams.

The sun was very high in the tropical sky when Sagua and Caoba awakened from their morning nap. Sagua was being shaken vigorously when he opened his eyes. "Time to rise sleepyhead" whispered the girl as she rattled him to consciousness. Sagua groaned and rubbed his face. "I want to sleep a little longer." He complained. "No Sagua..." answered Caoba shaking him even more vigorously. "We must rise now. We will travel during the day today. By night fall we should be able to reach the sacred cave."

"Do you think they have noticed our absence yet?" asked Sagua. "Not yours" answered Caoba. "They probably have not even missed you, but the master has probably been awake for almost an hour now. Soon he will be wondering where I am." "What will he do when he realizes that we are gone together?" The boy asked rising and brushing the leaves and grass that stuck to his flesh. "Oh, he will be furious." Answered Caoba. She rose also and pulled a tortoise shell comb from Sagua's bundle and began to untangle her luxuriant black mane.

Sagua looked back in the direction of the trail. He turned his eyes to the girl. "Do you think they will loose the killer war-dogs on us?" He asked nervously. Caoba leaned sideways and let her hair hang as she ran the comb through it. "The master is my uncle. He is the brother of the old pig who raped my mother. He probably does not want me dead for the simple reason that I'm a relative." "Your father never cared for you, did he?" Said Sagua softly approaching the girl. Caoba stopped combing her hair and straightened to face him. "I have no father! That pig, the master's brother is not my father." She answered in a whisper turning her eyes away and gazing past him into the distance. "He may have made my mother pregnant when he raped her; I happened to be the result of that event, that is all! That doesn't mean he is my father...He is not my father...He is not my father." She repeated morosely. I have not seen nor heard from him from a long time, and I don't care if he is alive or dead."

"I heard that he had run off to live by himself up in the mountain jungle." Sagua mumbled awkwardly. Caoba turned her face away from Sagua. "I heard he disappeared with all his armor." Sagua continued. "I heard he was chased off by your uncle for bringing some sort of embarrassment upon your family."

Caoba turned her head back to face Sagua and moved off a few steps. Sagua turned to pick up his bundle and continued. "I think he raped...or tried to rape somebody else years after he raped your mom." Now Caoba adopted a belligerent attitude and growled; "I don't want to talk about it." "Yea, but I heard he raped a relative, a member of his own family, didn't he?" Caoba took a step nearer and again growled, "I don't want to talk about it."

"But honey..." insisted the boy, "I'm just trying to remember what I heard about him...let's see, it was a young girl, wasn't it? A niece or a cousin, I think."

"Or a daughter!!" Screamed Caoba glaring at the boy.

Sagua froze. They stared at each other for what seemed an eternity, then Caoba stalked off towards the trail and began moving briskly uphill. Sagua remained immobile beneath the Ceiba tree and followed the girl with his eyes until she disappeared up the slope. Sagua was thunderstruck. Could it be true? Could it be true that his beloved was raped by her own father as a child?

Caoba continued up along the winding trail. Soon Sagua came running up from behind and joined her. He stared at her steadily as they climbed side by side through the jungle.

Finally the girl spoke. Her voice seemed breathless with the maddening pace of her walk. She spoke without looking at him as she moved along; "You will trip over a root if you don't watch where you're going." The boy continued to stare at her profile as they walked.

At last she stopped. Sagua stopped also. The girl turned to face him for an instant. Suddenly she lunged at him angrily. "You hate me now!" She screamed pushing Sagua violently up against a tree. "Now you know what I really am...deflowered, a white man's whore!"

Caught by surprise Sagua bumped his head sharply against the rough wood of the tree, then he fell to the grassy ground.

"I have been branded as the Delilah, the temptress who brought ruin to my father's honor and shame to his family! I am treated as the despoiler by my uncle even though I am the daughter of his only brother!" The girl screamed as she pounced on the dazed boy. "I know you hate me now! I know you loathe me now!" She continued to scream punching at him savagely as he struggled to crawl away from beneath her.

He pushed her roughly away in desperation, sending her rolling unto the floor of the forest. Then he crawled off rubbing the back of his head where a large bump was beginning to develop. The girl rolled on the grass and came to rest against a boulder. She lay there, her face bathed in tears, sobbing.

Sagua managed to focus his eyes on her. Her chest heaved as she stared back at him. "I didn't do anything..." She whimpered "I was only playing in the river with my friends that night. I did not want him there!" She buried her face in her hands and wept as she remembered the violent death of her childhood friend and her own sexual violation, both at the hands of her own father.

Sagua gazed at her for some time, then he said; "I don't hate you." He raised himself from the ground and walked over to her. He knelt at her side as she raised her tear-streaked face to look up at him. Embracing her tenderly he repeated; "I don't hate you." Then he added; "I was born into slavery. I have been a slave all of my life, but my slavery has been nothing compared to yours. Forgive me, I did not know, I did not know!"

Caoba threw her arms about the boy's neck and wept bitterly into his breast, washing out of her system the five years of suffering she had silently endured since her traumatic adolescent experience on the river-bank.

After a while they rose to their feet and resumed their trek hand in hand.

It was almost nightfall when Sagua spotted the mouth of the sacred cave partly obscured by thick jungle foliage in the distance above. They had walked all afternoon and into the evening rising ever higher into the Sierra. After reaching the summit of one peak they followed a ridge for many hours, which led them to the higher nearby peak.

Now, after climbing up this second mountain for some time they were nearing their destination. Their intention was to shelter themselves in the cave, making it their home while they established themselves more permanently upon the mountain. In the meantime they planned to make contact with other runnaways whom they had heard of, living free in the wild mountain fastness, barely eaking out an existance from the forest, but free!

"It is not far up ahead." Said Caoba panting as she climbed. "I'm hungry." Answered Sagua, also quite breathless. "You ate just a few hours ago, glutton! We will sup as soon as we have reached the cave." Caoba teased him. They huffed and puffed all the way to the mouth of the cave.

The evening star was shining in the darkening sky, when Sagua peered into the darkness within. "I can't see anything in there." He said. Caoba dropped down against a smooth outcrop of rock and began to undo their bundle. She picked through coils of rope, bone fish hooks, steel arrowheads, blankets and hammocks. She drew two guavas from the bag and spreading a cotton sheet on the grass, laid the fruit in the center of the cloth, then she found and took out a packet of dried fish and a glass flask full of spring water capped with a cork. She also laid a stack of Cassava bread wafers next to the guavas.

"You know..." Sagua remarked joining her on the grass, "I will probably get tired of dried fish and cassava bread in a very short time!" Knowing this was all they would have to eat for a few days Caoba ignored his quip and continued her work.

Then suddenly she stopped, pausing for a minute in thought. She looked up from what she was doing and said; "Do you think that cave still has spirits in it?" Sagua stared up at her in puzzlement for a minute as he sat down opposite to her on the grass. Then he looked up toward the mouth of the cave. "I don't know." He said "I had not thought of it. I guess spirits don't die, do they?" "No, I guess they don't." Caoba agreed turning to look at the cave also. Sagua turned back to her and asked; "Are you scared?" "Yes" she answered still staring at the dark cave mouth. "Aren't you?" she added. "Well, now I am!" he answered her looking again at the cave. Eventually they both stopped their mesmerized fixation on the cave and turned to look at each other simultaneously. Then they broke into a silly giggle and settled down to eat in the darkening twilight of evening.

The dawning of a new morning had brought the bright promise of a beautiful day. The sun was shining brightly through the branches of the trees above. The two youths ate a brunch of cassava and fish hunched over the embers of the previous night's fire.

Suddenly a savage war-dog sprang with a snarl out of the forest and into the cave at them. Caoba bounded away with a scream and was able to get past the animal and out of the cave. Sagua tried to cover her escape by turning to fight the large mastiff. She ran as fast as she could, overcome by a consuming terror. Behind her she heard the anguished screams of the dying boy as the dog tore him to pieces. She ran on feeling her legs get heavier as she moved. She screamed and wept desperately as she thought of the tragic end of her only love back in that cave. But the sheer intensity of self-preservation kept her running.

Then she heard the heavy panting of the war-dog right behind her. Its breath was hot on her bare thighs. She struggled to out distance him, but her legs felt like lead. Her breathing became labored and difficult. She began to gasp as the dog's growl turned nearly to a roar. She felt she could not run another step. She turned to face the monster.

When her eyes came to rest on the creature the first thing she saw was its distended jaws dripping blood an inch away from her throat. Then she looked into its cruel eyes. They were not the eyes of a dog! They were human! The dog stood on its hind legs and backed her up against the stone face of a cliff. Its countenance was dark with a vicious sneer, yes a sneer! It was a human face, a bearded man, a man she recognized, a man she knew.

He stood blocking her escape with his arms up against the rock trapping her, pinning her between the stone wall and himself. It was him! the fiend who had violated her when she was a child, the monster she thought she would never face again.

He began to chortle and giggle insanely. Heavy drops of blood fell from his lips, from his beard and splashed on her naked shoulders and breasts. His wild, high-pitched snicker rang painfully in her ears. I heard that sinister giggle in my dream and winced.

"Well what do you know, here you are frolicking naked in the forest again with one of these heathens. You thought I was gone" He hissed. "You thought my brother could drive me out of your life completely. I will never be gone. You will never be rid of me. I am a part of you. I took you just like I took your heathen mother before you. I told you then and I tell you now; you are mine, you don't belong to these animals. You belong to me! I own you. I will always own you, no matter how far you are from me."

She looked into his vile threatening countenance. His face approached her throat and she turned her head away nauseated. "No!" she sobbed closing her eyes. She could smell the wine on his breath. Could it be possible that the horror of that night, five years ago was going to be re-enacted now? now when freedom seemed so near.

"No, no, no!" She moaned hearing again his mad snicker. She felt his blood-smeared lips upon her neck. "No!" She screamed with her eyes still shut. She felt his hand on her hip. It really seemed as if this was going to be repetition of that foul night she had tried so hard to forget.

Then something happened. Even through her terror and revulsion she felt a strange heat growing in the pit of her stomach. As it grew she noticed the heavy touch of the man's hand fade from her body. She still had her eyes closed, but through the tightly sealed eyelids she saw something. It was a kind of drawing.

She concentrated on the vague image floating before her eyes. It seemed to glow and shimmer. She almost forgot the presence of her attacker, who was even then still slobbering on her neck and shoulder.

She focused on the drawing. Finally she made out its details. Its features became gradually clearer to her. It turned out to be a stylized linear rendering of a bird. Its shimmering made it appear to move. It did move!

She opened her eyes. The jungle was gone. The stone wall had vanished from behind her. The sun was gone from the sky, leaving her in the darkness of night. Before the girl the Spaniard stood, his threatening nakedness causing waves of revulsion to wash over her. He had backed away from her and stood with his hands at his sides, a vicious sneer on his face. And yet he seemed hesitant to approach her again or touch her.

Caoba sensed that they were no longer alone. She looked about. All around them a great circle of people surrounded them as she and the man stood facing each other. She looked up. Above him the great bird shimmered and glowed hovering with its huge wings outspread. She gazed intently at the bird and suddenly she broke into a song. It was the ancient melody that her mother had taught her long ago. The bird started to grow in size as she raised her voice in song. She continued to chant and the people began to dance around them in an enormous human hoop. They were Tainos, dressed in the old way with beads and feathers, with shell anklets and body paint.

The Spaniard looked around and saw the huge crowd. He looked back at her and said, "You filthy little half-breed, do you think I am afraid? One Spaniard is a match for a hundred of you heathens."

Suddenly he stood before her in full armor with a sword in his right hand. Caoba continued to sing. The people continued to dance around them holding hands in a friendship ring the hoop of Guaitiao, moving slowly in a clockwise direction.

The Spaniard lurched forward a step, lowering the visor on his helmet. She heard a muffled yell escape through an opening in his armor; the Spanish war-cry, "Santiagooooo!" The man screamed and charged at her with sword raised in both hands. Caoba sang louder and stood her ground. A sudden rush of wind and a deafening thunderclap filled the darkness. Caoba closed her eyes. As she did she saw her mother's face for an instant. She opened her eyes in time to see the armored Spaniard lifted bodily into the air and carried away in the talons of the great bird like an Allegheny River blue-gill fish in the claws of an osprey.

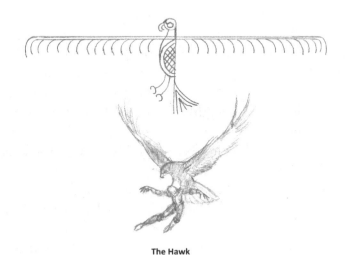

The Hawk

"I am not beaten so easily..." She heard him scream hoarsely as he was carried away. "I will come back. We shall face each other again and again."

60

His voice trailed off as he and the great being, which held him, vanished into the dream-gloom.

Caoba awakened in the darkness. She was covered with a layer of cool perspiration, which made her tremble violently in the mountain night chill. Her heart was pounding so loudly that she thought it would surely jump out of her breast. She looked down next to her. On the cave floor Sagua lay sleeping peacefully. It was just a dream! Just a nightmare!

She crawled slowly out from the thin cotton blanket, under which they had both been sleeping, and tiptoed a few paces away. She crouched down there quietly facing him from a few paces away and pondered the dream for a few minutes. Then she came back and squatted next to him. She hovered over the lad gazing into the serenity of his handsome face. Finally she approached him and stooping over the prone body kissed him softly on the lips. Sagua smiled in his sleep, stirred and sighed, then settled back to the calm breathing rhythm of heavy slumber.

Eventually Caoba stood and strode across the cave to the spot where Sagua had built their interior campfire that night. The embers were still quite hot and Caoba managed to reawaken the flames by throwing in a few sticks and fanning it forcefully.

She sat back against the wall of the cave staring into the flames and warming herself. Again she pondered the symbolism of her terrifying dream. Then she turned and peered into the gloom of the cave's interior. She could still see in her mind's eye the vision of the huge bird winging away with the armored Spaniard writhing in its talons.

Suddenly she stood. She crossed the cave again and looked at Sagua's bag. She drew out a long rag and a bottle of flammable lamp oil. She went outside and found a stick. She wrapped the rag tightly around the end of the stick, winding it about the wooden shaft, over and over many times. Then she dowsed the tightly bound rag with the oil. Having thus made a torch, she thrust it into the fire. It burst into flames. She re-corked the oil bottle and stood holding it and the torch ready to soak the rag anew once the oil upon it had been consumed. Armed with a light Caoba marched resolutely into the depths of the cave.

It was fairly easy going at first. The ground was packed soil and it sloped only gently downward. Then she came to a sheer drop of about five feet. Beyond that the ground slope was much steeper. She sat on the rim of the drop and pushed off holding the lit torch in one hand and the bottle in the other. As she dropped she prayed that the fall would not sprain one of her ankles. She broke the fall as best she could by bending her knees as she landed and continued on down into the heart of the mountain.

The slope was steep and slippery. Stalagmites and stalactites, slimy with mineral-rich water, became more and more numerous as she proceeded down. Then the slope leveled off. The passage began to widen until she arrived at a huge underground hall with a very high ceiling and subterranean stream running through its center.

Caoba focused on the walls of the hall and she knew that she had arrived at a sacred place. Most of the vertical surfaces were covered with hundreds of line drawings carved into the face of the living rock. The drawings depicted animals, birds abstract spiral patterns and people.

She knew intuitively that she would find her bird here, so she began to search. She studied each scratch carefully, trying to make out the cryptic significance of the old shamanic petroglyphs. She searched and searched, but the great line-drawing bird of her dream was nowhere to be found among the confusion of petroglyphs. She began to lose hope. Finally she gave up. "Pagan rubbish!" she mumbled sitting on a low rocky hump near the edge of the little stream. She set the oil bottle down near her foot and held the torch with both hands before her. She looked down into the sparkling waters and watched the flickering torchlight reflected on its crystalline surface. Then she looked up. There was something shining faintly up ahead by the light of her torch. She got up and crossed the shallow stream. She saw it more clearly. It was a piece of metal buried in the soil of the cave floor. It was lying outside the opening to a low narrow chamber. Caoba stooped and touched it. It was part of the gilt pommel of an old rapier still in its scabbard.

The girl felt a sudden mysterious thrill as she stared at the half buried weapon. Then she brushed away some soil and uncovered more of the sword's length. She kept working at it until the whole thing lay on the ground before her. Slowly she reached down and wrapped her fingers around the hilt. She pulled at it, but at first it refused to yield. Rust had begun its corrosive process. Nevertheless, the rust had somehow remained minimal and after a little tugging she managed to slide the blade out of its protective sheath.

The girl's eyes were fixed on the long, sharp, slightly rusted object, as she rose to her feet with it in hand.

After a few minutes of standing there staring at the thing in her hand, she looked up and shoved the torch ahead of her toward the opening of the dark chamber. She could make out some sort of shape on the floor far off at the other end of the narrow cavity. She dropped the sword and began to crawl in, striving to keep the torch high enough to illuminate the thing on the floor ahead. It was a long difficult crawl, but as she approached it the object looked more familiar. She suddenly realized what it was! Even before the distinct human shape of the full-body armor was completely clear to her. She knew what it was. She knew who it was.

Caoba broke again into a sweat. Her heart began to race. When she reached the armor sprawled out face up on the floor of the chamber, she instinctively looked at the helmet tilted down over his face. She knew it was not empty. She knew under that helmet there was a face covered by the rusted metal.

Caoba shifted over toward the head of the prone figure. She stretched out a trembling hand, half expecting the metal assemblage to rise suddenly and attack her. Finally, with her last ounce of faltering courage she tilted back the old helmet. The horrible death grin face of a dried up corpse lay behind the helmet staring up at the ceiling of the chamber, its hollow eye sockets fixed in an eternal gaze.

Caoba remained immobile for some time looking at the remains of the man who had, long ago, stolen her innocence. Then she looked up as if to find out what it was that the corpse was staring at. Craning her neck she finally made out upon the surface of the chamber's ceiling, the object of the dead man's fixation. Shimmering in the glow of the torchlight clearly chiseled into the face of the rock, a large stylized line drawing of a bird, a hawk, covered the entire ceiling of the chamber with its outspread wings.

5. THE VISITORS

I woke with a start. I felt overheated and restless making it unbearable to stay inside my sleeping bag. I couldn't remember the dream no matter how much I tried and I was troubled by a strange haunting feeling. I crawled out of the tent and walked around in the early pre-dawn half-light.

I approached the edge of the water and scooped up a handful of the clear cool liquid. It felt good on my face and chest. I sat at the river bank and took deep breaths.

Although I could not remember the dream I had just experienced any more than the first one, I knew that the last image of the dream featured a cave. As I sat there in growing light of dawn I remembered another childhood memory. Late in the year 1957, about seven months after my dramatic experience with the Cordon chants that emanated from the ceremonies in the home of my grandmother's next-door neighbor, my father decided to indulge the interest that I had always demonstrated in our Indigenous heritage. He took the whole family on a day trip to a famous archeological site in eastern Cuba called Patana Cave. This ancient Taino relic site is a set of caverns whose walls bear cryptic inscribed drawings in the shape of both abstract and representative images. As a young child, I stood dumbstruck before the sacred images that grace that place. Even as a totally unschooled innocent I instinctively understood the profound fundamental meaning of the holy native underground shrine. I emerged from there and felt like the re-born sun rising out of the primordial womb-cave of Iguanaboina in ancient Taino legend.

With these pleasant childhood memories floating through my thoughts and refreshed by the cool water on my face and chest I stood up and looked across the stream. To my left the muffled hiss of the water as it tumbled over spillway at the far end of the dam, created one of those monotonous numbing sound effects that can (if I let them) lull me into a trance. I let it. Soon I began to see unexpected things. On the far bank I saw two men climb into a canoe. They paddled forcefully straight across the river and pulled the canoe out unto the sand. They seemed familiar, although I had never met them before. One was very dark and short. His native features shaded by a wide brimmed straw hat. The other approached me bareheaded, tall, also Indian, but lighter skinned.

"Greetings" called out the shorter man, hailing me in the Taino language. The taller man likewise greeted me in his own Seneca language. I felt a little uncomfortable. Although I sensed they were a kind of vision or waking dream, I still realized that they were real and were thinking things about me, my appearance, perhaps my failure to return their greeting.

"Greetings" I finally answered back, choosing to use the language of my own ancestors. It was obvious who they were. The shorter man was the specter of Hatuei, while the taller gentleman was Corn Planter himself.

The Taino man smiled slightly at my badly pronounced greeting. They stood before me silently for some time without the slightest movement. Then the Seneca said "The time has come for the fulfillment of the prophecy of the twenty-four generations. The cycle is close to completion, the beginning of your struggle is at hand."

I stood speechless for a second. "What cycle?" I asked "What prophecy, what struggle?" Then Hatuei opened his mouth. "Five centuries of sleep have made the sacred magic very restless. The children of Kasibahagua are ready to re-awaken. The time has come for the people...your people, to reclaim their birth-right. And the people whose skin is the color of cassava, they who it was foretold would take control of our land, they are now ready to share in the sacred teachings, as well as others of different colors. They all shall come to learn this wisdom." I was more confused than ever before, though I realized that the color of cassava is white, so I assumed that he was referring to white men.

"The time of rebirth has arrived" The Taino continued. "But birth shall be wrought with pain. You and your people shall face a powerful foe. An adversary who has arisen from your own past shall challenge your work and ultimately try to defeat you." I realized they did not wish to be clear about their message. That I was simply going to have to decipher it myself, so I just continued to listen. "You will face a series of challenges in the years to come. It will be your Era of Personal Struggle" continued the Seneca." The adversary will present himself in many guises, in many shapes, but always remember his goal is to defeat the timeless human hope for brotherhood and sisterhood. His goal is to destroy the hope for reconciliation and his goal is to establish another five hundred years, maybe longer, of discord and despair. That is the hallmark of the colonized mind, the enslaved mind that exists hidden deep beneath layers of contemporary camuflage in each one of you. You, as many others like you have done already, can commit to be one of the warriors who will utilize the gifts of imaginative creativity and steadfast determination that were given to humankind long ago, to help bring about the culmination of an ancient prophecy of human reconciliation."

After those words the two men turned quickly and walked back to their canoe. "Wait!" I called after them. The Seneca stopped and turned to look back at me. He spoke in a very loud voice. "Beware the sorcery of discord in the village of tragedy." Then without another word, both men boarded their canoe and paddled back out to the middle of the river. There they appeared to vanish as if into a fog or mist. I walked back to the tent and crawled into my sleeping bag bewildered. I fell asleep and had no more dreams.

CHAPTER III

COLORS WE COME IN

1. THICK SKIN

Late on the morning of August 10 I awakened feeling like I was hung over. Sven had been up for hours but allowed me to sleep in, intuitively knowing I needed the rest. I knew I would pay dearly for my lack of sleep. In spite of this, I got up out of the tent eager to communicate with my wife in Pittsburgh. It was my son's birthday and naturally I wanted to wish him happiness on his day. I also wanted to share with them my experiences with the shooting star of the night before. I hoped to tell him that I thought it was a good luck sign to have such a beautiful thing seen in the sky on the very first hour of one's birthday. I tried to push out of my mind the troubling words of the two canoe-borne specters from my early pre-dawn vision. The monotonous paddling of the day and the river's beauty helped me stop thinking about it.

Soon we reached the city of Warren, Pennsylvania. We found a restaurant and ate there, and I succeeded in getting a call through to my wife in Pittsburgh. Nowadays I would simply reach for my cell-phone but at that time, an era before ubiquitous cellular towers, I had to haul the canoe out on the bank and drag myself into town in search of a pay-phone. I made the call. I was informed by my wife Leni that my son was, in fact enjoying his birthday, but the joy was being marred a little by some sort of rash that he seemed to be developing. I was concerned about the strange new ailment she described, but did not allow it to stop me from sharing his birthday happiness with him over the phone.

Little did I know at the time that the mysterious rash was the first signs of what would become for him a life-long personal struggle. He was destined to develop a particularly severe case of a frustrating skin disorder which would sometimes dominate elements of his life. Years later as the condition evolved we would learn all of its insidious qualities. It was almost always triggered by irritants and allergens of all kinds, and during his childhood we discovered that he was allergic to many things, from animal fur to several types of food. So the irritation and itching was never too far away at any time. Even when he moved into adulthood he would become intimatelly familiar with the offices of dermatologists. Then came the severe skin break-outs with infections and painful bleeding sores, the unpredictable trips to the hospital emergency room and a permanently scarred and thickened skin.

"Cha," as we would eventually come to nickname him, did not deserve to be cursed with the constant implacable, insatiable itch, irritation and downright pain of the vicious skin condition. Ointments, creams, balms, colloidal baths, oral medications, none of the doctor-prescribed or over-the-counter remedies gave him any permanent relief. He learned the tedious daily ritual of moisturizing his whole body and applying the many herbal and cortisone ointments. He learned to regiment his diet and carefully manage everything he put in his body. And of course he learned to deal with the cruel remarks of his schoolmates, the taunts, the name-calling from people who at that time and even now decades later do not fully understand his suffering. Most of us take our skin for granted. The thought of an itch is a simple temporary matter that is easily resolved with a little unconscious scratching and it goes away. It is almost impossible to comprehend the severity of Cha's condition. One has to understand that the human skin is a complex intricate system, known to experts as the "largest organ of the body". The first protective layer that separates the vulnerable human physical interior from the dangerous microorganisms that litteraly surround us every minute of the day and if compromised seriously, as has happened now many times during my son's life can have extremely serious consequences.

What is it about undeserved suffering that offends the human consciousness? Is it perhaps that we somehow expect fairness to be automatic? Do we feel it is a violation of some divine contract for nature to mete out suffering such as a serious chronic disease to an innocent who doesn't deserve it? Over the years I came to understand that injustice which descends from on high is always disconcerting to us because we are hard put to explain it or rationalize it. It can easily lead to loss of faith in a benevolent divine power.

However, unjust or unfair behavior acted out by a fellow human being is sometimes easier to grasp and we are better equipped to deal with it emotionally, even when we can't actually do anything to stop it because it is human-caused and, after all, humans, unlike a divine being, are so imperfect. That was what Cha encountered later in his life as he approached adolescence. A gang-related beating in a public school where his Hispanic ancestry made him a target of the local boys prompted my wife and I to withdraw him from his public school. We enrolled him in a predominately white parochial school where he heard racial epithets directed at him so many times they became indelibly branded in white-hot searing letters of hate upon his heart. At that time Pittsburgh was a town devoid of any real visible Hispanic community he had to make a truly herculean effort before he was able to find ways of fitting in. Eventually he did, but not without developing an emotional skin as thick and tough as his physical skin.

Of course Cha was not the first or last kid forced to grow up with the ugly specter of bullying, racial prejudice and the psychological scars left by it. From the minute my family arrived in the United States in 1961 I was made painfully conscious of the reality of prejudice. Growing up in the turbulent racially-charged sixties in Erie, a town which at that time lacked a Latino population, my adolescence was actually a precursor of Cha's. "Hey nigger, How' they hangin'?" "Hey spic, what color is your dick?" It wasn't so much their choice of insulting language which amused them, it was the inevitable look of puzzlement on my face as I struggled to decipher the unfamiliar slang of this new and alien language. I was newly arrived in the United States from Cuba and often times I didn't really know that they were insulting me. It was the dull glazed look in my eyes and foolish grin as I struggled to comprehend each rapidly delivered statement that reduced them to tears as they rolled on the floor of the boy's locker room convulsing with laughter.

2. BLACK RIBS

The one factor that made things a little more manegable at that time was my intense interest in my Indigenous heritage. At one point I became particularly interested in an old tradition that is still observed by some Indigenous people deep in the Amazon Rainforest where many of the ancestors of my Taino Indian forebears originated. This tradition is known as "Vision Quest". It involves periods of fasting and privation endured by young people as a vehicle for initiation into adulthood. As I approached my sixteenth birthday I became obsessed with that ceremony and came to the realization that there were powerful urges within me demanding that I perform the ritual of Vison Quest myself soon. I finally picked a warm summer weekend to retreat into a secluded place and fast for four days.

My experience on that weekend was intimately associated with the magic of insects, especially crickets. Their chirps sparkled in the darkness, like little stars. I heard that sound. I heard the voice of a spirit. It was the spirit of the sacred black cricket. It was my "semisaki," my guardian spirit. I met him for the first time on one of those evenings in the summer of 1968.

I had a friend at that time, his name was Dave. I had told my parents that I was going to spend Friday, Saturday, Sunday and Monday over at his house. Dave helped me raise a platform fashioned from an old door into the limbs of a great tree. The tree grew in a wooded area not far from Dave's house on the outskirts of the city of Erie, Pennsylvania. That night I fell asleep lying on the flat surface of the old wooden door suspended up there in that tree by ropes. As I lay there sleeping, I had a semiconscious feeling that strange things were happening to me. I was changing. I was becoming a new person. In a way, it was a kind of death. The old me was dying and the new me was being born. There was change and there was permanence. The two opposites complemented each other, functioning in unison, in harmony as they do in all aspects of the cosmic rhythm.

As I lay in a dream-like state I began to hear words. At first it was simply a casual disembodied voice holding a kind of monologue for my benefit. Eventually I began to answer and the affair turned into a conversation. I assumed that my hearing this voice was a result of my fasting. The lack of food made me feel weak and very hungry, and at times a little dizzy.

The voice continued droning on.

"Who are you?" I asked finally after half-listening for a while. "It doesn't matter who I am!" the voice answered. Then it continued. "Have you been listening to what I've been saying to you?" "Yes" I lied. "I heard every word." In fact, I couldn't recall a thing he had said. "I want to teach you something about yourself," continued the voice in the darkness. I began to get excited; it appeared that I would finally experience one of those sensational mystical communications that I had heard about from the old curanderos who follow the ancient native spiritual traditions of the islands.

As I lay happily waiting to be spoon-fed a dose of enlightenment; I began to sense a growing physical discomfort. I continued to wait patiently for the voice to speak again, but it didn't and in the mean time the distress in my abdomen grew to the point that I could feel myself squirming on the surface of my door bed. It was becoming increasingly obvious that I was going to pass gas. I held back the urge heroically. I certainly wasn't going to ruin this magical moment with such a gross expression of my bodily functions.

"Why don't you fart?" said the voice finally. "Uh?" I answered stunned. "I said, why don't you fart...if you need to pass some gas you should stop holding it in like some sort of valued possession and let it blow!" I was speechless. "But...but...I thought you were going to say something important." I finally managed to mumble. "I didn't want to fart while you were talking." "Why not?" he retorted. "Well...I don't know...it didn't seem appropriate." I said still fighting back the discomfort in my stomach. "You got some rule book that says you're not supposed to fart while holding a conversation with a spirit?" he continued. "No...no, I guess not." I answered suddenly letting go and cutting loose with a noisy honk. "Sometimes you do things and perceive things purely through the filter of your preconceptions. You are sure certain things are or should be a certain way. You assume it, but it's only your personal preconception which influences your vision and in fact things are not and do not need to be at all the way you think they are. To see things more truthfully you must free yourself from preconceptions because if you let them they will always cloud your perceptions. You should approach things with the innocence of a child, free of preconceptions." At that moment I thought of the nonchalant manner with which children pass gas in public unencumbered with the preconceptions and assumptions of politeness which we take for granted, I couldn't help smiling.

"That is the green lesson of the South, the innocence that frees you from preconceptions." he continued.

I mulled these things over for a moment. "Do you expect me to forget everything I have been conditioned to do and begin to fart in public like a kid?" I complained. "No fool...!" He answered. "I am simply telling you that you should temper the conditioning of your life experiences with the fresh outlook of the uncluttered child-mind."

He paused for a moment, then I heard him resume his discourse. "Do you love your father?" He asked. "Of course I love my father..." I responded "He is my most important role model." "But sometimes he makes you angry? He does not appear like such a wonderful guy to you at those times." The voice assumed a somewhat mischievous tone. "Well, sometimes he makes me so mad." I answered almost whining. "But isn't he the same man in any case?" "Yes, of course" I said "But when I'm mad at him I feel like I'm looking at a different man." "That's because people and situations reflect back to you your own state of mind. Often times what you perceive is not what's really there, but in fact, a reflection of your own anger or your own joy, or your own sadness. You need to crawl up inside your own self and understand what's in there before you can truly trust the veracity of your own perception. Much of what you think you see is in fact simply a reflection of yourself."

I listened enthralled as he concluded. "That is the lesson of the spirit of the west, the spirit whose sacred color is the black of night. The spirit of 'Introspection'. This is the spirit who provides you with the insight into your own soul."

"Are you teaching me now?" I asked naively wondering if the fabled wisdom of the ancient Indian spirits was in fact finally being imparted to me. "Where do you think wisdom comes from?" He asked. I thought about it for a minute then summoning up my sagest attitude I answered "Wisdom comes from the minds of the wise ancients." I felt pretty satisfied with my answer. "When you bump your head on a low hanging water pipe in the basement don't you learn to walk with your head low?" he said. When I heard this I was confused. "What does that have to do with wisdom?" I asked, "Oh, I don't know, I believe a man who learns not to bang his head is pretty wise, don't you think? That's the lesson of the North, the spirit of the color white. That's the spirit of the true wisdom. The wisdom that is attained through personal experiences, the lessons learned in the school of hard knocks."

This whole thing was not going at all the way I expected. I wasn't at all prepared for a wisecracking invisible teacher who would talk about farts and banging heads, and hard knocks. I had rather expected a vision of a tall old man with long white braids and sage sayings.

Then he spoke again: "When a hawk soars high above the ground and it looks down in search of prey, it takes in the whole panorama spread beneath it in clear sharp detail. The clarity of the daylight sky allows for a wholistic and inclusive image of reality. It sacrifices the detail of close inspection for the conclusive imagery that comes from seeing the whole picture. That is the lesson of the spirit of the East. It is the spirit of illumination, clear vision."

I waited for him to speak again but he didn't. Gradually I sank back into a deep sleep.

For four days I stayed in that wooded site praying and invoking the spirits of the forces of Nature. I was young, haughty and inexperienced in the inner workings of the spiritual system within which I was operating. In spite of the disconcerting experience with that flippant dream-voice on my first night, I still maintained many of my original expectations about the Vision Quest. I demanded a splendid vision. I expected to be visited by eagles, buffaloes and panthers just like I had read in the books.

On the second day I squatted on the ground facing west, the direction of introspection. I closed my eyes and prayed. All I was wearing was a brief loincloth. As the afternoon wore on and the sun approached the western horizon a great swarm of hungry mosquitoes surrounded me. I was bitten many times. I forced myself to endure the agony and humiliation as stoically as I could. The attack was probably not long, but it seemed to last for hours. I felt like I was losing a gallon of blood to the little suckers! Suddenly, the buzzing stopped and the infernal itching ceased.

I was surrounded by the twilight of early evening. The sky grew darker, then a single thin line of sound emerged from a spot behind me. I closed my eyes again and prayed. The sound was that of a cricket chirping rhythmically. It persisted, a veritable love song in the darkness. A second cricket began to sing on my right. I began to lapse into that hazy dream-state. I half expected to hear the disembodied voice I had heard on the first night, but it never came again that weekend. Instead, as more crickets added their voices to that of the first two I was enveloped in a blanket of sound. It wrapped me like a thin, fresh, cotton cloth sheet. It lifted me off the ground and held me aloft, above the crowns of the nearby trees. Each chirp was like a bright spark in the night sky. I began to vision. I saw myself identified with some large animal that had been killed for food by a tribe of hunters, a large sea cow, a manatee, slaughtered by ancient Tainos armed with spears and flint knives. The flesh had been consumed and there was nothing left but a great rib cage lying on the ground. I saw myself represented in this dead animal who had sacrificed his life for others. Then I saw myself as a man, approaching the big rib cage. Curiously enough instead of gleaming white, the bones were shiny black in color, the hue of introspection. I began to carve the ribs. I fashioned them into several utilitarian objects. One of those objects was a special spatula that the ancient Tainos used to induce vomiting for personal purification of their inner bodies. Then I gave the objects to some of the people who happened to be near-by. After providing the flesh and hide from its body, these bones were the last thing the great animal had to give for the sake of the people.

I sensed a feeling of continuity, a continuity that stretched back in time to the days of Hatuei, the days of Handsome Lake. I sensed a link between these and the self-sacrificing legendary characters of Indigenous mythology such as the Taino Yoka Hu, spirit of the life cycle, the soul of the yuca tuber plant that must die so that humans can eat and live, and the Maya divine twin Hun Ahpu, who sacrificed himself in the great bonfire so that he could be reconstituted as a victorious new being and triumph over the Lords of Negativity. I perceived each of these personages as a great animal, giving of itself even to the last rib for the welfare of the people. I saw them as examples of self-sacrificial altruism, which I would try to emulate. The symbolic color of the gift of the west spirit "Koromo" (Introspection/Self-understanding) is black in the tradition of my ancestors. At that moment I acquired a spirit name. I was taught the Taino language name Sobaoko Koromo. The word "sobaoko" is associated to the common slang term in modern Cuban Spanish "sobaco" (armpit). This term is derived from the Taino name for the portion of the ribcage in the area of the armpit.

Koromo is the name of the Taino spirit of the direction of the West whose symbolic color is black. So "Sobaokok Koromo can be translated as "Black Ribs".

I slowly returned to full awareness of my surroundings. I sensed the presence of some significant object lying behind me. I turned and saw on the ground a wooden dowel and nearby six feathers: four owl tail-plumes, the tail feather of a red-tailed hawk and a woodpecker tail feather. I gathered up these gifts from the Great Spirit and later fashioned my prayer headdress from them.

Learning the identity of my guardian spirit and having this entity clarify the meaning of my life journey made it a lot easier to cope with the spirit of intolerance and conflict whose presence I was beginning to feel more and more each day in my experience. My experience with the spirit of prejudice had followed me into high school. I attended a trade-oriented school in which the students were required to spend half of the day in shop and the other half in academics. My shop was Art. Mr. Plavcan, our Art teacher suggested that I take a diciplined technical drawing class to tighten up my somewhat sloppy work habits.

I was in my technical drawing class one afternoon experiencing the joys of proper drafting techniques. In a careless gesture of boredom I leaned over to whisper something to the kid sitting next to me. It was the fourth time I had done that this afternoon, and the fourth time Mr. Alessandro, the drafting teacher caught me.

"That does it, Mr. Sagoo..." (Mr. Alessandro never did get my name right) "I've had it with you, buddy. I told you I didn't want any talking during this project. You're outta here! Go down to Mr. Stepford's office right now!"

I knew I had it coming. He did give me three chances. And anyway he was still nursing a justified grudge from the previous day when a carefully whispered, but all too humorous joke about his choice of tie resulted in an explosion of laughter among the boys sitting all around my desk. I knew I had it coming!

I walked down the hall in shame. I had never been paddled, and that's what a trip to Mr. Stepford's office usually meant. I was aware of the old man's reputation with that piece of wood. He had a swing like Arnold

Palmer. My only consolation as I approached the Assistant Principal's office was the knowledge that I, in fact, richly deserved the punishment. What the heck! Alessandro didn't need my stupid clowning around, disrupting his class. The guy was just trying to do his job.

I entered the office. Stepford sat behind his desk working on something. When I came in he glanced up at me over his bifocals. I stepped up to the desk and handed him the note that Alessandro had entrusted me with. I felt like I was delivering my own order of execution.

Stepford read the note. He got up and faced me. "Oh well..." I thought. I was ready. I would take it like a man! I was resigned to my fate.

As the old World War II veteran glared at me I looked up past him and spotted the well-polished and beautifully varnished paddle hanging on the wall behind him. It had been a gift from the previous year's senior wood-shop class.

I looked at the paddle, but curiously, he didn't. He just kept staring at me. I finally turned my eyes back to him, a little puzzled. He had a strange look on his face. It wasn't the look of a disciplinarian. It was that look that says: "What I wouldn't do to be standing in the dark in my living room with my .45 in my hand and this asshole breaking in through a window."

When I deciphered the significance of his stare I was taken aback.

"Son, I don't care what color you are..."

Where the heck was this going? Why was this man making references to my color?

"I figure anybody can go bad; you know?" He continued "I call the white ones 'White Trash' same as I call the black ones 'Nigger'; you know what I mean?"

I understood perfectly well what he meant. I just never expected it from a school authority figure. I thought sentiments like these were expressed only by dumb kids and people in the South. I could deal with it from my peers. But coming from this man, this authority figure, this adult role-model, was a whole other matter.

"I'm not going to paddle you, because this is the first time you've been sent to my office. But I suggest you measure your behavior boy."

You don't want your teachers to think of you as a dumb spic, do you son? You want your teachers to see you as a good student." I stood there looking at him, wishing he had just paddled me.

I graduated from highschool that summer, and in the fall of that same year I began attending an art college in a neighboring state. I was walking home at about 2:00 A.M. one evening with my Navajo classmate Al Chee. In the East where fewer indians reside people unfamiliar with the way Indians look often mistook him for a Chinese person because of his high cheek bones and his Oriental-sounding name (In reality Chee is a very common Navajo surname) Al had come all the way East on a tribal scholarship to study art.

Al and I had spent about six hours that evening visiting most of the bars and clubs on the enormous campus of the local university far from our own little art school. We had spent most of that time checking out the college girls and drinking. It would be fair to say that we were not walking a perfectly straight line as we made our way back on the sidewalk to our own campus three miles away.

I guess it was the fact that it was such a dark night and I had a hat on making it difficult to discern the curl in my hair. The police officers who suddenly flashed their spot light on us from their cruiser thought we were both Chinese. It would soon become obvious that one of them didn't like Orientals. He was the one that got out of the car.

I don't remember very well how things got out of hand that night. It may have been that the alcohol made an usually shy and withdrawn Al a bit too cocky as the policeman inspected our college I.D. cards. All I remember is that fellow growling: "Don't you talk to me like that you fucking Gook!"

He caught Al hard on the chin with his flashlight. Al staggered backward and fell on the hard sidewalk, his lip bleeding.

"Our boys are dying over there in Nam, You sons 'a bitches come over here to this country, think your'e smarter than regular Americans..." He mumbled tossing Al's I.D. card at him on the ground.

I knelt next to Al. "Hey..." I complained trying to help my friend. "You can't do this. He didn't do anything! Anyway, he's not Chinese or Vietnamese or any of that...He's more American than you. He's an Indian."

The policeman glowered at me. I thought he was going to hit me too. Then I heard his partner answer a call on their police radio and suddenly whispering urgently: "Chuck, Chuck, come on let's go... Chuck, come on Chuck!"

The officer threw my I.D. card in my face and turned away still mumbling. "Well, you sure ain't no American you fucking wetback spic!" I could tell he had noticed my Spanish accent and had read my Spanish name, "Miguel" on my card.

He got back to his car and they drove away.

Was I somehow aware as I paddled my canoe on the river on the day of my son's third birthday, of the fact that I was poised between those two realities on the morning of August 10, 1982? Was I conscious of those two realities, the reality of my own past adolescent struggle with the demon of hate, and the reality of my son's future struggle with the same demon ten years hence? Maybe I was, at least vaguely aware. In any case I paddled on.

As I paddled I reflected on that demon and what he had done to me, the thick multi-textured layers of fears, suspicions, preconceptions and animosities which he had taught me over the years. They were layers, like thick layers of skin that I was aware of. They were layers which I was consciously trying to shed, with varying degrees of success.

I realized that we all carry these layers to a greater or lesser extent. I realized that those boys who delighted so much in tormenting me in the school locker room when I was twelve were victims just like me. I recognized this fact as I paddled and pushed the canoe forward.

Now, all these years later as I sit here recalling and typing all this into my word processor I also see my own son, also at the age of twelve, faced by the same enemy, and surrounded by a group of boys who beat him up because of the color of his skin. I see those boys also as victims. We're all victims of the same demon, a demon which seems to surface on many levels of interaction between humans all over the world; as if our species had been somehow desperately disconnected from the magic of what humanity truly ought to be, lost here in the midst of the Fifth Sun, and was sending out a great outcry, pleading for salvation.

3. PASKALOONSKA

After we left Warren we passed a place called "Buckaloons Campground." As we glided past this recreational area I called out to Sven: "How are we doing time-wise?" "Not bad" answered Sven checking his map. "I can see the Buckaloons right here on...." He wasn't able to finish his sentence. With a sickening loud scrape the canoe came to a sudden halt. We had become grounded on a gravel-studded sand bar. The river was at its late summer low-water mark and this area was veritably booby-trapped with shallow canoe-ripping rocks and sand bars. I winced at the thought of what the sharp gravel had done to the canvas-covered bottom of the fine old canoe. Then suddenly I felt a strange rush of anger rise up from the pit of my stomach. I glanced at Sven. "Shit man!" I screamed at him. We probably put a big tear in the canoe skin. You're supposed to stay on top of that situation. You're the navigator. Why didn't you find the deep water channel through here? Don't you have maps of the river's navigable areas?" Sven climbed out of the canoe, his sneakers soaking up the cool water as he stepped in the shallow.

"Hey! The water's too low at this time of the year, man. It's hard to judge where the deep water is." He answered. "Well, how the hell we gonna make a two hundred and fifty mile river trip in a canoe that may start leaking like a sieve?" I yelled, stepping out of my end of the craft. "I don't know Miguel. What do you want me to say? It's not completely my fault we're grounded, Ok? Just help me pull the canoe out of this mess and let's make some time. Just quit bitching at me, alright?" He said "just quit bitching at me" but what I heard in my anger-addled mind was "Just quit bitching at me, you spic!"

I developed and almost irresistible urge to lift my canoe paddle and bring it down on the head of this wise-ass white guy. When I realized what I was contemplating, I shivered. Quickly, I threw the paddle into the water. "What's the matter with you, Miguel?" Sven stared at me puzzled. The emotions churning inside me were frightening. As I stood there next to the grounded canoe with the water swirling around my ankles I felt a deep resonating hatred toward my friend. It was a hatred born of resentment, fear. I began to discover within me a dozen different kinds of bigotry I had never known I possessed, emotions I was not able or willing to identify. I wanted to talk about it, but I was afraid of what might come out of my mouth.

"Hey! Miguel, what you so mad about?" Sven asked taking a few steps toward me. I moved back away from him. As I did the canoe shifted and the river's current began to carry it off the sand and gravel bar. We both instinctively reached for the precious vessel inside which was all our camping gear. I looked up quickly at Sven.

"Hey! watch your end man." he yelled struggling to keep his side of the canoe from getting away. I turned my attention back to our task and soon we were on the river again. "What was that all about back there?" Sven asked as he paddled. "Uh!...I...Err... I just lost it that's all. I'm sorry." "Well what the hell!" he exclaimed and clammed up for a long time.

I looked over to my right at the site of the old campground, then something clicked in my brain. "Hey Sven!" I called out. "What!" he answered still irritated. "Aw come on." I insisted, "Don't be mad at me" "No?"... he turned to face me. "Well, you better cool that shit, you hear? cause I ain't gonna put up with it. You were acting like a fucking mad man back there."

"I'm sorry Sven" I pleaded. He turned and faced the front still fuming.

I kept silent for about five minutes as we continued to paddle past the Buckaloons. Then I ventured to address him again. "Hey Sven, I'm sorry man. It ain't gonna happen again." He grunted. "Hey Sven..." I addressed him again. "Hey man, look at your info booklet will ya...look up the Buckaloons for me. What does your historical informational map of the river say about the Buckaloons campground?"

Sven paused in his paddling and reached into the water-tight plastic pouch in which he carried our charts and maps. Thumbing through the pages of his little book he located the Buckaloons site and some notes on its history. "Hmm. Here it is!" He exclaimed. I listened intently although I somehow had a feeling I already knew something about the place.

Oh yea..." Sven continued, "This was the site of an eighteenth century Delaware Indian village..." He flipped through the pages. "A terrible battle took place here. Many Indians were killed."

I remembered the words of the ghost just before he vanished the night before. "Beware the sorcery of discord in the village of tragedy."

"What the hell happened here Sven?" I asked somberly. "Aw you know, the same old story of racial hatred and war... as it turns out these Delaware had been allowed to move into the Allegheny River valley by the Seneca's. They had been pushed out of Eastern Pennsylvania by the British settlers in Philadelphia and Harrisburg. Then when the European settlements kept moving west they again felt penned in by the white people."

I listened as Sven got the information from his book. "This village was called 'Paskaloonska'. That's where the word 'Buckaloons' comes from. Paskaloonska was one of the main resistance sites after the Revolutionary war, when the AngloAmerican settler's forced these Indians to fight for the last bits of western Pennsylvania where they still lived. Finally a detachment of troops of the U.S. continental army, led by a certain Colonel Broadhead, marched north from Pittsburgh in 1781.

After a bloody battle, in which many Indian men, women and children were literally massacred, the village was destroyed and the miserable remnants fled west into West Virginia and Ohio."

He looked up from his reading and turned to face me. "Well..." he continued "anyway; the name Broadhead ended up in Pittsburgh didn't it?" I thought about it for a minute, then I realized that there was, in fact at that time, a depressed slum neighborhood called Broadhead Manor in Pittsburgh's West End area where the residents struggled with the problems of poverty, drugs, gang violence, racial discrimination and general despair on a daily basis. Named after the 18'th century army officer who perpetrated the massacre at Paskaloonska, Broadhead Manor was a modern "Village of Tragedy". Years after our downriver adventure, in 1998, the blighted housing projects of Broadhead Manor were finally demolished and the residents were scattered against their will into a number of other urban ghettos in the area.

We paddled quietly down the river as the reality of what happened back at Buckaloons sank into my unconscious. I almost struck my friend on the head with the canoe paddle back there! I realized that the negativity, concentrated at Buckaloons, had energized something mysterious, some sinister entity which I felt was shadowing my steps. I realized that the nature of the strange presence was associated mainly with conflict, intolerance and despair. All these elements of hate had been foretold to me by the ghostly apparitions back near the dam. I began to dread my next encounter with whatever it was that was following me around, especially since I had a weird feeling that this thing had come looking for me from another time, another century.

4. THAT'S LIFE

After about an hour of paddling beyond the Buckaloons I began to daydream again. This time my daydreams carried me back to many of the Cuban traditions within which I had been raised. Intuitively I began to realize that many of these folkways that I had long written off as simple peasant customs passed down from the country upbringing of my grandmothers were, in fact, survivals from an Indigenous past. It began to dawn on me just how much of what I carried deep in my subconscious was truly a gift of my Native ancestors. That was the true beginning of my training for what I was to become later in my life. From these elders, my grandparents, my mother, my father, my aunts and uncles, I learned the basic foundations of ancient values which they had inherited and then passed on to me. They themselves did not realize just how much of this wisdom was inherited from our Indigenous ancestors. By the time I was growing up in this tradition most of my elders believed the ancient Tainos had been wiped off the face of the earth and nothing had survived of what they had once been.

My experiences listening to the ethereal chants, the beautiful rhythms of the Cordon tradition which wafted over the garden partition wall from the neighbor's house into my grandmother's courtyard on the nights that I stayed there added a powerful layer of musical magic to those early childhood experiences. Later on my father revealed to me his own experiences as a guest in Cordon spiritist gatherings which he had been invited to while he was working as a young newly-graduated teacher in a rural area of Oriente region in the 1940's.

My father also did a lot to add a whole other layer of cultural knowledge after we had immigrated to the United States. Not long after we arrived here in North America my dad landed a job as Spanish language and Latin American culture professor at Erie, Pennsylvania's Gannon College. Almost right away my father was given the opportunity to travel to the region of Yucatan in Mexico, and to the countries of Guatemala and Belize on professional sabbatical as part of an in-depth study of the culture of the ancient Maya civilization. My father's study and research in Central America was carried out in preparation for a course offered at Gannon. Later on I helped design and decorate the cover for the promotional brochure which was circulated around the campus to encourage students to take my father's course. It was a fascinating period in my life. I would sit for hours by his side at his desk at home and listen to his excited talk of sacred calendars and offerings of copal incense. As a former math teacher, the intricate arithmetic and mystical numerology of the Mayan calendar fixated my father with an infectious thrill which in turn affected me profoundly and permanently. This experience launched me on a journey of study of the Maya culture which paralleled my work with the culture of my own Taino people.

Then, early in the decade of the 1970's during several of the first years of my college career I met a number of people who played an enormous role in my spiritual formation. In the decade of the 1970's I befriended a young Yucatec Maya from Merida, Mexico. His name was Arturo. Arturo and I attended college classes together. He was extremely well-versed in the ancient traditions of his people. He spoke the Maya dialect of his region fluently as well as Spanish, which is how he and I communicated. Arturo did a lot to help me expand what I had learned from my father in the late 60's. This knowledge of Maya tradition that I picked up from Arturo confirmed for me the parallels I felt I was discovering between ancient Maya culture and the Native culture of Cuba.

In 1970 I also discovered an internationally circulated Indigenous newspaper that, in those days, had become one of the most prominent mouthpieces of the nascent Indian Power movement. Closely associated with the activities of the American Indian Movement, the most militant Native organization of that time, this journal was published in the St Regis Mohawk Reservation of upstate New York and was called Akwesasne Notes. Akwesasne Notes identified and expounded in its articles the deepest most visceral emotions of downtrodden Indians all over the United States. It also became a means via which Native people could express to the world how they felt about the injustices that they faced in their lives every day. I contacted the Notes and soon discovered that they were in need of an artist to illustrate some of their articles and also the independent pamphlets that they issued from time to time. I became a correspondent artist for the newspaper and for me it was a source of enormous pride whenever a new issue of the Notes was released with my illustrations.

My editor, the man who assigned me the illustration jobs wrote to me one day and asked me if I wished to provide illustrations for a similar newspaper based out of California called "Indigena". This newspaper was very interesting to me because it had a Spanish-language focus and dealt with the issues of Indigenous people in Spanish-speaking countries and other countries in Latin America.

An example of the author's illustration for the Native American publication Akwesasne Notes and his official correspondent artist ID card

When I began working for Indigena I began to correspond with an editor there who was of Haitian origin. Her name was Marie-Helene Laraque. Marie-Helene informed me that she was a Taino, a fact that thrilled me since in the 1970's I had not heard of anyone who identified themselves specifically as Taino.

During one particularly momentous telephone conversation between Marie-Helen and me, my complaints as to the lack of available information about the culture of the ancient Tainos made her pause briefly. Then she said to me: "What makes you believe there is no information available about our people?" "I have searched and there is really nothing about the beliefs of our people." I whined. At that point she simply responded: "Watch your mailbox." I did not know what she meant, but a few days later I received a heavy manila envelope from her in the mail. Inside I found a pack of carefully photocopied pages from a book. Marie-Helen had meticulously reproduced and sent me the full English translation of Ramon Pane's "Relacion Acerca De Las Antiguedades De Los Indios", a brief but detailed record of Taino culture, spiritual tradition and practices written by a monk who had been given that task by Christopher Columbus himself.

I had never heard of this book and was shocked at the amount of first-hand information about my ancestors that it placed at my disposal. Ultimately the most impressive aspect of the book is how similar many of those five-hundred-year old traditions were to traditions that I knew were still maintained by the peasants of Cuba today. This book contained my first introduction to the ancestral nature of the ancient Taino spirit Ioka-Hu the Lord of the Life Force and his relationship to his mother Ata Bei the Cosmic Matriarch. By reading the material that Marie-Helene had sent me I began to understand that this sacred being was, in fact, closely associated with the concept of energy and Life. His name was drawn from the word "Ioka" or "Yoka". This word is a close cognate of a word of Taino origin in the common Cuban dialect, "yuca". The word "yuca" identifies one of the most nutritious and energy-yielding food plants grown in that country as well as in the rest of the Caribbean to this day. In a sense, Ioka-Hu, the soul of the yuca plant, the son of Mother Ata Bei, is a being that grows from the fertile soil of the earth every year and is the very personification of all Life itself which emerges from the fertile pregnant underground womb of Mother Earth.

Ata Bei the Cosmic Matriarch and her two sons Yokahu and Guakar

My knowledge of the relationship between Ata Bei and Yoka Hu was expanded later in the decade of the 1970's after I met and began my long-distance relationship with my wife-to-be, Lenia Rodriguez. Lenia lived in a town of northern New Jersey that formed part of the unofficial greater New York metropolitan area. Whenever I traveled from Erie, Pennsylvania and visited Leni in New Jersey during the 1970's I took the opportunity to also visit near-by New York City. At that time the Big Apple boasted the largest and most complete Native American artifact collection in the world, the Heye Foundation Museum of the American Indian, located in the Washington Heights area of uptown Manhattan. On one of my many visits to the museum I met and befriended Federico, a Puerto Rican fast-food restaurant manager who, like me, was a frequent visitor at the museum. Federico was a high school drop-out, but I quickly realized that he possesed a rare wisdom that could not be acquired in a school. His knowledge came from years of life in the rural mountain country along the central highlands of his homeland.

Federico and I began to meet periodically in Central Park. There he taught me things about Taino culture that I could never have learned any place else. He introduced me to a unique world of spiritual ceremonialism that laid much of the foundation for everything I would later incorporate into my personal belief system.

Federico was the person in my life who gave me my clearest understanding of the sacred personality of Ioka Hu (Yokahu) the Taino spirit of yuca, the metaphoric representative of all Life and Energy. Federico introduced me to his unique insight on Ioka Hu on a warm Saturday afternoon as I sat next to him on the grass in Central Park. He laid down the guitar he had been playing and began to talk:

"You remember what I've told you about him?"

I nodded "yes"; Federico had shared many things with me about the Taino belief in Ioka-Hu.

"Ioka-Hu is the spirit of plants..." He continued.

"Ioka-Hu is the image of the yuca plant, the starchy, nutritious food that some people call 'cassava'. Cassava (or yuca) served as the dietary staple for our Taino ancestors.

As the top representation of Life, Ioka-Hu's most important symbol is the sun. The sacred narratives of the ancient Tainos, as recorded by Ramon Pane, speak of the spirit Ioka-Hu as dwelling in the heavens. He is the solar lord. The sun bathes our fertile planet with life-giving radiant light. Plants then use that radiant energy and convert it into calories, food energy (food-starch). They do this through a magical procedure called 'photosynthesis'. By doing all of this, plants establish the basis of all life on Earth. They do it through their relationship with the sun. They bring to earth and make the solar energy available to us.

Animals and people eat plants, and release into their own bodies the solar energy which plants went through so much trouble to store up in their tissues. We people and animals do this by digesting those plant tissues. In this way what was once solar energy is first transformed into plant energy and then finally into animal and human energy.

Taino belief recognizes a continuity of kinship between the sun, with its radiant life-giving light, then the plant, and finally the animals and people that eat the plants. This chain of continuity is manifested in the individual called 'Ioka-Hu'. The Taino spirit Ioka-Hu is associated with the most productive and energy-loded plant in the Taino menu, yuca, after which he was named. Beside that, the ancient Tainos also spoke of Ioka-Hu as dwelling in the sky. That confirms his identification with the sun.

Remember that Ioka-Hu is the plant spirit whose roots have to be eaten before he can manifest himself as a life-giver. He must sacrifice himself and die before he can fulfill his destiny. The yuca plant must be uprooted and killed before the yuca root can do what it does best, feed people!

Finally there is the issue of Hope. Being the Lord of Life and ultimate plant spirit, Ioka-Hu also holds out hope each year. As he dies at harvest-time, he holds out the hope that he will be reborn again as a new sprout, the following year at planting-time. He will be reborn along with the germinating plants of spring, reborn to grow and be there for us at many harvests to come. This theme of death followed by resurrection is, of course, paralleled by the Christian Jesus through his re-emergence from the grave on Easter Sunday, also in the spring."

Federico leaned back against the trunk of a tree as I mulled over in my mind the concepts he had just shared with me.

"Of course..." I exclaimed after some thought. "Spring is the season chosen to celebrate Ioka-Hu's rebirth. He is a solar spirit so he embodies the same symbolism as that image which the archaeologists discovered scratched into a stone in Utuado, Puerto Rico, the one they dubbed 'The Sun of Utuado'."

"Exactly..." affirmed Federico. "That image of a sun with a human face represents the 'Hope Child' of ancient prophecy. It is that 'Hope Child', expressed as the spirit of Light, the spirit of Life.

But that's not all there is to this 'Spirit of Life' business, Miguel..."

"You mean there's more!" I was genuinely surprised.

He leaned toward me. "In the legends and historical records of your own country, Cuba, there are more parallels. Ioka-Hu, the Taino sun spirit of Light, Life, and Hope bears yet another resemblance to Jesus. You see... They are both born of a virgin mother!

I have heard that the anthropologists and archeologists who study the culture of our Taino ancestors all agree that the title 'Ma-Orokoti' which that Spanish monk Ramon Pané said was one of the names for Ioka-Hu, means 'Without Male Ancestor', in other words, without a father. It is obvious that our Taino ancestors believed that Ioka-Hu was born of a mother who had no previous sexual contact, a virgin.

You know the story of your country's 'Virgin of Charity'. Remember how there's folks that say that the statue was first brought to Cuba by a shipwrecked sailor?"

I nodded "Yes" in response to his question.

"That sailor's name was Ojeda, and he gave that statue to the Indians of Cueiba. It is no wonder that those Indians welcomed the statue to their village with such enthusiasm. After all, the Spanish told those villagers that the woman portrayed by the statue was the virgin Mother of the World. They also told the Indians that the child she held in her left hand was a boy born without the benefit of sexual intercourse with a man.

Knowing now what we know about the ancient Taino belief that Ioka-Hu, the son of Ata-Bei had no father, we can well understand why those Indians immediately made the connection between Ojeda's statue and their own Mother divinity, Ata-Bei. And we can also understand how they made the connection between the Virgin Mary's baby and their own Ioka-Hu, Lord of Life, Light, and Hope."

I learned a lot from Federico those two years that I spent hanging out with him.

In 1976 Federico passed away.

That same year I was married. On that cloudy June afternoon as Federico lay struggling for his last breath in a bed of the intensive care unit of a New York City hospital, I stood unaware of his predicament, beside my bride, before the mayor of West New York, New Jersey just across the Hudson River. By the time we finished saying our vows, he was dead.

5. THE INDIAN CENTER

As we continued to progress slowly downstream on the afternoon of August 10 I again began to fret about our limited time and the fact that I had promised my boss at the Indian center that I would be back to work after only two weeks. The excecutive director, Russ Simms, had been very understanding and had given me the two weeks without hesitation wisely comprehending just how important this trip was to me.

I discovered the existance of this organization while I was still living in Erie. I had just gotten married and was working in the educational component of a minority health advocacy agency when one day a friend approached me and informed me of the center's existance in Pittsburgh, about three hours car ride away. I struck up a long distance relationship during the following months with the Pittsburgh agency which ultimately culminated in my being offered a job there. I promptly quit my job in Erie and moved to Pittsburgh.

In September of 1977 I arrived in Pittsburgh, a city originally built near the site of an important Delaware Indian village called Shannopin's Town. This city later became the epicenter of the Andrew Carnegie multimillion dollar steel manufacturing empire, built on the backs of generations of thousands of overworked underpaid immigrant steel workers.

Almost immediately I went to work as an educational researcher for the Indian center's Native American Cultural Curriculum project. My new job required me to spend long hours of research at the Hillman Library of the University of Pittsburgh.

It was there at the Hillman Library that I discovered how intimately ancient Taino tradition permeated the culture within which I had been raised. It was there that I discovered the subtle relationships between that Taino tradition and the traditions of the high mesoamerican and Mexican civilizations, especially the Maya.

It was there also that I began to get the first inkling of the five hundred year prophecy of the resurgence of Taino culture and its potential impact on humanity. It was through my experience as an employee of the Indian center that I became inspired to make the canoe journey in which I now found myself. This canoe trip was, in some ways, the logical outgrowth of my many hours of study at the Hillman Library.

The year before I went on this canoe trip, I and others in the Pittsburgh area, who wished to follow in the ancient path of Taino tradition, formed the spiritual group named, "Caney Indigenous Spiritual Circle." It grew slowly like something alive. The members were both people of Caribbean Indigenous origin and others who were not. I never saw any reason why our group should deny membership to a person based on that person's ethnic origin.

Some of the early period of the Caney Circle's history was plagued with controversy within the Native American community of Pittsburgh.

Unfortunately there was a conservative Christian element in the center's membership who resented what they saw as "pagan" activity in the work that I was doing there. That all was complicated by the fact that, even though this religious conflict existed, the principal Christian family that objected to our activity contained a member who claimed to be trained by a "real", "authentic" medicine man back on their reservation. The young man's name was Jimmy and he demonstrated particular contempt for me and the Caney Circle. Evidently they did not consider his work "pagan". The ironic contradiction of a Christian family objecting to the activities of the Caney Circle at the Indian center on the grounds that it was "pagan", and yet promoting their relative Jimmy as a traditional Native medicine man seemed to be lost on them all.

With the support of our center director, who had become my personal friend, we prevailed and our circle eventually came to be tolerated by the wider Native community of the region. With time my activities and the Caney Circle became more acceptable to most of the Pittsburgh Indians. Some of them even began to attend the circle ceremonies. A couple of the more inspired members of the community even led special prayers and ceremonies based upon their own tribal traditions as guest spiritual leaders by invitation. Our small circle continued to develop turning into the focus of a small community of Indian and non-Indian earth-minded people. Soon we were meeting on a regular basis on the hilltop site of the Indian center.

6. THE WOODEN FLOOR

Around the time when I was making my way down the Allegheny River in Pennsylvania in 1982 a group of fishermen in Cuba were making some of the most extraordinary archeological discoveries of the Caribbean in the twentieth century. In a place called Buchillones they discovered the remains of a huge Taino Indian village. Some of the buildings of this Indigenous community had been built elevated above the ground supported on heavy log pilons, rather like houses on stilts. The reason the Indians built these houses up off the ground was to guard against periodic flooding. The floors of these structures were made of wood, a fact that made them different from the typical Taino bohio home in higher or drier parts of the country with its packed dirt floor.

I did not find out about these archeological discoveries until many years after my river journey but even without knowing about the discoveries at Buchillones, I was aware that sometimes my ancestors built houses on stilts and with solid wooden floors. But wooden floors were not on my mind on August 10 1982. I was thinking about food. After a few more miles paddling down the river I began thinking about the Cuban tradition of the "Pig Roast" with its accompanying music and fraternal camaraderie. As I paddled I meditated on a long-held desire of some day holding my own pig roast. Two years later, when this two-week river voyage had become but a fond memory, I got the opportunity to throw just such a party.

It was a Fourth of July party and it would take place in my own back yard on a sunny afternoon in July of 1984. I would find myself surrounded by a group of Cuban and Puerto Rican friends who I had managed to acquire during the two years after my river trip. Hispanic friends were hard to come by in Pittsburgh in those days.

"Pass me a beer, Juan." Tony called out in Spanish as he sat down next to me on a stool. He picked up the big conga drum he had brought with him and laid it sideways on his lap. He looked over at me and smiled with a wink. "Lets show these guys how it's done." He whispered to me. Juan walked over holding two bottles he had just fished out of the cooler. Tony snatched one of the bottles, opened it and knocked it back, gulping down its content in one draught. "Man, it's hot out there!" he exclaimed wiping the sweat off his face with his sleeve. He had gotten done with his turn at the firepit and the heat of the coals had taken their toll on him.

Tony began a slow six-eight cadence on the conga, while Juan sat down and accompanied him on the claves. Over by the hot coals, Eddie shifted to look at the drummers and smiled. He turned the spit slowly. The pig rotated gradually over the hot coals, its color changing perceptively to a golden brown.

The pig had come cheap. Tony worked in the butcher's section of Foodland supermarket in the West End. They gave him a discount on an eighty-pounder and we all pitched in on the cost. Now, we were celebrating the Fourth of July 1984, Cuban style!

I sat back and enjoyed the rhythm of Tony's "Bata" beat: "Ide were were nita Ochun Ide were nita ya..." The African words flowed from Tony's tongue like a magical incantation, his ebony hands dancing like butterflies on the tight skin of his drum. The rhythm of the chant took hold of everyone in our little backyard.

Leni, my wife, who had spent all night seasoning the large bulk of the pig in preparation for the day's roasting, suddenly got up to dance. The exhaustion from the night's work fell from her like a heavy burden shed.

Eddie over by the coals, began to shake his behind rhythmically. Then he turned to look at me and yelled: "What does all that stuff mean?" His Spanish was very strongly accented by his many years in English-speaking Philadelphia. "Oh..." I answered getting up and walking over to him. "That's just a Santeria chant; Tony is singing in the Lucumi language."

Even as I said that I realized that Eddie wouldn't know what the hell I was talking about. At that time few Puerto Ricans were acquainted with Afro-Cuban culture.

"Lucumi" is the common term used in Cuba for the Yoruba language spoken by the African slaves who had been brought to that country over a period of four hundred years. The language had survived, little changed in the chants of a unique spiritual tradition called, "Santeria."

Over the centuries that these people were forced to work in the sugar cane and coffee plantations, and in the tobacco fields they developed a synchretic hybrid which neatly blended traditional Catholic concepts from Spain with aspects of their polytheistic African mysticism.

"It's just an African language..." I began to explain as I noticed the puzzled look on Eddie's face. "Oh yeah, yeah, sure, It's all that AfroCuban Yoruba stuff, right? I've heard something about that." He smiled as he looked at the singer on the other side of the yard. I nodded and patted him on the back, then I moved away from the intense heat of the coals.

When Eddie was a child his family moved from Puerto Rico into a Puerto Rican barrio of North Philadelphia. He lived there for several years with his family. Now he was a tall handsome nineteen-year-old with as many girlfriends as any one man could handle.

He had only recently moved to Pittsburgh. The circumstances relating to his move were obscure, but it seemed obvious to many of us who knew him that he had been in trouble with the law several times back in Philly. All he ever offered by way of explanation was that his mom had moved back to their home town of Utuado in Puerto Rico. Without any remaining family ties in the city of brotherly love, he decided to move out.

Eddie's uncle, a social service worker in Philadelphia knew another social service worker who served a brief stint as translator for hundreds of Cuban refugees interned at the processing camp of Fort Indiantown Gap hear Harrisburg in 1980 during the historic Mariel Boat Lift phenomenon.

Eddie had accompanied his uncle on numerous visits to the camp. During those visits Eddie got to meet some of the young men who had just recently arrived on the Mariel boat lift. He was impressed by their macho swagger and had struck up friendships with several of them.

Now, here in Pittsburgh, he resumed that friendship in the public housing projects and ghettos of the West End where several of the Mariel immigrants had relocated.

Mario walked over and sat by me. He swallowed a couple of gulps of Iron City beer and then switched the bottle over to his disabled hand. "If it wasn't for this stupid shriveled-up arm of mine I'd probably be playing the drums like that also." He complained pointing at his left hand.

I looked down at it. The little deformed fingers curled awkwardly around the half-empty I.C. bottle

"What was it you told me that did this to you?" I asked him reaching for a glass of rum and coke. "Don't you remember?" He answered. "I got polio when I was a kid back in Cuba. It left my whole arm all shriveled up like this... Even the operation I had, when they sent me to Russia, helped only a little."

"Well, at least now you can hold a beer bottle with that hand." I retorted. "Yeah that's true. He sighed, "But I can't bring it up to my mouth." He reached over with his good hand and took the bottle, finishing the last drop of beer. Then he walked over to Eddie.

Tony was done with his chant and motioned me to pick up my guitar, but I had already been singing for hours and was determined to take a nice long break before my turn came up at the spit.

"Hey Eddie, how eess dat peeg comin' along?" Mario asked Eddie in English. Eddie answered in his broken Spanish. "Talk to me in Spanish, Mario. You know I'm trying to get better at it." "O.K. O.K." Mario responded. "Don't get touchy. Just trying out my English on you, that's all."

"I'll tell you what Mario..." answered Eddie. "If that shit you're talking is English this country's in big trouble." Eddie threw his head back and let out a big guffaw. Mario shook his head and walked over to get another beer. "Everybody's a comedian." He muttered good naturedly. Eddie laughed even louder.

"What's going on out there?" Called Odalis from the kitchen, hearing the loud laughter. Leni started toward the door. She stood there looking in at Tony's wife. "It's nothing honey, just Mario and Eddie horsing around." "Well you tell them guys to behave or they won't get any of this black bean congri I'm making."

The aroma of the traditional Cuban rice and black bean dish that Odalis was preparing had been wafting gently out the kitchen window for some time, saturating the whole backyard with a delicious tropical essence.

"You better hurry up and get that stuff out here before we all start chewing on each other's arms." I yelled at Odalis. Leni turned to look at me and smiled.

"Yeah, yeah, keep your pants on." Odalis retorted in English. Then she emerged holding a huge steaming platter of congri. Leni rushed over and snatched up a handful of paper towels to be used as napkins and a stack of paper plates we bought that morning. Soon we were all sitting around holding heavily laden paper plates and shoveling plastic spoonfuls of congri and roast pork into our mouths. My five-year-old son Cha darted to and fro grabbing bits of food from Leni's plate and from mine.

"When are you and Odalis going to have your first?" I asked Tony. "It's not like we're not trying, Miguel." He answered.

"Maybe he doesn't have what it takes." Kidded Juan getting up for another beer. Tony turned around and shot him a dirty look. "I got more of it than you ever will, sonny." He sneered. "In fact, I still haven't met any guy from Havana that can measure up to the cojones of a man from Santiago." Tony winked at me. Tony was from Santiago like me and so was Leni my wife; although she had come at a very early age and for all intents and purposes was as American as the president.

"Now don't you guys start with all that regional rivalry stuff." chimed in Tenanche, who until now had been characteristically quiet. "Here in the U.S. you aren't Havanan or Santiagoans, you're all a bunch of 'Latinos'."

We all laughed. She was right, of course, we were all acutely aware of the fact that to AngloAmericans in Pittsburgh we're all the same.

Tenanche is an American, but she is unique. She is a mixed blood Powhatan-Taino Indian. She is keenly interested in Latino culture, has lived in Mexico for several years and taught English in a Mexican school.

She can speak our language fluently, although her years in Mexico had flavored her Spanish with a heavy Mexican drawl. Now she was picking up our Cuban accent quite readily.

Tenanche turned to me. "Miguel, are you still making plans to write a book about your experiences on that canoe trip you took with Sven two years ago?"

I looked up from my plate and frowned. "I'd like to, but it's hard when one doesn't remember the most important thing that happened!" Tenanche cocked her head to the side and her face screwed up with a puzzled look.

"What do you mean you can't remember what happened, I thought you told me you had taken notes during that trip. Didn't you say you kept a diary?"

"Well yeah..." I answered gulping down another mouthful of congri. "I did write down many of the things we did but it wasn't the daytime events that concerned me so much, it was what happened when I fell asleep. During the whole trip I had a series of dreams. I dreamed almost every night. I know the dreams were weird and important, but I can't remember them. I feel that without the dreams my book about the river journey would be meaningless.

"So what's so important about these dreams?" She retorted. "Can't you write the book without them? You can't even remember them. Why are you so worried about them?"

I looked down at my plate and began to push the food around with my fork. "I don't know, Tenanche, I just don't think the book would be complete without the dreams."

"So who is this Sven that you traveled with for two weeks?" Asked Tony. I looked up at him and watched him set down the conga drum he had been playing.

"Sven is a friend of mine. We work together now and then in the Imaginarium." I answered Tony. "Oh yeah. That's the clown group you work with." Tony mumbled through a mouthfull of food. I hesitated for a minute.

"Well, yes. I guess you could call it that. Actually the Imaginarium is a children's art, music and movement troupe which happens to include a clown."

Tony looked up at me and smiled. "That's what I said."

Eddie got up to serve himself seconds. "You trusted some dumb gringo in your canoe with you?" He sneered. "I'm surprised he didn't tip the canoe over and drown you both up there in the woods."

Tony turned to Eddie and laughed; "I wonder how close we all came to watching Miguel's soggy hat come floating down the Allegheny river past Three River Football Stadium."

Eddie laughed also; "Yeah, all the way from Warren, past a Steeler's game, with Miguel and his dumb gringo buddy chasing behind it doing the doggy paddle." The whole back yard exploded with laughter.

I took off my expensive white wide-brimmed Beaver brand panama and looked lovingly down at it. "This baby stayed right here in Pittsburgh safe when I went on my trip with Sven." I said. "And as for Sven; I trust him in a canoe with me any day over any of you clowns! The only boats you guys ever sailed in were the ones that brought you over from Cuba, and I heard they almost sank!" Everybody laughed again.

"Hey keep me out of all that mess..." protested Eddie. "I ain't never been no shark-bait, I'm not from Cuba, and I didn't come over in any boat. I'm from Puerto Rico and I came legal, in a plane, with a ticket!" He grinned haughtily at us.

"Listen to Mister U.S. citizen over there..." Snapped back Tony. "Aren't you proud to be from a fucking colony?"

"I'm not from a colony..." Eddie argued.

"Puerto Rico is a colony of the United States, kid, look it up." Insisted Tony.

"No it isn't a colony, it's a 'Free, Associated State'. That's the official title." returned Eddie.

"Oh, yeah, yeah...Free, Associated State, that's English for 'colony'." sneered Tony.

"Ok you guys pipe down over there..." I yelled at them. "I don't want any arguments today." "Ain't no argument, Miguel, I just had to straighten out the wetback over there that Puerto Rico ain't no colony of the gringos." Eddie insisted.

I rolled my eyes and went back to eating. Tony wadded up a paper napkin and threw it at Eddie. Eddie swatted the paper ball with his hand and sent it right back at him. They both ended up laughing.

Tenanche turned to Eddie; "What do you have against us Americans." She asked him teasingly in her cute Mexican-accented Spanish. Eddie turned to face her, a kind of wounded defensive look on his face. "Aw, there's nothing wrong with you, Tenanche. I wasn't talking about you. You're not one of them." The tone of his voice was apologetic. You're Indian, and part black. You speak our language. You're not one of them!"

The telephone rang inside the house. I laid my sagging paper plate on the chair and ran in to answer it. It was a familiar woman's voice.

"Oh, hi Chris, how are you doing?" I greeted the mother of one of the children enrolled at the preschool that my wife and I owned at that time.

"Hi Miguel..." Chris answered. "I hope you guys are taking it easy on your day off." Oh yeah, in fact I've got a backyard full of people here right now. We are having a holiday pig roast!" I answered.

"Oh, no, I'm intruding. I'll call some other time."

"Heck no, Chris, what are you talking about?..." I responded. "You're no bother at all. What did you need?"

"Oh well, It's just that I need some carpentry work done at my house. I know you have that friend of yours from Cuba... What's his name?" I knew instantly whom she was talking about. Mario, in spite of his physical disability, was an able carpenter. He had built child-sized furniture for the preschool, had put in a drywall partition in the teaching area and was at that time in the process of extensive remodeling of his own house.

"Oh yeah..." I responded "It's Mario you want. What do you need from him? I'll translate for you because he doesn't speak much English."

"It's our front porch. It's really getting dilapidated and could use a thorough rebuilding." I reached for a pen and a piece of paper. "OK, Chris, no problem, I'll pass the word along to Mario. I'm sure he'll be interested in this. In fact I have him right here at my house now."

I took down Chris' number and went back outside to join the others. "Looks like a job for you." I said handing Mario the slip of paper containing Chris' telephone number. He looked down at it. "What's this?" He asked looking up at me. "This is the number of the parents of that little blond kid, Nathaniel, in the day care." I answered. I knew he would remember that child because he would often hang around the daycare and do odd jobs. He knew most of the children by name.

"Oh, yeah, I remember the kid... so what's this all about?"

"His mom just called... wants you to fix her porch. She knows how handy you're with tools." I smiled at him. "Could be a nice piece of change."

"Right!..." Exclaimed Eddie skeptically. "You better watch your step with these damned white Anglos... They'll rip you off as soon as look at you." I glanced over at Eddie. "Don't jump to conclusions Ed. I've known Chris for over a year now. I know she's on the level."

"Hey, All I'm saying to the man is to watch himself..." Eddie countered. "That's all, Watch yourself boy! You can't trust them." Mario got caught up in the emotion of what Eddie was saying. He began to nod energetically. "Yeah, Eddie's right, Miguel. You can't trust any of these creeps. They're all a bunch of racists no matter what they say."

I shook my head and sat down to finish the food on my plate. "Well, I did my job, I delivered the message. You do whatever you want with it. If you decide you're interested in this opportunity let me know. I'll translate for you."

"Just watch yourself, that's all, just watch your step." Insisted Eddie.

About three days later Mario called me at the daycare. Alright, Miguel, go ahead and call this gringa. We'll see what she wants." I hooked Mario up with the job on Chris' front porch. I got into the habit of visiting him almost every day at the work site so I was able to appreciate the progress of the job.

"Couldn't get Eddie out here to give you a hand, eh Mario?" I asked, getting out of my car and walking over to the partially completed porch one overcast Friday afternoon. "Naw, he doesn't trust these gringos..." He paused for a moment in mid sentence and looked up at me, then added; "Neither do I... why, if it weren't for the money in this here job..." His statement of suspicion and animosity was interrupted at that moment. Chris appeared at the door holding a glass of lemonade for Mario.

"Oh hi Miguel, if I had known you were here I would have brought you a glass also." She exclaimed as Mario sheepishly accepted the refreshing drink from her. "Hold on, Miguel..." she continued "I'll go back in and ..."

"No, no, please Chris..." I interrupted. "Don't worry, I have to move on I still have a bunch of things to do. Please say hello to your husband and to little Nathaniel for me." I said moving down the steps of the porch.

Just as I turned to leave I whispered in Spanish to Mario, as he obviously enjoyed his cold drink. "I can see how shabbily you're being treated here by the big bad gringa!" Mario suddenly choked on his drink. He began to gag and cough blowing lemonade out his nose. As I walked back to my car I could hear Chris patting him on the back and asking: "Are you all right? What did Miguel just say to you." I giggled quietly to myself as I entered my car and drove away.

Mario was never able to persuade Eddie to help him out with Chris' porch, but eventually he did convince Juan to give him a hand with the job. The progress was dramatic. In a very short time the porch was finished. On a bright Tuesday morning in August of that year Mario found himself standing on the wooden floor planks of the porch he and Juan had repaired. Before him stood Chris. She looked down in admiration at the work my friend had completed for her. I was there that day as these two people from vastly different worlds extended their hands to each other in friendship and trust, and shook. As that handshake occurred Mario was no longer a black Cuban. Chris was no longer a White Anglo-American. They were simply two fellow humans. They stood there on that wooden stage and were transformed into the main protagonists of a sacred drama.

7. THE MEDAL

Well, anyway, I did eventually have my pig roast in July of 1984, but in August of 1982 when I found myself alone with Sven on the Allegheny river that pig roast was still two years in the future. I had not yet met Mario or the others. In 1982 they were still being detained in internment camps or had recently been released under the supervision of various sponsors.

The historical events which brought Mario, Juan and Tony to the United States were a significant chapter in the ongoing saga of the relationship between the United States and Latin America.

I had first been made aware of the Mariel Boatlift incident as I sat one day working at my desk in the library of the Council of Three Rivers American Indian Center in Pittsburgh. It was a bleak overcast day in 1980 when I turned on the radio in my office and heard the astonishing news. The Cuban government had suddenly announced a lifting of the foreign emigration restrictions. Practically anyone that wanted to leave Cuba, could leave.

They set up an official departure site in Mariel harbor near Havana for Cubans who wanted to go. Vessels coming from Florida were allowed to enter the harbor and pick up these people. This event came to be known as the "Mariel Boat Lift".

Hundreds of boats sailed out of Miami and Key West to pick up these Cubans. Relatives residing in the United States were willing to pay large amounts of money to bring them over to Florida.

Cubans with relatives in the U.S. began to receive urgent messages all over the island ordering them to report to Mariel harbor for embarkation. As they arrived there from every corner of the country they were herded through stream-lined emigration proceedings and loaded unto the boats. Unfortunately, hardened criminals also managed to board some of the boats at Mariel Harbor. Many of the boats carried way more people than could safely travel on them. The overloaded boats struggled to cross the ninety miles of ocean from Cuba to Florida. Some boats did not make it. Many drowned.

The Mariel immigrants faced an atmosphere of hostility and suspicion in the United States, when the word got out in regard to the number of criminals that had managed to sneak in undetected among the legitimate immigrants. In the mentality of the average American, guilty or not, all Mariel Immigrants were a threat.

Eventually a motion picture named "Scarface" starringthe famous actor Al Pacino in the title role and based on this event was filmed in the United States in the mid 1980's and became a cult classic.

Historically, the established aristocratic and middle-class Cuban-American community of South Florida, scions of pure-bred, mostly white, Spanish-descended, Havana cigar entrepreneurs, sugar cane plantation barons, tropical rum distillers, lawyers and former demagogues that had left Cuba when Castro's revolution triumphed had traditionally perceived any attempt to leave the island as a heroic act. These attempts were always compared to East Germans attempting to cross the Berlin Wall from the

Communist East to the Capitalist West of the Iron Curtain, and any Cuban who succeeded was lionized when he arrived in the United States. It was a testament to their commitment against the Communist Castro government which they felt, had forced them to leave. Cubans desiring to exit Cuba were seen as one of their own, the hard-working successful type that had immigrated to South Florida in the sixties and built the prosperous Little Havana community in Miami. These were the hard-core conservative Republican Cubans who had been so instrumental in the re-election of President Nixon a few years before.

But the presence of so many obvious delinquents among the Mariel immigrants, and so many blacks and mulattos made many of them nervous. Some Miami Cubans began to distance themselves from the Mariel refugees. Like their Anglo counterparts, they developed a fear and suspicion of the whole Mariel immigration. The whole episode became an embarrassment to them.

As for the Anglo-American community, these were strange new times. Throughout the sixties and most of the seventies a Cold-War mentality influenced the attitude toward Cuban refugees. Cubans struggling to make it to the United States were perceived as heroic anti-communists who were fleeing what they portrayed as the horror of a Socialist system and escaping to the "Free World".

At the beginning of the Mariel Boat-Lift phenomenon the heroic East German, Iron Curtain comparison remained steadfastly in place, but things quickly changed as the thousands of new refugees began to arrrive in South Florida. Increasingly these new refugees began to be seen as no better than the hordes of dark-skinned Haitians fleeing their country not because they were political refugees from Communism but simply because they were oppressively poor.

Back in the sixties the typical Cuban refugee was light skinned, college-educated, professional, and inclined to succeed.

Now twenty years later this new influx of Cubans was quite different. Many of them were young, blue-collar laborers. They had grown up in a socialist environment and did not understand the capitalist system of their new country. Many of them were black and contrasted sharply with the predominantly Spanish-descent white Cubans of Florida's little

Havana. The discrimination that they received came not only from Anglo-Americans, but also from some of the lighter complected Cubans. These saw them as an embarrassing blemish on the well-cultivated image of the "Good Latinos" which they had for years struggled to create in the minds of Anglo Americans. It was an image which strove at a sharp demarcation and separation between this community of Cuban-American bankers, lawyers, doctors and entrepreneurs who strove to look as American as they possibly could, and the large disenfranchised populations of New York Puerto Ricans and West Coast Mexicans. Some of these Florida Cubans with their staunch conservative Republican mindset and their considerable financial and political influence had never wanted to be identified with the poor migrant workers of California or the tenement dwellers of New York.

Rejected by a large portion of U.S. society, the Mariel Cubans of 1980, who where scornfully dubbed "Marielitos" by some in the older Cuban community, had to work very hard to find their niche in the North American society. Many of these newcomers from Havana felt much more at home with the street-smart South Bronx Puerto Ricans than with the Cuban-Americans of South Florida who drove around Southwest Miami in Mercedes Benz's and Cadillacs talking into their car phones at a time when only rich people owned cell telephones.

Eddie had watched the movie I mentioned earlier, "Scarface". He was fascinated by its story of the fictional character, Tony Montana, a smart, violent Mariel immigrant played by the actor Al Pacino, who rises quickly through the ranks in the underworld and becomes a powerful Miami drug kingpin. This was the era of the Medillin and Cali Cartels. This movie captured Eddie's imagination. Then he met our Tony. The black Santiago native was a Mariel immigrant just like the Pacino character and had a very similar attitude toward making money illicitly, which he covered up with a slick good natured humor. Even though Tony's race differed from that of the Pacino character the coincidence of the names was enough to convince Eddie that their meeting had been pre-ordained by fate.

For his part, Tony did nothing to dissuade him from his fascination. Tony enjoyed the coincidence of the movie. He owned a videotaped version of the film which he played for everyone who visited him at his apartment in the depressed Broadhead Manor public housing projects of Pittsburgh's West End.

Eddie and Tony could never understand Mario's rapprochement with Chris, a member of the race that had shown them all so much contempt. Mario's handshake with Chris on that wooden porch floor meant nothing to them. The tough streets of the North Philadelphia barrio had hardened Eddie and the disillusionment at not finding the American Dream had made Tony synical.

Even as Mario began to receive more carpentry jobs, Tony and Eddie drifted gradually into the shadowy realm of drug trafficking. Still styling himself in the Al Pacino role, Tony began to drive around Pittsburgh in expensive cars and wore extravagant gold jewelry like a character from theTV series "Miami Vice". Eddie soon joined the Crips gang of the West End.

In 1986, about four years after my canoe trip I ran into him on the street. By then he was deeply embroiled in the violent netherworld of thousand-dollar crack cocaine deals and drive-by shootings. For my part, I was so preoccupied with preparations for a momentous metaphysical event in which I planned to participate during the month of August of the following year that I almost walked right past him in the street without saying hello.

"Hey Miguel, you gonna ignore me?" I looked up and saw that mischievous smile of his. "Oh hi Eddie..." I greeted him. "What's up?" "Nothing much..." He smiled. We stood there looking at each other with nothing to say for a minute, then he broke the tense silence. "Well, gotta go Miguel, see ya around!" As he strode briskly down the street I wondered how long it would take for his perilous life to catch up with him.

Eddie's problems were soon pushed out of my mind. I was involved in preparations for a major event in the history of the spiritual circle that I helped found in 1981. I had become the spiritual leader of the circle, sharing teachings that had come to me via the Puerto Rican Taino Native medicine teacher whom I had known in New York City back in the 1970's, and via years of study and prayer. We were planning to participate in a world-wide observance called "Harmonic Convergence."

My interest in participating in this global event arose from my fascination with the wisdom of the ancient Maya people who had traded and exchanged ideas with my Taino ancestors in pre-colonial times. Now, I was caught up in the excitement stirred up by the concepts set forth in a remarkable book called "The Mayan Factor". The book's author, José

Arguelles, proclaimed the impending onset of a new era in human history, an era of constructive positivity which had the potential to bring about a time of millennial reconciliation. He gleaned these assertions from his own personal studies of the ancient Mayan calendar.

In his book, he had singled out a particular date in August of 1987 as "Harmonic Convergence", a mystical shift-time, a time when large numbers of people all over the world would be called upon to organize earth-aligning ritual and other significant activity to help begin the shift toward the eventual new era.

Knowing of the historical links between the ancient Yucatec Mayas and my Taino forbears I joined the movement enthusiastically, leading our Caney Spiritual Circle into a fuller consciousness of the significance of the Mayan system. Guided by what I had learned from my father's 1960's research, and the wisdom shared with me later by my college friend, Arturo, I became a "Day Keeper" for our Pittsburgh group, meticulously maintaining a written record of the ancient Central American Indian calendrical divination device. I also used the old resrach material that I had inherited from my father after he discontinued his Maya culture course. My life during the year of 1987 was filled with the preparations for the big event. It kept me busy through the whole spring and early summer of that year.

One Saturday afternoon I was sitting at my desk at home poring over the complicated arithmetic of the ancient calendrical "Long Count" used by the priests of the ancient Mayan city of Tikal. I was suddenly interrupted by the telephone. Eddie's voice sounded distant and weak. "Hey Miguel, you gotta do me a favor..." He started in English. Then he switched to Spanish. Speaking slowly in a language that still gave him lots of trouble, he continued. "I'm calling you from 'La Casa De Piedra' (the Stone House)." I knew immediately that he was making his call from the Allegheny county jail. The massive stone masonry architecture of the old building had earned it that nickname in our little circle of friends. "Back in jail Eddie?" I asked casually. "When you gonna wise up...?" Eddie interrupted me. "Never mind all that bullshit, Miguel; I don't have much time now for your lectures, so just be quiet and listen. This time it's for keeps. They're putting me away for a long time..." I gasped. "Oh No! What...?" "Miguel don't talk, just listen to me..." Eddie continued. "They're moving me to Huntingdon State Pen Tomorrow. Do you still hold those Indian ceremonies up at your Indian center in Dorseyville?" "Yes Eddie..." I answered. "In fact we're getting ready for a big event next month, in August." "Good..." He continued. "I want you to go to my apartment and talk to my girlfriend. She's got something of mine that I want you to take." I was still somewhat taken aback by the fact that I was probably never going to see Eddie again in the street. "What is it Eddie?" I asked him. "It's a little medal, Miguel, just a little medal. I want you to promise me that you'll take the medal up to the Indian center with you and purify it, cleanse it of my sins. Then, if you ever go to Puerto Rico, promise me that you'll visit my home town of Utuado. There is an old abandoned Indian village site there that I want you to visit." I was confused, but I continued to listen. "You gotta take the medal there, Miguel. When you get there you'll know what to do with it."

I didn't know what to make of all of this. "Who gave you that medal?" I asked him. "I got it from my grandmother when I was a kid. Now it ain't gonna do me no good here in the joint, it must be taken home. Will you do me this favor Miguel?" "Eddie, take the medal with you to the prison. Maybe it will bring you better luck." "No, I can't do that. I can't take it to that nasty place. It has to go home!" Ye yelled over the phone. I thought for a minute. "Sure, Eddie don't worry about it, I'll get your medal..." "Thanks Miguel, I owe you one." He exclaimed somewhat sadly.

Then his voice changed and rang with that mischievous tone that was typical of him. "Hey Miguel, did you ever write that book about the canoe trip you took with your gringo friend back in '82?" "Oh no!" I answered, taken aback by the sudden change in topic. "I'm still having trouble remembering all those mysterious dreams I had during the trip. Without that information I can't write my book!" "Boy that is weird!" he exclaimed. "Well, of course, you did tell me once that the gringo did all the cooking during your trip." I was confused. "Yeah, Eddie, Sven did cook, but what does that have to do with my strange dreams?" I asked him. "Well..." I heard the smile in his voice as he answered. "Are you sure those dreams weren't just indigestion nightmares brought on by your gringo friend's cooking?" He exploded into laughter. I couldn't help smiling.

"I gotta go Miguel, Thank you for the favor, I owe you! I'll see you around O.K.?" "Sure, yea, see you around, Eddie." I hung up the phone. I sat thinking about Eddie for a long time, his words ringing in my head.

About a week later I visited Tony in his Broadhead Manor apartment. The little welfare dwelling was decorated with expensive furnishings. A huge wide-screen television set sitting in the corner of the living room roared with the sounds of machine gun fire as one of the drug cartel thugs attacking Al Pacino's "Tony Montana" character bit the dust for the millionth time.

"Hey, hi Miguel, wuzzup?" Tony greeted me", his thick Cuban accent coming through his imitation of the popular 1980's African-American street greeting. "Not much, Tony not much. Just happened to be driving through and decided to drop in say hello." I yelled over the noise of the T.V. Tony waved me in and sat me down in the kitchen-dinning room. He handed me a bottle of beer, then he walked into the living room and turned off the television set before the scene in which the Al Pacino character finally got killed. That was a part of the movie he never watched.

"Hey Tony, did you know Eddie got sent up to Huntingdon?" I asked when he came back into the room. "Yea, I know..." Tony answered me pulling another beer out of the refrigerator. "His girlfriend wants to talk to you. She says Eddie gave her something for you." I leaned forward "Yea he called me about it, a medal; right?" Tony took a gulp of Budweiser and said: "I don't know what it is, she just says it's important." That afternoon Tony led me to the apartment of Eddie's girlfriend. She stood at the door, Eddie's little two-year-old boy hanging on to her skirt, and handed me a delicate silver chain. From the chain hung a small silver medal bearing the etched replica of the ancient Taino Indian petroglyph called "El Sol De Utuado." It represents the Sun Spirit of the Tainos, "Guey-Boinael," as envisioned by the pre-columbian Indians of Puerto Rico. I took the little medal home that afternoon and placed it in my spirit pouch.

After my visit to Broadhead Manor I became more and more involved with the Caney Circle activities. As part of these activities I began to participate in social justice and political activism which I felt was part of my spiritual responsibility. Soon, local organizations such as the Thomas Merton Center, The Hunger Action Coalition and other similar outfits dedicated to the righting of injustice in the United States and around the world, began to count on me and the Caney Circle for support in public demonstrations and activities that furthered their programs. Not long after that I formed a salsa musical group called Guaracha Latin Dance Band.

As our band gained acceptance and acknowledgement in the area we made the services of the group available to those social justice movement groups and the name of our band became closely associated with the cause of justice and peace.

It was at a rally sponsored partially by the Thomas Merton Center in 1989 that I learned the depth of the tragedy taking place in the land of the Mayas. On that day I found myself standing in the crowd grasping my guitar surrounded by people holding up placards that read "U.S. out of Central America". I was approached by Sally, a good friend and fellow movement supporter. Sally greeted me: "Miguel, I loved your song today, You have such a beautiful voice!" "Thanks…" I answered. "Hey did you read the book by Rigoberta Menchu? Its so sad!" I had not heard of the famous Guatemalan Maya woman. "What's the book about?" I asked. "It's an account of personal experiences by a Guatemalan Indian woman who participated in the resistance against the U.S. supported dictatorship."

This was a subject that was extremely relevant to everything I believed in. I was aware that since the early 1980's thousands of Mayas were being systematically massacred in remote highland villages by the Guatemalan armed forces with the military assistance of President Raegan's government. Every day horror stories filtered out of the most affected areas, of rape and torture and of mass killings among the country's poorest and most vulnerable. These were the same people my father had met and talked with during his research trip in Central America back in the 1970's when he was preparing for his course on ancient civilizations. Now they were the target of the most inhumane of persecution and I felt a profound sense of helplessness that I could not do more to help in some way.

After my conversation with Sally we, the participants of the rally, were treated to first-hand witness narrative by a diminutive Guatemalan Kiche Maya woman, garbed in beautifully multi-colored native huipil and corte dress, who had been flown in by the organizers to talk about what was happening in her country. The heart-rending account delivered in her soft yet determined voice was one of the most important catalysts that helped crystalize in my mind some of the most important elements of my political and social world-view in the late 1980's and fanned the fire in me to do something, ANYTHING, to change the way things were.

I bought the book "I Rigoberta" the next day.

8. A GIFT OF SUFFERING

The ancient sacred narratives of the Tainos say that in a far-off time, in the past, the men of the tribe found themselves with no women. The women had run off with a misguided chief, a selfish unjust despot called Guaguyona, who took all of the females for himself, leaving the tribe out of balance and in danger of destruction. Then, after the chief had returned, alone, abandoned by his female companions, chastened and humiliated, and had been allowed to reassume his position of authority in the community he set about undoing the harm he had caused.

At that time the lonely solitary lives of these men were being disturbed by some magical jungle beings who lived in the trees of the forest. These beings were neither male nor female, but possessed nubile feminine human-like bodies with which they teased and tormented the men with no wives. The forest beings danced and frolicked flaunting their naked bodies close to the men when these went to the river to bathe. They moved provocatively near the men but when the men reached out to touch them they ran away or slipped out of their grasp laughing and teasing. The forest beings were heartless and without ethical sensitivity. But actually they possessed the capacity of being transformed into ethical human beings if only the men could catch them.

Hoping to turn these beings into women so that they could take their place as the wives, mothers and grandmothers of the tribe, the reformed chief, Guaguyona, devised a plan to catch them. He called upon some men of the community who were afflicted by a skin condition that made the skin of their arms thick and rough like the bark of the cohoba tree. They were known as "caracaracol". These men soon captured four of the slippery beings. The slippery beings were not able to slip out of their rough abrasive arms. The creatures were tied struggling to some trees and the medicine men of the tribe began to chant for the sacred bird of transformation, Inriri the woodpecker. Thinking that these beings were part of the tree trunks, Inriri arrived and alighted on the forest beings, one by one. Inriri pecked and carved into the beings as it would into the trunk of a tree, shaping their bodies into the bodies of true females. As he did so the creatures underwent a metamorphosis and became virtuous ethical human beings, no longer disposed to torment and tease. They maintained a memory of the forest wisdom which was their origin and so when they became members of the human community they brought with them the knowledge of forest medicine and healing, a gift that they shared with the men. Because of this, Guaguyona, the wayward chief became reconciled with the community. Justice had been wrenched from the jaws of an unjust selfish act.

9. DONA NESTORA

On the evening of Monday, August 10, 1982, Sven and I camped on an island near Tidiute, Pennsylvania. We had earlier stopped at Warren, the largest town in the vicinity. It was in Warren that I made the telephone call to Pittsburgh which I mentioned earlier. That night I slept somewhat uneasily, bothered by the unpleasant incident with Sven near the Buckaloons and the news of my son's skin rash.

August 11 passed without any significant development. On August 12 we reached the town of Tionesta. In Tionesta I decided to call my parents in Erie. The call turned out to be a very unpleasant and alarming experience. They had recently been in touch with one of my wife's friends in Pittsburgh. She informed them that my son was very ill. His skin rash had taken a turn for the worse and he had been rushed to the hospital emergency room. The illness was nothing life threatening, but it was something the baby had never had before. He was showing signs of a relatively severe allergic reaction and everyone was worried. I called Pittsburgh but I couldn't get through to Leni. I returned to camp with the intention of calling Leni again that night. I would decide then whether to abort the trip and take a Greyhound bus back to my family.

When I arrived back at our campsite the world seemed gloomy and unsympathetic. I shared the news with Sven and we discussed possible scenarios. After my conversation with Sven I sat alone and depressed on the darkening river bank and contemplated parenthood, that awesome responsibility some of us humans accept. I thought of <u>my</u> parents, and of my parents' parents. My father's mother was born back in Cuba at the end of the nineteenth century. That island was, at the time, one of the last vestiges of the once mighty Spanish empire. During her lifetime there she witnessed momentous historical events. For instance, as a young girl she once heard the news that at a place not far from her humble peasant

110

village a United States volunteer army unit named the "Rough Riders" led by a man called Teddy Roosevelt had finally overrun the Spanish military garrison of San Juan Hill. This was a Spanish army installation, which Cuban rebels had been softening for years with a withering guerrilla action. The rebellion against Spain had been going on many years before the Americans decided to intervene. After the U.S. intervention the war was named "Spanish-American War" totally ignoring the years of valiant rebellion of the local Cuban patriots and their invaluable assistance once the North-Americans decided to join the fray. Of course the identity of the famous future President Roosevelt was of little interest to the young girl who would some day become my grandmother. To her it was far more important that the long brutal war that had killed so many Cubans and the colonial tyranny that had ruled her country since 1511 should come to a just end. Moreover, she had personal concerns more important to her than the identity of a rich New York adventurer who had come to play war in her country. These concerns had to do with survival. My grandmother was born into poverty. She did nothing to deserve that fate. She grew up in poverty. Later in her life she proceeded to raise a large family on her husband's humble income. Throughout her life she maintained rigid adherence to ethical values, which are a legacy of that peasant upbringing. She was born in quiet humility, lived in quiet resignation and died in quiet dignity.

Sitting there in the twilight gloom watching the river I suddenly felt an irresistible urge to be near my dead grandmother, Doña Nestora. She might have an answer to the problem of my son's ailment. I realized the river might provide a conduit of communication between her and I, if I could only talk to it. I made a great effort. I learned the language of the waters. In the unceasing babble of the turbulent current I found I could hear words from another world. And so I raised my eyes from the pebbly bank and looked out upon the darkening panorama of the forest dusk. The timeless music of the river filled my ears as the water flowed past our campsite. The river beckoned me. "Come with me!" It said "Flow with me down past the industrial cities of the North, Pittsburgh, Cincinnati. We will merge with the waters of streams that have meandered through the fertile western prairies, with the Missouri. We will glide together south upon the back of the mighty Mississippi past the heartland of this great nation, past St Louis, and then flow past New Orleans into the wide gulf of Mexico. There, mixed with the salty waters of the Caribbean we will lap at the shores of your grandmother's birthplace Cuba's Oriente region." In the voice of the river I heard the voice of a humble country woman, my ancestress, the woman who had given birth to my father. I spoke to her.

"Revered grandmother, daughter of ancient native farmers and fishermen; why does the Divine Power allow you to fade so ill rewarded back into the obscurity where you sprang? In your lifetime you were never granted any favors or special recognition in consideration of your goodness? Was that just?" I complained. The river water answered with my grandmother's voice. "Justice is not heaven-sent. It is established by human hands. It flows from a sense of morality and ethics, neither of which grow on the guava tree. You must shape these from your instincts. You must strive for fairness so that there may be fairness. The Creator gives us the capacity to establish fairness but we have to make it happen."

I didn't understand that answer, but the river murmured on. "Men less worthy than I shall reap greater fruits from their lives than I did simply because they were born in the right place at the right time or simply because they chose to ignore the rules the rest of us live by. No natural law of fairness will impede them. No supernatural power from heaven will come down at the nick of time and save the victim from the predator as it happens in the movies. Thieves, murderers, oppressors and swindlers, unjust and dishonest men, abusers and bullies are destined to thrive while the innocent suffer if honest folk do not act justly. Fairness is not sparked spontaneously. It must be coaxed laboriously from the tinder, fanned patiently to life, and kept glowing with infinite care by humans. Otherwise the helpless will suffer and the undeserving will prosper."

I heard the river sigh. "Suffering is the legacy of humankind. It is as much part of our nature as our ability to think and to love. Some suffering, such as the illness that has struck your son, has always been, shall always be unavoidable. That kind of suffering will continue to strike indiscriminately the guilty and the innocent. Much of it can serve to strengthen, to toughen us. You will find that your son will eventually learn valuable lessons from his affliction. He will learn to keep himself healthy and pay closer attention to the requirements of his body than most others. He will also become more sensitive to the suffering of others. He will grow to be more sensitive than boys with no personal affliction to teach them compassion and an uncompromising sense of fairness. Ultimately he will develop a thick skin. He will grow tough. His rough skin will be his vehicle to victory, like the skin of the legendary ancestors, the caracaracol men who helped bring balance back to the primordial tribe. But other kinds of sufferings are brought about through people's negligence for the care of justice. That sort of suffering has no value at all."

I could no longer see the river. The sun had set behind the dark forest-wrapped hills. "What is our relationship with God then? Doesn't God provide justice?" I insisted.

The spirit of my grandmother, a woman who had been raised in a hybrid cultural tradition of ancient native lore and European Christianity all mixed together, answered me. "The Creator is not a procurer of victories. The Creator is a giver of opportunities. We are all armed with a set of assets and then placed on the Earth. Among those assets is your guardian spirit. When I was a girl we called it the "guardian angel". It is a source of great power. Seek its aid often. Guard its powers jealously. It is the source of your spirit strength."

I was still somewhat confused, but was beginning to perceive that there was a direct relationship between my aspirations to attain spiritual transcendence and the need to help others. I realized that the medicine man's quest for power is useless if that power is not utilized in the aiding of a neighbor in need, especially if that neighbor had been wronged. Only through helping fellow humans in avoiding suffering and injustice, and assisting others in their quest for joy and self-accomplishment does the beike, the spiritual leader, truly reach his or her full potential. The medicine man had to become the great Giving Beast, the generous manatee of my Black Ribs Vision Quest dream to achieve ultimate manifestation of his destiny.

The river was now only a mass of darkness in the moonless night. It withdrew beyond my reach taking with it the "hupia," the soul of my ancestress, sequestering her to a far-off "Koai-bai," The Taino abode of the dead. I became very drowsy, so I bundled myself in my sleeping bag and slept.

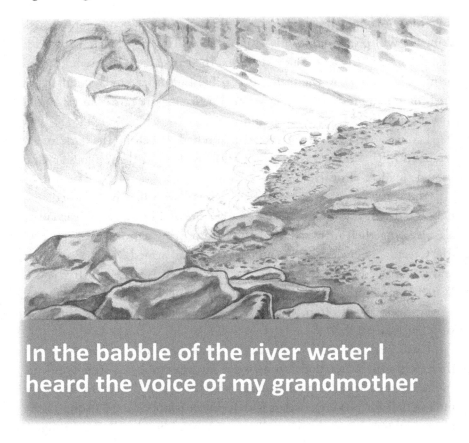

In the babble of the river water I heard the voice of my grandmother

10. SPLINTERS

Late on the night of August 12, 1982, I awoke after having slept a few hours. I crawled out of the tent and wandered off into the night away from our campsite. I walked in the dark along the riverbank and eventually located a small riverside community not far from where we were spending the night. A road ran near the riverbank there. I found a gas station that was closed, with solitary phone booth near the road and managed to get a long-distance phone call through to my wife. She assured me that our son was fine and feeling much better. The occurrence of Cha's rash that day was only the early precursor of the life-long physical condition which would haunt my son for the rest of his days, erupting in full-blown attacks and then subsiding periodically. But at that point I was oblivious to that fact, and all I knew was that when Leni talked to me he seemed to be doing better. I slept well the rest of that night dismissing all further thoughts of Greyhound busses.

On the morning of August 13, 1982, I woke up in our camp near a place called Henry's Bend. During the course of the morning our campsite area was visited several times by deer. We enjoyed their company as we went about our morning activities. I was feeling relaxed and happy that morning.

We felt we should have been a little further downstream by now. So we launched the canoe that morning with the resolve to cover lots of ground during the day.

As we glided quietly down the stream large herons along the riverbank spread their long graceful wings and took to the air. They broke their earth bonds and soared effortlessly. I paddled in unison with my canoe partner as I watched the beautiful creatures rise in majestic flight. As they flew they were followed upward by my own spirit.

One summer I broke some bonds of my own and embarked on a flight of self-discovery. That flight took me thousands of miles over North America. I traveled to the land of the Mohawk Indian people in Eastern New York State. From there my journey took me to the impressive Black Hills of the Lakota Indian people in South Dakota and then south through the everglades of the Seminole Indians in Florida.

At that time I was still professionally associated as an artist with the radical Indian-movement oriented periodical called Akwesasne Notes. Until that year my dealings with that Indian newspaper had been strictly by mail and phone. I supplied them with illustrations which accompanied their articles on Central American Indian issues. I also illustrated several of their independent pamphlets.

The Mohawks are one of the Iroquois nations. They share a common ancestry with the Seneca Indians of Western Pennsylvania. That summer I got the opportunity to visit for the first time the home offices of the newspaper for which I had drawn so many pictures. I arrived on a bus which left me far from my destination. I walked and hitch-hiked from the town of Messina asking for direction and following my instincts. Eventually I arrived at a large house in a town inside the reservation. I marveled at the modesty of the home of one of the most noted and world-renowned

American Indian publications in circulation at that time. I was received warmly, fed and put up for the night. During my stay I volunteered to work on a special maize crop that the Akwesasne Indians were growing in a field nearby. I spent hours that day weeding and cultivating in the hot sun. This corn was destined for shipment south to feed some fellow tribes people who were at that time engaging in peaceful civil disobedience by occupying an abandoned tract of woodland in the Adirondack Mountains. The Mohawks called that place "Genienke."

The protesters were squatting on that tract of land in defiance of state and local authorities. They had created an occupation camp on the site maintaining that the area was part of a Mohawk Indian land plot never legally ceded away by the Mohawk Indian nation. The local authorities and the state of New York threatened forced removal. The Mohawks have a history of steadfast determination. The families dug in and the warriors prepared for any eventuality. Back on the reservation, family and friends of the occupiers grew food for them, supplied them with medicine, blankets, weapons and many other necessities.

As time passed the situation went through a series of ups and downs with both the Indians and the non-Indian authorities fighting a battle of wills. Negotiations were at a standstill when I arrived at Akwesasne. South of the town at Genienke the Mohawks dug in and prepared for a siege.

I have always prided in considering myself a member of the global community. That which affects my fellow human beings affects me.

When I was back in high school I had read the story of the Mohawks. Like that of many other Native American tribes this was a sad story. Their history closely paralleled the history of their tribal cousins the Seneca Indians of the Erie region. The injustices heaped upon the Mohawk Indian people over the course of time were so profound that they affected forever the character of that nation.

In helping their cause I added in small measure to their ongoing effort at attaining justice. In so doing, I also was indirectly helping myself because, as I have been taught, that which affects my fellow human being affects me.

That same evening, as I prepared for bed, miles to the south the sun set behind the lush summer vegetation in the Adirondack mountain woodlands. In the occupation camp young mothers hushed their little ones to sleep. Warriors discussed the possibility of an armed rush upon the camp by the state authorities.

Back up at Akwesasne I settled down in a modest cot and wrapped myself in my sleeping bag, my fingernails still dark from the soil in which I had toiled that afternoon. I thought of those young men and women not far away, hunkering down for the evening in their primitive camp up in the mountains among hostile local farmers and other gun-toting townspeople. I thought of them huddling with their children with the threat of an armed state police raid hanging over their heads.

I looked up from my pillow. Across the room from me sat a young Mohawk woman dressed in blue jeans and an old olive drab army shirt that bore insignias indicating it had recently belonged to a Viet Nam veteran. She was absorbed in a book. Earlier that day I had shaken hands with her as a sign of friendship. Under our feet the floorboards of the house silently echoed the footsteps of some Mohawks who a few months before had made this building their last preparation point before going south to join the occupation camp in the Adirondacks.

I had felt the reverberation of those footsteps. They vibrated under my feet, up my body and out through my outstretched arm. They had emanated a magic warmth that created a bond between the people and the heritage of the woman whose hand I was shaking and my own people, my own heritage. We were truly members of the same family. Like each board making up the floor upon which we stood, we were wooden planks split from the same trunk.

My people, the Taino Indians of the Caribbean islands, had in very early times split off from a mother tribe dwelling on the northern coast of South America. My ancestors had taken to canoes and abandoning the South American continental homeland, sailed out to settle the islands. The people of the mother tribe which stayed behind are known as "Arawaks." They shared a common culture with my island-dwelling Taino ancestors.

One group of the Arawaks lives in what is now the South American country called Guyana.

In 1984 I traveled to Canada to visit my sister. There I met an Arawak Indian from Guyana named David Campbell. He is a singer who moved to Canada years ago and has written protest songs on the current Indian experience of the Americas.

117

David Campbell wrote a song that spoke of splinters. It likened the different Indian nations of North, Central and South America to slivers of wood; "Splinters" he called us. He envisioned all the Indian peoples as part of some great mystical tree; "Splinters of the Tree" He sang. Slices of the same wood, a magic wood of unity and strength, A wood of common kinship, which like the great mystical peace tree of Iroquois tradition extends its protection and brotherhood to people of all colors.

In David Campbell's imagery I see all peoples, not just Indians, joined together in brotherhood and sisterhood like planks laid side by side upon some polished mahogany floor, unflawed by the imperfections of injustice, greed, prejudice and suspicion, a firm base where our children and children's children can stand and grow.

Curiously, I don't see this imagery as hopelessly romantic wishful thinking, but actually as a perfectly attainable future state of affairs toward which we should all be striving as part of the history of our species.

CHAPTER IV

THE LANGUAGE OF STONES

1. INDIAN GOD ROCK

At around 3:00 p.m. on August 13,1982 we pulled the canoe up on the right bank and I climbed out to the highway above the river. The road ran parallel to the stream. At this particular point it came very close to the water's edge. By the road there was a small shopping plaza with a telephone booth. I tried to call my family in Pittsburgh, but did not get through.

We continued on down the river. We had learned from the informational maps in Sven's plastic chart pouch that not far beyond the mouth of French creek there was a large stone covered with petroglyphs, drawings chiseled into the surface of the rock. These drawings had been executed long ago in prehistoric times by Indian holy men of the area. The whole Allegheny and Ohio River valley is dotted with these illustrated rocks.

We reached the mouth of French Creek, a stream that flows south from Erie County and empties its waters into the Allegheny River. The volume of creek water flowing in at this point created an underwater sandbar, which we had to avoid carefully as we passed by. I began to look out for the illustrated stone, which as I said earlier, is known by the locals as "Indian God Rock."

It was not long before we spotted the archeological relic on our left. It was a prodigious boulder which lay heavily on the bank of the river as if some divine hand had deposited it there for all to see. It sat there, prominently and clearly visible from the river. To the early Indian inhabitants of this area the river was an important transportation route. This rock must have been as conspicuous a landmark to those river travellers as a large billboard is now to a motorist on a modern highway.

Indian God Rock

To my dismay I discovered that the visibility of the sacred drawings had been badly obscured by a jumble of historic-era graffiti. The graffiti, chiseled over the years into the rock right on top of the more ancient petroglyphs, presented the names of generations of locals eager to absorb some measure of the immortality inherent in the ancient etchings. Fortunately someone had outlined the old drawings in white paint. Thus aided, the magic shapes fought through the tangle of contemporary ignorance, springing forth from the stone surface to bless us as we passed beneath it.

Indian God Rock spoke to me as I passed alongside of it. I can't really describe how. It spoke without words, in its own language, the language of endurance, the language of permanence. The cryptic drawings etched upon its surface communicated with me in that brief instant when our canoe glided near it, and it touched my consciousness, opening it to the subtle nuances of meaning in the language of the stone people.

Indian God Rock was my introduction to the rock folk and their stories. Many times since, I have been touched by the silent images evoked in their messages.

Sven and I managed to travel a few more miles before we were forced to camp for the evening.

I kept thinking of Indian God Rock as we pulled the canoe up on the riverbank.

2. CIRCLES OF STONES

From my vantage point high above the river I watched canoes and other boats as they floated downstream. I sat near our campsite. Not far from where I sat stood the tent in which I would sleep that night. Closer still lay the ring of stones surrounding the tiny campfire that Sven had prepared some hours earlier.

I sat there with a pad of paper on my lap and a pen in my hand trying to compose a new song. It was not going well. The lyrics came slowly and laboriously.

I was attempting to set to music an experience that I'd had recently on my last trip to New York City, where I often went to visit my aunt Adela in Washington Heights. The graffiti on the walls of the bathroom stall of the Port Authority bus terminal in Manhattan documented a vicious war of words between a Puerto Rican and a Mexican from competing street-gangs. The exchange of badly-spelled insults reflected a hate and rage that seemed to me incomprehensible. How could we expect the respect of others when we did not respect each other?

I struggled with the lyrics of my new song for a while until I became distracted by the majestic beauty of our campsite. It was a unique campsite. It soared 50 feet above the river and gave us a breath-taking view of the forest landscape both up and downstream. High up here above the river where we were, the cliff was topped by a flat area covered with pines.

We had set up our camp among the tall evergreens. Having first carefully stashed the canoe in a hidden stand of brush near the river bank, we had climbed a steep trail to the top. The flat pine needle-covered floor made a good surface upon which to prepare the campfire. We cleared an area clean of pine needles and kindled our fire on the bare ground. The stones around the flame created a natural shield protecting the flammable pine needle floor outside the circle of stones.

I looked into the flames of our little campfire and realized that it epitomized the very essence of our whole trek. This trip was, in fact a series of campsites. It was a series of small evening camp fires separated by periods of daylight filled with a hundred little adventures and personal discoveries which gelled and were properly digested only after the sun had set and we had settled ourselves around the glow of the small flame surrounded by a ring of stones. It was the nightly fires that provided the constant, the one defining factor of the whole experience.

The flames of this campfire would become a symbol of my constant personal struggle to evolve. In my life, many future fires would mark important milestones in that progress much like our little campfires marked the miles of progress down-river. The enduring theme of my life during those coming years would become the nurturing of the Caney Circle that my friends and I had created in 1981. As the spiritual community grew and developed in later years its evolution also could be measured in terms of a journey down a series of fires surrounded by rings of stones. Eventually these would turn out to be great ceremonial bonfires, burning with the sacred life of Ioka-Hu himself, the fiery solar energy spirit, the food deity of my ancestors who kindles the flame of life within human beings. Around each one of those future fires stands a circle of cobbles or boulders, stones that represent the all-encompassing, protective enclosure of Mother Ata-Bei's eternal womb.

As I sit now writing these words I am reminded again of all the future fires which were later born of the heat that emanated that night from that magical little flame, and all the stone rings associated with those fires. I am particularly reminded of an occasion in 1987, five years after my downriver journey. On this day I found myself standing before a much larger conflagration. It was a blazing bonfire.

This much larger fire was also ringed with a protective circle of stones.

In the flames of this later fire I watched a large heap of stones slowly become hot enough to glow. These stones were being prepared for use in a "sweatlodge" ceremony. In Taino we call these ceremonies "guanara".

The Guatemalan Mayas call them "tuj" and the Mexica Aztecs call them "temazcal". Sweatlodge ceremonies are ancient Indian healing rituals of purification and rebirth which utilize heated stones. The celebrants sit in a circle inside a small lodge and the stones are brought in from the fire outside. They are placed in a pit in the earthen floor at the center or the back of the lodge. Water is poured over them and the whole space fills with hot purifying steam drenching everyone in perspiration.

As I stood there watching the bonfire that evening, I saw in the stones at its center a kinship to the stone circle of our little campfire up on top of the pine-covered cliff by the Allegheny river back in 1982.

I felt the intense heat of the bonfire, which roared fiercely before me. I knew that later that night I would be sitting inside the lodge pouring water on those hot stones. But before that happened I was to find myself at the center of an even wider circle of large rocks, a much larger stone ring than that one by the river in 1982, or even the one around the sweatlodge rocks in 1987. This stone circle also had a fire inside it, but the fire was at the center and the circle of stones was so wide that there was plenty of room for people to dance inside it around that central fire. It was a ceremonial arena outlined with big cobbles. Here we would gather and dance and sing in a sacred ceremony of hope and faith. Then when that ceremony was concluded we planned to file down to the sweatlodge.

I turned away from the hungry heat and saw a man carry in the last couple of stones to complete the great circle. He laid them on the ground. The cobbles he had positioned lay half-hidden in the tall grass as he strived to mark out the final outline of a perfect circle. When the great stone hoop was complete it contained twenty-eight stones representing the approximately twenty eight day-long span of the lunar phases, the twenty eight days of a woman's menstrual cycle. Stones were everywhere; cold ones on the grass, hot ones in the fire. I walked calmly into the circular perimeter of the stones and felt the power of the sacred space. To my left the bonfire continued to rage fiercely, turning the stones in its center into red hot glowing children of the sun. It seemed as if there was a conversation between the cold stones composing the sacred ceremonial circle upon the grass and the glowing cobbles in the bonfire.

As I walked about within the sacred ceremonial space I felt a comfortable connection between this big circle of my present and the much smaller stone circle high above the river in my past. Only five years had elapsed between those two fires but it felt like it was a hundred. I had learned so much. I listened carefully and heard the stones silently speaking. Twenty-eight stones, as many stones as there are days in the lunar cycle, they spoke of the menstrual blood, the liquid of life. They spoke of the sacred red fluid which surges and ebbs within our veins like the waves of a living ocean dancing in tidal rhythm to the music of the lunar orb. The stones spoke of the predictable gyre of the moon. The stones spoke of permanence. They spoke of immortality, of creatures gyrating about the spinning hoop of life and death, changing, molting, flowing, arranging and rearranging themselves in a marvelous glory of flexibility and growth. They spoke of countless living beings dancing the dance of existence, and experience, and evolution, and transformation as each one strove to guarantee itself its own special place in the greater cosmic scheme, as each one refused to cease.

I walked out of the sacred space and away from the bonfire. I entered the main building of the Council of Three Rivers American Indian Center and began to change into my white cotton ceremonial clothing and feather regalia.

It was the weekend of August 17, 1987. On that date I found myself surrounded by about two hundred people up on the Indian center hill. We were engaged in ritual festival of hope which was being observed by groups of people all over the world. It was called "Harmonic Convergence". The whole hill-top area of the Council of Three Rivers American Indian Center buzzed with activity as hundreds of participants took in the wonderful positive energy of the event.

Towards the edges of the ceremonial field informational tables had been set up to be manned by representatives of organizations such as the international Rain Forest Action Coallition, TheThomas Merten Peace and Justice Organization, and the local Pittsburgh Hunger Action Network. The presence of these persons at our event highlighted the fact that the global shifts which were being initiated on that day included very practical and substantial changes in attitude, and real action that would impact human beings and the world's environment in a fundamental way.

As I put on the white Taino-inspired cotton cloth regalia which I wear at rituals I reflected on the five years of intense study of the ancient Mayan calendar to which I had dedicated myself since my two-week long canoe trip with Sven. I saw how those five years had culminated in the event in which I was now participating.

That study of the calendar's mystical symbolism and its profound numerological permutations brought me to the cosmology of those ancient people. I was doing all of this research on the Maya Calendar at the same time that I was educating myself about the culture of my own Taino people.

My research augmented what I had learned during my adolecence in the 1960's when my father had taught me the fundamentals of the Maya Calendar. The whole prophetic image brought to light by the research that I had carried out is based on the premise that our era is marked by the allegorical return of a special spirit of reconciliation. In the Mexican Indian mythical complex this spirit has been named "Quetzalcoatl," also known as the "Feathered Serpent."

In the incarnation of a great king of antiquity, this legendary Toltec Indian entity reputed to have brought art, literature, poetry, medicine and magic to the ancient Indians, immolated himself by jumping into a giant bonfire. It was an ultimate act of self-sacrifice which he performed for his people, much like the sacrifice of A-tuei or the great Giving Beast in my Black Ribs dream. The legend says that Quetzalcoatl's burning body turned into a cloud of butterflies which floated out of the flames as he was consumed. The legend also states that he would return during our era.

Some participants in our August 17th ceremony went as far as to identify Quetzalcoatl with Jesus because of the obvious parallels of self-sacrifice, millennial return and ultimate redemption.

About Two hundred people joined us over the weekend to celebrate Harmonic Convergence.

And yet this series of Mexica and Maya-inspired shamanic vision and ceremony was to be but a prelude to an even more dramatic sequence of prophetic events. These would be dominated by the symbology of Taino Indian spirituality as well as Maya spirituality, confirming in my mind the close connection between those two traditions. It was a trail of metaphysical phenomena which would lead right to two other fateful dates of reckoning, October 14, 1992, five hundred years and twenty four generation since the arrival of Europeans upon the shores of this continent, and beyond that via a series of significant nexus dates leading up to the even more climactic date, December 21st of 2012.

The year 1992 is a date which commemorates the 500th anniversary of the first permanently sustained encounter between the Native peoples of the Americas and the people of Europe who would eventually conquer and subjugate them. It is particularly significant to people of Taino Indian descent because the first Indians that met Columbus were the Tainos of what is now Dominican Republic, Haiti, Puerto Rico, Jamaica, Cuba and other islands of the Caribbean.

The year 1992 was to mark the conclusion of the five-century long, twentyfour generations of tragic discord established in the Americas in 1492, a period initiated by Columbus. My mission was to help in some small personal measure in bringing to a satisfactory close the twenty-four generation historical phase of ferocious conflict and hate, prejudice and discrimination which has ruled the Americas for five centuries since Columbus made his fateful transoceanic voyage.

This phase includes a history of wanton massacre, slavery, racial and class oppression, and the legacy of colonization that enslaves minds and souls long after actual physical slavery has been abolished. I strove to be a meaningful participant in the effort not only to bring that phase to a close, but to give birth to a new phase, a phase of re-synchronization which would begin in 1992 and culminate with a hoped-for launching of a newly re-synchronized Timeship-Earth twenty years later, in the year 2012. I was soon to realize that this was easier said than done, since the colonization and enslavement of the mind is subtle and perniscious, and most of us carry it deep within us even if we don't know it.

The ancient Mayas had designated that year, 2012, as the ultimate cycle-transition milestone when humanity was destined to step into a new and marvelous phase in the evolution of its consciousness. Once that new cycle was achieved I expected to work very hard to overcome the effects of colonization within my own mind and to assist in allowing the new cycle to evolve into full fruition in the years beyond 2012.

I share this dream with visionaries all over the world and along with them continue our efforts daily toward that end for the sake of our descendants.

As I write these words now, I think not only of a small stone circle which accommodated our little campfire in the pines high above the river. I think not only of those little stones near which I sat and meditated on the evening in 1982 as I prepared to crawl into my warm bedroll for the night. I also think not only of the larger stone circle built five years later to accommodate the Harmonic Convergence Ceremony. But now I also remember an even larger stone circle. This third stone circle came into my life as a result of a death in my family.

Late in the Autumn of 1987, three months after the Harmonic Convergence event, my uncle Anibal died. I traveled to Puerto Rico to attend his funeral. While there, I had the opportunity to make the pilgrimage that Eddie had asked me to make. After the funeral in the coastal town of Arecibo where my uncle had lived since he emmigrated from Cuba, I rented a car and drove up the tortuous little roads that led up into the highlands in the interior of the island.

In the central mountain region of the island, near Eddie's hometown of Utuado there is an Eden-like river valley crowned with palms, festooned with a chaotic avalanche of green jungle foliage, bromeliads, and the red blossoms of the flamboyan tree.

I brought with me the silver medal that I had acquired from Eddie's girlfriend. There amid the luxuriance of the rain forest stands the site of an ancient Taino Indian ceremonial center now known as "Caguana". The traditional wood and thatch huts are long since rotted and gone but the site is marked by a number of enormous rectangular courts which once served as sacred ceremonial ground.

The wood and thatch huts of the ancient Taino village were long gone

All of the fields are outlined by rows of standing stones of varying sizes neatly arranged around the dance areas. Many of the large basalts bear line drawings of important spirits etched upon their surface that look very much like the line drawings on Indian God Rock back in Pennsylvania, and like the drawings on the walls in La Patana cave in Cuba that I had visited as a child with my family.

The most impressive of these petroglyphs is a depiction of the ancient Taino mother spirit, Ata Bei, the Earth Matriarch, the Lady of the Terrestial Waters. The ancient Tainos envisioned this entity as the supreme mother of all that is. She is even the mother of the most important male deity, Ioka Hu the Lord of Life. The image of Ata Bei engraved on the surface of the principal stone at Caguana features a curious circular structure on her abdomen. The round image resembles the image of a round globular higuera gourd which the ancient Tainos utilized as receptacles for enclosing the bones of the dead. The higuera gourd was a metaphor for the Taino Abode of the Dead. The ancient Tainos perceived the Abode of the Dead, a place called "Koai Bai" to be a mystical region located at the very center of existence in the core of Creation. They imaged it under the ground and it was a watery place submerged in an ocean of amniotic fluid since it was actually in the uterine belly of Ata Bei the All-Mother. This place was, in fact, a kind of recycling center in which souls at times can swim around in the form of fish waiting to be re-born. Koai Bai was also a place from whence the ancestors could emerge temporarily at night in the form of bats, and ocasionally transform into human-like beings who could communicate with the living in the darkness of the night.

I approached the holy place with a profound sense of awe, and in the hush of the tropical afternoon, I began to transcend ordinary reality. The experience brought back memories of my conversation with Grandmother Nestora back on the Allegheny River. And I just knew that this experience now was going to be exactly like that one.

I entered as in a trance. When I emerged from my trance I found myself in the center of a circle of standing stones approximately 30 feet in diameter. I knelt there in the middle of the sacred hoop and placed my hands on a low flat stone standing in the center of the circle. I closed my eyes and felt the heartbeat of the boulder. I felt its rhythmic breathing and heard its song. Its song mingled with that of the forest songbirds in the trees around me. I shut out the brightenss of the sun above and gradually I was enveloped in a calm magical darkness, a mental night in the middle of the afternoon. In the midst of that darkness I heard the wing-beats and the shrill calls of a bat flying around my head. I stayed very still.

At the center of the sacred circle of stones

Again my thoughts traveled back to my riverside stone circle back up there on the pine covered heights above the Allegheny River in 1982. I thought of it, alive with its glowing little campfire in the middle. I also thought about the big ceremonial stone circle at Harmonic Convergence just a few months earlier, and the other stones glowing there in the guanara sweatlodge bonfire.

All those stone circles were epitomized by the ancient ring of boulders within which I stood now. This ring of stones here in Puerto Rico was the ancestral model for all those other stone circles.

I knelt before the central rock. Around me I visioned the men and women who had sat with me three months earlier at Harmonic Convergence. Above the central stone I visioned a fire much like the little fire which had burned in the campsite above the Allegheny River five years earlier. I stared into the flames of the imaginary fire hovering over the center boulder. And still all around me I heard the same shrill call of the bat.

I knew that there was magic in the glow of that vision flame. It was alive. It quivered like a spirit caught in the throes of passionate ecstasy. It spoke to me. It spoke to me with my grandmother's voice.

"What is it about my immortality that puzzles you?" she asked me. "It's just the simple fact that I know that you died," I answered. "Your death is not an illusion. Its palpable reality emanated from every feature of my father's face on the day he got the news of your death. I remember that day vividly! It washed over him and left him a different man. He was no longer a man with a living mother. Now he was a man with a dead mother. He had changed. I saw this and it changed me also."

"What does that have to do with my immortality?" she insisted. "Well, if you are immortal why did you die?" I queried impatiently. "For that matter; why did Uncle Anibal die yesterday...?"

I became sullen. "Uncle Anibal was one of the people who did the most to bring me close to the reality and the magic of my art. He spent patient time and energy during my childhood demonstrating to me the value of my talent. He helped me come to terms with it. He lovingly gathered up my childhood drawings and saved them for decades. I own those old drawings now because of him. Now he's gone! like he had never been!" My voice cracked as I realized that I was talking out loud to the stones and crying. I opened my eyes and looked about me through the haze of my tears, to make sure I was still alone. Then her answer came.

"That's because this is not about immortality at all. Is it? It is better than immortality. It will feel like immortality because certain elements of this will never go away. But it is not about a man or a woman living forever. It is more important than that. It is about the impact that a man or a woman's life has on the world around him or her. That is the REAL immortality. Your ancestors knew a spirit called 'Maketaurie Guaiaba', the Lord of Death, the lord of Koai Bai, a very powerful spiritual entity". She said. "He controls the relationship between the living and the dead. He is your ability to remember me to venerate my memory and the memory of your beloved uncle, your ability to conjure up my presence in the glow of this imaginary fire which your mind has created in the midst of this sacred circle of stones."

I thought about all this for a minute then I asked, "How long will you continue? Will you only last as long as I can remember you?" To this she answered; "My immortality is not entirely contingent on your very faulty memory. I live on in the things that I left behind. I live on in your own existence. Look at my face. You will see mirrored there your own features because I bore the child who came to be your father. My life force lives on in you. It is your legacy from me and from millions of men and women who came before me. You carry this life legacy from your ancestors as your descendants shall carry it from you, each generation taking up the torch of life as in a huge cyclical relay race."

But the grandmother I remembered from my childhood was warm. Her kiss was moist and remained on one's cheek long after it had been administered. She was tangible and real. The specter read my thoughts and said; "There was once for me a time of oblivion, a period when I was only the potential for life. At that time I existed in the soil and the air, and in the aroma of a flower, and in the buzz of a hummingbird. My essence, my potential was a mystical fish swimming in the salty amniotic seas, encapsulated in the womb of the Cosmic Mother, the legendary hanging higuera gourd of the past and the present and the future. Then I was born, and I became manifest as a woman. My life was rich, and full, and bitter-sweet, and finally it ended in the bosom of my family. Death came as a transition, not as an end, even as my birth had also come as a transition, not as a beginning. My spiritual essence, like a fish, returned to the salty sea within the uterine higuera gourd, within the cosmic female belly. You see, I am perennial. I never really die. I go on and on through history. In a sense I stood witness to the birth of the cosmos billions of years ago, just as surely as I was witness to the uphill charge of Teddy Roosevelt's Rough-Riders at San Juan Hill in 1898.

You, moreover, share in my permanence. I am aware that you carry the vivid childhood memories of house-to-house fighting and revolution sixty years after San Juan Hill. That was your life experience. You feel confident in talking about those events because, as a child, you lived through that era. You feel they are part of your personal experience." She was alluding to the fact that in the 1950's, as I was growing up in Cuba, the island was rocked by the most extraordinary political upheaval of my life, the Cuban Revolution that triumphed in 1959.

"What you don't seem to realize," she continued, "Is that in sharing my immortality, you share in my transcendence of time. That is the most important lesson of the timeless stone circle of permanence, the circle of infinity, the circle of transcendence. You share in my experience as well as in your own. You live in a timeless space where dates matter little except as guideposts. You also make the endless perennial cyclical journeys back and forth to and from the uterine higuera gourd, and you are as much a witness to the birth of the Fifth Sun at the beginning of time as you are to the rebel raid on Moncada barracks in Santiago Cuba, in 1953. All living things share in this. As a result of this we shall all be witness to the birth of the physical Sixth Sun billions of years hence, or the spiritual First Sun in the sequence of the human evolution of consciousness that the ancient Mayas prophesied for December 21st 2012. So it may not be physical immortality in the sense that I did not last forever as one woman and you will not last forever as one man. But we are immortal in the spirit of the cycles that mark our journeys back and forth in and out of Mother Ata Bei's sacred uterine higuera gourd.

Everything that exists now has always been in one form or another, constantly undergoing changes and transitions. You and I, although separated by two generations, are contemporaries. But more significant still, you also share in the experience of even more distant ancestors. As their ancient struggle has likewise transcended time you are now facing the same foe they faced ages ago. My grandson, it is your duty to prepare yourself for the ultimate battle with that great enemy. Because when you, at last, face him, your battle shall culminate a struggle which has spanned five centuries."

Her voice echoed down the valley amid the shrill calls of a bat that fluttered on erratic wings above me in the tropical darkness, then faded. As it faded so did the imaginary coals which had materialized upon the boulder in the center of the ancient Taino stone ring. The energy of those imaginary coals slowly dissipated into the obscurity and privacy of the tropical afternoon.

I stayed there for a long time squatting before the large stone at the center of the ring of boulders. The stones arrayed around me in a circle at that moment seemed to form a protective uterine enclosure, and I imagined myself floating in a sea of amniotic fluid within that enclosure. I pondered the words of my grandmother and as I did that I imaged myself as if I were a fetus rather than an adult man, or as a swimming creature circulating within the enclosure's warm, liquid, saline environment. The words of the specter echoed in my head.

After staying there immobile for some time I finally came out of my semi-trance. I stood up and looked down on the large flat stone where my vision had manifested.

I reached into the pocket of my pants and withdrew my spirit pouch. I opened it and pulled out Eddie's medal. Earlier in the day I had stopped in at the humble home of his relatives in the near-by town of Utuado. They had given me directions to the ancient archeological site.

Now I held the medal in my hands and it began to vibrate and glow eerily. A weird mix of emotions gripped me. Then I sensed a clarity of vision I had rarely experienced before.

The image of the sun on the little medal, with its enigmatic face, radiated an aura of enlightenment which spoke eloquently to me. I knew at that point that the brilliant light of the sun with its fundamental representation of cyclical power would be a symbol to me from then on. It would represent the metaphoric connection between circles and the cycles of nature, ephemeral and changing yet eternal. It would be a symbol closely related to the significance of the campfire of my river journey, a symbol of hope, a symbol of the potential for good to come out of so much evil that existed in the world, the hope for reconciliation between seemingly irreconcilable adversaries, the hope that things could some day come full circle and be turned around. I saw hope for the Eddies and the Tonys of the world. At that moment I felt truly optimistic. The threat of the ancient enemy did not seem as frightening. I rose to my feet. A strong compelling force controlled my next act. I walked to a near-by annatto tree and buried the little medal in the loose soil next to its roots as if I were planting the seed of hope under the sheltering protective branches of the great tree. I stood there for a brief instant and prayed.

In later years I would continue to enter great ceremonial circles bounded by stone hoops. Every year since then we created stone circles on the grounds of Pittsburgh's Indian Center to celebrate the various ceremonies of the Caney Circle.

CHAPTER V

THE JOURNEY OF GROWTH

1. INSECTS UPON THE WATER

On august 14, 1982 we traveled down a portion of the river which meandered tortuously among a number of lofty green-carpeted hills. We passed the towns of Kennerdell and Emlenton, and finally made it to Parker, Pennsylvania, near the mouth of the Clarion River. We camped on an island close to the town of Parker. Having settled ourselves in for the night I took out my paper pad and continued to work on the song which I had started the day before. I had decided to work on the difficult lyrics throughout the rest of our trip until I got the song finished.

As I sat there writing on the large pad of drawing paper, things began to fall upon its white surface. When the first one landed I realized it was some sort of insect so I casually brushed it off. Then two more landed. I brushed them off. Eventually they were falling at a rate of about one per ten seconds. They were landing on my shoulders, on my head and on my boots. I looked up into the darkening evening sky. There was a huge cloud of them over the whole island, over the river, as far as the eye could see. They were delicate spindly creatures dancing in midair. When one landed on my paper it would sit there and quiver for a while, then slowly it would pull its wings back and begin pumping its body literally out of its skin.

Gradually it pushed itself out, crawling from inside its outgrown old coat. As its wings became freed from the old skin they would spread and the insect lifted off still dragging the old skin dangling at the end of its tail.

I guess it was necessary for them to land on something before they could to go through this procedure, they could not do it in flight. The interesting thing is that they were not very particular about where they landed because next morning when we launched the canoe the river was covered with a thick layer of dead insects many of which lay partially out of their skins. They landed on the water and tried to molt even as they drowned.

In my childhood I had owned a fascinating book about insects. From it I had learned that as an insect develops it goes through one or more body changes. Different insects perform these operations in different ways. Some, like the butterfly undergo a complex change in shape called "metamorphosis." These insects are born as worm-like larvae, popularly known as "caterpillars" in no way resembling their adult form. After a period of growth the larva goes through a phase called "pupa" and then transforms itself into the adult fully developed.

Other insects, such as the grasshopper emerge from the egg as tiny immature replicas of their parents. Instead of undergoing the larval stage and subsequent process of metamorphosis they are simply born like people, as babies called "nymphs", and as they develop they outgrow several layers of skin like a child outgrows blue jeans. Their life is a series of molts.

In a way, much the same thing was occuring to me that week. I was molting. A kind of metamorphosis was taking place during that downriver trip. I was transforming and becoming. And the end result for me was growth, growth in unexpected forms.

2. DREAMS OF GROWTH

On Saturday August 15, 1982 we traveled down the river in a driving downpour. The rain stayed with us for hours and turned the experience into a long surrealistic dream. All around us the dead bodies of those molting insects from the night before floated on the surface of the water in a thick layer turning the river into a giant watery graveyard of failed transformations.

It all really did have a bizarre dreamlike quality.

I happen to believe that real dreams sometimes reflect messages from a guardian spirit. Each human being possesses such a metaphysical protector, a guide charged with the responsibility of providing not only a shield in time of danger but also a source of inspiration and encouragement in times of difficulties and a conduit for communication with a realm of trans-dimentional wisdom known to some as "the spirit realm". It is this entity which is in fact communicating with a person when that person dreams.

As I paddled in the rain that afternoon, covered in my rain poncho, I contemplated in silence the meaning and symbolism of several of my most recent dreams. The dreams I was concentrating on that day reflected the aspect of my humanity which demonstrated my capacity to create, change and become. It is that uniquely female, motherly side of us all, men and women, which allows us, through change and transition, to evolve into new beings. When a person evolves and changes he or she ceases to be the person that he or she was before. He or she, in essence gives birth to a new person. On that day that new person is in fact "born". This is a creative act, as is any birth. And the person that is responsible for that birth, in a manner of speaking, can be considered a "mother", whether it is a man or a woman.

My thoughts of dreams transported me back to my childhood. I was born into a Hispanic culture inherited from the European Spanish conquistador mentality that had long ago conquered my country, marked by the typical "machismo" which most people associate with Latin America. The Roman Catholic tradition which thinly veils the ancient Native and African beliefs of Latin America still maintains all the male dominance Christian characteristics of European Spain.

But deep in the heart of that tradition the heritage of an older spiritual reality thrives and survives through the ages. It was the sculptor and art historian, Merlin Stone, who first seemed to expose the secrets of early European culture's less macho past. In a ground-breaking book published in 1976 "When God Was a Woman" she put forth compelling evidence that most of the ancient Middle Eastern and European cradles of Western civilization had once preferred worshipping female deities as opposed to the male ones that dominate the area now. In essence, those early Neolithic and Chalcolithic civilizations still recognized the fundamental importance of the female quality of creativity within a spiritual context that they had inherited from their primordial Paleolithic past.

I was, at first a little puzzled by her assertions when I read her book back in 1978. But later reflection of my own religious upbringing and the kinds of soul-revealing dreams that upbringing had spawned began to confirm her theory. Both in Europe and in the Americas, Mother Nature was worshiped in ancient times as the "Cosmic Matriarch." When her worship was persecuted by newer male-deity-oriented conquerors, the followers of her rite, inspired by persistent mystical dreams of their goddess, found ways of worshipping her under a different more acceptable identity.

Upon the advent of Christianity in Europe many followers of the ancient Cosmic Matriarch tradition adopted the Virgin Mary as the identity of the sacred mother. Mary and several other female saints took on the spiritual characteristics of the Matriarch's ancient religious complex. In Mexico, the Aztec people were forbidden to venerate their Indigenous mother spirit, Tonanzin, by the Christian conquistadors. So they adopted the Christian image called "Our Lady of Guadalupe" as the new representation of their ancestral divine matriarch. This icon was reputed to have appeared on the hilltop site of an ancient Aztec Tonanzin temple in Tepeyac.

In my homeland of the Caribbean islands the ancient Taino Indians venerated ATA-BEI as the personification of the Cosmic Matriarch. After the Spanish conquered the islands and forced the Indigenous people to convert to Christianity the Indians of one of those islands, Cuba, adopted the Virgin Mary as a new manifestation of their ancient female deity. This mother manifested herself in the form of the icon that was brought by the shipwrecked sailor Ojeda and given to the chief of the village of Cueiba. That image would eventually emerge as an important symbol of veneration for the downtrodden of Caribbean history for 500 years until 1992 when the ancient Mother Spirits honored by the various peoples of the region would finally have the opportunity to rise again in their original forms.

Throughout my childhood I was taught by the Spanish priests who staffed Trinidad Church in my neighborhood of Los Hoyos in the city of Santiago that God the Father was the master of the universe. But the wise elders among whom I grew up and developed knew that "Our Lady of

Charity" was the true mistress of my native land. Our Lady of Charity was non other than the ancient Ata-Bei in a more acceptable non-pagan guise.

Ata-bei has always been associated with the moon. The moon marks the twenty-eight day monthly cycles which are Ata-bei's hallmark. The particular dream which I recollected on that rainy Saturday came to me during my early adolescence when I was living in Erie. In my dream, which was obviously influenced by my Roman Catholic upbringing, I found myself in the midst of a huge crowd outdoors. The people were assembled in expectation of some sort of miraculous event.

I waited along with everyone else until the image of the Virgin of Charity gradually appeared on the branch of a tree. The vision shimmered in the darkness of the night before the large multitude. Then it began to rise into the air. She floated up into the sky until all that was distinguishable of her was a silvery triangular wedge-shaped silhouette shimmering against the dark sky, created by the contour of her veil.

In the night sky it looked very much like one wedge-shaped section from a silver pie.

We all stood gaping up at the white shimmering wedge of silver hanging high over us. Suddenly the wedge began to change as if we were all witnessing a divine metamorphosis. The lower rounded base of the wedge slowly became broader. The two sloping sides pivoting out as if other new wedges were being added to either side of the original one, gradually completing the "Pie," the circular shape from which the original wedge had come. As this metamorphosis manifested itself the crowd continued to gaze adoringly at the vision.

Soon the process was complete. What had once been a wedge shaped section of a circle was now a full circle, a silver disc upon the dark heavenly mantle. It had transformed itself into the image of the full moon. In my dream, the Virgin had clearly identified herself with the mistress of the moon, a symbol of creative fertility.

These thoughts of my adolecent dream brought into my mind the words of the apostle John in chapter 12, verse 1 of his famous biblical book "Revelations"; "...And a great sign appeared in heaven: a woman clothed with the sun, and the moon was under her feet..."

Certainly the apparition in my dream had demonstrated that as well as compassion and love, she represented inventiveness and ingenuity, in other words "creativity", the motherly creativity and potential for creativity that manifests itself monthly in the womb a menstruating woman. These are attributes that manifest themselves in the adaptability that humans use as they change and transform to conform to changing survival situations. It invokes the old adage "Nececity is the mother of Invention" in a demonstration of how vital to survival is the power to come up with the new. CREATIVITY!

The moon goes through cycles of changes and metamorphoses called "phases". In this dream of becoming, of changing, of evolving, I eventually recognized the lesson of the conch sea-snail whose shell the ancient Taino Indians called "cobo". I wondered at the creative capacity of the mollusk who first made the shell and became its initial tenant. This creature formed that marvelous piece of structural art from her own body secretions, enlarging it, adding to it, making it anew and adapting its size and shape to her own gradual stages of growth, what a powerful act of artistic creativity!

Then after her death, if she died when her shell was still of manageable size, a large hermit crab might find shelter in her discarded shell allowing the mollusk to transcend her original identity as creator and assume a new mantle as selfless nurturer or protector, even beyond death, Nature's own "Lady of Charity". She becomes the great "Giving Beast" who transcends mortality and keeps on giving, even its bones, even after dying, like the manatee of my Vision Quest, giving away everything all the way down to its ribs after its demise.

Like the manatee in my Vision Quest dream, the sea shell conch is the great giving beast who transcends death and offers shelter to the hermit crab even after its demise

The conch seashell became for me a symbol of the feminine principle of creativity, and creative generosity, and creative compassion, personified by Ata-bei and by the Virgin of Charity. The Shell came to symbolize for me the ability to become, to creatively and imaginatively evolve, to adapt, and then later, to give, and even to nurture and protect, like Oshun nurtured and protected Babalu by using her creative ingenuity.

Now as I paddled down the river in my canoe I cherished this powerful symbol because I sensed that in the personal creativity of my art and music I would find an ultimate weapon with which to confront the sinister phantom that still seemed to be dogging my steps.

The Seashell Lady

CHAPTER VI

SACRED IMAGES

1. RETURN OF THE SEASHELL LADY

The rain had been so pervasive that day that it seemed dry weather would never return. But it did. In fact, although we never did see the sun we had enough of a respite to make it possible to set up camp, build our evening campfire and sit there to enjoy it. As usual I sat working on my song lyrics before the small blaze that Sven had so skillfully prepared. The nightly campfire always held a sort of fascination for me at the end of each day. It gave me a sense of presence in the midst of the vastness of the forest. It represented a modest statement of my existence even as I felt dwarfed by the sacred wonder of its untamed beauty.

I knew the glow of our little fire would be unable to illuminate the work I was trying to accomplish on my paper pad. So as usual I worked furiously trying to milk from the last vestiges of sunlight the couple of seconds needed to finish a few more lines of the song.

When the last faint glimmer of twilight disappeared I finally gave up. I set down my pad of paper, leaned back and allowed myself to get lost in the glow of the fire. Eventually I grew so drowsy that I decided to call it a night. I bid my friend good evening and withdrew to the darkness of the tent. I fell asleep and began to dream about a fire.

The light of that huge dream fire, that great victory bonfire, cast an orange glow on the faces of the group of dancers gathered around it. Among these, Caoba closed her eyes and allowed the rhythm of the drum to flow through her as her bare feet alternated in kissing the hard-packed earth. Her ears were filled with the trembling jingle of hundreds of shell anklets adorning the fast moving limbs, ankles and wrists, of the many participants. The behike medicine man's voice accompanied by that of the dancers rose shrilly into the night air and mingled with the song of the crickets and tree frogs. Caoba opened her eyes again and took in the emotional panorama revealed to her by the fire's glow. She saw men and women of all ages abandoning themselves to the ecstasy of the moment. An old grandfather wearing nothing but a loincloth heaved to the music while beside him a young warrior clad in knee-length cotton cloth breeches and a captured steel breastplate emitted war-whoops as he danced.

Not far along the arching line of dancers a half-naked adolescent girl threw her head back and released a long high pitched howl which floated over the treetops and wafted down from the Sierra all the way to the ears of frightened Spanish officials, blending eerily into their nightmares as they slept fitfully in their richly adorned beds.

The defiant "areito" dance lasted all night. It echoed thousands of areito rituals of centuries passed and forecasted future areito rituals to come. Caoba felt the grip of her husband's hand on her own as her soul soared through magic trance states. The ritual was powerful and permanent. Its features were meaningful and relevant. The areito had begun!

Then the lead singer raised his voice in a high-pitched crescendo. The verses of the ancient ancestral chant began to flow from his lips in a current of energy which touched each dancer. As the singer began to intone the first few notes of the melody I realized it sounded familiar to me. I lay there dreaming and in that dream I experienced a song that I had actually heard many years before. It was the familiar melody of the Cordon dance that had come to my rescue wafting over the partition wall of my grandmother's patio all those years ago to rescue me from the dream-shark dog monster. I heard the vigorous rhythm, felt the strenuous foot-stamping and ecstatic grunts and shouts. The singer's voice rang out and I marvelled at the energy and hypnotic quality of the experience. The singer sang of the first

Mother, Ata Bei, the great divine progenitor. He sang of the birth of her twin sons, Yoka Hu, the Lord of the Life Force, and Guakar, the Lord of Teaching Trials.

The song flowed like a river and the current carried the areito participants into the soul of Taino sacred narration. The singer wove a tapestry of colors, painting images of the primordial cave, Kasibahagua, the uterine enclosure place where the original embryonic ancestors dwelled before the earth was populated. The singer's voice unfurled sequential images. The singer's voice intoned the story of the first sentinel, Macocael, his assigned task to keep watch at the entrance of the primordial cave home so that the chief of the community could determine what portion of the new earth was fit for human habitation. He sang of Macocael's failure to carry out his duty and his punitive transformation into a pile of rocks at the entrance of the cavern. He sang of those who were sent out to search for food for the hungry ones in the cave. He sang of their failure to return and their transformation into trees, of Yaubaba the one who was sent out to search for healing herbs, of his failure to return and his transformation into a mockingbird.

The current of the singer's voice throbbed to the rhythm of the mayohuakan log drum, the maraca rattles and the hundreds of seashell anklets as the participants stamped their feet to the hectic tempo. His melody led the dancers down the dramatic trail of the hallowed story. And they danced. They danced as ecstatically as the Cordon dancers in the ceremony at my grandmother's neighbor's house. They danced the sacred story. They danced the journey of the despotic chief, Guaguyona, as he led the women of the cave away from their husbands and children leaving the primordial community devoid of the magic of the female. The dancers followed the trek of the false leader, Anakakuya as he attemped to fill the power vacuum left by Guaguyona. The singer's voice rose dramatically at the moment when he retold how Guaguyona, realizing his great error, eliminated the false leader and threw him into the ocean as the Big Dipper constellation dives into the marine horizon.

Then the song cycled back to the community, carrying the areito participants to Guaguyona's repentance from his great misdeed, his suffering under the weight of the illness he contracted as punishment for his evil acts, an illness that could only be healed by Guabonito the primordial curandera healer woman, his recovery in her guanara sweatlodge, and his triumphant return back to the cave, empowered by the magic of the sacred crystals and ciba stones, and the chief"'s guanin necklace given him by the holy woman.

Then the singer's voice grew husky and guttural as he processed the images of provocative, unethical forest beings who were neither male nor female, with slippery, human-like, naked bodies, who taunted and teased the men of the community, desperate men who had not been with women for a long time, and the recovery of the women of the community via the assistance of the tribesmen with abrasive skins from which the slippery forest beings could not escape, and the transformational power of the magic bird, Inriri, the woodpecker, when it sculpted new virtuous, ethical human females from the sexually ambiguous bodies of the captured forest beings.

It was an emotional and adrenalin-filled ride as the dancers were carried by the singer's voice, into the homestead of the primordial god-like human, Yaya-Lokuo, and witnessed the violent rebellion of Yaya-Lokuo's son, Yayael, and witnessed Yayael's death. Then the dirge-like wailing rose dramatically upon the narration of the interment of Yayael's bones in the funerary gourd, the mystic metaphoric symbol of Ata-Bei's womb, and the transformation of the bones into mythic fish and salty sea water.

The singer finally concluded his epic narration as he swept the dancers into the great global flood that occurred when the mischievous quadruplet sons of the sacred woman Itaba Iaubaba, knocked down Yayael's magic funerary gourd and spilled the salty fluid within it where the fish were swimming, creating the Caribbean Sea. It was the dramatic culmination of the legendary narrative that lifted the crowd of participants as Deminan, the leader of the quadruplets challenged the authority of the elder medicine man Baiamanako, and the old sage caused a great turtle to break out painfully from a suddenly emerging hump on the impudent youth's back. The story arrived at its destination when the turtle that had emerged from Deminan's back became transformed into a woman that represented the gift of compassion that the four sons of Itaba had repressed within themselves for a long time and which the medicine man had released out of Deminan's body with his magic power. This was the moment of the ancient narrative's resolution as the singer presented it in his song, when the four boys, representing the four cardinal virtues of humanity were united into one integrated human and this man became the husband of Turtle Woman, and she became the mother, and he the father of all Tainos.

The dancers moved to the rhytm of victory and perseverance and the ultimate emergence into a new era of glory and life.

And they chanted in ecstatic unison with the singer, and they became part of the story.

"Old Hutia-Woman had the appearance this evening, of someone who is destroyed." Sagua commented as he and Caoba trudged wearily along the narrow mountain foot-path that led to their little thatch-roofed hut. "She lapses in and out of her melancholy. I don't think she will ever recover from the loss of her son."

Caoba pondered her husband's words for a while as she walked, then answered: "Andres was her only son. He was born into slavery and she went through great hardship to ransom him from the slave's whip. Now he's gone."

Sagua listened quietly to her pessimistic words. Then, after a short pause he said: "Andres was a good kid but he couldn't fight."

"Yes!" Caoba sighed. "I saw him that morning when we attacked Don Isidro's hacienda. He waved that war-club like a toy and didn't hit anything. The rest of us had to keep looking after him. When the Spaniards loosed the war-dogs he unwisely decided to take on all three of them." "Yes, I saw that too." mumbled Sagua. "That's why Antonio and I rushed to his side. But by the time we reached him it was too late. The dogs tore him to pieces!"

Caoba and Sagua continued their walk in silence all the way to their humble home.

Caoba fingered the hilt of the old Toledo sword she had found in the cave the day after her escape as it hung in its scabbard from a belt at her waist. She found plenty of opportunity to put it to good use. She had become a warrior. Both she and Sagua had joined a band of renegades who, from their mountain hideaways in the Sierra De Purial mountain range, sustained an ongoing guerrilla struggle against the haciendas and small towns in the whole south-eastern portion of Oriente territory. They terrorized the Spanish settlers from Baracoa in the east, to Santiago city on the foothills of the Sierra Maestra range in the west.

Led by an intrepid chief known only by the title "Guamá" (leader), the band had grown quickly, swelled by scores of escaped Indian and half-breed slaves.

On that evening the face of the hacienda lord, the local "encomendador" flushed red as the veins swelled at his neck. He pounded his fist on the hardwood table-top and screamed at a scribe who scribbled hurriedly and nervously upon a piece of parchment on the other side of the table. "Don't they understand that we are sinking in blood out here? What is Santiago thinking? What is Santiago doing? Have those city loafers forgotten about us out here in the hinterland". The scribe fidgeted tensely with his paper and dared not look up into the angry face of the nobleman. "Sir…Is there anything else you wish me to add to this letter?" he finally stammered cautiously. "NO! damn it!…Just send the letter. Let's hope they do something this time. Let's hope they send an army or something! These savages are killing white men, killing Christians, for God's sake! and any Indians who demonstrate loyalty to the whites. It's a disgrace. It's a disaster! WE ARE LOSING A FORTUNE! They are ruining us! The tobacco crops are going unharvested, the copper ore stays in the mines and there is no one to dig it out! All the hacienda lords have complained loud and long to the colonial authorities about this Indian rebellion raging in our district but all official measures taken against them have proven unsuccessful. These rebels sweep out of the dense highland forests all smeared-up in bija paint, howling like rabid beasts, burning, looting and killing. It's a disaster!" The scribe rose nervously from his seat at the table and rushed out the door of the chamber to mail the letter from his master, leaving the encomendador fuming behind him. The letter went out the next morning in the satchel of the mounted messenger to the city of Santiago.

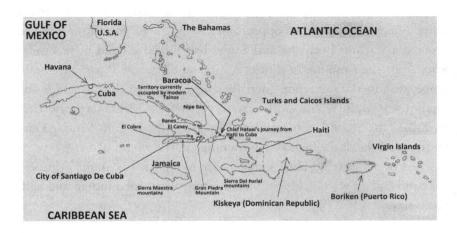

Caoba always wore a little white cotton-cloth bag full of anamu leaves on the war raids for good luck. She was wearing it during the dance that night.

The great ceremony that Caoba and Sagua had attended that cool November evening was in celebration of the maize harvest. It was led by Guiro, the old behike medicine man who always accompanied Chief Guamá.

Guiro was a mighty "Brujo," as the Spaniards called the Indian medicine men. He was one of the few who still practiced the visionary cohoba ceremony and one of the few members of Guamá's rebel band who had never felt the slave whip's bite. There were still a few Indians living in isolated regions of the mountain forests and other remote sites, who had eluded the encomienda all these years. He had attained his great magic from a series of powerful dreams and visions. His most important semisaki spirit-guide was a green parrot and he wore a parrot skin covered in green feathers attached to the back of his head. He had led the funerary ceremony for young Andres a few months earlier. At that ceremony Caoba and Sagua experienced for the first time the ancient burial rites of their Taino Indian ancestors, the cleaning of the bones, the partial cremation and finally the interring of the remains in a large higuera gourd and a clay bowl.

One morning as he walked past the old brujo's hut on his way to the cassava fields, Sagua spotted the medicine man sitting on one of those old time "duho" stools, the kind that Taino chiefs and behikes had used for centuries. He stopped to greet the elder.

"Greetings grandfather." He remarked with a smile. "Greetings grandson." The old man answered, using also the kinship terminology that was traditional among the Indians. "You pass by my bohio early this morning." The old man added removing a crudely rolled cigar from his mouth. "I want to finish work early today, grandfather because I need to make an offering at the old spirit cave on El Gato Mountain," said the young man. "And what might be the reason for this offering, if I may ask?" Inquired the old man with an air of unabashed curiosity.

The young man lowered his head shyly. "I think Caoba is with child, grandfather." he said in a whisper. "Eh!...a father, we have a father here!" exclaimed Guiro, his squinty eyes twinkling with mischievous delight. He rose from his stool and bringing the cigar back up to his mouth clamped it between the few teeth he still retained. "Sit down, sit daddy... a man in your condition should not strain himself. Sit here on my duho." He cried out waving his hand at the low wooden seat.

"Aw come on grandfather, don't tease me. At first I was overcome with joy but now I've grown worried. I have never been a father before."

The old man doubled over with laughter. "Really...?" he spurted amid guffaws. "Really...you never had this experience before, eh? I am amazed! How old are you, eighteen, nineteen seasons old? A mature gentleman like you ought to be well informed on matters of paternity." He struggled to bring his laughter under control.

Sagua saw no humor in the situation. These were hard times. The rebellion had made life very complicated for Indians in the district, He was convinced that what they were doing was the only right thing to do, but their life was the desperate life of fugitive guerrillas, and it was a very uncertain world into which to bring a new child or to start a family. The old man continued a bit more soberly but with a wide smile on his face. "Look grandson, to worry a bit is natural in your position, specially having grown up in the hacienda like you did. Most of us fathers go through much the same thing you are going through."

He approached Sagua and threw an arm about his broad brown shoulder. "Don't be embarrassed by your awkwardness, there is a first time for everyone. The first time will always seem frightening and overwhelming because you are facing the unknown." Sagua felt the reassuring touch of the old man's hand on his shoulder and the slight loosening of a tight knot he had been carrying in his stomach since Caoba had informed him of her pregnancy. He smiled faintly back at old Guiro for an instant then said.

"Blessings to you, grandfather.".

"Blessings to you, grandson." The old man responded, still smiling past his big cigar. Sagua continued on down to the cultivated fields.

In June of the following year Caoba miscarried her baby. The sadness of that event was somewhat alleviated by news of the imperial edict from Spain abolishing Indian encomienda system of compulsory labor for Indians throughout the Caribbean. Unfortunately this joy was temporary. The energy with which Chief Guamás followers continued to carry out their rebellion forced the Spanish authorities to temporarily re-introduce the Indian forced-labor system to justify the ruthless hunting down of Guamá's rebels throughout the following years.

By the time of the first anniversary of Caoba's miscarriage many of Guamá's warriors had been captured or killed and several of his mountain stronghold camps had been destroyed. His people's fields were burned and families dispersed. It was later suspected that Guamá's own brother finally killed him.

Fortunately for Sagua and Caoba their own camp was never discovered. After Chief Guamá's death Sagua and Caoba continued participating in raids on Spanish settlements. They continued joining first one impromptu warrior band then another. Their activities in these raids finally ended about ten years later when a sweeping imperial edict backed by a papal bull permanently abolished all Indian compulsory labor in all Spanish America once and for all.

Soon after the new law was passed the Santiago city authorities began to organize well trained, well armed and well paid Indian mercenary brigades, made up of loyal Indian men. These divisions, men who no longer felt the ignominy of the slaver's whip and who were motivated by the irresistible lure of money, quickly tracked down the remaining rebel groups and systematically eliminated them.

In the midst of all this turmoil Caoba kept trying to bear another child without success. Finally, in the spring of the eighth year after her first miscarriage, just before the ruthless Indian mercenary operations shifted into high gear, she gave birth to a beautiful baby boy.

The child was born in the early morning hours just as the sun spirit, Guey, began peering over the eastern hills. There were two midwives attending the event and the Brujo Guiro himself came to sing his powerful chants next to the birthing bed adding to the atmosphere of hallowed dignity which reigned throughout Caoba's labor and delivery.

It was after the midwife, Caona had thoroughly cleansed the vigorous little newborn with fresh spring water that Guiro finally approached to gaze into the child's face.

At first sight of the baby's eyes Guiro blanched and froze as if stricken by some invisible seizure. "It is he...!" The old man finally moaned after a long mysterious silence. All in attendance were too awed by the profound impact the child's face had made on the powerful old brujo to make any inquiries as to whom "He" was. "It is he, it is he!" Guiro repeated excitedly, bringing his hand over his mouth. "It is he..!"

"Who?" Caoba finally gasped clutching her child protectively as she stared at the weird expression on Guiro's face. "Yes, Guiro, come out with it man! Stop frightening the girl and tell us all what mystery you see in this child's face." Scolded the midwife Caona as she pulled the old man away from the young mother and child. Guiro allowed himself to be dragged back still staring at the baby, then turned and walked to a nearby hammock which hung between a supporting upright pole of the hut and a hook in the wall. He slumped heavily into the hammock lost in contemplation, even as every eye in the house rested on him with impatient anticipation.

"Guiro, for the love of everything that is sacred to you tell us what is the matter. You look like you are about to faint!" Insisted Caona.

The wizened old brujo stared at the thatch of the hut's ceiling for a few more minutes. Then he turned to face the small group of people and began to speak in a strange monotone.

"Years ago in a place not far from here there was a large village in a district called Cueiba. That was back in the days before the white men had taken possession of our land.

In that village there was a powerful clay statue of our Cosmic Matriarch. Ata Bei, depicting her in the position of birthing, with her legs spread wide and her face straining in the midst of childbirth delivery.

That statue was kept in a beike's hut. The beike was an old woman called, "Guaricheanao" whose care for the sacred image absorbed most of her waking time. Her home was a shrine to Atabei, with offerings of shells, flowers, tobacco and bowls of pineapple wine wreathing the matriach's altar like a crown.

That image of the Earth Mother was the source of great pride to the people of the village. Pilgrims flocked to that settlement from distant villages to sing the praises of the Matriach and ask her favors at the altar in the beike's hut.

Then a series of events forever changed the lives of those villagers. First Guaricheanao became ill. For months she languished in her hammock unable to care for the altar of the wonderful statue. At last the old woman lapsed into a deep coma in which she remained for four days. On the fifth day she awakened and spoke to the people in a weak trembling voice. She said she had traveled to the land of the spirits and was returned with a message that she had to share with her fellow villagers. In her dream she had been visited by a seer from another island, a prophetic priestess who told her that the country of her people would be taken away from them by white-skinned foreigners.

"You will suffer!" The ghost had warned. "Your treasured icon will be lost to you. It will vanish from its altar. It will retreat to the sea mother!"

The old lady told her people not to grieve, for their sacred statue which had represented the Divine Love Matriarch as a fertile pregnant mother in the creative act of giving birth, would be transformed during its brief absence, and then would return among them in a strange new manifestation.

It would come back in the image of a new mother who had just given birth, with her new-born baby at her hip.

Ironically this new incarnation of their ancient icon, returning to them from the ocean into which she had retreated, would be borne to them by the foreign conquerors themselves as they emerged from the eastern sea, in their huge alien crafts with white wings. The new image will rise to the exulted position held by the old one. She will temporarily replace the old image and reign over a span of twenty four generations, representing the twenty four pebbles that are placed between the four cardinal directional stones of the Taino Medicine Wheel.

The newborn child at her hip will be the Hope-Child. He will represent the promise of the future redemption of all humam beings. During the period of twentyfour generations the people will suffer slavery, persecution, oppression, war, exploitation, and near extinction. They will find hope only in the serene smiles on the faces of the new spiritual mother and her child. Then, after 500 turbulent years the Hope-Child will mature and grow up. On that day he shall come to the people in all his native glory as Ioka-hu, Lord of life.

At that time there will be a great struggle. Justice, Hope and Reconciliation shall battle Injustice, Despair and Discord. The winner of that struggle shall rule humanity for the rest of its tenure on Earth.

The ancient traditions will be kept alive by various leaders and holy people during 500 years of trials and will again be ready to bring the people together when the hope child comes of age!

When the old woman finished that speech to her people she died." Added Guiro; and then he continued.

"Not long after her death the old statue of the pregnant Ata-Bei did indeed vanish mysteriously from its altar in spite of the many precautions taken by the chief and the council of nitainos.

It is said that a few days later a fisherman returned to the village after a canoe trip to a neighboring island. He claimed to have seen the little statue floating as if it was made of wood on the water in a large harbor to the north called Nipe Bay.

He said that when he spotted it bobbing on the surface of the choppy water he recognized it as the missing idol. He says he approached it but suddenly the clay figure transformed itself into a large conch shell and sank quickly to the bottom of the sea. As it vanished beneath the waves the fisherman heard the deep boom of a shell trumpet being blown in the distance."

The old medicine man now rose to a sitting position on the hammock and gazed past the faces of the little group gathered around him. He continued:

"Soon after that, the village was visited by white men from across the ocean. They were the first Spaniards those Indians had ever laid eyes on. The white men were lost. They were a small group of explorers from a capsized ship, starving and sick.

The villagers treated them kindly, giving them food and nursing them back to health. In gratitude the leader of the exploration group, a man named Ojeda, presented the village chief with a statue depicting the Virgin Mary holding her son Jesus at her hip.

The Indians realized this was their matriarch returning to them from the sea in a new form to comfort them in this temporary manifestation for the next twentyfour disastrous generations, til her son grew to adulthood to redeem them. They welcomed her with overwhelming joy. As they re-instated her in her new form to her proper place at the altar they blew dozens of conch shell trumpets symbolizing the Matriarch's gift of creativity and her connection to the sea. A large conch shell was placed at the foot of the altar and a new beike, the young daughter of the previous caretaker, was given her mother's old responsibility. The new image took the place of the old one. People again began to journey from distant villages to make offerings of gratitude and praise at the altar of the matriarch. They called her 'Lady of Charity' because they saw in her the model of compassion symbolized by the ancient Turtle Woman who had emerged from the back of Deminan in the time of legends. In fact, since they had acquired the new little icon by compassionately helping the shipwrecked sailors, they perceived her presence among them as the fruit of an act of compassion, an act of charity. They also called her the 'Shell Lady' because she represented the selfless compassion of the conch snail who, like the great Giving Beast, continues giving as it wraps its hard shell mantle of protection around the hermit crab, even after death."

At this point old Guiro looked again at the new-born's face. Then he said: "Some time passed before the conquistadors finally came back in force to conquer our land. This time the Spaniards did not need our compassion or our charity. They came as conquerors. They burned the village of Cueiba, where the sacred statue resided. Before she was hunted down and killed the young beike managed to hide the statue of the Lady of Charity in the forest. No one knows where.

I was one of the survivors of the destruction of Cueiba. I was there when the Spanish destroyed our homes, killed my relatives and rounded up the majority of those who were still alive to work for them against our will. I escaped into the mountains with a few others. We made it to a place far to the west where the local Indians had built a whole village on stilts right on the shoreline. I lived there and apprenticed under the local beike. I learned the way of the cemies. I became a spiritual guide. During a great fast and cohoba ceremony that I carried out years later I was approached by the spirit of the Cueiba beike who had been murdered by the Spanish. She revealed to me the secrets that would eventually make me a respected medicine man. She told me that I would some day meet the man who was destined to bring back to the people the sacred image of Shell Lady, the Lady of Charity. She told me that not long after I met this man I would die."

At this point, old Guiro climbed down from the hammock. "The man who is to return the image to the people has a great mission, for after its return it is destined to become a great icon to all the inhabitants of this land, Indians and non-Indians. It shall be a symbol of the responsibility that each human has for the welfare of all his brothers and sisters. She will represent compassion in all its manifestations.

The name by which it shall be known is 'Our Lady of Charity'. That name will reflect that law of self-sacrifice and altruism which guided those villagers who so long ago saved the lives of the men that embodied the forces which would eventually enslave them."

A deadly hush hung over the group gathered there in that little one-room hut as Guiro again approached the new mother and her child. "The man who shall fulfill the prophecy shall find the image in the forest right where the Cueiba behike hid her. Upon finding it he shall take it home and offer to it the smoke of sacred tobacco and the food of cassava meal. It shall speak to him. The words of the ancient ancestress, the virgin mother of all people, she who gave birth to Yoka Hu without the benefit of a father, shall guide that chosen man in the task before him. That man shall be the bringer of a great power focus to our people. His contribution shall be anonymous for they shall never know that it was he who was responsible for returning to them the object of their veneration."

Guiro stared intently at the calm face of the sleeping baby. "I am now looking at that man!"

"What?" exclaimed Caona as all eyes turned to the baby. "Do you mean this child here?" she added.

"Yes!" answered Guiro emphatically.

"Does this mean your death is imminent?" Caona ventured. "Yes!" repeated the old man squatting next to the birthing bed. "Little one..." he murmured tenderly, "I never dreamed I would some day attend to your birth!" He brought up his gnarled brown hand and gently caressed the sleeping infant. "I spent my whole life waiting to meet you. I had nearly given up hope. My death is of no concern." He smiled turning to the others. "I am an old man. My task upon the earth is finished and it is time to go back to her womb. This child's mission is just beginning and it was my duty to reveal the nature of that mission. It is also my duty to reveal his name to you. This child shall restore the Shell Lady to her rightful place, his name shall be Cobo, 'The Shell'."

Guiro died peacefully in his hammock that night.

Little Cobo grew among the untamed native people of the Sierra Maestra.

After the passage of the Indian emancipation law and the beginning of serious African slave trade in the Caribbean, and after the victories of the notorious Indian mercenaries against the rebels, most of the wild warriors gave up the fight. They decided to leave the mountains and settle in the more populous low-lying areas around the growing towns of Santiago in the South and Baracoa in the East and in the surrounding villages, where Indians and whites were already living side by side. Many took refuge in the missionary settlements set up by the Jesuits at Caridad de los Indios, Yateras and El Caney. Here, enlightened clerics showed them skills which would enable them to survive in the alien new system that had established permanent root in their country.

But Caoba and Sagua never returned to the lowland. They lived out their lives in the mountain fastness of the Sierra, cultivating cassava, tomatos and maize, hunting ducks and jutias, raising their little boy in the old traditions within the understanding of the sacred mission which had been revealed by Guiro upon the child's birth.

On a dark, dreary December afternoon seventeen years later Cobo, now a young man, trudged slowly home from a hunting foray in the valley swamplands. A brace of ducks lay slung over his shoulder as he walked. Along the trail he met a criolla woman with a child at her hip. She was clearly a meztiza of mixed ancestry with dark skin but European features and wearing European garb. The lad wondered why this mother should be walking alone so late in the afternoon, way out here in the wild mountains so far away from the nearest white community.

"Mistress..." He called out, "Are you lost? We are far from any settlement. Dusk will overtake you soon and the night is not safe for a criolla woman with a child."

"You are right..." answered the young mother. "I am lost and the night will be dangerous for me and my baby."

Cobo gazed into her clear sweet face. He had never seen such a beautiful woman. Then she did something that left him speechless. She began speaking in the Taino Indian language.

"My child is chilled we must find a warm, dry place to spend the night." She sighed. When he had recovered from the shock of hearing a criolla speaking a language that even some of the Indians were forgetting he stammered:

"We have a room on our bohio, mistress. My parents and I can shelter you tonight. Tomorrow I can guide you to Santiago city."

The mysterious lady nodded and followed Cobo up the trail. Cobo and the woman walked for several hours.

"You have shown me great kindness considering that to you I am no different from a white woman, a member of the race which has subjugated your people and stolen your land." The woman suddenly commented as she walked along behind him. Cobo turned his head around and looked at her suspiciously but continued to walk in silence.

"I am sincere in my words, young man. I am grateful." Cobo looked ahead at the path before him and answered calmly. "I have been raised to show kindness and compassion to all people, no matter what their color. True, my people fought a long bitter war in a failed attempt at independence but now the war is over. My people have returned to their tradition of peace. Within this tradition we believe that charity is an obligation, not an option." The woman fell silent as she walked in his footsteps behind him. Then she echoed his words: "Charity is an obligation not an option." after another pause she continued: "Charity is important to your people, isn't it?" Cobo turned his head again to face her. "My people are historically famous for their charitable nature. After all, didn't we practically hand our country over to you on a silver platter?" There was acid sarcasm in his words. The woman returned his angry glare with a disarming gentle smile.

"I understand your bitterness..." She said softly.

"Hah! That's a laugh." Retorted the boy turning his face away from her. What could you, practically a white woman, possibly understand?

"And, of course that bitterness is justified." She continued, ignoring his synicism. "But that does not invalidate charity. It is the hallmark of the human being. It is the great lesson that your culture shall leave to posterity. Charity, along with compassion and reconciliation is the strength of your people's magic and the true power behind your medicine men and women. It is a virtue to be guarded and cherished."

It was odd to hear a criolla speaking in this way about the ancient Taino spiritual tradition that was banned by theSpanish. Cobo felt a strange intensity in the voice behind him. The last words seemed to rise in volume and then trail off as if disappearing in the distance. He stopped in his tracks and turned to face the woman, but she was no longer there. Cobo looked around in utter bewilderment then he heard a voice which seemed to emanate from every quarter of the forest.

"I am the image of the creative spirit of selflessness and generosity." The mysterious voice murmured: "I am the mother who, in the ancient legend, conceived the Lord of the Life Force, without a father's participation. I am the mother of all Life. My womb is the center of the galaxy. At my feet is the image of the moon for I walk the sacred path of the twenty-eigh day cycle of fertility and creativity. I am 'The Shell Lady'." I am the Virgin of Charity.

A soft warmth washed over the lad. "My Lady, you are she who was foretold at my birth. You are she whom I am charged to return to the people. Please guide me. How am I to fulfill my mission? How am I to serve you?" He pleaded recognizing now the identity of the young mother.

"Don't rush..." The woman's gentle voice reverberated through the woods. "There is plenty of time. For now the most important way in which you may serve me is in continuing the tradition of your forebears, the traditions of mercy and sharing. We shall meet once more in due time. When our paths cross again I shall tell you what to do."

Cobo grew to manhood among the mountain peasants. He never told anyone of his amazing encounter on the forest trail. Secretly he burned with anticipation, looking forward to the day when he would carry out old Guiro's prophecy.

A few years later Sagua died of pneumonia. The aging Caoba grieved her loss and not even the company of her devoted son, Cobo, seemed to fully cheer her. Finally two years after the death of her husband, she also died in Cobo's arms.

As Caoba lay dying in her son's embrace she spoke to him for the last time:

"Son, my time has arrived and I am ready to make the long journey to Coai-Bai, the land of the spirits. It is up to you now to pass on the tradition which your father and I, and so many others tried to reawaken in our people. The task is not an easy one and the odds are against you. But with the help of your guardian spirit and the protection of our mother Ata-Bei and our father Ioka-Hu you can persevere.

You in particular have been given a huge responsibility, for you have been entrusted with bringing to the people of our island a new symbol.

Our island is a new place, a different place now. Our people are quickly becoming a hybrid mixture of three races, three cultures. Old Guiro foresaw that our people were going to need a new image to maintain everpresent in their minds their age-old relationship to our Cosmic Mother even as the Spanish oppressors oblige us to accept their god of war.

We are now in the midst of the twenty-four generation period which his prophesy foresaw. Our people suffer greatly. You are destined to bring to them the sacred image of hope which Guiro said would provide a bright beacon in these dark times, the beacon which will guide our people through this gloomy tunnel and out into the daylight at the other end. That image may be very different from the ancient semi statues which our ancestors held sacred, but for the time being she must be representative of ALL the people of this land. There will be time enough later for our sacred images to return to our descendants when it is safe for them to be honored again".

The old woman gasped and coughed up blood. Cobo wiped the corners of her mouth with a cotton rag. She struggled to finish her final message to her son. She painfully pushed herself up on one elbow and pointed to a box which sat on the ground in the corner at the far end of the room.

"My son..." She continued. "In that box are the two weapons which our family has inherited from the sacred forces. A vile enemy seeks to thwart the plans of the high spirits. A vile enemy seeks to slam shut the door at the end of the dark tunnel. He seeks to trap humanity in the darkness forever. The weapons in that box are magical and posses the power to conquer the vile enemy. One of those weapons is the conch shell of artistic creativity, ingenuity, and compassion, the cobo that is your namesake, that represents the creative gifts of the past, of the ancestors; the other weapon is the sharp sword of undaunted determination and justice, the technological advancement tool of the foreigner that you will take hold of and transform, that can be molded into the vehicle of future victory. Guard these two mighty tools, and care for them, because they will be of use to your descendants."

That said Caoba lay back and expired in her son's arms.

That night Cobo buried his mother in a plot of land behind their family shack next to Sagua's grave. He was weeping quietly as he entered the house. It seemed strangely quiet, as if the soul of the house had decided to leave once the soul of Caoba was no longer present there.

He lay in his hammock awake for hours that night thinking. He thought about his mother's last words. Eventually he climbed down from his hammock and crossed the room. He knelt before the large wooden chest his mother had pointed to and opened it. It was full of old clothes.

He began carefully to pull out the garments one by one and laying them on the floor beside the chest until he got down to the very bottom of the box. Lying there at the bottom were two objects. One of the objects was a magnificent gleaming white conch shell and the other was a sparkling Toledo rapier sword in a guilt scabbard. Cobo looked down at the two objects for a long time, then he shut the lid of the chest, walked back to his hammock and went to sleep.

Cobo made an important decision that summer. He left behind the wild mountains where he had been raised and moved to the city of Santiago. He had heard that there was a little money to be made on the busy docks of the growing harbor town. A year after his mother's death he packed some belongings in two large canvas bags, he loaded down an old mule that Caoba had bought from a half-breed living near Gran Piedra mountain, and descended from the Sierra never to return.

In town he worked unloading transoceanic vessels with goods from Spain that had first docked at the port of Havana and then had sailed around the western cape, and along the southern coast to Santiago harbor. He helped load tobacco, which was becoming the region's main export bound for Havana and then from there back to Spain.

He saved enough money to lease, and then buy a plot of land near the harbor. He built a small wood shack on that land. Eventually he met and married Carlota, a witty mulatto former slave girl who had bought her freedom with money earned from her performance of lively Afro-Caribbean tunes in the inns and public houses of the city.

Cobo with his wife established himself permanently in Santiago. He never forgot his mission to which he was born or the vision which had confirmed it. He and Carlota only had one child, a beautiful girl called Marina. Because of Cobo's fanatic secretiveness, neither his wife nor his daughter ever learned of his life-long obsession with the lost statue. However, the little family went regularly into the forest and performed the old Taino ceremonies far from the religious persecution of the city officials and parish clerics.

Cobo kept up the spiritual traditions he inherited from his mother and father

2. MARINA

In my dream, I watched Marina grow up and become one of the most beautiful women on the waterfront. Every man at the docks begged her to marry him. But the dark-eyed beauty dreamed of pearl necklaces and jeweled rings.

One morning Marina set out on one of her leisurely walks along the narrow streets of the waterfront. As usual, the muscled stevedores, slave men and free men, black, Indian and mixed-blood, filled the air with the poetry of the "piropo," a kind of lyrical folk-art form used in Cuba by men to complement attractive women. Marina relished the experience and tossed back the long luxuriant mane of jet-black curls cascading down her back, and the men sighed and groaned. The more she was compared to flowers and to the various female saints of the Catholic pantheon the less notice she appeared to take of the ardent would-be suitors.

She turned the corner of one particularly narrow alley and ran full into the arms of a tall blond stranger. Startled for a moment Marina looked up into the blue eyes of the young man. Then she cowered back.

"My, aren't we bold? Not only are we walking the streets without a chaperon, but to make matter worse we throw ourselves into the arms of the first stranger we run into."

The girl felt a burning flush of embarrassment wash over her face. The man was well dressed, obviously a nobleman or the son of a rich merchant. He approached Marina and putting a knuckle under her chin, lifted the cherubic face. "Well, no harm done, and certainly a woman of your charms can easily be forgiven a minor social impropriety; don't you think?" Marina was lost in the pale aquamarine sparkle of the stranger's eyes. She nodded absently.

"Yes, of course...well... señorita, do you live around here?" "Yes" gasped the girl hoarsely, then clearing her throat she repeated: "Yes... uh, yes señor; I live near the waterfront."

"I see", the stranger muttered turning pensively. The girl felt awkward.

"I have to go now." She exclaimed suddenly and started moving down the street.

"Wait!" His voice rang out. "Don't leave." Marina stopped and covered her face modestly with her veil. She did not turn to face him. "What is your name? When can I see you again?" The girl felt that flush on her face again.

"My name is Marina. I'll meet with you in the plaza in front of the cathedral, if it pleases you señor." She said almost in a whisper. Then she hurried on down the street.

"Noon, tomorrow!" She heard him call after her.

When Marina arrived home she rushed past her mother, hung up her veil and silently sat down near the stove to chuck corn. Carlota followed her with her eyes. "What's wrong with you?" Carlota asked her daughter, then she got up and walked across the room to where the young woman sat working nervously at the corn husks. "It's nothing" Marina whimpered without looking up from her work.

"Well, it seems to me like a lot more than nothing. Something's eating you today!" Carlota insisted looking down at the girl.

"It's nothing mamma, I swear by the Blessed Mother!" Marina pleaded, finally looking up. The old woman stared down at her daughter for a moment and then walked away muttering. Marina looked after her and relaxed just a little, letting out a sigh of relief. Then she crossed herself and silently asked the Virgin Mary's forgiveness for making a false oath in her name.

Next morning Marina wore a snow-white cotton dress embroidered along the hem with a row of little red and purple flowers. It was the finest garment she owned. Her mother had sown it herself and given it to her on her fifteenth birthday.

The girl combed her rich mane of ebony curls back away from her face and wrapped a modest shawl around her head and shoulders. She sneaked out of the little house when her mother went to the chicken coop to fetch a couple of eggs for the noon meal. The girl's heart thumped wildly in her breast as she hurried down the dirt streets to the center of town.

The old governor's mansion built by the conquistador, Don Diego Velazquez, almost a century earlier stood before the square market place. On another side of the plaza workers were already busy at that day's labor on the construction of the city's new cathedral.

Marina spotted the handsome young man walking non-chalantly in front of the construction site. He turned and saw her. She froze in her tracks. Her eyes downcast and her face tightly covered by her shawl, she waited as he approached her.

"Well, buenos dias (good morning) to you, señorita. I swear, you have humbled the sunrise itself today with your beauty. Let's be moving on before the sun turns around and dips back down behind the eastern horizon for shame of being outshined by a mere maiden!"

Marina smiled shyly from behind her shawl and turned to follow the young man down the street.

"I feel very embarrassed to be meeting a man alone señor!" The girl exclaimed through her veil.

"Hmmm...My dear..." the man answered. "What harm can come of a little walk with me?"

"But, I don't know you." She insisted. "I've never seen you in town before." The man turned to face her as they walked side by side.

"That's because I'm new in these parts. My name is Rodrigo. My Lord, Don Alvarado, just moved here for a while on business and as his squire, I will be staying in this city as long as he does." The girl smiled.

"Have you had breakfast?" The man asked.

"No." The girl answered.

"Ah, well my dear, then I would like to invite you to breakfast with me at Don Alvarado's home." Marina's eyes widened and she stopped dead in her tracks, the veil dropping from her face. Rodrigo stopped also and turned to face her with a broad smile.

"I...I couldn't!" Stammered the girl. "I am not a fine elegant woman..." She looked at her bare feet. "And I have no shoes. How could you get me inside a rich nobleman's home?" Rodrigo gently took her hand in his and whispered;

"I'll tell them you're a new servant, they'll believe me." He turned and started walking again leading her by the hand. "We will sneak into the kitchen. I will order the cook to prepare you a delicious morning meal." Marina relaxed a little and allowed herself to be led up and down the narrow streets of the bustling colonial town. As he walked, Rodrigo kept up a reassuring chatter. "You will see the inside of the home of Don Alvarado himself. You know, he is no ordinary nobleman. Don Alvarado once met the great Diego Velazquez himself." Marina had never heard of Diego Velazquez. Rodrigo sensed her lack of historical knowledge.

"You know, Diego Velazquez, the man who led the conquest of the island eighty years ago; the man who founded this city." Marina nodded quietly, bringing her veil back up around her face as she walked behind the young man. She really was not interested in Diego Velazquez. Her mind was on more immediate concerns. She had heard of poor mixed-blood girls like herself who had caught rich noblemen's fancy. She had heard that at times these powerful men had discreetly set their mistresses up in quite acceptable comfort, well-taken care of. Many of these mistresses had their own house and family with children by their wealthy lovers. These children, under Spanish law might even inherit part of their father's estate.

The excitement welled up inside her as she considered the future that seemed to be presenting itself before her. These tantalizing visions danced before Marina's eyes as Rodrigo continued to lead her up one street and down the other.

They arrived finally at the grand house not far from the mayor's mansion. Rodrigo knocked on the heavy oak door. Presently a dark black man dressed in the moorish garb of the peoples of North Africa answered.

"It is I..." snapped the young nobleman as he stepped briskly in through the open door. The slave bowed and let them in. Marina followed Rodrigo, trying to keep up with his fast pace. She looked up into the servant's face as she passed him. The African flashed her a brief but melancholy look of pity which unsettled her.

Rodrigo led Marina back through several huge and lavishly decorated rooms, richly hung with expensive Oriental wall hangings and furnished with exotically carved furniture made of the finest native hardwoods.

Together they approached a closed door. Rodrigo knocked on this door. His knock had an odd code-like character. He turned to Marina and smiled, winking at her reassuringly. The door opened only slightly. Marina saw the ruddy complexion of a young freckled-face man of about 18 years.

"Everything alright?"

"See for yourself." Rodrigo answered nodding in Marina's direction. Marina looked up at Rodrigo, a puzzled look on her innocent face. The red-faced man inside the room opened the door a bit wider and spotted Marina.

"Ah!" He exclaimed, his eyes widening. More puzzled than ever Marina lowered her gaze timidly, covering her face with her shawl. The man inside threw the door wide open. Rodrigo took Marina's hand firmly and stepped in, leading her along. The freckled-faced fellow, his face split in half by a broad lascivious grin, shut the heavy door behind them.

Marina found herself in a medium-sized chamber with tall windows draped over. There was a book-shelf at the end of the room and a large oak desk nearby. Several heavy wooden chairs had obviously been moved to create a wide empty space in the middle of the floor.

As Marina stood there and looked around she counted four young men. They all stood about her in a circle looking in at her. Some of the men held goblets of cognac in their hands. Rodrigo stepped back away from her and stood in a corner of the room. She turned to him and sent one desperate pleading look in his direction but his face had turned stone cold and she realized she would find no sympathy there, just a cruel open-mouth smile. As she stared at him for a moment she had the bizarre impression that his smiling face resembled that of a shark, his heartless smirk the toothy grin of the marine predator.

The freckled-faced Spaniard moved toward her first. "Rodrigo, you old dog you, I don't know how you do it. How do you find these girls? This one is more than well worth what we paid you. She is positively stunning!"

Marina stared at the young man paralyzed with terror. Then the men all closed in on her.

Rodrigo did not participate in the gang rape of the young woman, he just watched. Apparently his interest in the matter was purely financial.

I woke up in my sleeping bag with a start. For a brief instant Marina's terrified expression floated vividly before my eyes, then it faded!

"What's the matter buddy..." Sven mumbled drowsily. "Did you have another nightmare?"

"Yea..." I answered frustrated. "But I lost it. I had it for a second, then I lost it, dammit!"

"Whatcha mean you lost it?" He asked shifting up on one elbow and reaching for his water canteen.

"Yea..." I continued. "You know, just like before... I woke up with the image of my nightmare clearly in my head, then I lost it. It just vanished!"

"You mean, you forgot it?" He said taking a couple of gulps of luke warm water.

"Yea, Sven, just like before, I can't remember anything at all. It's so damned frustrating!"

"Well, watcha complaining about? Who wants to remember a nightmare anyways? Close your eyes again and try to get back to sleep. Maybe the next dream will be better." I sensed his smile in the darkness of the tent as he patted me on the shoulder. Then he rolled over and went back to sleep.

I lay in the sleeping bag wide awake next to Sven for about an hour. Then, slowly, inperceptively I drifted back to sleep again.

I dreamed again, but it wasn't any more pleasant than before. Again the scene was the richly furnished room in Don Alvarado's home. The men were finished with Marina. They had left her there alone lying in the middle of the cold tile floor, battered, bruised, her beautiful white dress in tatters.

She managed to drag herself to her feet. After struggling with the heavy chamber door for what seemed an eternity she exited the room and stumbled through the empty hallways of the cavernous mansion. She eventually found her way out into the glare of the sun-drenched street. She managed to return to her home on the waterfront.

Marina never spoke again. Her parents tried to help her bear the trauma of that terrible morning, but she never recovered.

A month later she was found to be pregnant. There was no way of knowing who the father of her baby was. At the end of her pregnancy, she gave birth to a beautiful baby boy.

The labor was long and difficult so the consensus was that the young mother needed some quiet time after it was all over, to rest alone with her newborn child.

The midwife laid the infant on Marina's breast and left her alone in the room to nurse her little one in peace. However within fifteen minutes the loud insistent wail of the baby drew Marina's mother back to the door of her room.

"Are you alright in there honey? Why is the baby crying so?" Carlota opened the door slowly then drew back in horror. She pierced the stillness of the afternoon with a shrill desperate scream. While several other members of the family rushed to her side, she sobbed softly as she watched the dead body of her only daughter swinging gently at the end of a rope in the middle of the room. The baby cried and cried as it lay on Marina's bed unfed.

In a tearful dedication ceremony deep in the woods Cobo both mourned the death of his daughter and celebrated the presentation of his new grandson to the Moon Spirit "Karaia." He named the baby "Guzman" in honor of a kind young sailor he had once met on the docks.

3. CHARITY

Guzman was raised by his grandparents and developed a special bond with Cobo. Cobo taught him to hunt with a bow and arrows, to fish and to tell stories. As he had once done with his daughter, Cobo introduced Guzman to the world of peasant spirituality. Together the three of them, Cobo, Carlota and Guzman, traveled several miles every month to the Indian areito gatherings held in the small rural farmstead of an old medicine man of El Caney district. These were hodge-podge affairs in which the participants practiced a mixture of the old Taino tribal ceremonies interspersed with Catholic prayers and, as more and more Africans were brought into the country through the brisk slave trade, some of the areitos were recited in African dialects and the names of African deities were invoked during the rituals.

Guzman's attachment to his grandfather intensified with the years. Then he married an Indian peasant girl from El Caney, and begged the old man to let him alter the house so that he and his new bride could live under the same roof as his grandparents.

Flattered by his grandson's devotion Cobo, now seventy-four years old and still strong, helped him enlarge the wooden shack.

As I watched those two men working together to enlarge that little shack, I began slowly to realize that what I was watching was actually a dream.

I have often heard the term "lucid dreaming". It's a term that describes a dream which the dreamer knows is only a night time vision. The dreamer is aware that he is asleep and the experiences before him are not real.

At this point in my dream I began to realize I was dreaming, I knew I could wake myself up but did not want to. I was enthralled by the fascinating story unfolding before my closed eyes.

In particular, as an avid history enthusiast and a relatively knowledgable period costume buff, I was captivated by the clothing worn by the protagonists of the dream-drama.

I recognized by the clothing what century these people were living in. I sometimes was even able to discern the decade of each event. It was evident, for example, in the next series of scenes in my dream, by looking at his shirt and trousers, that it was late in the sixteen twenties when Cobo turned 88 years old. He had lived surprisingly long for someone in the profession that he had occupied for such a large part of his life. His vision was dim and he had trouble walking. His grandson worked on the docks and supported himself, his wife and the old man. Carlota had died tragically three years earlier in the market when a violent earthquake shook the city and brought hundreds of pounds of debris down on her head.

One night while every one slept in the house Cobo was awakened by a sweet and gentle whisper:

"Cobo...Cobo awaken my son. Your mission awaits you."

Cobo recognized the voice instantly. He struggled out of bed and leaning heavily on his walking cane stumbled out of the house and into the deserted street holding a lit lamp. He hobbled painfully out through the darkness led by the irresistible call of a life-long obsession.

"Cobo...I am here. Come to me my child." The musical voice beckoned him to the outskirts of the city and the blackness of the forest. Cobo walked up a narrow forest trail for almost an hour. The sound of the woman's voice grew and became more intense. The very earth was talking to him, urging him on. Finally he arrived at a large bush that grew on the side of the trail backed by a rocky hillside. He knew instictively to look behind the bush, and caught a glimpse of a small dark man-sized hole on the side of the hill. Cobo raised his oil lamp and peered into the cavity. He could see that the hole was more of a tunnel down there, and it beckoned to him. He stooped, groaning, and began to crawl into the opening, leaving the lamp behind, groping in the pitch-black darkness. As he progressed into the tight little cave his heart began to beat faster and faster. Eventually the cavity widened into a small chamber about the size of his own bedroom. He rose painfully to his feet in the scant glimmer of light that managed to struggle into the place from his lamp outside. He continued to grope around practically blind, searching for anything of importance that may be in there. Suddenly his fingers touched something hard. It was a long cylindrical wooden object crammed up against the wall of the small chamber, a hollow log carved into intricate relief that Cobo could feel with his fingers. He tried to move it but it was too large and heavy for him to budge so he kept feeling his way around it until he found the other end. It was open and, running the risk of encountering a poisonous spider or scorpion living within it, Cobo reached inside the wooden object and immediately his fingers touched the soft pliable texture of oil-cloth. It was something carefully wrapped and hidden within the wooden cylinder, covered in cobwebs and dust. He tugged and pulled at the object until it yielded and he was able to slide it carefully out of the hollow log. Cobo crawled laboriously back out of the dark tunnel carrying the mysterious bundle until he finally emerged into the flickering light of his oil-lamp outside. He slowly unwrapped the thing he had found and laid it out on the ground.

Before him on the trail, at last, lay the object of his long search. Cobo knelt before the small statue and gazed lovingly into her face. It was the same gentle countenance of the beautiful half-breed meztizo woman he had aided so many years ago. To Spaniard, to Indian, to slave, to master, to black man, to white man, she was destined to be the same mother, The Cosmic Ancestress, the Shell Lady, the Lady of Mercy, a powerful symbol of hope in a hopeless brutal world.

"Remember my words, Cobo, remember who I am. Remember that the power of your people's magic lies in the creative character of their generous and unselfish nature. I am the symbol of that spirit. I am the Lady of Charity."

Those were the last words the old man heard from the enchanted sculpture that night. He tenderly gathered it in his arms and conveyed it back to his little shack on the waterfront. There, as Guzman and his wife slept in the adjacent room, Cobo found a wooden board and a chisel. He marveled as his eyesight temporarily returned to its former clarity and the tremor in his hands died away while he carved into the wood. Upon the board he engraved the words of the Shell lady; "I am the Lady of Charity." Cobo burned incense before her and made offerings of flowers, shells, liquor and tobacco, as he had done in his youth for years in his remote mountain retreat to his old clay statue of Ata Bei.

As he stood there watching the smoke of the tabonuco incense rising from the wooden bowl in front of the little statue Cobo heard the sound of rain begin to fall outside. He walked to the window and noticed the distant flash of lightning to the south. He felt a breeze begin to pick up and move the curtains. Cobo knew instinctively that the mood of the night was changing. The rain intensified and the wind began to yank at the shutters. He reached out and pulled the window shut. Then he heard the wind begin to shake the branches of the trees outside. The sound of the creaking wood and rustling leaves filtered into the house through the cracks between the window shutters. He looked up at the statue and began to pray in Spanish. He prayed for his family. He prayed for his people. He prayed that he would somehow understand what he was supposed to do next. He looked deep into the eyes of the little statue and began to weep softly as the sound of the rain became louder outside.

Suddenly Cobo was startled by a gruff voice behind him, "What are you doing old man?" Cobo turned to see who was there. He thought perhaps the intensifying storm outside had awakened Guzman and his daughter-in-law, but there was no one there in the shadows of his little chamber.

"Haven't you lost enough to the white man; your country, your daughter, and now your religion? Why are you pampering this image of a Spanish woman?" Cobo stopped his prayer, he felt confused. As the intensity of the storm outside continued to grow, another storm began to brew within his own heart. Profound resentment began to well up deep within him. He looked at the little statue, its fine yellow dress glittering in the flickering candlelight. He began to think of the rich merchants and aristocrats who venerated Christian icons similar to this one, the same men who scorned him, looked down on him all his life. He thought of his daughter, the way she looked, destroyed and otherworldly, when she stumbled back into their humble home on the day she was violated, the way she looked hanging by the neck on the day when she killed herself. He reached up slowly with a trembling hand. Then the shutters of the window slammed open, the wind rushed in, blew out the candle, and whipped the curtains violently as the rain invaded the interior space. The bowl of burning tabonuco was blown to the floor in the darkness, and the lit charcoal hissed in a small puddle of water where the rain that was entering through the open window was beginning to pool on the floor. Cobo did not seem to notice. In the semi-darkness his eyes were still focused on the statue as the wind fluttered the yellow fabric of her dress. A bright flash of lightning lit up the inside of his room and his ear-drums were slammed by a tremendous thunderclap that seemed to shake the ground beneath him like an earthquake. He began to approach the statue, his hands still extended out toward it. He was going to pick up the little ceramic statue and smash it in a million pieces. Another flash of lightning and the room again shook with the sudden explosive roar of thunder. As Cobo's hands touched the little statue the sound of a high-pitched snicker began to rise gradually amidst the loud howl of the wind swirling around inside his room, and the torrents of water pouring through the open window. Outside, the world was boiling, caught in the fury of the tropical storm. Inside Cobo's soul was also boiling as he picked up the delicate object in his hands.

"Abuelo!" The unexpected sound of Guzman's voice snapped Cobo out of the melancholy trance into which he had fallen. He looked up, dazed, his long gray hair whipping around his wet face as the young man rushed into his room and hurried to the window to shut it and secure it with a latch. Cobo stood there, dripping, looking dazed with the little statue in his hands. Guzman's young wife, Amada, appeared at the door and yelled at her husband over the din of another thunderclap. "Guzman, the mare, the mare!" Guzman rushed out of the room and into the stormy night to lead the family's one and only beast of burden into the safety of the shelter behind the house. Amada walked over to the old man, throwing her arms around his shoulders. "Come abuelo, you are wet! And where did you get this pretty statue of our holy mother?" Cobo just looked up at her and closed his eyes a tear rolled down one of his cheeks as the girl led him gently to the rough-hewn wooden chest on the floor by his bed where he kept his clothes. She drew a clean cloth out of the chest and began to dab his wet face and arms gently. Then she pulled his wet shirt off and put a clean dry one on him. Then she went back to wiping his arms and face dry. Cobo raised his eyes again and took in the full sweetness in the face of his grandson's wife as she fussed over him. He raised one hand from the statue and put it on hers. She stopped wiping the old man's face. "It's OK baby…I'm allright. Go back to your husband." He smiled calmly. Another loud thunderclap rent the serenity of the moment and Amada jumped, startled. Cobo squeezed her hand gently. "Go, go to your husband I am allright." "Are you sure abuelo? You don't seem yourself." Amada laid the damp cloth on the bed. Cobo let go of her hand and answered: "I will be fine." He smiled again. The shutters of the window shook against the force of the wind and Amada stood and walked over to make sure the window was still secure. Then she moved on to the door and turned. She gave the old man one last look. He smiled up at her. She parted the curtain and exited.

Outside, Guzman had led the frightened horse to the shelter and secured the gate. Then he fought the howling wind back to the house. Amada's long black braids swung wildly over her breast as she helped him back into the house and slammed the door shut. Cobo could hear his grandson and his gradson's wife muttering in the other room as the wind howled outside, and then he looked down again at the little statue that was still clutched in his hands. The confusion and doubt that had materialized in his heart just moments before vanished as if it had never been, and the wild sinister laughing that had emanated from the corner of the room had ceased. His vision cleared and he saw the future.

In the little icon he saw an unifying, uplifting symbol which brought together the three races of his land. In this little icon of reconciliation the Indians still saw Ata-Bei, as they always had, since the day Ojeda handed her to the chief of the village of Cueiba in gratitude over a century earlier. She was the Earth Mother, ever fruitful, the fountain of nature. In her, the Black man would some day see Ochun, the orisha, the sacred river goddess of compassion, love and affection of Africa's Yoruba tribesmen, the goddess who in the complex syncretic religious mixture of the African and Catholic tradition called "Santeria", incorporated the ancient Yoruba tribal magic of Africa into Caribbean culture. In her, the Catholic European white man subconsciously saw the modern manifestation of the age-old pre-Christian Earth Mother of his European ancestors, Gaiia, as the writer Merlin Stone would later confirm. Three sacred mother spirits for three races were joined in one.

The old man reached down into the open wooden chest at his feet. He drew out his old worn canvas rain-cape and pulled it on. He put on his tattered broad-brimmed straw hat. Then he picked up the statue and wrapped it back up in the oilcloth that had held it when he found it. After that he slipped out the back door of the hut without alerting his son and daughter-in-law. He stumbled against the furious wind and rain, holding on tightly to the little bundle in his arms. He went out to the horse shelter, and saddled the old sway-back mare that his son utilized to travel to the outlying villages to purchase vegetables. The animal was still skittish and wide-eyed as Cobo led her back out into the wild wind-swept night.

Cobo set out on the road through the raging tempest, north toward an old settlement called Banes. It was a village near the northern Atlantic sea-shore, built on the site of an ancient Taino community called Bani. As he travelled on the muddy road the storm began to abate. But even as the wind slowly died down the torrential downpour continued on all night long.

The sunrise caught the old man still plodding slowly northward on his equally old mare, and in the dim early morning light of the heavily overcast day the rain continued. It persisted, falling in thick sheets all day long and making Cobo's journey north very difficult.

Finally, after spending the whole miserable rainy day on the road, several hours after sunset he arrived in Banes. The town was quiet and deserted as most of the villagers attempted to get a good night's sleep after spending the whole day cleaning up the storm damage left behind by the terrible night and day of wind and rain. It was obvious to Cobo that they had only gotten started at that task and would have to finish it the next day. However he was surprised that the storm damage in the village was not more severe. Here and there an up-rooted tree lay amid broken branches and lots of debris and trash all over the street but the majority of the buildings seemed to have escaped the worst of the storm.

Cobo made his way in the pouring rain through the middle of the silent village, a village that had been built on the site of an important ancient Taino community called Bani. He stopped in the darkness in the center of the storm-ravaged town and stood there holding the mare's rein. As he paused for a moment he felt as if he was being given special instructions by some powerful sentient entity left behind there by the ancient indigenous inhabitants of that place. Suddenly he knew what to do next. He led the mare out the other side of the town and continued on straight through cultivated fields and woods to the the sea-shore. The waves lapped at the shore as he walked along the rim of Banes Harbor where the locals had built an embarcadero. He was exhausted but there was a kind of other-worldly energy to his step as he led the mare along the sea-shore plodding along the soggy spongy ground. He walked and walked, moving farther and farther south along the rim of the harbor. Eventually, just as the first rays of the sun began again to peek along the eastern horizon, Cobo reached the base of Ramon Peninsula. Ramon Peninsula separated Banes harbor from Nipe Bay. At this point Cobo had gone two days and nights without sleep, water or food, but somehow still he pushed on. He kept walking, across the peninsula, until he reached the northern shore of the big bay. He found a small cluster of houses built by some fishermen near the shore. He followed a narrow trail to the edge of the sea. The rain finally slowed down as he reached the end of the trail which terminated in a wooden pier at the water's edge. The sea seemed calm and he wondered if there had been any shipwrecks during the storm. He looked down at the water lapping at the thick cylindrical, barnacle-encrusted pilons beneath him. Slowly, Cobo unwrapped the sacred icon that he had carried there and laid it on the board he had engraved. Then he lowered it gently into the water. He stood quietly on the wooden pier in the star-lit night as the tide carried the floating treasure out to the heart of Mother Sea.

I shifted in my sleep but still realizing that this was a lucid dream I took care not to wake up. I watched old Cobo standing on that pier in the darkness of the tropical night, looking out on the bay. I began to remember a piece of Cuban historical literature I had once come across in my father's library. It was a book by Emilio Bacardi.

In his acclaimed work "Chronicles of Santiago De Cuba", the grand scion of Cuba's most notable rum-distilling family, and once mayor of the city of Santiago, Emilio Bacardi, noted something to the effect that on the morning following a strong storm in 1627 two young Indian men and a black slave child sighted a small ceramic statue dressed in yellow, miraculously floating upon a wooden board as they rowed their boat across Nipe Bay in search of salt, on the northern shore of Oriente Province, in the eastern part of Cuba.

Rescued and returned to land, the icon was installed in the altar of a church above the old copper mines of El Cobre district. There it eventually became the most revered religious object on the island, and a beacon of hope and solace to all Cubans of all races, especially the poor and oppressed, for centuries to come. She has seen her people through good times and bad to the present day.

On Friday January 16, 1998 Pope John Paul II visited Santiago, Cuba. He was the first reigning Roman Catholic pontiff in history to ever do so. On the occasion of his visit the miraculous little statue was brought to him to be blessed. As I watched the momentous historical event on television I remembered my 1982 dream and I realized that, in fact, it was not the little statue receiving a blessing from him, but he who was receiving the blessing from her.

The Virgin of El Cobre

CHARITY and COMPASSION

Among the vast majority of the inhabitants of the island and later far beyond the island's limits this statue came to stand for all of the various ancient divine mother spirits who had been revered by their ancestors. Eventually at the turn of the new millenium as people of Indigenous ancestry began to reclaim their ethnic and cultural legacy, her regency as the substitute for Ata Bei was destined to end and she would again give way to allow for the revitalization and renewed blossoming of artistic representations of the original Taino divine matriarch. The old Taino mother spirit Ata Bei would return from the sea and nurture her Native children again in her original Native form, the ancient clay effigy of a pregnant woman. After that there would no longer be a need for the syncretic little Spanish statue with its yellow dress. The reawakening descendants of the ancient Taino rediscovered the beauty and grace of the old Taino clay Mother Spirit figurine, and they ceased to venerate the little mestiza statue housed in the shrine on top of the copper mines.

For 500 years the little statue at the top of the altar in the chapel of El Cobre stood in behalf of all the divine mother spirits revered by all of the diverse people who came to call the Spanish Caribbean their home. Now her regency had come to an end. The primordial cosmic matriarch could finally again manifest in her original Indigenous forms.

CHAPTER VII

RAINY NIGHT OF VISION AND CONFLICT

1. CEREMONIES

The break in the rain on the night of August 15, 1982 was short-lived. At about 2:00 in the morning, as we lay rolled up in our sleeping bags we heard the first tap-tap of the rain drops on the tent as the storm resumed. Once the rain returned it hammered us with such a fury that at times the very din of the downpour upon the tent canvas literally kept us awake. Soon the water began to seep through the floor of the tent making comfortable sleep an impossibility.

I lay awake in what seemed a pool of water staring into the darkness. All I could do is simply exist there that night in my own private little spot of wet misery and tough it out till morning. Then something unexpected began to take place. As I lay there wet and uncomfortable I began to receive messages from my spirit guides. The cricket sang in my ear and whispered secrets. The hawk's image entered my field of vision even with my eyes closed and I saw images of ceremonies.

In my vision I saw myself standing on a slight rise atop the Indian center hill back in Pittsburgh. I was surrounded by a group of men. We huddled together near a bonfire in the cool of a September evening.

Wafted up to us upon the evening breeze we could hear the haunting tones of the women's chant as the Boa Constrictor dancers wound their way up the trail toward us. With the hot haze of our bonfire as backdrop the long line of women danced around us tracing a sinuous path all over the ritual area.

Led by an honored lady clad in a special robe and feathered crown representing none other than Ata-Bei, the Cosmic Mother herself, the women danced and chanted a beautiful song.

I was so mesmerized by my vision of this ritual that I forgot all about the wet sleeping bag. All I could think of was my desire to return home to Pittsburgh and share the beautiful vision with the members of the newly-formed spiritual group.

I continued to witness the spectral ceremony. Behind the resplendent leader of the Boa Constrictor dance came a row of women whom the spirits identified as "Food Mothers", each holding a basket of food; yellow maize, black beans, green squash and white cassava. They were followed by the rest of the women. All of them wore shell anklets which jingled rhythmically as they danced.

As they moved around our tight little circle the women held fast to a long thick rope along the length of which they were arranged like a long necklace of living jewels, each adorned in her own personal ensemble of feathers, shells, woven sashes and beads. The ceremony culminated in a short but powerful ritual whereby the outer circle of women faced the inner circle of men and painted their faces with biha juice extracted from achiote seed (annatto). In doing this the women imparted a powerful blessing upon the men.

Women's Ritual of Equinox

The Boa Snake Dance of the Equinox Ceremony

Ancient Taino crafted life-like wooden sculptures of boa constrictor snakes to honor the Earth Mother Spirit

Caney Indigenous Spiritual Circle Boa Snake Dance

At the completion of the Boa Snake Dance the rope serpent is given as a gift to the woman who performed the role of Ata Bei

All this I saw in my mind's eye as I lay in my wet sleeping bag.

I believe that the rain brought a vivid vision that night, a vision of a ceremony which we would eventually name the Boa Constrictor Dance. Furthermore later that night I received a second vision illustrating yet another ceremony. In this instance I witnessed a dance in which a masked medicine man wearing symbols of the shark spirit faced off against a man who personified the Lord of Life.

The man wore a fan-shaped feather headdress symbolizing the rays of the sun and the yuca plant spirit, "Iokahu". In his hands he brandished a bow and an arrow. The medicine man in the shark vestments wielded a shark effigy in one hand constructed of bundles of twigs ingeniously bound together in a long oblong shape with bent twigs for fins and tail. In his other hand the medicine man threateningly swung a wooden hatchet carved in a manner identical to the Taino Indian artifacts found in Archeological sites all over the Caribbean.

The two men, one the incarnation of life and joy; the other, the incarnation of suffering and challenge, wheeled around each other locked in ritual combat. Several times the shark-man swung and connected with his weapon delivering gentle token blows of his hatchet at his adversary as the latter maneuvered for better aim.

Then finally the man representing the shark-spirit of challenge set down the wrapped-twig effigy on the ground. The archer approached the effigy, pulled back the bowstring and released the projectile, sending it deep into the bundle of twigs which made up the shark effigy's body. The dance was over. Wounded in his symbolic soul, the shark man dropped his weapon and fell with a scream to the ground. As he lay on the grass twitching the sun-man approached his prone body and let out a triumphant yell. Life and joy must overcome the perennial challenges of suffering and despair.

Those visions of what might someday be, made the discomfort of my soggy night a little easier to bear. Little did I know then how accurate those visions of the future would eventually turn out. In fact, not long after my canoe trip with Sven I incorporated both of those ceremonies which I had daydreamed into the ritual lore of our spiritual circle.

SHARK DANCE

In the fall of that year I initiated the first Boa Constrictor dance. A few months after participating in that Boa Constrictor dance, in the winter of 1982, the other rainy night dream also materialized. I found myself actually dressed in the shark regalia that I had visioned, holding a shark effigy and a hatchet, both of which I had hand-crafted myself, identical to the ones in my vision and facing an archer chosen from the male participants of our ceremony. The dance is a ritual of conflict and represents the struggles which manifest themselves in the lives of human beings. They are unavoidable learning and growing experiences. They are also the ongoing internal struggle between potentially destructive urges, and the wiser, well-thought-out process of ethical behavior.

Kahaia the Shark Spirit

The Solstice Ceremony's SHARK DANCE requires the creation of a shark effigy which is used in the ritual. In the Miami area Winter Ceremony this effigy is usually constructed of palm fronds.

The powerful ceremonies that manifested themselves to me that wet evening became an integral part of our circle's tradition and as our group grew and flourished the participants were blessed with the symbolism and energy that those two dances manifested. We performed them in 1982 and in 1983 and on every year right up to 1987 when we celebrated the great Harmonic Convergence of August. These sacred ceremonies continued after Harmonic Convergence and are still being celebrated by the Caney Circle to this day.

2. HEAVEN GAZER

Our Caney Circle and I personally endured two major challenges during the years between my canoe trip of 1982 and the great Harmonic Convergence gathering of 1987. The only way that we were able to survive these life-or-death challenges was through the energy that we had acquired by the periodic celebrations of the powerful ceremonies that I received from the spirit realm during my visions on the rain-drenched night of August 15.

The ultimate symbolism of those rainy night visions gradually materialized years later in my own life.

It was a night in December of 1984 at the Indian Center's Singing Winds site. I had quit my job at the Indian Center and accepted a position of art teacher at a private elementary school in a suburb north of Pittsburgh. I remained a loyal community member of the Indian Center and continued holding ceremonies there.

That's how I came to find myself there that winter night of 1984, surrounded by a circle of men and women celebrating the Winter Solstice.

I was sweating under the hood of my shark-mask as I lay on the floor of the Indian center building known to all of us as the "Mess Hall". It carried that name because it had once served as the officer dining room of the old military installation which stood on this hilltop back in the 1950's.

It was cold outside so I had compensated earlier that evening by turning the building's thermostat up as far as it would go. Now, as I felt the dampness of perspiration pooling on the fabric of my shirt I repented my actions.

We had just played out the most exciting part of the ceremony. My friend David had finally found his mark and had shot the slender arrow into the body of the five foot shark effigy I had been carrying throughout the dance. The mock battle came suddenly to an end. A great cheer went up as I dropped to the floor.

I welcomed the coolness of the tile on my bare arms and waited for David to stride toward me triumphantly and sound off his victory yell. He looked impressive in the tall macaw feather headdress. The hat, with its pattern of radiating plumes, represented the face of the sun symbolizing his impersonation of "Iokahu" the solar lord of life of Taino Indian spiritual tradition.

The Boa Constrictor dance, invoked the regenerative powers of Mother Earth by appealing to her through the creature that lives closest to her surface, the snake. Likewise this SHARK DANCE invoked the strength of the sun spirit, and his ability to overcome the challenges of the Lord of Trails.

The Boa dance appeals to the Mother of all life, Ata Bei. She is the ancient Caribbean Indian female spirit which I had learned had returned to my native country after the near-destruction of Taino culture in the new identity of a Christian saint, the so-called "Virgin of Charity". On the other hand the shark dance appeals to her son, the Lord of Life, the child of Hope.

Once the shark dance was over, David helped me get up off the floor. The twig bundle shark effigy was later thrown into our bonfire. I stood in the chill of the December evening and thought of the rainy-night dream which had taught me this ceremony two years earlier. I watched the flames devour the bundles of twigs that made up the effigy.

Around the bonfire the illuminated faces of the ceremony's other participants danced and twinkled as they, like me, stood mesmerized by the magic and warmth of the flames. All around the circle I looked at the faces, each one staring at the fire, every face but one. It was the face of a woman. I paused in the midst of my casual scanning of the crowd to look back at her. She was staring right at me!

I hadn't seen Heaven Gazer for months. I wondered how I had missed her presence in the group earlier. I nodded a greeting to her across the bonfire. She smiled back and turned, walking into the darkness and heading down toward the warmth and light of the main building of the Indian center.

I had met Heaven Gazer almost a year earlier. She had been introduced to me by a friend at one of our Indian center's Pow Wow's.

I was serving as Master of Ceremonies that year and just finished introducing a Seneca dance group from the Allegheny Indian reservation. I leaned against one of the poles of the arbor under which the Pow Wow drummers sat. I prepared to enjoy the excellent performance of the young Seneca dancers.

As I watched the dance my friend Lawrence approached me accompanied by a young woman with striking features and long dark braids. She was fair-skinned and did not present a particularly Indian appearance save for her braids, but upon introduction she claimed to be a member of the remnant of the Delaware Indian tribe.

The woman introduced herself as Heaven Gazer and soon began to attend the ceremonies of the Caney circle with great regularity.

Heaven Gazer always claimed to be a spiritual leader. She often spoke of having apprenticed under an important North American Indian medicine man. In our circle we treated her with respect and deference, although in many ways she exhibited certain disturbing qualities.

She imperiously began to demand a leading role in our circle and insisted that she must be allowed to lead ceremonies. We allowed her to do so as a guest ritual leader. Soon we noticed that she placed an increasing degree of importance on money. She advocated the requirement of a fee for attending our ceremony and set up a complete payment schedule for "spiritual services".

Our teachings are very clear on such matters. We in this tradition are forbidden to profit from any public Caney Circle ceremony, so her ideas were anathema.

Heaven Gazer never seemed quite happy with any allowance we made for her in the circle. She always asked for more control. Eventually she and I began to quarrel. After one unusually strident disagreement, Heaven Gazer stopped coming to the ceremonies. She stayed away for months.

Now, on this winter evening, Heaven Gazer was back. I had a weird insecure feeling as I watched her melt into the darkness of the crisp December night. I knew that when I returned to the main building to share in our usual post-ceremony meal she would be there waiting for me.

Later that evening I sat on blanket spread out on the floor of the main building surrounded by fellow participants. We shared the delicious dishes that had been contributed by the celebrants for the post-ceremony meal. Eventually Heaven Gazer approached our little knot of people and casually sat down right next to me.

"The ceremony was very nice," She said.

"Yes," I answered cautiously. "Tonight was a powerful night." She Looked down at her paper plate and picked at a sprig of celery. "There is no need for us to be arguing all the time." She continued in that hurried, machine-gun tone that was so characteristic of her speech.

"Well, Heaven Gazer..." I answered realizing that the topic was unavoidable. "I think we here at the Caney Circle have made more than a fair effort at accommodating you." I set my plate down next to me on the floor and shifted around to face her. Then I continued, "However, we simply can not turn the circle over to a person who has repeatedly avoided learning the specific teachings of the Caney. After all if you truly want to be a full leader of our group you should become an expert in our tradition. You are not even a Taino by birth so you should make an attempt to become one by adoption through learning our ways and earning that priviledge".

At that point she launched herself unto her usual tirade on how all Indian traditions are basically the same. She insisted she must be made a full leader of the group immediately without further training and implied that my reluctance to do so may be based on sexist reasons.

As in so many previous similar discussions I held fast to my position and braced myself for the inevitable argument. It never came. Surprisingly, Heaven Gazer stood up and walked away calmly.

My friend Tenanche, who had by then reached the status of "beike" (full leadership in the Caney Circle) walked over to me and put her hand on my shoulder. We both watched Heaven Gazer leave.

I spent the rest of that year very busy, my mind focused on my responsibilities at work in the school where I was teaching, and within the Caney Spiritual Circle, which was growing and flourishing. I had also become more active in the Imaginarium children's art music and movement troupe.

In addition to all these activities I began to paint a lot more. Most of my paintings featured aspects of Taino spiritual iconography as subject matter.

I really didn't have much time to think about Heaven Gazer between preparing lesson plans for my classroom and leading circle ceremonies and performing with the Imaginarium in one venue or another around the city. But if I thought she had walked out of our lives on that chilly December night I was dead wrong!

The following Summer Heaven Gazer telephoned me. She consented to receive training and learn the sacred teachings which had been handed down to me by my elders from Cuba and Puerto Rico. She said she wanted to do this in preparation to becoming a "beike" or full spiritual leader of our circle.

Naturally I was very surprised by her sudden change of mind but consented to begin meeting with her on a regular basis.

For our first session I suggested a meeting date and my home as meeting site. I offered the hospitality of my family and an evening meal.

She refused to meet at my house. She insisted that the most appropriate location for the session was a wooded tourist campsite by a lake about fifty miles south of the city. I didn't want to meet that far from town on a week night but she insisted adamantly. Finally I consented.

I began to have a series of strange dreams on the nights leading up to our first meeting date. My memories of the dreams are vague but the most distinctive and memorable feature of the dreams is a recurring theme of torrential rain. In each dream the rain would eventually turn into a flood and I would find myself swimming in the water. As I floated about I would invariably be gripped by a heavy sensation of foreboding and danger, and an awful feeling that there was some ominous presence in the water with me.

Finally the day came for our meeting. Heaven Gazer showed up at my house in her car. She suggested I ride with her instead of taking my own car. She insisted that we approach this activity in a relaxed informal attitude. "Bring your bathing suit, it's a sunny afternoon and the lake has a nice man-made beach." She suggested. There was a friendly casual tone in her voice which I had never heard from her before. It had a strange calming effect on me.

Heaven Gazer talked incessantly throughout the duration of the trip to the lake. Since she seemed in the mood to discuss the different concepts of Native culture as she drove, I made a few attempts to discuss topics of Indigenous history in the car. Her stream of chatter was so seamless it was impossible to insert even the minutest idea into the one-sided conversation without interrupting it. So finally I decided to interrupt her. That was the only way I was able to get a few words in.

She demonstrated great annoyance at being interrupted so our conversation in the car was not productive.

I gave up trying to communicate with her and fell silent as the steady droning of her hurried monologue began to lull me into a kind of trance. With my eyes open I began to recede into a dream-state. Heaven Gazer's voice and the hum of the car's engine as it sped down the highway began to merge into a smooth pattern of sound in my mind, a pattern that felt more and more like raindrops. Soon I was surrounded by the strikingly vivid vision of a warm summer rainstorm. The rain fell about me in sheets punctuated by occasional claps of thunder.

As in the recurring dreams of the previous nights, I soon found myself swimming in the resulting flood of the rain water. I glided through the clear liquid and it gradually turned into a broad estuary, transformed into a salt-water expanse of alternating deep pools and shallow mangrove stands. I assumed this was what it would feel like to swim in the lake where we were now heading. Moreover I began to sense a kind of identification with the marine "Giving Beast" of my Black Ribs dream, the manatee who gives of himself for the survival of the people. Then I began to get that uneasy feeling again, the same feeling I got in my dreams the preceding days. I was haunted by the vague fear that there was something dangerous in the water with me, something unseen.

I pulled myself along the water with long leisurely overhand strokes. I didn't think of holding my breath or of getting water in my nose or mouth. I simply swam through the primordial fluid like some amphibious beast to whom both land and water were home. I swam in lazy circles blowing long streams of silvery bubbles behind me. Staring through the murky haze of the water, I searched for something I couldn't quite identify. Suddenly, without warning I realized the circles I was tracing in the water were no longer under my control. I stopped moving my arms and proceeded to relax my body. I felt myself pulled along by a current of increasing speed. The water all about me was moving around by itself carrying me along in its spirals.

I began to flail my arms wildly trying to regain control of my body's movements, trying to return to the surface. But the circular motion of the water grew stronger and faster and began to pull me further down into the depths of the lagoon.

I was gripped by a frantic desperation. I became oblivious to my physical presence in Heaven Gazer's car. Somehow, at that moment the only reality I was able to accept was that of the watery vision in which I now found myself helplessly ensnared. It was a desperate vision of inexorable downward spirals which seemed to pull me deeper and deeper into the nightmare pool of salt water.

I tried to cry out but the briny liquid entered my mouth and throat choking me. I looked down. I could see into the depth of the water. Way down in the murky fathoms I managed to discern some movement. I stopped struggling long enough to stare at the activity beneath me. In the depths of the pool I made out several long undulating shadows circling below. I recognized the shapes immediately. It was a school of sharks!

Again I began to flail the water wildly with my arms. I did it as hard as I could but it was to no avail. I continued to be sucked down toward the pack of killers below.

My body was a whirl of motion as the desperation increased. Beneath me the undulating shadows grew bigger and the water still continued to pull me toward them. I stared up at the surface and watched the brightness of the sky dim gradually as I was pulled away from it.

I looked down again, beneath me the sharks seemed to be circling around something. I focused on the central object amidst the circle of makos, white-tips and hammerheads. I made out a dark amorphous shape, like a clump of fibers or tentacles radiating from a round central form. Then, as I was pulled down closer I recognized a slender human leg extending out from under the dark shapeless mass. Then another leg and a set of arms made me realize that I was looking down at the head of a woman from above. Her long dark hair floated like a canopy over her, shielding most of her body from my overhead view. I was alarmed. Were the sharks about to attack her? Did she know how close she was to death?

Without warning the woman arched her body and performed a back somersault beneath me. Her pale nakedness became suddenly starkly evident and I was momentarily distracted by the sight of her breasts and the dark triangle of her pubis. Her shapely legs kicked leisurely as she finished her turn.

I was confused. What was this nude person doing down here in the depths of my nightmare? How did she keep the sharks from tearing her to pieces? I was again seized by that same mysterious feeling of dread that I had felt before. It wasn't the desperation of being pulled helplessly toward the pack of sharks as much as the weird, threatening fear of being in the water with some unseen terror, unidentifiable and more frightening than any shark.

As the current pulled me closer to the enigmatic character below the sensation of dread grew. I realized that it wasn't as much the sharks as the woman herself who seemed to threaten me. She floated calmly among what were obviously her pets and awaited my inevitable arrival. She did not look up with expectation but simply waited so that all I could see was, again, the top of her head.

I began to sense something like words in my mind. The voice seemed close to me and it definitely was a woman's voice.

"Why don't you relax? Come to me. I will share my pleasures with you." The voice insisted. "Come on, it will be easy. You won't have to work for it."

I stopped struggling. My body continued sinking toward her. Suddenly she performed another provocative back somersault. Again she displayed her nakedness to me, this time a little slower.

"All you need to do is relax your grip a little on that organization of yours." I was mesmerized by the irresistible allure of her voice. I thought to myself. "Why do I have to be so committed to the spiritual group? What am I really getting out of this, all the work, the frustrations, the effort." I let myself drift downward.

"What are you trying to prove anyway?" She continued."...all that Latin American Indian mumbo jumbo. You and I could make a lot of money off of this Indian spirituality scam. Just let me take over a little. Loosen up, relax. You have no instinct for profitability. I'm better at this than you, baby. Look, you can take care of the hokum, I'll take care of business. What a team! We'll make a killing! Aw, come on honey; don't you see we can gouge these affluent suckers for all they are worth. We can set up expensive workshops and graduate lots of "Indian shamans". Let's charge them big-time for ceremonies. They're just a bunch of dumb confused New Age white people with money to burn. Think of all the bad things they have done to our people. It's time for payback, we can make a bundle!"

Somehow in a twisted bizarre way, her words seemed to make more and more sense. I thought of my unpaid bills. "Yea..." I said to myself. "They owe it to me anyway; Why not?"

"That's it honey, come to my arms. Come to mamma!" I could see her shapely legs. "You know, babe..." The voice continued. "Money is not the only thing we could make together." The voice had grown irresistibly suggestive, blatantly sexual.

Suddenly I snapped out of my temporary hypnosis. I realized I must fight this powerful seductive sorcery. But my sudden desire to struggle was not as firm and righteous as I would have liked it to be. Just as I prepared to fight back I wondered for an instant if my desire to struggle was really motivated by a pure ethical urge to resist the temptation of greed and lust or just an instinctive aversion to feeling controlled! I still wonder to this day what exactly motivated me to resist.

For whatever reason, I decided to struggle. I called my spirit magic for help. I opened my mouth to sing my personal magic song, the song of the cricket and the hawk, but only succeeded in choking on a throatful of water. I didn't give up. Again, I opened my mouth to sing. This time a burst of bubbles exploded from my mouth accompanied by a series of toneless yelps. "What are you trying to do babe? Relax, ease up." She crooned seductively. "Think of the money...Think of this great body in your hands... You don't know what I can do for you, baby!"

Again I tried to give voice to a chant. This time I heard my own voice. It flowed out not so much from my lungs as from my soul. I saw the woman shudder violently when she heard my song. It was the power chant. The one I had learned from, the spirits on my vision quest, the one which appeals to my guardian spirit for protection.

I initiated the slow methodical rhythm of my power melody and by doing so I began to slow down the rate of my descent. I feared that it might already be too late, since I had gone down so far that some of the sharks were no longer below me. Some were already circling around me and within seconds I would be close enough to reach out and touch the mysterious shark woman.

I chanted louder and with more vigor. The creature beneath me began to kick and flail her arms violently. It was obvious that my chant angered her but she never looked up at me. The sharks, which now were all around, closed their circle in tighter on me. Some of them swam menacingly close, their toothy grins passing within inches of my arms and legs.

I sang louder. Mingled with the sound of my own voice I began to make out the crystal-like chirps of a cricket. Nonetheless, even though it was obvious that I was now under the protection of my guardian spirit. I could still sense the feeling of dread growing inside me. Is it possible that my spirit guide could really save me from all this?

I continued to sing. The shark woman, now quite near me was still frantically writhing amidst a whirl of 20-foot-long sharks. Then, almost unexpectedly, I was there, right next to her. She turned her back to me as I continued to sing, as if she was attempting to shut my song out.

Since she was still flailing her arms violently I had to do my best to maneuver out of the way of her frantic activity.

The strange shark woman kept her back to me as I stared in horror at her weird underwater gyrations, and I kept singing. I tried to swim around to get a look at her face but she kept turning around also always giving me her back.

At that point I got the impression that, with my spirit so near, I might have enough strength to swim away, or at least wake up. I stopped singing and began a powerful crawl stroke upward. But soon it became evident that my swimming was useless. I wasn't able to rise an inch. The unearthly underwater drama was obviously not yet done with me.

The minute I tried to swim away the woman's violent motion stopped. She calmed and began to appear more stable in the water. Then, she started to turn, her arms and legs gesticulating slowly. She maneuvered her body around to face me. I braced myself to come face to face with my tormentor. But before she had turned completely around my ears were blasted by a tearing high-pitched wail. I instinctively brought my hands up and covered my ears, my eyes tightly shut against the sharp pain cutting through my brain while I kicked to stabilize myself. The wail grew in intensity and formed itself gradually into the unmistakable rise and fall pattern of a wolf-howl as we two hung there suspended in the water facing each other. The canine howl made me think of Reti, the big scary mastiff who guarded my grandmother's patio at night when I was a child. I doubled over while the pain reached into my head and gripped the insides of my skull. As my agony increased I thought again of my guardian spirit. With a tremendous effort I managed to resume my singing, again appealing to my guardian spirit for support. My voice was drowned out by the thin piercing wail of the wolf howl, the terrifying vision of the shark-dog from my childhood nightmares. I sang louder and noticed that even though I could not hear my own voice, the pain in my head was reduced as I sang.

Finally I felt the pressure in my head relieved sufficiently enough to allow me to open me eyes. In the midst of the awful din created by the continuing wolf-howl I decided to focus my eyes on the figure before me. I sang as my eyes zeroed in but to my surprise there was no longer a naked woman here. Instead, I was confronted with a hazy dark shape whose image I couldn't focus completely.

The wolf-howl began to tone down. It became gradually less piercing till the canine voice deepened to a loud booming growl just like the ones emitted by Reti whenever we kids used to approach his portion of my grandmother's garden so long ago. It was a low vicious snarl that reached out and enveloped me. I continued to sing, and my singing did something strange. The texture of my song began, in an unusual manner, to actually take visible form before me. I hung there, suspended helplessly in the water a threatening, growling darkness just a few feet before me. I watched as my own song materialized between me and the awful vision.

The growling was very intense and continued steadily, angrily. Meanwhile my song continued to take physical shape in the water. Each note added to its form.

Finally my song image became recognizable. Gradually I began to make out the shape of a person. A young dusky woman hovered there before me, wearing a plain white calf-length cotton dress, cinched at the waist with a wide white cotton cloth belt. She wore a broad white headband that kept her long straight black hair off her face.

She smiled at me serenely. Nonetheless, the calm of her demeanor did not succeed in allaying my fear. Behind her the dark growling figure continued to grow in intensely and now it began to shimmer and fluctuate angrily. The growl grew deeper and more threatening, like a quiet roar.

Then the apparition of the young Indian woman moved. She extended her arm toward me. Her fist was clenched as if holding something. Behind her the awful dark figure grew still bigger and throbbed. The growling became fiercer still.

I looked again at the calm young woman floating bravely there with her back toward that thing, facing me, staying steadfastly between me and the thing threatening me. Her face radiated with a subtle beauty. She still held her fist out to me. Then a pale ray gradually emanated up and out of her closed hand. Extending out toward me the bright line slowly formed itself into the shape of a sparkling Toledo sword.

The rate of growth of the ominous shape looming behind the girl accelerated. It created a black gaping void which now threatened to engulf us both.

I reached out toward the sword that was being offered to me. As I did she lifted her other hand. In it was a large snow-white conch shell. I felt a rush of frigid cold all about me as the darkness behind the girl extended around her and began to reach me. My feet started to get numb. My lips began to lose feeling also. A dark gloom surrounded me quickly. My right hand reached the sword. I felt its sharp edge with my fingertips. My other hand also reached out, going for the shell.

The numbness crawled quickly up my legs and to my groin. I gripped the sharp blade with one hand. I wrapped the fingers of my other hand desperately around the shell. The minute my hands held the two objects a brilliant flash of yellow light enveloped both the girl and myself, blasting the darkness from around us. I was able to make out in the burst of light the unexpected image of the famous little icon which has so long ago come to represent generosity and compassion among my country's Indians. A vivid image of the Lady of Charity burst for a moment through the sudden glow, then it took on the shape of an ancient clay Taino mother-spirit statue, Ata-Bei. Then it faded.

And then it was all over. My eyes focused on the faint glint of sunlight reflecting off the edge of Heaven Gazer's rear view mirror. I realized I was back in her car. I turned to look at her. She was driving in silence. A cold clammy feeling lay heavily upon the whole lower half of my body. I looked down at my pants. My fly lay wide open, the white of my underwear showing plainly. I looked back at her face, quickly fumbling my zipper shut. She ignored me and continued to drive.

The mysterious young woman with the sword in one hand and a seashell in the other floated there protectively between me and the threatening manifestation behind her.

"Dozed off eh?" she finally said turning to me with a grin. I stared at her. She had put on her sunglasses so I could not see her eyes. "Yeah...I guess so," was my answer although I couldn't remember having my eyes closed at that point. I thought about it for an instant and realized that my eyes had stayed open throughout the whole dream episode.

I shifted in my seat and noticed that both my legs were only just gradually recovering from a cold deep numbness. Then I felt a sharp pain on the index finger of my right hand. I brought it up to my mouth and sucked on it instinctively. I looked at it. It bore a fresh cut, the kind of cut made by a sharp blade.

We arrived at the campground in the heat of the early afternoon. Heaven Gazer picked out a picnic spot. We had brought food and drink.

As we carried the soda-pop cooler and clothes bags I suddenly remembered that Heaven Gazer had once mentioned something about possessing a powerful shamanic ally in the person of a wolf. I thought of the eerie wolf-howl which dominated the last part of my day-dream vision in her car.

Heaven Gazer laid the picnic things on the table then preceded away toward a near-by women's changing room. She emerged in a very brief one-piece bathing suit. She returned casually and insisted that I also change. I felt awkward but finally against my better judgement I also retired to a men's room and changed.

When I returned she was already busy cutting bread and preparing other items of our meal. I began to help her, still feeling very akward about having this weird bathing suit picnic, me a married man and her a divorcee.

I put paper plates and cups on the picnic table in silence. As I worked I occasionally looked up at her. Her eyes were fixed on me every time. She stared at me the whole time that she prepared the meal. And she stared at me the whole time that we ate.

When we were done eating I lit a charcoal brickette and laid it in a bivalve seashell on the table. Then I placed a piece of copal on the glowing coal waving the aromatic smoke to the four directions with a hawk tailfeather and said. "OK, now we can begin with the names of the main Taino spirits; 'Ata-Bei' is the female spirit of creation, love and nurturing..." I began to rattle off the information nervously trying to ignore the intensity of those two burning eyes still staring at me in silence.

"Er...Ioka-Hu..He's the male spirit of Life, Energy...eh...ah..." I stuttered, and she smiled, her eyes still riveted on me. Then during a brief pause as I tried to clear my throat she leaned forward over the table at me propping her elbow on the table and resting her cheek demurely on her hand. The deep cleavage of her breast came into full view. I coughed. Then I cleared my throat again and looked awkwardly up past her at the branches of a tree.

"Guakar is the spirit of trials..." I mumbled looking back down at her face. She shifted in her seat and I was able to make out below through the gaps between the wooden boards of the picnic table as she crossed her bare legs "accidentally" rubbing her ankle on my left thigh. I stopped talking and glared at her.

"Look..." I finally remarked angrily. "I think I'm going to go for a swim."

"Ok". She answered... "I feel like lying out in the sun for awhile anyway, you don't mind do you?"

"Suit yourself..." I answered turning away.

As I walked away from her and entered the water she spread a towel on the sand and proceeded to cover her arms and legs with lotion. Once in the water I felt a little more in control of myself. I concentrated on enjoying my swim and tried to put aside my fears and apprehensions about Heaven Gazer. At first I succeeded in accomplishing this but soon she was back on my mind. As I swam through the cool water of the lake I began to think about the frightening vision in the car. Only then did I really realize how much the shark woman in my dream resembled Heaven Gazer.

I emerged from the water and looked over in her direction. She lay face up on the towel, her eyes closed and one shapely leg slightly flexed. Suddenly my thoughts began to become confused. I was having trouble focusing on the image of her prone form out there on the sand. My body felt weak and the water seemed to grow colder. I looked down and shook my head. Then I looked up at her again. I couldn't really see her. She seemed hazy and indistinct, not much more than a vague blur out there on the sand. I had to strain my eyes painfully to finally clear up my vision. As her form came back into focus I realized she was no longer lying down. In fact she was now sitting up. She was out there sitting staring at me with a bizarre look on her face!

Without warning my arms and legs went limp. I collapsed into the water and sank like a stone. It was shallow where I was but without the use of my limbs I could not raise my head back out into the air. This was no dream. If I didn't get rid of this sudden paralysis quickly I was going to die there!

The thought of drowning in four feet of water was ludicrous, and I got a fleeting urge to chuckle as I struggled to hold my breath. I felt the water cool down even further until I was shivering violently. I saw a kind of darkness envelop me. It engulfed me so thoroughly that I could no longer see my own legs and arms in the water. I realized with horror how similar this experience was to the dream episode in Heaven Gazer's car.

Then I heard the voice again, that syrupy-sweet beckoning woman's crooning. "Why are you fighting me? I am powerful and I know your weaknesses. You can be putty in my hands".

A chill rose up my spine as I heard the woman's voice deepen to the tone of a man's...then a silence...then...a giggle, a weird, high-pitched laugh. I felt myself passing out. I began to inhale water. It was now or never. I clenched my teeth and made one last effort to move. Suddenly my legs uncoiled like tight springs. My body shot through the surface of the water making a big splash. I coughed. I sputtered, gagging and choking but alive.

I crawled up on the little artificial beach of the man-made lake and retched for a while. I could still hear the giggle, that infernal vicious laugh that wouldn't go away. I spat and dry-heaved on the sand, my eyes shut tightly. I covered my ears much like I had done in the dream in Heaven Gazer's car. I lay for a while with half of my body still in the water. I panted and tried to concentrate on formulating an image of my guardian spirit in my mind's eye. It didn't come easily. I had to work at making the image appear. It was hard work but finally it happened. I visualized the welcome figure of the magical insect, the cricket, and behind him my helping spirit, the hawk.

"Why don't you give it up already?" Her voice sounded distant, weaker.

"Because I can beat you!" I whispered "Because I know my real enemy is not that woman lying over there on the sand. She's just your tool. You're using her to do your dirty work because she's weak and lets you! I know you. You are much older than her. I know what you want, and you aren't going to get it! The spiritual community that I lead is a threat to you. Those men and women with whom I work are dedicated and committed. They are committed to the dignity of this tradition. My group and other groups around the world like it which constantly manifest aspirations of love and reconciliation are dangerous to your mission. I know we are the potential purveyors of your ultimate defeat, so I will not allow you to destroy us. Whether it happens sooner or later we will defeat you."

The voice did not respond to my last remark. I didn't realize when the giggling had stopped, or when I had stopped gagging and choking. I was calm, no longer afraid. I stood and walked back to the car.

We made the whole trip home in silence. She took me home and I never saw her in person again. It was the last time Heaven Gazer approached us for any reason. Not long after that incident I was able to confirm that she had become a professional "exotic dancer" and was performing in all the local strip-tease joints of the city. That, in itself, did not shock me. I recognize that unconventional careers and life-paths which appear to be inappropriate to one person may not necessarily indicate a lack of character in another person, but in her case it was different.

Soon after that, I heard rumors that she had slowly descended into the shadowy dangerous world of drugs and prostitution. I do know for a fact that Heaven Gazer developed something of a reputation among the Native American craftspeople who occasionally passed through Pittsburgh for pow wows and festivals.

Many Native men soon learned that she was the woman who would willingly spend a couple of nights with you in your motel room while you stayed in Pittsburgh if you told her you were an Indian medicine man.

She spent a period of time living this dangerous promiscuous lifestyle during the height of the AIDS epidemic, and I actually heard about her from time to time over the next couple of years. And then I never heard from her again.

As for me, after that experience, water became a strong personal vehicle of purification and a symbol of self-testing through difficult trial. In the sweat-lodge it not only reflects the cleansing powers of the spirits but also the purging and teaching effect of suffering and conflict.

I had confronted the first all-out attack of what I soon realized was my hereditary enemy, a fiendish being whose existence was closely associated with the prophecy of the twenty-four generations. I knew he was committed to enmity, jealousy, discord, intolerance, suspicion, hatred, prejudice and victimization.

This entity had chosen to manifest itself through the centuries in the image of Kahaia, the trickster shark spirit of Taino sacred tradition. He was the challenge, the test that every human must pass or fail. As a manifestation of Kahaia it had approached me shrouded in the aura of torrential rain and flooding which is closely associated with this spirit. Was I up to the challenge? Would I eventually pass or fail?

Over the years since this first encounter with the spirit of challenge I had the misfortune of having to face him time after time under various circumstances and each experience has been of increasing intensity. Each time I faced him I found something in the encounter that would remind me of the long wet night I had spent in my tent on the evening of August 15, 1982, lying there next to Sven in my own little spot of water.

3. SURVIVING SORCERY

It continued to rain throughout the night of August 15, 1982, on the Allegheny River. At dawn the next day, Sven and I awoke beneath a dark brooding sky. It was Sunday morning, August 16. The rain had stopped momentarily so we were able to strike camp in relative dry comfort. But the rain resumed once we got under way.

Paddling down the river in the rain was not quite as bad as trying to sleep in it. We wore our water-proof hood capes and the exercise kept us warm in the cool dampness. We reached the area of the river where the U.S. Army Corps of Engineers had erected a series of low dams. This line of dams continued in sequence all the way down to Pittsburgh. Each dam was accompanied by a boat lock. Boat locks are contrivances built next to a dam on a navigable river. They are used to transport boats across from the high water on the upriver side of the dam to the low water on the down river side or viceversa. We had locked through the first of these dam and lock combinations on Saturday. Today we knew we would not be able to lock through the next one a bit downstream until noon. So we lounged around on a grassy spot on the riverbank killing some time.

We were technically out of the Allegheny National Forest portion of the trip. Naturally that portion of the journey had been the most scenic; since we were travelling through some of the most pristine and beautiful country in Pennsylvania. That afternoon Sven and I had to portage around the lock and dam near Templeton because the lock mechanism was malfunctioning. During the rest of the afternoon the sky cleared progressively. By 4:00 we were finally paddling under completely blue skies. At around 6:00 we reached the lock and dam combination near Kittanning. We were still four days away from Pittsburgh. After locking through we began looking for a campsite. We had to paddle five miles further before a suitable rest stop came into view. It was a small island at the mouth of Crooked Creek just down from Ford City.

That night was cold but as we settled into our sleeping bags the stars sparkled overhead like they hadn't done for ages. There is something very special about sleeping in a dry tent after two consecutive rainy days and one long miserable rainy night.

My mind drifted and I began to think about my work at the Indian Center. I thought it might be a good idea to call long distance the next day and speak to somebody back at the center, let them know how my trip was coming along. Then I thought of Jimmy. Jimmy's contempt for me and the Caney Circle had intensified since the early days. His family also had grown more distant and cold. As I lay in my dry sleeping bag I wondered why my relationship with Jimmy and his family had soured. Was there any hope for repair?

Of course I did not know then that in future years my relationship with Jimmy and his family would deteriorate to the point of bitter rivalry, a rivalry that I regret to this day. Events would begin precipitating about four years after my canoe trip in the spring of 1986. I had spent most of that winter quite busy, in part, trying to forget my terrifying experience with Heaven Gazer. Again, my responsibilities at the school where I taught, my activities with the Spiritual Circle and my work with the Imaginarium consumed every bit of my attention.

Unfortunately trouble had erupted that year at our Indian center and we found ourselves in the midst of a bitter power struggle. On one hand there was the faction headed by our executive director, Russ, a member of one of the founding families of the center. Our Caney Circle threw its support behind him because he had always been a rock-steady captain of the fragile ship which was our Indian center. On the other hand there was the faction led by Jimmy's family. We had all seen other Indian centers come and go buffeted by the violent seas of external discrimination, internal discord and the fickle political ambiguities of federal funding. Now, the Indian center we belonged to faced its toughest test ever. It was Jimmy's family. They had always disagreed with Russ's leadership technique. Now they had finally decided to make a takeover bid to depose him.

The whole thing culminated in a decisive election for board of directors. In spite of the fact that during the elections the board of directors was practically controlled by the opposing faction and that their people manned the poll, our faction won. Our candidates swept into office and I was elected chairperson of the board. Most of the members of the other faction responded by resigning their membership in the Indian center. Jimmy promptly founded a competing organization. He attracted a lot of publicity to legitimize its existence by raising the visibility of his family's drumming and dancing group, a group that never failed to attract a lot of attention with picturesque Native dancers dressed in colorful feather pow wow outfits.

As soon as Heaven Gazer found out about the trouble between Jimmy and myself she tried to lure him into some sort of sexual dalliance in an attempt to join forces against the Indian Center and the Caney Circle. Jimmy was not interested in an alliance with her and rejected her scornfully. He never had entertained much respect for self-assertive women. And if nothing else could be said about her, Heaven Gazer was definitelly self assertive.

As a result of my success with the Native spiritual work that I was carrying out in the city among Indians and non-Indians alike at that time I believe that Jimmy developed a violent jealousy toward me and everything I stood for. I think that now that I had become the leader of the Indian center also, I assumed Number One position of his enemy list.

In the spring of 1986 I participated in a public event held in downtown Pittsburgh along with several other members of the Indian center. The event was called "The Mayor's Heritage Day Parade", and was designed to showcase the beauty and diversity of the city's ethnic communities. There, along with Ukrainian and German dancers, along with Polish floats and

African-American marching bands our Indian center was featuring a group of marchers in full regalia. Predictably, Jimmy entered his dancers in the event in competition with our Indian center's entry. They entered in behalf of the new rival Indian center which he had just founded.

It so happened that during the weekend of the parade I was hosting a visit at my home from my sister Rosa and her husband Melvin. They had flown in from Canada with their children to spend a few days with us in Pittsburgh. Melvin is a full-blood Cree Indian from the Kehewen reserve in Alberta. He has always been very active in the tribal cultural activities of his people and is a renowned Pow Wow dancer. During their stay in Pittsburgh he decided to participate in the downtown event in behalf of our Indian center.

That's how I came to find myself on that sunny morning in May, watching my brother-in-law as he prepared for his dance. I observed in silence as he solemnly unwrapped his eagle feathers.

My vehicle at that time was a converted Dodge work-van. The carpeted interior of the back cargo area afforded excellent privacy for the brief ritual he was performing. Outside the van, in the street, hundreds of people waited the commencement of the festivities. Melvin burned some sage in a large bivalve seashell that I had given him from my medicine bundle. Over the sacred smoke he blessed the feathers he was about to add to his colorful red, white and blue fancy-dance pow wow outfit.

As he hung the last feather unto the center of the shoulder bustle he looked at me and said quietly: "You know, Miguel, I sense a lot of bad feelings over this event. I feel that jealousy is playing a big role here." I listened thoughtfully to his words and hoped that my spirit protectors would shield me during the conflicts which I knew were still ahead.

Soon after that, Melvin stepped out of the van and joined me in the parade. I approached Jimmy before the parade began, extended my open hand to him, and offered to join our two contingents in the parade, but he rejected my overture as decisively as he had done to Heaven Gazer before me.

The parade began and our participation in it was received by the Pittsburgh crowds with much more enthusiasm than Jimmy's group. Later, when the festivities had ended I caught sight of him. He wore a dark threatening expression on his face.

The look on Jimmy's face that afternoon made me very uneasy, and I must admit that I lost sleep over it during the next couple of nights. Jimmy's group had as its main objectives, goals which were in direct opposition to everything I was being taught by the spirits of positivity. The young man had, in fact, received training in Indian medicine ways back on his reservation, training which should have inclined him to cooperation and reconciliation. Instead he was using all his medicine powers to advance the forces of antagonism and division.

The next week after the parade was quite chaotic many of the members of our Caney spiritual circle were afflicted by sudden strange nightmares. In addition to this, a number of other strange mishaps and setbacks affected the lives of several members of the Indian center. At around that time, Spider, an unusually perceptive woman in our group experienced a strange unexplained dream. The dream featured, above everything else, a scene of hard persistent rainstorm.

I began to sense that the time had come for my old enemy's next attack. I felt very strongly that now he had chosen Jimmy as his instrument of aggression. He would try to use Jimmy to derail our work of reconciliation. More importantly, I also sensed that he was going to tempt me into behaving vengefully or vindictively.

I contacted Tenanche and a few of the other more powerful and insightful members of our spiritual circle's leadership. The time had come for a "Digo" ritual. This is a powerful trance-inducing behike ceremony based on an ancient Taino visioning procedure. The ceremony appeals to the guide spirits of certain sacred plant-seeds to usher the participants into the spirit world. In doing this the behikes of the group are given revelations and enlightenments which help them in their work.

We met in the upstairs ritual room of Spider's house in Sharpsburg, Pennsylvania. It was Thursday, May 29. There were four of us there. We sat in circle on the blanket-covered floor of the attic and began the Digo ceremony chant. At first it was hard for me to concentrate. My mind was filled with apprehension at the possibility of another spirit conflict. I fidgeted nervously as I sat there. I tried to keep my mind on the ritual but everything distracted me, the stars shining outside the attic window, the many posters and decorations which Spider had covering the walls of her ritual room, Even the sound of the crickets outside in the backyard distracted me.

Finally my mind began to click with the rhythm of the chant. The sound of the drum and the rattles intertwined in a pounding harmony, every beat pulled us deeper along the path of the netherworld of shamanic trance called "Koai-Bai". As I descended into my own personal corner of Koai-bai I sensed an unusual tingle of alarm. My danger sensors were suddenly on full alert. I visioned myself entering a familiar underground cave of immense proportions, a high-vaulted hall which I had visited many times before. I was amazed to find the place flooded hip-deep in water. As I waded through the spacious chambers of the huge subterranean hall the feeling of peril intensified. Then I began to catch fleeting glimpses of a frightening shape which appeared and then vanished furtively behind great pillars of stone.

Suddenly the creature came out in full view and confronted me, blocking my path to the far end of the hall where I would have emerged into the forested exterior of the spirit realm. I faced the being with terrible apprehension and insecurity. He was imposing. He towered above me, standing seven feet tall. He possessed a lithe muscular man's body like that of a heavyweight boxer. The athletic torso was topped with a bizarre shark's head which grew quite naturally from his muscle-wrapped shoulders. His cold emotionless fish-eyes were fixed on me in a steady gaze, his crescent-shaped mouth grinning multiple rows of sharp triangular teeth.

I didn't see the thing's mouth move, but it talked. It talked and I heard his voice inside my head. "Ready for a fight shaman…shame-man?" I stood paralyzed with fear in the pool of water.

"Ready for a fight, descendant of a whore? I know you saw her in your vision last time we met. Did you like her? Didn't she look virginal in her white gown? I guess she must have looked a damned sight better to you than that naked bitch I tried to tempt you with on the beach, eh?

Well, I don't blame you the naked bitch was kind of pushy, and, oh boy! was she ever a sad case of sloppy seconds. She sure spent a lot of time flat on her back eh?" He giggled "Maybe that's why they called her 'Heaven Gazer'…Always looking up…" He emitted a loud guffaw. I kept staring at his ugly face as he spoke of my experience with Heaven Gazer. At that point, hearing the way this demon was dehumanizing Heaven Gazer with his obscene words, I actually felt sorry for her.

"Well, anyhow..." he continued after laughing for a minute. "Anyhow, I still call you a descendant of a whore 'cause your little Miss Virginal-White Gown is, after all, a woman, and all women are potential whores!"

He paused for a minute to gauge the effects of his disgusting words. I was all confused. I knew he was referring to the incident where I had daydreamed in Heaven-Gazer's car. It was that bizarre daydream in which I was threatened by a seductive naked shark-woman, and rescued by a white-gowned young Indian with a sword in one of her hands and a seashell in her other. But now I guess he was trying to imply that this young woman in the white gown was an ancestor of mine!

"Yea, yea, Mr. Shit-for-brains... You heard me right. She was your ancestor. Like I said, I don't blame you for preferring her. She did look better. Didn't seem as easy a lay as Heaven Gazer...know what I mean? She probably would have put up a fight before she'd let you fuck her".

He laughed again. "Yea she would have been a little more trouble to get to but she did look cleaner than the bitch I tried to sell you. Oh hell, I would have preferred her too."

"I'll tell you what..." He moved closer to me, his hands balling into fists, his forearm muscles knotting.

"I'll tell you what; I'll give her to you.

I can do it, you know. I can give you a big juicy wet dream and you can fuck her brains out, right here, right now.

Then I'll kill you.

What a way to go! What do you say, eh Shaman?. You want to pork your own ancestor?"

I began to feel uncontrollable anger welling up in the pit of my stomach. "Hey, you getting mad? Didn't you know she was your ancestor? Yea, babe and didn't she look good? The fuck of ages! Just think of it, the very idea; to shtupp her, of all people, your own great, great, great goddam, great, great fucking super-dooper great grandma, from the seventeenth century, man! How many people get an opportunity like that. Here she is back in the land of the living just to get laid by you. Now isn't that down right shamanic of her. Why don't you tell that one to your feminist girlfriends playing "Ghost-Buster" in that attic with you?"

My anger was beginning to come to full boil. He raised his hands making a beckoning motion to me.

"Yea that's it, come to papa babe. I'm going to eat you up tonight. They're going to bring you down out of this attic on a stretcher!"

Taunting challenges are one of my weaknesses. I think he knew that. For that matter, I think he knew an awful lot about me. He seemed to be pushing all my buttons. I didn't notice my own hands clench into fists. He did. He began to snicker. It was a familiar giggle. I had heard that diabolical giggle before. I had heard it again when I felt trapped in my desperate vision in Heaven-Gazer's car, and although I couldn't remember it now, that giggle had been the horrid background symphony for the nightmares of rape that I experienced during my canoe journey with Sven four years earlier.

The foul monster took another step toward me.

Somehow I sensed when it decided to attack but couldn't do anything about it. He was lightning-quick. I felt his fist in my stomach before I even saw him move. All the wind was knocked out of me as I splashed into the water face-first.

The pain in my abdomen was indescribable. Then, after he punched me I saw him dive at me. All I was able to do was ward off the second attack with my hands and twist out of the way of the deadly jaws. Even so, I received a painful abrasion in my left shoulder as the rough surface of his shark-skin rubbed past and he fell headlong in the water.

I struggled quickly back up on my feet and turned to face him, my body still contorted in pain, my lungs still gasping for breath. Far away in the distance, as if they were sitting miles from me I could still faintly make out the rhythm of Spider's drum and the sweet melodic tones of Tenanche's singing. The sound gave me strength.

I saw the creature get back up out of the water, dripping, after having unsuccessfully lunged at me. It turned to face me. The giggle began again to ring inside my own head like a radio broadcast of his amusement.

I closed my eyes and began to sing along with the chant Tenanche and Spider were intoning. I began to vision. I thought of the young woman with the two sacred objects in her hands. As my adversary stood there preparing his next move I sang and brought my hands up in front of me. I began to image those objects in my own hands.

"Hey, shaman... Who do you think you are, Crazy Horse? Hey! Hey! Don't you hear me... I'm talking to you." I ignored him and continued singing.

"Hey, you... hey, Shit-for-Brains, Don't you hear me? Quit that singing and listen. What you closing your eyes for? Ain't I pretty enough for you? Look at me! You weren't afraid to look at me when I put you in that little trance last summer back in Heaven-Gazer's car. You didn't close your eyes then! Oh well, maybe it's because back then that day I had tits, and a cunt!" He laughed again.

I was only partially successful in shutting out his foul, obscenity-ridden talk. Meanwhile, I continued to visualize the two sacred objects in my hands. In my right, a long sparkling sword began to materialize, in my left, a shiny white conch shell.

I began to feel the soul of the red-tailed hawk fluttering inside me. Then I began to hear the clear chirps of the cricket spirit.

"Playing around with animals again, Mr. Wannabe Sitting Bull." He laughed again.

It was all I could do to contain myself from lunging at him. I knew the only way to beat him was self-control. Not with Hate or Anger, but with Faith.

"Hey, maybe you don't want to fuck your great-great-great-great-great-great grandma, eh? Maybe your problem is that you really don't like girls anymore. What do you think? Is that you problem bub? You tired of girls? You want a guy? Did you turn into a fag now?

Doesn't surprise me, what with you hanging around all them goddamned feminist dykes! Looks to me like you lost your balls!

I think they've turned you into a goddamned queer! Maybe you'd prefer to fuck a boy!"

I kept my eyes closed, the objects in my hands were almost ready.

"Hey Black Ribs, or should I say; 'Black Spare-Ribs'. Hey, you half-Indian, half-nigger sonovabitch, open your eyes and look at me!"

I opened my eyes, my face flushed with rage.

"That's better..." He giggled again.

"Did you hear me? Maybe you wanna make it with a guy, how about Chief Hatuei? He'd probably make a great lay..."

His talk began to choke with laughter.

"Of course, he'll be a little crispy around the edges. It was kinda hot up there on that stake when he died."

The creature could barely make himself understood as he choked on his own hysterical laughter.

"But don't worry you can pretend you're fucking a giant roasted marshmallow, they're always soft and mushy on the inside!" He punctuated his gruesome gag with great peals of laughter.

I lunged at him, the sword flashing before me. He dodged me deftly and delivered another gut-bursting blow to my abdomen. Again I splashed into the water, fighting back tears of pain and frustration. I turned around as fast as I could. He was almost on me, rushing ferociously at my throat, his jaws wide open, they protruded from the lower part of his face. I knew that the practice of the behike was serious business. I had heard that medicine men have died in the midst of intense trances such as this one. I managed to move fast and evade the deadly teeth again. This time I was able to turn around and deliver a glancing blow to the side of his head with my sword. He flew past me with a groan and faltered. Then it was his turn to splash into the water on his knees. He was dazed.

I struggled to my feet and brought the conch shell to my lips. With my stomach still throbbing in pain I somehow managed to let out four blasts of the shell trumpet. Then I let the shell fall into the water and grasped the sword in both hands. I lifted the weapon high above my head and stumbled painfully toward my dazed adversary who was kneeling there, head lowered, swaying back and forth now. "Take this with my compliments, you sonnovabitch" I gasped hoarsely as the monster turned to look up at me. Then I brought the sword down as hard as I could on his neck at the gill area. He fell back and his face splashed into the water.

Typically a rapier has no appreciable edge near the hilt, since it is mostly a stabbing tool, but I knew the end of my weapon was very sharp, nevertheless, it didn't cut him. It dented the rubbery flesh and thick trickles of blood began to ooze from the gill-slits. The keen edge at the end of the blade did not slice off his head as I had hoped.

The monster slumped limply in the water and lay submerged on the flooded floor of the cavern. A stream of bubbles rose from the corner of his mouth, a cloud of red billowed from his injured gills.

I stooped over him in a semi-crouch trying to catch my breath, my stomach still burning with pain.

I stood there for a few minutes panting. Then I reached down into the water and grabbed his arm. It was limp, but I knew he wasn't dead. This entity couldn't die. But it could be defeated.

I lifted him out of the water and positioned him sitting upright.

I didn't know where the rope came from. Did it materialize in my hands? I didn't care. I was just happy it was there. I knew it wasn't a physical rope. It was a spectral one just like the creature it was designed to immobilize. In a few minutes he was securely tied up, his hands bound behind his back.

All throughout my battle my companions sitting there next to me up in that attic had maintained a steady cadence on their drums and rattles. I sensed it viscerally, sort of like the recognition of one's own heartbeat. Now as I finished tying up the dazed monster's hands behind his back I noticed that they changed the beat. It was time to return from the medicine journey. I grabbed my prisoner and carried him back out of my dreams.

As I returned from my trance I sensed the invisible presence of the immobilized monster near me. I couldn't see him anymore but I knew he was there beside me on the blanket, stunned and groggy but very much alive.

I rose from my spot on the floor and walked over to my medicine bundle. I withdrew a little bottle of malaguetta herbal alcohol. I looked at the bottle's label. "Alcoholado 70" It read. I doused my hands thoroughly in the stuff. It is a pretty powerful psychic cleanser which I usually acquired at the Latin herbalist "botanica" shops in the Little Havana sector of Northeastern New Jersey

As I stood there and rubbed the alcohol all over my hands I began to feel very faint and dizzy. The pain in my stomach was overwhelming. I must have staggered a little because Tenanche looked up at me from her place on the big blanket and asked; "Are you alright, Miguel?"

"Yea, yea..." I answered, "I'll be OK... don't worry about me. Just concentrate on the magic.

Once my hands were thoroughly rubbed with alcohol and thus protected, I took a small dry squash gourd and willed the defeated monster into it.

He went inside the gourd reluctantly. I sealed the gourd with a wad of cotton cloth soaked in malagetta alcohol and placed it atop an upright pole. Then I grasped a sacred bow and a power arrow tipped with a quartz crystal.

I began a powerful dance around the pole. As I danced I sang my spirit song. Then I attacked the gourd with the bow and arrow. My first shot missed and flew past the gourd bouncing against the wall of the attic. I walked over and picked it up. My second shot missed also, and so did my third. On the fourth shot the arrow found its mark. The little gourd exploded into a hundred pieces when the arrow struck it. With this act the enemy's power was disabled, temporarily at least. At that moment my actions, with the help of the people sitting there next to me in that attic and the sacred spirits of my ancestors, effectively created a powerful shield of protection around all the members of the Caney Circle and the people of our Indian center.

That night I returned late to my house and went to sleep right away. I was exhausted. I had another weird dream. In the dream I saw an image of Jimmy standing before me. He had a big grin on his face. "You think you stopped me, eh. Just you wait Buddy!" He began to laugh. At first I heard his laugh in his own voice, Jimmy's voice. But then it changed, it rose in pitch and the old familiar giggle of my persistent foe took its place. His image changed also. The slightly pudgy, heavy set build of Jimmy's body gradually slimmed down and turned into the athletic boxer I had battled earlier that night. Then he metamorphosed again and before me stood Heaven-Gazer, naked and still laughing in her own voice. She changed also and finally before me stood a Spanish conquistador in full armor, his laughter so loud it hurt my ears!

I was beginning to realize just what I was up against, how determined our spirit enemy was to stop us from continuing the work of reconciliation, and to elicit in us a sense of vindictiveness which would feed into his scheme. I knew that it would be natural for me to be filled with anger at Jimmy for what he had sent our way. I could have reacted vengefully, sending the same kind of venomous energy right back at him.

But I realized that my real enemy was not really Jimmy but someone who was manipulating him. I could not afford to make mistakes. Again, I was fully aware that Jimmy, like Heaven Gazer before him, was no more than a human tool for the vile work of a very old, very cunning and very determined demonic being.

He seemed to seek out ambitious individuals with flexible scruples. He used them to launch his devastating attacks against us, then discarded them to their fate. I have talked to many other people who are involved in the mission of millenial reconciliation and they share similar experiences.

Not long after the episode in Spiders attic Jimmy began to run afoul of the law. I heard rumors of Illicit or improper use of government funds in association with his work as a medicine man ministering to Indian inmates of state prisons, improper use of the Indian center name for shady deals which may have gotten him in trouble with government authorities in the other side of the state. Some people that I knew even spoke to me of blatant illegal sale of feathers and other parts of eagles. I did not know what to believe or what not to believe. It seemed that the ancient enemy, once finished with Jimmy decided to leave him to his sad self-destructive patterns.

Finally one day Jimmy was arrested on suspicion of rape. The being against whom I stood was ruthless and did not hesitate to wear his human accomplices into the ground and leave them destroyed behind him. This entity was as dangerous to those with whom he allied himself as he was to the targets of his attacks. The demon left a trail of shattered lives behind him.

Jimmy somehow survived his problems with the law. The new Indian center that he founded eventually failed and closed down. He ultimately moved away from Pittsburgh. I heard about him from time to time, and on certain ocasions I even ran into him in person. We managed polite greetings between each

CHAPTER VIII

SANTIAGO

1. ISABEL

It must have been eleven o'clock at night when I finally dozed off on the evening of August 16, 1982. Sven had been fast asleep for hours. He snored next to me. I had fought hard to stay awake, trying to avoid the mysterious dreams which tormented me nightly, and which then, I could never recall in the morning. But of course, eventually I had to succumb. The night was pleasant, my bedroll was comfortable (and more importantly, it was DRY!). It was inevitable. I had to fall asleep.

Before I knew what had happened I was again witnessing a scene from a time gone by. I was asleep. I was dreaming once more. I could see a young boy. It was a lad named "Santi". Immediately I noticed the boy's period clothing, the traditional white cotton garb of a late seventeen century Cuban peasant. I was again being transported to another era, and in my lucid dream I felt I knew this child intimately.

I knew his name was Santi. I knew that young Santi was a very good swimmer. He had been born in a fishing village on the northern coast of the island near the town of Banes, and had spent his whole life near the sea.

His name, "Santi", was the diminutive of the word "Santiago." That word means St. James, and was the name of the important town to the south. Santi's mother, Elena had been born in that southern port city. She had lived there all her life but just before her son was born she had decided to abandon the comforts of civilization in her hometown for the rigors of a rural fishing village. She had done that because she was mortally afraid.

In the 1600's, life in Santiago had become dangerous. The brisk commerce in the town, with ships sailing in and out of its excellent harbor, had made it a prime target for pirates. The port of Santiago became the primary embarkation point for the valuable tobacco traffic that originated in the rich vegas of Holguin destined for Havana and from there, the world. There was also a brisk unauthorized contraband trade out of the harbor that lined the pockets of local merchants and was largely ignored by the regional authorities as long as they also were given a cut of the illegal profits.

The traffic in and out of Santiago harbor beckoned like a magnet to French and British pirates and privateers who at that time sought great overnight riches and saw the city as a vulnerable target that was not as well protected as the capital of Havana to the west.

The Spanish authorities in the town of Santiago had finally taken some precautions, including the building of a ponderous fort bearing the unwieldy name "San Pedro De La Roca El Morro de Santiago." El Morro had been built when Elena was only 2 years old. Unfortunately that fortification later proved useless in saving her husband's life.

I watched as Oscar Hernandez, Elena's husband, rose very early on the morning of October 15, 1662. He was a cabinetmaker and had fallen behind on his schedule. There was a large oaken chest which had to be finished in two days for a wealthy town merchant.

Just before dawn the craftsman headed drowsily down a dirt road leading his horse and cart out of the city to the sawmill near a place called "Las Lagunas."

As he trudged along Oscar came to the gradual realization that he was not alone. He stopped and looked around in alarm. He could not make out what was hiding in the early morning twilight shadows of the wilderness around him. Suddenly there was a flash of gunpowder, then the roar of musketry. Oscar lay bleeding on the ground. He twitched weakly and groaned his wife's name; "Elena". Then Oscar died.

In the city the military garrison had been alerted earlier in the night that an army of British pirates, headed by Captain Henry Morgan, had landed near the mouth of the Aguadores River.

The pirates spent the night in Las Lagunas and attacked at dawn. A column of Spanish regular army troops met the enemy on the road to the city and were soundly defeated. The whole town was in chaos. Church bells rang the alarm. Citizens dashed madly to and fro in a desperate effort to flee the city before the pirates arrived.

Elena ran down the road toward the sawmill screaming her husband's name. She was met by a ragged bunch of wounded Spanish soldiers. They urged her to turn and escape. Returning to the city she joined her mother and the two of them fled to the Indigenous community of El Caney, where the old woman had been born. Most of the townspeople joined them and a large contingent of the surviving Spanish soldiers from the city came there also. Meanwhile the pirates indulged in an orgy of destruction and plunder in the deserted city. It lasted for a month. The nightmare of that month never left Elena. Long after the pirates finally departed, she continued to mourn her dead husband even though no one was ever able to give her an account of his body or its final resting place.

She moped around town sadly for months. Eventually her sad beauty attracted the attention of a fishmonger at the local market. "Señora, would you like some large, freshly caught flounder for your dinner table tonight?" The man asked as she absentmindedly browsed through the piles of sea produce, her mind only partially on her task. Elena looked up at him through a haze of tears, reluctantly disturbed from her permanent reverie.

The powerful muscles of the fishmonger's bare chest rippled under his ebony skin.

"Señora..." He added. "Such beautiful eyes should never cry!"

She turned angrily away and walked home in a flurry of indignation. She wondered how he could be so oblivious to her loss. Didn't he notice her black mourning clothes? "These free blacks, just because they no longer wore the slaver's mark, they thought they weren't black anymore. They seemed to forget their place!"

In the highly stratified society of seventeen-century Cuba a dark-skinned Negro usually did not approach a light-skinned Mestizo (a mixture of Indians and whites).

Elena avoided the fish market after that. She had moved in with her mother since the tragedy, so from that day onward her mother was forced to take care of all the fish buying.

"Why do you refuse to go down to the sea food vendor, Elena?" Her mother had asked.

"I don't know Mami," she whispered with downcast eyes. "I guess the fish smell makes me sick."

Her mother smiled an understanding smile. "That is just your pregnancy my dear, morning sickness, it will soon go away."

In spite of her apparent aversion to her experience with the fishmonger, Elena began on occasion to stop and study her own facial features on her mother's hand-held mirror. She searched for the meaning behind the fishmonger's comment about her eyes. As she gazed into the mystery of her own face she began to discover a new sense of hope.

One afternoon Elena was walking along the main street in front of the cathedral. She stopped before the ruined shrine. The pirates had set fire to the old temple, having first plundered the rich gold and silver furnishings. They even took the bells!

Elena watched intently as the workmen contracted by Bishop Saenz swarmed over the gutted building clambering over a network of wooden scaffolding. She was engrossed in the vivid memories of that terrible October morning that had taken the life of her husband. Seven months had passed since the tragic event.

Her hand rested on the gentle swelling of her pregnant abdomen. Suddenly all the fear and sadness of that day rushed back in on her and a flood of tears began to wash over her smooth tanned cheeks.

"I must insist Doña Elena, tears don't become those lovely eyes." Quickly, the young woman's head turned at the sound of the familiar voice. There, standing scarcely four feet from her was the irreverent fishmonger.

"You!" She gasped drawing her vail modestly across her eyes. The man looked up at the gutted building. "Those men are experts at what they do. They will have the church looking like new in a year."

"Sta...stay away from me." stammered the young woman, stepping back away from him. The man turned to look back at her.

"Do you find me repulsive because of my color?" He said quietly. He took a step toward her. Actually her heart was racing and a strange forbidden desire began to grow in her breast.

"I'm a recent widow...you should not talk to me, you should not approach me...I am in mourning." Elena took another step back.

"My grandfather was brought in chains from Africa," The man answered. "When I was little I spent a lot of time listening to his stories. He talked to me of his people's customs back in the old country." The fishmonger took another step in her direction "He told me that the Yuruba people of his ancestral land don't mourn for years like the Spanish do. A woman as beautiful as you need not remain alone without a man throughout the best years of her life just because her first husband died."

Elena brought her hand up to her bosom. Her breathing was fast and her heart seemed ready to jump out of her. Then a strong dizziness overwhelmed her. The whole world seemed to spin out of control around her. Then everything went dark.

Elena opened her eyes. Her mother's face hung over her like a welcome full moon. Underneath her own head she could feel the soft smoothness of her pillow. She was lying on her own bed, in her own home.

"Mami!" She moaned weakly.

"Ah so, she finally came around." The shrill squeaky voice of Doña Ramona, the healer, rang out from behind her mother's face. Elena rose from the pillow and leaned forward perplexed and saw the old lady standing back there at the foot of her bed. Elena's mother turned to look at Doña Ramona.

"Yes, she's up now." Amada answered. Then she turned back to her daughter and caressed the young woman's forehead with a gentle maternal stroke of her hand, brushing from her face a thick lock of jet-black hair.

"You have your father's hair". She said softly. "Do you remember him?"

"Oh yes Mami, I remember Papi. He used to hold me on his lap and tell me stories of that old Indian witch-man, Cobo"

Doña Amada's eyes welled up. She smiled sadly as a silver tear ran down her cheek. "Oh, you remember those stories." She exclaimed pulling a chair up to the young woman's bedside. "Yes" continued Elena in a dreamy voice. "I remember he talked about that old Indian like he was a saint or something, maybe a great hero. It's strange how Papi spoke that way about an old pagan. I remember he told me the old man was his grandfather. He told me that old Indian had been born in the old days, when Indians were slaves in chains..."

Suddenly Elena's voice trailed off as she became lost in a new thought. "grandfather...slave, chains.."

She paused. Then she said "Slaves in chains, Yoruba....Africa!" The fishmonger's words began to dance in her head.

"Slave grandfather in chains...Africa." She raised herself quickly to a sitting position on the bed.

"What happened to me?" She demanded looking around the room nervously.

"You dropped like a stone in front of the cathedral." Squawked the old healer moving around to the other side of the bed.

"And no wonder..." She continued, wagging a thin knobby finger at her, "you eat like a bird! Don't you know you're eating for two now? Do you want to give birth to another sickly infant who will die within a week of birth, like your last one when you were in mourning for your great Aunt Elvira."

"Ramona!" yelped Doña Amada angrily to the old healer.

"Oh, shush, Amada! It's time your daughter heard the truth. A respectable period of mourning doesn't mean you must starve your unborn child right inside your belly..."

"How did I get here?" interrupted Elena, her heart beginning to pound, suddenly remembering her emotional encounter with the fishmonger in front of the cathedral. Doña Ramona turned to face her.

"What?" she asked.

"Who brought me here when I fainted?" insisted Elena.

"Oh!" responded the old lady. "That young Armando from Banes district happened to be passing by when you lost consciousness...and lucky for you that he was there, because he is strong. He caught you before you hit the ground."

Doña Ramona picked up her veil and moved toward the door.

"Well, I'm leaving now, and a fat lot of good my services do you. You never follow my directions."

The old woman wrapped the veil around her head. She stopped at the door and turned around to look at Elena. "You must take care of yourself if you expect my cures to stick!"

Ramona picked up a coin that Dona Amada had laid on a small table by the door, payment for her healing services. Then she shuffled out and slammed the door behind herself.

"Oh don't mind her, sweetheart" cooed Amada turning back to her daughter. "She means well. Now lie back down and get some rest."

"Mami, who is Armando? Is he the black fishmonger?"

Amada stooped over and kissed her daughter on the cheek, then she rose and walked to the window, she closed the shutters.

"Yes, honey. You know... the young man from the little village near Banes. He moved into town last year."

Elena sank back into her pillow with a sigh. "Mother, would you please bring me my hand mirror?"

Doña Amada stood and looked at her filled with delight. "Would you like your comb also?" She asked hopefully as she turned to fetch the two items. Since the pirate attack, Elena had shown no interest in her appearance, never fixing her hair or trying in any way to look attractive. She was a widow, the older woman had thought, but she wasn't dead.

"Yes Mami, bring me the comb also."

Elena's health improved rapidly after that day. She assumed again her fish-buying responsibilities and showed a genuine enthusiasm about going to the fish market which she had never exhibited before. Soon Elena began taking mysterious nightime walks. Her mother was aghast.

"It is not proper for a young woman to be walking alone at night. What will the neighbors say?" complained the old woman. She was genuinely alarmed but she could not help noticing the new glow in her daughter's face.

"But mother, all I do is go to the harbor and watch the waves roll in the darkness." Elena said. But her mother answered sternly: "You have been keeping rendezvous with the fishmonger, Elena. Don't try to fool me. What will happen to your child when it is born my dear, if you become this man's mate? Will this fishmonger agree to care for another man's baby?"

"I don't know." Answered Elena softly, "I don't know." She repeated turning and stepping into the moonlit darkness.

"May the Virgin of Charity of El Cobre protect you!" She heard her mother call after her.

"How can you love a woman already pregnant with another man's child?" Asked Elena as she walked hand in hand with her tall ebony lover.

"Because I know it only lasts nine months." He laughed.

"You tease me!" Elena smiled. Then she turned serious again. "I know you don't mind that I am pregnant. In fact you find my present condition so attractive that I wonder if you will still love me once I've lost this great belly. No, my question is not if you can love a pregnant woman, my question is; can you truly love a woman pregnant with someone else's child? Can you learn to love that child, Armando, love that child as your own?"

Her voice cracked. Armando stopped walking and turned to look into her beautiful face. He held her by both hands and spoke softly. His words reached Elena's ears accompanied by a refreshing sea-breeze which sent tingles up her spine.

"I love you, Elena, and everything of you!" He stood gazing into her eyes for a long time. Then he leaned over and planted ever so gentle a kiss upon her lips. The young woman threw her arms around his neck and drew herself as close to his chest as her pregnant belly would allow. She felt his strong protective arms encircle her, his rough calloused, yet gentle hand caress her hair.

They kissed again. This time it was a long sweet kiss, a kiss that spread a penetrating wave of warmth throughout her whole body. That kiss seemed to lift from her shoulders a heavy debilitating doubt which had gnawed at her from the inside since she started seeing the young man.

She closed her eyes and laid her face on Armando's broad chest. Her arms slid down from his neck and she began to run her fingers in little circles on his chest close to her face.

"Take me out of here, Armando. Take me away from this city." She whispered.

Armando pulled back and asked, "Why?"

Elena looked up at the puzzled expression on his face. "Because this place holds only memories of death for me. My father died here in a fire leaving my mother a widow. Now my husband is killed leaving me a widow. I live in fear, Armando. I fear death. Those terrible pirates will return some day. I just know it! I don't want to stay here any longer. Take me to your village in the north!"

Armando turned back to continue the walk.

"Life is hard in my village." Armando commented.

"I don't care." She answered stubbornly.

Armando added. "Sometimes there is no fish harvest. When there is no catch there is no money." Armando insisted.

"Let's leave next month." was Elena's defiant response. "Before my pregnancy makes it impossible to travel."

"But Elena, I make good money here in the city selling the fish my cousins bring down from the northern fisheries. Why should I abandon such a profitable trade?" Armando complained weakly. "Please Armando, please!" The girl stopped walking and stared into his eyes with a wild look of pleading desperation. Armando paused for a moment. He looked back at her. He drank in the full measure of her agony. Finally, he said:

"Fine, fine, I won't try to argue. I'm totally outmatched. I never imagined that I would ever return to the hard life of a fisherman." Elena let out a laugh of relief. She buried her face in his chest again and wept tears of joy.

As her handsome dark lover walked her home. Elena bubbled with the excitement of bringing up her child in a remote spot far away from earthquakes and pirates.

Elena and Armando moved to a fishing village not far fom the town of Banes where he had grown up. There she gave birth to a boy. She called him Santiago after the city of her birth. Everyone took to calling the boy "Santi."

Young Santi was a good swimmer because he had spent all of his nine years of life in a place where children learned to swim practically before they could walk. He knew the sea like a relative. The sea was a nurturing mother whom his people approached daily for their livelihood.

So, when he saw the child fall into the water, he did not hesitate to jump right in after her. That little girl was the five-year-old granddaughter of one of the most influential persons in his community, a powerful black curandera woman, a magician-healer named "Doña Isabel."

The old woman and the child had been sitting on a wooden pier watching a jellyfish in the water. Santiago happened to be sitting about five yards from them on the same wooden platform.

Suddenly the girl's squeal had startled him and he saw her splash into the sea. He was in the water and at her side in a matter of seconds.

Bringing the little girl to the surface, Santi swam in long easy sidestrokes as he kept her head out of the water. Soon he reached the wooden platform.

Once there the frightened grandmother helped him hoist the child out of the water. He pulled himself out as the old lady fussed over the wet little girl. Eventually she turned to him and holding on to her granddaughter, stared at him hard, her lips quivering without saying a word. Her emotion-filled eyes spoke eloquently enough.

Finally Doña Isabel reached out to the young lad and placed her hand on his shoulder for a brief instant. Then she turned silently and led her wet granddaughter home.

That evening the old magician showed up at the Alonzo home. She came alone but she brought her famous "Jabuco," a sack in which she carried the tools of her esoteric trade.

Armando was particularly tired that evening, and quite irritable. He had fished all day long but the catch had not been good. He was really in no mood for evening visitors. But Doña Isabel was an important guest so he was polite.

Santi was somewhat alarmed by the unexpected visit. The old woman had always struck him as mysterious and weird. He had never seen her smile except to her granddaughter.

After dinner and some polite conversation the old woman settled into a modest wooden chair which Armando himself had made. She asked Santi to sit on the floor before her. She shoved one brown age-weathered hand into the canvas sack and pulled out a handful of bones. Santi began to feel his apprehension turning to fear.

"I'm going to do this, not only because you saved my grandaughter, but because for some time, I have been watching you" These words made Santi even more uneasy. The very idea that the scary old woman had been harboring some sort of special interest in him was extremely alarming. "I have seen something in you which I have seen in very few people before. It is an unusual light which illuminates your face, a kind of glow which surges out of you and can only be seen by people like me!"

Santi's eyes widened. Armando dragged in a chair from the other room.

"What's so special about him?" He asked settling into the chair. The old woman turned to him and quietly hushed him with a simple gesture of her finger to her lips. Then turning again to Santi she continued.

"You have the gift." She said using a tone of voice hung heavy with a sober intensity. She stooped and brought her puckered, nearly toothless mouth close to him. "There is a spirit who accompanies you wherever you go. She is an ancestor. She has chosen you because she has found in you a powerful force through which you are destined to play an important role in a great spiritual drama."

Santi knitted his smooth young brow in confusion.

The old woman leaned over and blew out the flame from oil the lamp on a nearby table. A small candle that burned upon the wall was left as the only illumination in the room. All was dark and shadowy.

Santiago could barely make out the movement of the holy woman as she began an intricate set of preparations which preceded the divination ritual. Finally after all the preparationswere completed she pulled a gourd rattle from the bag and started shaking it in a slow steady rhythm.

"This rattle was given to me by an old Indian magician before he died back in 1612." She said, and then she began to sing an African chant.

With a quick movement she tossed the bones to the ground. The light in the room was so dim that Santi found it difficult to read the expression on her face as she stared at the pattern on the floor.

The slow pulsating beat of the rattle began to fill his whole consciousness to the exclusion of anything else that was happening around him.

Finally the old woman stopped her singing and raised her head. Her eyes were closed and she began to speak in a strong purposeful voice. "There is a great bird hovering over you, my child. It is a bird of power, a hawk."

She fell silent for a minute then she looked down again and gathered up her bones. She made some passes with her hands and again threw the bones down. After studying the new pattern for some time she again raised her face and closed her eyes.

"You are the descendant of a sea-shell spirit. The sea-shell accompanies you wherever you go."

She opened her eyes and again her time-weathered face came very close to the young boy. "Listen well to my words. In twenty years' time you will encounter me in the woods. When you least expect me, long after you have forgotten me and the events of this night, I shall come to you in the forest. I shall not be alone. With me shall be your sea-shell spirit ancestor.

Together we two shall give you a pair of magical objects, not gifts, but in fact your spiritual inheritance."

Again the old woman gathered up her divining bones, and again she tossed them upon the floor, reading from them yet further prophetic messages. "You must visit the town that is your namesake, 'Santiago'. There you will go to the grave of your grandfather. Beneath the ground, deep beyond the resting place of your mother's father you will begin to discover the true nature of your destiny." Doña Isabel leaned back in her chair and heaved a deep sigh. Then she stooped again and gathered her bones up for the last time. Quietly she wrapped them in a white cotton kerchief and replaced them in her sack.

Seeing that the old woman's work was finished Armando rose from his chair and lit several lamps around the room.

Doña Isabel finished gathering her things together and stood facing Santi.

"I want to say one last thing." She exclaimed, her piercing brown eyes riveted on the boy's face. "I am a leader here. Many people in this village respect me. Some even fear me. They would never expect me to humble myself to any man. But you have done something extraordinary today. You saved the life of the most important person in my world. I will feel indebted to you for the rest of my life and beyond my death. Forever after this day, every time I look into the laughing eyes of my beloved granddaughter..."

An awkward knot formed in her throat and she was forced to wipe a sparkling tear which appeared beneath her left eye. Eventually she composed herself and continued.

"Every time I look into her eyes I will remember your selfless deed today. I will remember that it is because of you that my treasure is with me still!"

Then the old woman approached Santi and stooping toward him, kissed his hand. Quietly she turned and disappeared into the night.

That event on the night of December 12, 1672 transformed young Santi. He developed a growing restlessness which occupied each one of his days and intensified as time wore on. As he helped his stepfather in the task of repairing the fishnets his conversation never strayed from the subject of the old lady's predictions and more importantly, the possibility of a visit to the city of Santiago.

His mother listened with mounting apprehension as her son pressured her daily about visiting her hometown. Elena did not want to return. Santiago town was a place she never wanted to see again. The city held only bad memories for her. In fact, her mother Doña Amada had to travel the 80 odd miles north to Banes to visit her daughter's family because Elena refused to return to her childhood home.

Young Santi had traveled to El Caney, a village situated quite close to Santiago. Elena's mother still had many relatives who lived in this predominantly Indian district. Often Elena would hitch a mule to Armando's buckboard and take Santi to visit her cousins. It was during one of these family visits that Santi met little Luis.

Luis was a quiet little boy. He was only five months younger than Santi, yet he stood a full head shorter. His arms and legs were by far thinner than those of most boys his age and he seemed always to be suffering from some sickness. Luis was the kind of child who in those days did not survive to see his fifth birthday. Somehow he had beaten the odds.

The little lad seemed always to be in the company of his older sister, Rosa, an overprotective girl who smothered little Luis with her excessive mothering and fiercely defended her self-appointed position as his guardian angel. From the very first time that they met, Luis and Santi became fast friends. The two boys would spend hours together whenever Santi came to visit his relatives in El Caney. It was a long trip from Banes but Elena and her son made the journey at least once every two months, and Elena's mother took the opportunity whenever she came to walk up from the near-by city of Santiago to see her since the young woman still refused to visit her in the city.

At first her brother's new friendship with Santi was a catastrophe for Rosa. She tried her best to break up the relationship. For months the rivalry between the Santi and the girl over the affections of the sickly child raged until Rosa began to discover the mysteries of adolescence. Soon she was spending less and less time on her conflict with Santi and more time with the older girls of the village, talking about boys and flirting. Santi realized that he finally had Luis all to himself whenever he came to visit with his mother.

Santi's friendship with Luis alienated him even further from his life in Banes. Armando found the boy increasingly reluctant to participate in the routines of the fishing trade. Soon Santi found excuses to hitch rides with villagers who were heading south. Spending so much time away from home and so close to Santiago made him even more eager to someday come face to face with the sights and sounds of the city after which he had been named. His mother remained steadfastly reluctant to make any kind of trip to the town which for her held so many ugly memories.

"If you will not take me to Santiago city at least take me to El Caney." Santi complained to his mother one afternoon late that summer. "I will persuade Cousin Leonor to take Luis and me the rest of the way to the city."

After thinking about it for a minute Elena sighed in resignation. "Very well, my son, next month we shall go to El Caney. Tomorrow I will speak to some men who are leaving for Santiago soon. I will send word to your grandmother in the city that you will be visiting for a short spell. She will speak to Leonor in your behalf. I'm sure your cousin Leonor will not mind taking you to grandma's house."

The boy threw his arms about his mother's neck nearly choking her with an emotional embrace.

The sky was overcast on the morning of August 12, 1672 but in Santi's heart the sun was shining radiantly. The young boy's excitement was contagious. Even Elena herself, for the first time in nine years was beginning to consider a visit to her native town.

The roads to El Caney were dry and dusty. It had not rained in weeks. That made travel easier. Muddy roads meant mired wagon wheels.

"Now, when we reach your cousin's house in El Caney you remember to be polite. Greet her graciously. Ask about her health and the health of her children. Don't accost her with questions of how soon she will take you to Santiago city. Don't press her, remember she's doing you a favor."

They traveled with a little group of fisherman who were headed to the city to sell their catch. The trail to Santiago passed through El Caney just north of the city. The woman and the child took advantage of the relative safety afforded to them by traveling on the dangerous road in the company of five strong men.

In El Caney they would reach their destination while the fishermen continued on the rest of their journey to the large town. Of course Santi fully expected to follow in those men's footsteps some days later in the company of his older cousin Leonor and her son Luis.

It was early evening when they were finally knocking at Doña Leonor's door. Leonor was actually a cousin of his own grandmother Amada. Most of Amada's family still lived in her hometown of El Caney. Visiting that town was always a pleasant immersion into his distant maternal roots.

Doña Leonor's face lit up when she opened the door and discovered who was standing there.

"Muchacha!" She exclaimed and threw herself upon Elena in an ebullient embrace. Even as she was still squeezing her newly arrived guest she called over her shoulder; "Rosita, Luisito, come here, greet your out-of-town relatives."

She dragged Elena into the house followed by Santi who took the whole thing in with a certain amount of amusement.

Doña Leonor lived in a modest peasant shack of wood and thatch, the kind that the country people called "bohio." It was a fairly simple structure, roofed with palm fronds such as the Indians of the Caribbean islands had inhabited for centuries. Inside it was clean and orderly, with simple handcrafted wooden furnishings and hand-woven cotton cloth curtains on the windows.

Dona Amada was an excellent cook and in a surprisingly short time they were all sitting around a neatly laid table covered with the palatable succulence that the El Caney district was famous for. Santi did not hesitate to dive into the rich bounty before him; stewed duck, boiled yuca smothered in garlic, ajiaco stew, piles of cassava wafers, fresh tomatoes. On the table lay large locally crafted earthenware crockpots heaped with cornmeal-hallacas wrapped in their own husks. He reached for honey-glazed sweet potatoes, and black bean soup flavored with chunks of jutia meat and green peppers.

Santi stuffed himself as he always did when he visited Doña Leonor. He more than made up for the predictable finickiness of his cousin Luis on the other side of the table; even as his excited non-stop talking made up for Luis' customary shy silence.

Luis' eyes widened with amazement as the story of the old healer woman and her prophetic predictions came tumbling out of Santi's lips.

"Did you say she promised to meet you again in twenty years?" exclaimed Leonor. "Why, that old witch is almost eighty years old. I know her well. I have friends in Banes whom I visit. I have met the old curandera. Does she expect to last another twenty years so she can rendezvous with you at the age of a hundred and one? and in the woods yet!" She laughed. Santi's face darkened. "She might live to be a hundred." He said hopefully looking at his mother,

Elena smiled back at him and answered. "Honey I have never heard of anyone living to the age of a hundred years. Well, except, of course the people in the Bible which old Padre Jacinto used to tell us about at church when I was a little girl in Santiago city."

Santi turned triumphantly to his incredulous cousins. "You see, Mami knows this Padre Jacinto guy from a town called 'Bible' who knows people that have lived to be a hundred."

It took a couple of minutes for the absurdity of his last statement to sink in. Then the whole house exploded with laughter and Elena embraced her bewildered boy realizing that their isolation in the northern village had deprived him of a proper Catholic upbringing. He did not know what the Bible was.

The next morning something happened which dramatically changed the plans that Elena and her son had so neatly laid for his visit to Santiago. Late in the morning Santi found himself strolling alongside his cousin Luis on a narrow path next to a cornfield. They were absorbed in conversation when suddenly Luis spotted a large wasp nest hanging from the lowest branch of a guava tree.

For reasons that Luis would never be able to satisfactorily explain, he quickly picked up a large pebble and whipped it at the large gray egg-shape.

The wasp nest fell heavily to the ground and immediately the air was filled with an angry cloud of wasps. The furious hum of the insects made the air vibrate around the boys' ears as they both took to their heels in a desperate attempt to reach a nearby stream.

Santi quickly outdistanced his smaller companion. Even as he plunged into the water he could hear the shrieks of the other child who stumbled and fell, overtaken by the swarm.

That night Doña Leonor's house was deathly quiet. The normal bustle and laughter of the jolly woman's household was replaced with the incantations of a local healer and the sobs of Doña Leonor as she gazed down at her little boy's misshapen features. His face was horribly swollen and distorted from the many stings.

The healer worked long and hard applying his homemade salves and ointments to Luis' reddened sores. Anybody else would have had some trouble weathering this crisis, but Luis was a sickly child and there was real consternation in the household, and a palpable unuttered concern that he might not survive the night.

Santi drifted in and out of consciousness as he struggled to stay awake throughout the terrible night. He turned slowly away from the scene of the healer bent over his cousin's bed. He stared hard at the window. The darkness outside was impenetrable. Did he see a face at the window? Did he see a sickly white shimmering apparition? A toothy grin! As he drifted off to sleep the faint sound of a maddening snicker reached his ear as if from a distant place. It was a weird high pitched giggle more sinister and filled with hate than anything he had ever heard in his life.

That night Santi floated in a dreamy haze which carried him into remote regions of the night. Gradually he found himself in a large richly decorated hall. The windows hung with silk and gold brocade. In the center of the room, sprawled on a multicolored tile floor he saw a young woman, her long curly mane wildly disheveled about her tear streaked face. Her clothes hung in tatters all about her, and her thighs and arms were covered with ugly bruises.

Then there was that giggle again. There was that nasty heartless snicker, a high-pitched mockery of the pitiful sight before him.

Santi looked around the room to see where the laughter was coming from. At that same moment the girl reached for her scarf lying on the floor near her. Santi watched her wrap the torn rags that had once been her beautiful dress around herself as well she could, and struggle to her feet

When she stumbled the laughter increased. When she limped toward the door the laughter became a deafening din.

Santi struggled to discern the source of the laughter.

As the young woman wrestled with the heavy door in her attempt to get out, Santi finally realized where the laughter was coming from.

The huge portraits hanging all around the room were laughing! The richly dressed gentlemen in their well-coifed hairdos convulsed in their mocking humor, each one from his designated place upon the wall.

Santi watched helplessly as the anguished girl pulled and pushed at the huge door, the laughter now so loud that it hurt his ears. It rose in a crescendo of horror. He instinctively covered his ears.

The girl began to pound the door with her fists. The sound of her sobs was drowned out by the ferocious din of the laughter that filled every corner of the room.

Santi awoke suddenly, his breathing was rapid, his heart thumped almost audibly. A hot clammy layer of sweat covered his whole body.

This was the most frightening dream he had ever experienced.

Then his eyes grew accustomed to the light of the sunshine streaming in through the window. Finally he realized where he was and what had happened the night before, the wasps. Rubbing the neck stiffness that had been caused by his akward sleeping position sitting in a chair by Luis' bed, he leapt to his feet.

Before him Luisito lay quietly on his bed, his face and hands still grotesquely swollen from the wasp-stings. Next to him Doña Leonor sat and held Luisito's hand as she had all night long.

"Is he going to be alright?" Santi asked approaching the bed. Leonor raised her face and flashed a tired smile at him. "Yes honey, he'll be fine. He's resting quietly now but it was a very close call!"

She choked a little on the words, then wiping a tear with her veil she continued. "Santi, little man...I don't know how to tell you this." She stood up and held the boy's hands. "I'm sorry. Please understand, I can not go to Santiago city. I can't leave my little boy like this. He is still very weak. He needs me."

She grimaced as she saw the look of pain that washed over Santi's face. He tried to be brave about the whole thing. Throwing himself at her he embraced her and fought back the tears.

"It's alright cousin. I understand, really." Leonor squeezed him tightly.

Later that morning Santi stood outside the hut looking at the bright flowers growing next to Leonor's home. He leaned on the broad trunk of a flamboyan tree whose red-splashed branches spread their brilliant-blossomed foliage out over the little house.

Not surprisingly the image of the miserable battered young woman in his nightmare filled his depressed thoughts that morning. As he stood immersed in his private thoughts he heard someone approaching from behind. He turned and saw his mother. She came close and embraced him.

"Leonor told me."

Santi looked down and nodded. Elena glanced up at the beautiful flowers of the flamboyan.

"You know..." She said quietly; "When I look around at the beauty of this place it's hard to remember fear."

"Uh?" Santi looked up into her face quizzically. She continued to look into the branches of the huge tree.

"What I mean is that it's hard to remember why I am so afraid to return to Santiago city when I find myself surrounded by so much beauty."

Santi continued to stare at his mother's face, there was a puzzled look on his young face. Then Elena looked down at her son. "I shall go to Santiago city with you my son. We'll leave tomorrow." Santi's heart leapt with joy.

"Oh Mami, you will do this thing for me?"

"My son, I have strong feelings that there is a great destiny awaiting you in Santiago city, you are fated to return there and I must help you do it." Elena returned her son's embrace and she sighed.

The next morning found mother and son again on the road south to the city. They walked along the dusty path in silence. The two-hour walk felt more like eight hours to Santi.

At noon they arrived in the jumble of whitewashed, red tile-roofed buildings that clustered up and down among the foothills of the Sierra Maestra range, and arranged around the fine old harbor, constituted the seventeenth century port town of Santiago de Cuba. They walked down the narrow dirt streets lined with turned wood barred and wrought iron covered balconies that gave the city its unmistakable Iberian colonial flavor.

The streets of Santiago city were bustling with activity. Merchants hawked their goods in a loud voice as they led horse-drawn carts up and down the congested avenues announcing fruits, vegetables and other produce of the fertile Cuban soil to their prospective customers.

In the center of town, the main plaza, a large rectangular paved area fronted by the cathedral buzzed with the noises of trade. As he passed the crowded plaza Santi strained to hear the rapid-fire discourse of an auctioneer as several black slaves were put up on the block for bidding. As the fast-talking caller expertly maneuvered the bidders into offering higher and higher amounts, two men stood discreetly in the background guarding a small group of chained men and women. Keeping a wary eye on their wards the two men eyed the passers by. Lost in the hubbub of finely dressed landowners clustered around the auction block the two men had the advantage of a fairly good view of the square and the street.

As Santi and his mother passed by the scene of the auction the eyes of the two men followed them up the street. "My friend, there goes the reason why I will never leave the Indies." The short balding man licked his lips and mopped the sweat off his brow with his sleeve as he took in the gentle sway of Elena's hips.

Two pairs of eyes followed them up the street past the slave auction

"Women like that are impossible to find in Madrid." He continued looking up at the taller man.

The other looked down at his dumpy companion with a look of disdain.

"Hernando your whole life is guided by your loins..." He sneered. "That's why you have not amounted to much in the nine years that you have lived here."

The older man turned angrily to the tall Galician but the latter continued unaffected by the impact his insults had on his companion and ignored his enraged look.

"I, on the other hand, have used the relatively short time that I have spent in this land much more profitably."

"Listen here you impudent whelp..." growled Hernando. "I am respected in this community. My master is one of the most powerful slave traders in this region..."

"And you're his go-fer." Interrupted the Galican turning his back on him. "Today you are making barely enough to keep you in rum and wenches for three days baby-sitting these blacks while they wait to go on the auction block. That's all you're good for, a glorified babysitter. Yesterday I got four times as much for just one of the three runaways which I brought in from the bush.

They keep running away, God bless them, and I keep bringing them back in. I set my price and the landowners pay it."

The Galican turned to face Hernando. The shorter man stood silent with his fists clenched but still.

"Can you claim as much my fat friend?"

There was a brief silence as the two men glared at each other. Then the Galician smiled and turned to walk away. "I did not think so."

Hernando's anger was a simmering cauldron inside him. But he knew better than to cross the Galician. He had seen him run three men through in one fight with his sharp Toledo sword. All three men had been armed and it had all happened very quickly. The Galician was a very dangerous man. So Hernando simply muttered to himself as the Galician, looking to me for all the world like one of the Three Musketeers as I watched him in my dream, walked up to his horse, mounted it, and with a flourish of his broad-brimmed hat galloped away.

Galicia was a remote northern corner of Spain which bred hardy adventurers. José was one of these. After a brief stint as a mercenary he had come to the islands to join the growing ranks of fortune hunters that were profiting from the lively slave trade of the Caribbean.

ELENA AND HER SON

Elena

Santi

Santi and Elena reached the end of the little avenue that would one day become Heredia street in downtown Santiago city. Soon they were down at the waterfront. It was the site of row after row of humble one-story wood-frame homes and ramshackle firetraps which marked the neighborhood of the free black and mixed-blood dock workers and market laborers of the city.

Eventually, they arrived at the modest two-room dwelling where Elena had been born. After a warm welcome they sat around the table; Elena, Santi, his grandmother Doña Amada, and Adriana, a young god-daughter who began apprenticing the seamstress' art under Amada upon the death of her own parents.

Doña Amada was all atwitter about the whole thing. Her daughter Elena had not set foot in her house for over nine years and she felt an overwhelming feeling of gratitude toward her grandson who she knew had caused her prodigal daughter's return.

After lunch Adriana went back to her sowing and the others moved outside where they set up chairs and stools in front of the house and sat together sipping strong coffee.

"The first thing I want to show you is the new cathedral." Amada commented with excitement.

"We passed next to it as we went by the main plaza." Answered Santi with eyes full of expectation. "Can we go inside it?"

"Sure my grandson; I can't wait to give you the grand tour." Amada smiled at her daughter's son. The boy beamed a radiant grin right back at her.

It was almost three o'clock when Amada led her daughter and grandson up the dirt avenue which would one day become Enramada street. She was still shaking cobwebs out of her head since the inevitable drowsiness of Siesta time had finally overtaken her in spite of the coffee.

Elena and Santi had allowed her to sleep for several hours. Now, as she walked she yawned every three steps

Santi could feel the breeze from the bay helping the city recover from the broiling heat of noontime. His youthful impatience made the walk up Enramada street a personal ordeal. It appeared to him that his grandmother was inching along at a snail's pace. He wanted to see everything at once; the Cathedral, his grandfather's grave, the bay!

Suddenly the huge church loomed before them. It was a magnificent Romanesque temple which hung suspended above the level of the street, rising from a raised masonry platform that contained stores and sundry compartments underneath it. Climbing up the richly adorned steps of the religious edifice Santi felt as if he was climbing into the kingdom of heaven itself.

Inside, the heavy scent of frankincense enveloped him, slowly transporting him into a zone of consciousness he had never before experienced.

The three of them stepped quietly up the side isle of the church. The stillness of the building's interior was powerful, entrancing. The enormous altar towered in all its majesty over the nave of the church creating an awe-inspiring sense of otherworldly splendor which left the young boy breathless.

He gasped at the magnificence that surrounded him, a kind of divine opulence he had never dreamed of.

That night Santi could not sleep. There was something stirring deep in the pit of his stomach that he could not quite understand, a kind of yearning, a hunger for something that was not quite clear in his consciousness.

The next day as Doña Amada led him and his mother through the streets of the city his eyes sought out the glint of gold upon the jewelry of the urban aristocrats. He noticed the well-fed indolence of the market merchants. He compared the rich footwear of a nobleman's mulatto servant to his humble worn-out sandals.

In his mind here indeed was the true magic of the big city, a monument to wealth and power, to a wholly alien transcendence. Could he become part of this enchanted world? He had always dreamed that there must be more to life than the toil and drudgery of the fishing village. Could this be his escape?

Santi stood before the simple grave of his grandfather. "This is the resting place of my Guzman." Amada whispered kneeling to tenderly remove some dried-up flowers from her husband's grave and replace them with a bunch she had bought on the way.

The three of them stood in silence for some time gazing at the hand-carved white cross which marked Guzman's final resting-place.

"You know, Santi, in this same grave there is an even older burial down below your grandfather's."

Elena looked at her mother in puzzlement. "Do you mean there is somebody down there beside daddy?" She asked.

Amada looked at her daughter and then at the wide upturned eyes of her grandson. "Yes, there is someone else down there, someone who lived a totally different life."

"Who is down there grandma, what are you talking about?" piped the boy excitedly.

"Yes mama, who is down there?"

Amada smiled and looked up at the sky. "He was a mysterious, almost spooky old man. He didn't speak Spanish very well; he had that funny Taino accent you don't hear anymore. And all those crazy words he used, sometimes he was almost impossible to understand!" Elena began to realize what her mother was getting a.

"Do you mean to tell me daddy's Indian grandfather is down here with him?" She asked incredulously.

"That's exactly what I'm saying. I understood why you don't remember your father's funeral darling. Don't feel guilty about that. You were so young when he died"

Elena looked down in shame. Her mother embraced her. "You don't remember because you were too young but long before the terrible earthquake that took his life he had often mentioned that he wanted to be buried in the same grave as his half-civilized ancestor."

Santi's mouth dropped in amazement. He suddenly remembered old Doña Isabel's prediction... "Beneath the ground, deep beyond the resting place of your mother's father you will begin to discover the true nature of your destiny."

The rich dark tone of the old sorceress' age-lined face appeared before him as he stared at the white cross that stood over the grave.

"You are the descendant of a seashell spirit..." He remembered her words.

"Grandma what was the name of this man that is buried down here with my grandfather?" He asked breathlessly looking up at Doña Amada.

"His name was Cobo, honey, Cobo...It's an old Indian word. It is the name of those big conch shells the fishermen use to signal to each other over great distances."

The journey back to Banes seemed longer than any journey Santi had ever undertaken. Leaving the exciting exotic sights and sounds of the city was painful and made the prospect of returning to the commonplace life of the fishing community quite unbearable. That was bad enough, but leaving Santiago City so soon after discovering these new elements of his own personal heritage was almost umbearable for the young boy.

He knew that he would never feel the same about his lot in life and decided that someday, someday soon he would live in Santiago. He would leave the humdrum world of Banes behind and join the enchanted universe of the big city with its connections to his family past.

Santi's relationship with Armando worsened that summer. After his journey to Santiago he was often restless and uncooperative. His mind was not on his work, and he was proving more a nuisance than a help to his adoptive father.

About a year of this and Elena decided that the only solution was for him to leave the Banes district. Her mother Amada was an old woman who had by now lived far longer than was normally expected. She was being cared for by her young apprentice who was even younger than Santi. Amada was in no position to take in and raise this restless boy.

Santi moved to El Caney with Doña Leonor. Close to his cousin Luis he finally felt at home. And although he sometimes missed his mother, the thrill of living so close to the big city more than made up for it.

Leonor maintained a well-tended mango orchard on a modest plot of land she had inherited from her father. Together with her children she raised enough mangos to make a simple living.

Every season at harvest time a local merchant from the district came up the trail to their neat little peasant hut and bought her whole crop. This, along with an assortment of other locally grown fruit was taken to Santiago and sold in the busy markets of the city. The fruit harvest of El Caney district was considered the finest in the whole island.

Leonor also managed to grow small crops of vegetables for her family's consumption. There was always enough cassava, beans, corn, potatoes and yams to keep the larder well stocked. In addition she would occasionally get her hands on a wild duck or a jutia from some of her male relatives who were expert bow hunters and trappers.

Santi learned the skills of the farmer, the cyclical routines of the planting and harvesting seasons. Working alongside his cousin Luis he learned the tricks of a successful crop, the dangers of blights and insect pests, the ancient Indian technique of interplanting, and many other secrets of the peasant lifestyle which sustained the people of the region.

And yet the most important thing about his new life was its proximity to the city. Now, just as he had done in the past when he had visited El Caney from Banes, he began to find ways of getting away from El Caney to visit Santiago. He and Luis managed to squeeze in at least one visit to old Doña Amada's house once every three months. During those visits things got a little easier for Adriana, Doña Leonor's young apprentice. Santi and Luis would wait on the old woman hand and foot, helping her around the house, cleaning up for her and running countless errands. Adriana began to look forward to their visits.

On one of those pleasant visits Santi found himself alone in the small back room of his grandmother's little two-room house. Luis had returned to El Caney that night but Santi had stayed an extra day.

He lay in the hammock that he had just slung from hooks driven into the walls of the room. A cool breeze wafted in through the window making the hot tropical night much more bearable. Slowly he drifted off to sleep.

First there was darkness and hazy half-consciousness. Then slowly there was sound, the shrill call of a hawk. Then suddenly a startling scene unfolded before him, a dramatic dream panorama of tropical jungle lushness.

In his vision he stood atop a high point looking down upon a huge expanse of forest wilderness. Different kinds of palms competed desperately for space with mahogany and a thick undergrowth of low branches.

He turned to look behind him. On the other side of the peak upon which he stood lay a sandy tropical beach from which the green-blue mantle of the sea spread out to the horizon.

As he looked down at the never-ending cycles of surf which took their turns one by one over the wet sand, a bird appeared on the distant horizon. Where sea met sky the small, silhouetted figure soared and grew in size as it approached his mountain-top position. The bird reached him, whizzing past so swiftly that he was almost knocked down. It was a medium sized red-tailed hawk, the rufous of his tail feathers flashed orange as it flew by.

Santi followed the creature's flight with his vision until it took a sharp dip and disappeared into the verdant canopy of treetops.

All was still for what seemed an eternity. Santi kept his eyes fixed upon the spot in the forest where the bird had vanished. Then softly at first, and then more loudly, a repetitive chant began to emanate from that place. Santi waited with growing anticipation as the volume of the song rose to a majestic choir.

Then amid the din and thrilling emotions of the experience a great figure rose out of the forest, a huge bird with great outspread wings emerged from the green blanket like a reborn phoenix.

Santi watched the majestic form as it soared high above the forest. It took him a minute to realize that the great bird was holding something in its talons, a writhing figure securely imprisoned in the deadly grasp of its sharp claws. Santi stared at the helpless captive struggling violently to free itself from the bird. The bird beat its enormous wings several times, and with a graceful motion began a sweeping trajectory past Santi's position on the high peak. As the bird swung past him Santi got a good look at the captive in its claws. It was a man dressed entirely in fine Spanish plate-armor. The visor of his helmet was raised and as he was swept past, Santi's eyes met his. They were cold eyes, emotionless eyes.

Santi felt touched by an icy finger as the man's impassive glance reached him. The armored figure was swept away by the giant hawk.

The primordial chorus rose and it seemed to lift Santi from the mountain. I heard the music in my dream state and again the memory of the song and stomping feet that had wafted over the partition wall into my grandmother's house during my childhood came back to bless me. In my dream I saw Santi's dream. He felt light and buoyant. He spread his arms and was lifted off the mountain by a gust of wind. Rising above the forest he felt the spirit of the magic hawk, the "GUARAGUAO" palpitating within him to the rhythm of the omnipresent maiohuakan drum. He was now the hawk. Below him he spotted a small clearing in the midst of the forest. He dived gracefully down for a closer look. As he approached the clearing he spotted a small figure at its center. He descended and circled over the treeless space. He saw a woman standing down there tall and proud. She wore a beautiful white dress, cinched at the waist and covered with intricate white cord applique patterns. She looked up at him and flashed a glorious smile full of tropical sunshine. Her long black wavy hair played gracefully about her shoulders in the soft sea breeze.

Santi felt a warm relaxed wave sweep over his whole body as he continued to circle over the figure of the young woman. Then she raised her arms and held two objects up toward him. In her right hand she bore a long glistening Toledo sword, in her left hand she held a shining white conch shell. On the ground by her feet he saw a simple but elegant line drawing of a bird with outstretched wings scratched into the dirt.

As Santi continued to circle over the young woman he heard the sound of a conch shell trumpet rising over the din of the mighty chant. It blasted out in the distance and created a layer of sound which covered the primordial chant with a harmonious upper stratum blending with it and then descending, taking the chant with it as it withdrew into the distance. The sound of the chant and the shell horn diminished until it was barely discernible. As that happened the boy was surrounded by a smooth sweet night softness, a kind of private concealing secrecy studded with stars. It wrapped itself around him and drew him back gently until he opened his eyes and found himself swinging in his hammock within the familiar walls of his grandmother's house. Outside, the crickets intoned their chorus and in the distance a fisherman blew long blasts upon a conch-shell trumpet.

2. THE MOVE TO SANTIAGO

I awoke in the middle of the night fully aware I'd had another one of those mysterious dreams, but as in every one of the previous nights, I couldn't remember what it had been all about. At this point it was really no longer as much frustrating as it was a nuisance. I no longer cared whether I could remember these annoying dreams. I knew I wouldn't. I just wanted to sleep in peace! The dreams wouldn't let me. I would awaken from each one with powerful emotional forces pulling me apart. And then it took me hours to settle down. And that's how I felt this evening; my heart racing, lying in my bedroll, afraid to go back to sleep.

I lay awake, staring out through the mosquito net covering the window opening of our little pup tent. Just for the hell of it, and because I had nothing better to do, I closed my eyes and made one last attempt at remembering the dream I had just had. Instead I dozed off.

Predictably, I began to dream again picking up the thread of the story right where I had left off.

Again, images of dimly perceived characters from an ancestral memory inhabited my dreams. Again my mind was filled with people and events from the distant past, people and events that I had never heard of before.

This part of the dream began with the somber scene of a funeral. A small knot of people dressed in very modest attire gathered around a very plain wooden coffin.

As the white Spanish priest recited the familiar words "dust to dust ashes to ashes..." Santi stood riveted to his spot, his eyes focused on his mother's contorted face. Santi had never seen her so distraught.

To Elena, Amada had represented the last firm anchor to her childhood. The only person she had ever truly felt safe with, safe and protected. Now she was gone. It was as if the principal pillar holding up her world had given way and the very ground was crumbling beneath her. Elena clung like an inconsolable child to her husband's arm, sobbing, trying to somehow draw from him the sense of security and protection she had always felt with her mother.

It was a spectacle Santi would not easily forget, for as he saw the desperate look on his mother's face, his own world suddenly seemed unsafe and insecure.

The next day, on the morning of November second of 1677 Elena and Santi accompanied an old missionary Jesuit monk who had worked most of his life with the Indians of El Caney. The three of them trudged up the narrow streets of Santiago to the offices where properties and deeds were disposed of.

The monk was ancient and quite hard of hearing, very difficult to communicate with, but he knew about transferring deeds and was well-acquainted with Elena and her whole family, having seen the childhood and growing up of practically every one of her relatives in her generation.

It took a long time for the process to be completed as Elena and the clerk in charge of the records took turns screaming into the old monk's ear. But when it was all over Elena had succeeded in transferring her title as sole inheritor of her mother's property to her son. It wasn't much, just a minuscule plot of land down on the waterfront and the very modest structure that stood upon it. But to Santi it was everything. This was the house that Cobo had built; it was the place where his grandfather had grown up listening to the exciting adventures of the old mountain Indian. He imagined himself in his grandfather's place sitting at Cobo's feet reliving the dangerous, sometimes tragic events of the old man's youth up in the mountains when he witnessed the great Indian rebellion of the past. He thought of how lucky his grandfather was to have been raised by such an interesting person.

3. RUNAWAYS

It was a little after dawn. The morning sun had just cleared the uppermost peaks of the eastern mountains. On the rise overlooking one of the tributaries of the Aguadores River, Jose the Galician crouched behind a luxuriant growth of aromatic yerbabuena bushes. The minty fragrance of the plant's leaves filled his nostrils as he watched.

He stared intently at the homely little scene below. Down in the hollow the creek marked several wide bends before flowing south for several miles to eventually join the larger Aguadores River near the town of Santiago. In one of those bends a black peasant couple had built their simple thatched hut, a pleasant little bohio partially obscured by a stand of royal palms. As the Galician watched, a slight young woman of about 17 years of age emerged from the palm-frond-roofed wooden structure. She headed for the stream with a bundle of clothes on her head.

Beyond her in the distant background the Spaniard could make out the figure of a man stooped over a small tobacco patch. The dark-skinned peasant carefully weeded his emerging crop. As he worked, he made plans for the money that it would bring at the city market.

The Spaniard waited till the woman settled down to her laundering work. Slowly he moved down and back off the knoll. Then he sneaked around to her blind side. He positioned himself and looked over his shoulder. Pursing his lips he produced a perfect imitation of a mockingbird's mating call. It was a signal to attack.

Santi's eyes snapped open with a jolt as a sudden explosion of noises burst rudely through his sleep. The whole world outside the wooden hut seemed to be falling to pieces. A din of screams and dog barks mixed with the boom of a musket's discharge and the thunder of a horse's hooves blasted in through the open door of the one-room hut.

Santi fell with a heavy thud from the hammock and lay on the floor trembling and rubbing his eyes as the racket outside got louder. Luis bolted up out of the cot at the corner of the room in which he had spent the night and ran crouching to the door. He peered out at the violent drama unfolding itself by the riverbank. Santi crept nearer to him and cried out: "What's going on out there?"

Luis yelled back at him struggling to be heard over the loud commotion: "Santi, we're caught up in something very serious...Come here, look at this!"

Santi crept up next to his cousin at the door and watched. To the far left at the edge of the tobacco patch he saw Antonio standing his ground wielding his hoe like a weapon. Before the young black man a dog of massive proportions crouched menacingly, its teeth set in an alarming snarl. The huge animal lunged at Antonio from time to time trying to get past the hoe.

"Santi, I think Antonio and his lady are escaped slaves. Last night I caught a glimpse of a property brand burned into his left shoulder," whispered Luis.

"Oh my God, are you sure?" muttered Santi still trembling. "Yes, Santi, look at those fellows there. They are obviously slave-hunters. We could be in very big trouble!"

Santi caught sight of a figure which emerged from a thicket and galloped into the scene astride a brown stallion. The rider was a well dressed light-skinned mulatto no more than eighteen years of age.

The young half-caste lad reined his horse in as he reached the spot where Antonio stood at bay with his hoe. The horseman swung viciously at Antonio with a long machete. Antonio ducked the blow but stumbled and a large spurt of blood gushed out of his right thigh where a musket ball had nicked his femoral artery turning his white calf-length cotton cloth trousers crimson.

The dog, mad with the scent of blood lunged at him again but Antonio quickly regained his balance and found enough strength to deliver a glancing whack at the beast's face with his hoe. The dog yelped and fell dazed. Even as the rider with the machete wheeled to position himself for a second blow, Antonio fell upon the dog and delivered three more quick whacks to its head.

He felt his knees give way beneath him and his head became faint as huge quantities of blood flowed out of his wound with each beat of his heart. He realized he was bleeding to death. Then he stiffened and let out a gut-wrenching scream when the mounted mulatto rushed in and brought his weapon down hard on his shoulder. The machete sliced deep into the young dark skinned man's flesh snapping his collarbone with an audible crack. Santi convulsed with nausea, his eyes widening as he watched Antonio crash face first unto the neatly cultivated soil.

Out of the forest another black man emerged running. He carried a spear. He approached the spot where Antonio lay writhing, clawing desperately at his mangled shoulder, and watched the mulatto dismount.

Down by the creek out of sight, another violent struggle was playing itself out. Santi and Luis could hear the anguished screams of the young woman rising from the riverbank.

The mulatto strode up to the prone form of the fallen runaway, leading his horse by the reins. He approached the other man, the one with the spear, and handed him the rope to his horse's bridle. He stood over Antonio and began to speak.

"You shouldn't have run off Antonio: I told you it would not take long for us to find you..."

The wounded man moaned. Blood flowed freely from his shoulder. "Your biggest mistake was to take Leonor with you. I told you she was mine. You knew the master had given her to me. How could I let you get away with this insult? You stole my woman!"

The mulatto delivered a viscous kick at the fallen man.

The black man with the spear shook his head in disgust then walked up and stood over the body of the dead dog. The horse snorted following behind.

"Did you think a black bastard like you could just walk off with my property?" continued the mulatto and kicked Antonio again. Antonio barely groaned. He lay in a veritable pool of his own blood and was now more dead than alive. "Now the master's hired slave-hunter has found you and I came along to see you fall!" he delivered a third kick at Antonio.

The man with the spear got up holding the limp body of the dog. "Kill him already!" he barked at the mulatto.

The mulatto looked up and glared at him. "Back off nigger!" The mulatto growled. "Go to your slave-hunter master, take him his dead mutt...this here business is between Antonio and me."

The man with the spear rolled his eyes in disgust, shook his head again and walked off in the direction of the creek carrying the dead dog and leading the mulatto's horse away with him. The mulatto knelt down beside Antonio and stooping over him whispered something inaudible into his ear. Then he raised the machete high in the air with both hands and brought it down hard on Antonio's neck three times, hacking at it as if it were a stand of weeds. Blood spurted high in the air as Antonio's head rolled away a few feet.

Back in the shack Santi pulled backwards away from the door and puked repeatedly upon the earthen floor of the hut. The mulatto heard something and raised his eyes staring at the house.

"Quiet!" hissed Luis, still peering out the door at the young killer. "I think he heard you". Santi clasped his hand over his own mouth and smeared his fingers with vomit. He reached up and snatched a rag that hung from a peg on the wall. Wiping his face and hands he crept back next to Luis. He saw the mulatto still staring at the house trying to make out any movement or sound within.

He was still staring at the house when he rose to his feet and wiped the blade of his machete on Antonio's headless corpse. He walked over and picked up the severed head, holding it by the black wool of the dead man's hair. At that moment the tall white Spaniard came striding up from the creek bank. Behind him his black slave followed, still holding the dead dog and leading the mulatto's horse. On the horse rode the girl, her arms bound behind her back and her dress disheveled. The girl sobbed as she swayed to and fro to the rhythm of the horse's walk. When she saw Antonio's head dangling from the mulatto's fist her face contorted into a horrible grimace and she let out a scream that reverberated from the nearby mountains.

The Spaniard glanced over at the mulatto.

"My friend, do you realize that you have destroyed a very valuable slave? That is a very expensive head you are holding there." He muttered casually.

"Never mind that, Spaniard!" snapped the mulatto walking up to the white man and brandishing the severed head. "You will be well paid for your work today. I am the master's nephew. He is my godfather. I will tell him how efficiently you fulfilled his orders today..."

The Spaniard walked right past him ignoring him completely. "Hey, Spaniard, Did you hear me? I'm telling you that I will report your work to my master." He called out after the tall Galician, following him up the slope.

The Galician still ignored him.

"Hey...Are you deaf?" He yelled, approaching him from behind. Suddenly the Galician whirled about and drew his sword all in one swift motion. The mulatto dropped the severed head and stumbled backwards falling flat on his hind end. He found himself looking up the length of the Galician's sharp Toledo rapier. He gulped as he felt its point digging into his throat. But he didn't move an inch. The Galician held him at sword point for a minute and glared down at him.

"If you ever again use that tone of voice with me I'll gut you where you stand, by God!" The white man growled quietly.

The mulatto's eyes widened and he let out a barely audible whimper.

Jose, the Galician relaxed his stance and pulling back away from his frightened companion, threw back his head and let out a howl of laughter. Then still snickering a little he turned and slipped his weapon back in its scabbard.

"You know, Tomas, I don't give a horse's ass whose nephew you are, who's godson you are." he murmured in a cold low tone of voice as he strode up the rest of the hill.

Tomas arose slowly, his head hanging in shame. He stood for a minute, mortified. Then still flushed with embarrassment he got up on his feet and recovered his grisly trophy. Up ahead the Galician continued:

"You represent the most disgusting aspect of our colonial system. I am a Galician. My country was never dominated by the filthy Moors." He referred to the fact that dark-skinned Muslim conquerors from North Africa had succeeded in overrunning southern Spain over eight hundred years earlier. They had ruled most of the country from their stronghold in the southern region of Granada for centuries. Then, after many years of gradual southward progress of the European Christian re-conquest in the Iberian Peninsula, King Ferdinand and Queen Isabela, the fighting Catholic monarchs of the united kingdoms of Leon and Castille finally defeated the last Moslem ruler in battle in the year 1492. That was the same year they authorized Columbus' historical voyage.

Tomas knew little and cared less about Spanish history. He had been born and raised all his life here in Cuba and had never been to the colonial metropolis. But he listened in prudent silence as the Galician droned on.

"Here in this savage hinterland, rich Castillians like your uncle rule. They all come from a land tainted with the disgusting legacy of Moorish domination. Their ancestors mixed with the dark-skinned conquerors, no longer real Spaniards, they are a breed of mongrels!"

The mulatto winced at the stinging words. Jose reached the top of the rise. He stooped and picked up his satchel where he had left it before the attack. Then he strode back down past Tomas.

"You are a prime example of the malaise which characterizes our colonial system." He stopped in his tracks and turned to look up at Tomas. "Do you think for a minute that the hardy, efficient English tobacco planters of Virginia up in North America mix with their slaves?"

He glared fiercely at the dazed mulatto.

"I've been to the English colonies; I know. Up in Virginia they don't countenance the kind of foolishness that is rife here in Cuba. Up there white men marry white women. They raise healthy white families. Sure, sure they are all a pack of Protestant heathens, but for God's sake, they know the law of nature.

Oh certainly, an English plantation owner will give one of his black wenches a little pop now and then, that's normal, that's natural; a man has needs. But he doesn't feel inclined to dress her in fine silks, to bring her into the big house, to make her little bastard son his heir! Only in a Spanish colony do you find such unnatural abomination...It almost tempts me to become a Protestant!"

The Galician looked Tomas up and down with disdain. "And look at you." he hissed through a sneer. "Just look at you. You big high-yellow nigger. You think you're something; dressed in your fine clothes, riding your brown stallion. Do you think any of this makes you any more white? You're a big yellow mongrel nigger, you have always been a big yellow mongrel nigger, and you will always be a big yellow mongrel nigger."

He stared at Tomas for a minute. Then he shook his head and turned away. He walked back the rest of the way down to the spot where his dark-complexioned black slave stood still holding the dead mastiff. He looked down at the body of his dog and muttered: "Best dog I ever had, a real warrior. Put him down, you African ape, you don't deserve to touch him."

The black man set the dead mastiff gently on the ground.

"Now, get away. Go give that strutting peacock back his nag and fetch me my own mount."

The slave jumped dutifully to action. He led the chesnut stallion up the hill and handed the reins back to Tomas. Tomas glanced up at the sobbing girl astride his horse, then walked it back down away from the Galician and toward the trail. Meanwhile, the black slave continued up and over the hill. He plunged into a thicket and re-emerged leading the Galician's white charger and his own mule.

Luis and Santi remained huddled in the hut. They watched as the tall Galician swung up onto his horse and led his party down the trail toward the distant hacienda.

Santi fell back against a wall and covered his face with his hands. Luis walked across the room and sat down to pull on his boots.

"If they had found us they would have killed us for sure." he exclaimed looking up at Santi. "Or worse, they would have kidnapped us and sold us in Jamaica to the English."

Santi looked up in bewilderment. "I don't understand all this..."

Only the day before they had arrived at the peasant couple's little shack. Luis' mother had given them a sack of mangos to trade for some cured tobacco leaves.

The black couple had moved into the area a few years earlier and had settled down in the valley, growing their tobacco and keeping mainly to themselves. No one in the area knew where they had come from and they volunteered little information about their past. Of course everybody suspected that they might be runaways but nobody saw any need to make anything of it. Now they were gone, and the scenes that had just played themselves out in front of Santi were burned into his memory forever.

Santi and Luis walked together in silence all morning. By noon they reached the fork in the trail. Here they parted ways. Santi headed west into the city while Luis turned north toward El Caney.

Santi reached his new home on the waterfront by early evening. He found Adriana sowing in the main room. The girl looked up at him and smiled. That smile had been a source of many a sleepless night for Santi. He had stayed awake in his hammock pondering the sweet mysteries of the young woman lying in the adjoining room. The girl had no family. She had been his grandmother's apprentice and upon Amada's death when he inherited the house he allowed her to stay and to carry on with her seamstress trade. Her modest little cot was pushed into a corner next to her piles of cloth.

But none of this was part of Santi' awareness today. He stumbled past Adriana without returning her greeting and headed right to his room. His mind reeled with the events of that morning's violent adventure.

He slumped into his hammock and sank into a nightmare-ridden slumber.

CHAPTER IX

THE SWORD AND THE SEASHELL

1. THE SWORD

The scenery along the banks of the Allegheny River had changed dramatically during the last couple of days. Lush forests had given way to heavily settled summer resort riverfront property, and then, just ugly industrial sprawl. We went from gravel-dredging works to river-polluting oil refineries lined up along the banks like dark brooding monuments to inappropriate technology.

That night we camped near Freeport, Pennsylvania. The sky had stayed clear and we had perspired profusely all day under the hot August sun. As Sven tended the fireplace I finished setting up our tent and sat down to scribble the day's notes, and attempted to add a few more verses to the song I was writing by the dim light of the fire.

It was about twelve midnight on the morning of Tuesday, August 17, 1982. The lights of the town of Freeport glowed in the night blotting out most of the stars as we prepared to turn in for the night on the left bank. We had come back very close to civilization. I could tell we were on the last legs of our trip, approaching the environs of the Pittsburgh greater metropolitan area.

I drifted gradually to sleep, the sounds of the night blending neatly with the images of my dreams. I did not fight the dreaming this time. I welcomed it. Slowly the images came into focus. I saw a young man dressed modestly but neatly in white cotton shirt with ample sleeves rolled halfway up his forearms and a pair of white cotton trousers with the legs reaching down only to his calves. His bare calves and feet were tanned brown by the constant exposure. The lad wore a wide brim straw hat which kept the fierce tropical sun from his face. He stood listening attentively to the words of an older man who was addressing him as he wiped the perspiration from his brow with his sleeve. The older man was dressed in fine silk and velvet and stood under the shade of an umbrella held by a slave over his head.

"I have been watching you out here on the docks for some time as you work, young man. Every time I come down to supervise the shipment of the tobacco from my brother's plantation. You are different from the other men. You are not coarse and rude like them but you seem to bear yourself with a kind of quiet dignity that is rare in your race."

Santi shifted nervously from one foot to the other. He glanced up past the rich old man's face. He could see his foreman watching from a distance. The hired boss stared impatiently at him because he had not lifted a sack of tobacco for the last five minutes.

"Anyway, what I mean to say is that I am interested in hiring you to be my personal man-servant. You are very strong and young. I have slaves, but I believe only a free man can truly be trusted to be loyal."

Santi's eyes widened. He forgot all about the impatient foreman. He looked hard at the old nobleman and said; "You want me to work for you?"

"Yes, yes..." answered the elegant gentleman. "You can start today if you wish! I have already made arrangements for you to move into my home near the central plaza."

Santi was overwhelmed. This was an undreamed-of opportunity to escape the backbreaking toil of the docks, a life-long daily struggle which aged men quickly and killed them early.

About two hours later, hat in hand, his callused bare feet standing on the coolness of the multicolored tile floor, Santi waited patiently for the chief house servant to return. The old black man reappeared, the shiny cloth of his trousers swishing as he walked. Behind him, a pretty mulatto girl scurried to keep up with his long dignified stride. In her hands she held a set of brilliantly colored servant's clothing.

As they approached Santi the girl stepped behind the chief servant and peeked around him at Santi with a giggle.

"You may follow me. I shall show you to your quarters." said the gray-haired black man. Without waiting for a response from Santi he turned smartly and marched out of the room, the giggly girl and Santi keeping up behind him as best they could.

They filed down a narrow corridor with walls covered partway up from the floor with beautiful glazed tiles. At intervals, the upper white-washed stucco portion of the wall bore large paintings of elegantly dressed men and women that reminded Santi of the frightening dream he had experienced years earlier featuring the young woman in tattered clothes lying on the elegant tiled floor and the portraits lining the walls, laughing at her.

At the end of the hallway they filed out through a door that led into a broad open walled-in garden patio. The bases of the walls were lined with enormous clay vases overflowing with a colorful explosion of potted plants. Plants also dangled in smaller pots which hung from large brass hooks upon the wall. Overhead the curved red tiles of the mansion's roofs all around the patio framed the bright tropical sky.

The tall old black man led Santi to a door on the other side of the patio. He removed a large key ring that jingled at his waist and opened the heavy wooden door.

"This is your room, boy..." He said imperiously. "You will sleep here for eight months each year, except when you are traveling with the master. The other four months of the year you will be allowed to return to your family and spend the feasts of our Lord's holy birth, his passion and death, and his resurrection among your loved ones."

Santi had no intention of travelling all the way north to his mother and Armando in Banes for Christmas and Easter, but the prospect of spending the holidays with his cousin Luis in El Caney was very exciting, and with money in his pocket! His mother would willingly travel to El Caney for the holidays anyway where all her cousins lived. His only regret was the beautiful young seamstress who had shared his home for a year and a half.

Adriana had captured Santi's heart. Although his strong sense of honor had maintained him at a respectable distance from her during that time, he felt a powerful attraction to her.

She slept every night in one room and in the other room he spent sleepless hours lying awake and thinking of her. Many times he had thought of proposing marriage. Now with this new position in the service of a rich man he had the money to start a family, but he was going to be separated from her for long periods of time by the necessity of living in his master's house!

The days that followed were full of excitement like Santi had never experienced before. He accompanied the old man from business engagement to social event, to trips into the countryside in luxurious horse-drawn carriages, and even overseas to Santo Domingo and Puerto Rico. He saw places he never dreamed existed.

Every year the old Spaniard, whose name was Don Fernando, employed Santi until the month of December. Then around the 20th of the month just before Christmas the old man would hand Santi a bag full of coins and they would part company for the holidays.

"See you again in April, God willing..." the old gentleman would always call out as he headed for his carriage and as Santi headed for the road to El Caney. "And have a blessed holiday."

Every year Santi would wave goodbye at the old man and walk the country roads to his cousin's home in the rural Indian village. There in El Caney he would spend Christmas with Luis and his family. Then he would return to the city and spend the mild, dry tropical winter there. Eventually, in the spring when the rains returned he would observe Lent and Easter with his beloved Adriana.

It was on one of those occasions, or perhaps it was just on a special day that Don Fernando had given him the day off, Santi would later have difficulty remembering; anyway, it was one of those nights that he was sleeping in his own hammock at his own home on the waterfront that the pirate attack took place.

Santi had arrived late that night after a leisurely walk alone along the docks. Adriana lay sleeping in her cot in the corner of the main room; her day's stitching folded neatly by the window.

As he swayed gently in his hammock in the back room, he thought of ways that he might convince Don Fernando to let him marry and bring Adriana into the old gentleman's house to live with him in his little room at the back. He missed her so much during the eight long months of separation each year!

Eventually Santi's thoughts blurred and he drifted slowly into a state of half-sleep.

The sharp staccato reports of distant musket fire intruded rudely into his dreams. He probably would have slept right through the faint racket had the gunshots not been immediately answered by the deep boom of the main cannon at El Morro fort down over the entrance of the bay.

The cannon-shot was the general alarm. It signaled an attack on the city. Suddenly the whole town was submerged in a din of alarmed voices, shrieks of panic, church bells and the stamping of boots on the city streets.

Santi jumped out of his hammock, pulled on his shoes and blouse in one quick motion and rushed out of the room almost crashing into Adriana who had stumbled bleary-eyed out of her cot. "What's happening?" She asked trembling.

"Pirates!" shouted Santiago over his shoulder as he opened the front door and launched himself out into the chaos of the streets. He headed straight for Don Fernando's house.

Don Fernando stood in the middle of the street in front of his residence, fully dressed and brandishing his sword. As soon as Santi reached him Don Fernando waved him to follow and marched up the street to the town hall.

At the municipal building, In the city council meeting chamber Lord Mayor Ramos as well as several council members were already assembled and awaiting an official report from the commander of the garrison at El Morro fort.

Soon after Don Fernando and Santi had arrived, Don Francisco De La Vega, the territorial governor showed up in the council chambers. Within an hour the local militia was ranged outside the building in the Town Square below. The militia commanders stood awaiting orders from the men gathered inside. These in turn continued to wait patiently for some word from the garrison commander at El Morro fort.

Finally the voice of a garrison soldier was heard outside asking leave to enter the council chamber. Santi was ordered to open the door and as he swung it open he stood face to face with a local town character known to everyone as "Juan Bobo" (Juan-the-fool).

The mentally challenged young man stood caked in mud, dressed in tatters and with a heavy smell of gunpowder hanging about him. He was certainly the last person Santi expected to see at the door. A soldier shoved poor Juan into the room and behind them marched the El Morro fort garrison commander.

Governor De La Vega was livid with rage. "What is the meaning of this? Why has this idiot been brought into our council chamber? And why are you, sir, not at your post down on the harbor? We are presently under attack!"

The garrison commander bowed respectfully and answered: "With all due respect, your grace, but the threat to the city is quite over, I assure you. I left a very able second-in-command in charge at the fort and I have come because I felt I should be present here to corroborate in person the amazing story this lad must relate to your Excellencies."

At that, everyone in the room turned to the wretched figure of the mentally challenged man.

"Well, speak up boy! What happened out there?" urged Mayor Ramos.

"Uh?" asked Juan looking up at the mayor with a puzzled look on his face.

The commander moved across the room to stand by Juan's side. "Tell these illustrious gentlemen what you told me, Juan, Don't be afraid." whispered the commander into the young man's ear.

Juan took off his hat and looked around at the councilmen spread out throughout the room.

"They wuz a bunch of ferriners...uhuh... a bunch of ferriners they wuz!...I could tell...They wuzn't from 'round these parts...nope, not them! They spoke funny..."

He wiped his nose on his shirtsleeve. "I could barely make out whut they wuz saying. They spoke so funny...they offered me money to guide them into the city, but they was such a bunch of dumb ferriners that I fooled them!..."

"Your excellencies..." interrupted the fort commander. "If I may be permitted...We captured one of the French pirates. He was wounded but he was able to talk. These were French corsairs led by the Marquis De

Franquesnay from their stronghold in Haiti." "Yea...yea, I told you they wuzn't from around these parts, I knew, I knew! I took them up the forked road..." Continued Juan, "They went and split theirselves up into two groups...one went up the right fork, the other bunch followed me up the left fork..." The councilmen fidgeted impatiently.

"Hee, hee, hee, hee..." Juan giggled nervously.

"Get on with the story, man. What happened next." yelled the mayor.

"Oh yea, well it's like this..." continued the young man. Santi smiled to himself as he watched the elegant old coots squirm with impatience, hanging on every word of the town fool.

"They's fools more than me! It was so dark out there that the one bunch didn't know what the other one was doin'. I knew that they wuz all confused so I yelled out our war cry..."

And then Juan opened his mouth wide and screamed out the Spanish war cry: "Santiagooooooooo!" (which, of course, happened to be the name of the city) The dignified men all jumped, startled By Juan's sudden scream. Santi turned his face away from the group as he stifled a sudden explosion of laughter, his hands cupped tightly over his mouth.

"Yea, I fixed them..." Juan continued. "Them ferriners, they wuz all shitting their pants out there in the dark..."

A hush fell upon the assembled group all around the room as they began to realize the importance of the fool's story.

"Yea, yea...They thought it was our brave men coming to do battle with them."

Santi stopped laughing. He realized that he was hearing the story of how a town fool had saved the city. Juan began to prance about the room in a comic imitation of men fighting a battle.

"Them ferriners started a-shooting every which way, they did...They commenced ta swearing an' cussin' in their language till it wuz pitiful ta hear...They wuz shootin' at each other in the dark and screaming so bad I had to drop down to the ground and cover my ears. They didn't see me down there on the ground. They didn't see anything! They couldn't, it wuz so cursed dark out there they couldn't even see their own hands in front of their faces.

Well, sir... They kilt a bunch of their own men before they realized they wuz shooting at each other. Their wounded men wuz rolling around on the ground moaning and groaning and making a general racket. Then I heard our men coming down the trail for real from the fort. I knew it was safe! Them ferriners hightailed it outta there likkity-split back to their boats!"

At that point the fort commander walked up to Juan and put his hand on the young man's shoulder. "Gentlemen, this youngster is telling the truth. We found him just as he has related, cowering on the ground, surrounded by scores of the enemy dead and dying. The bodies of the Frenchmen were riddled by musket balls shot by their own comrades in the dark. I'm afraid we all owe this man a debt of gratitude."

Eventually Juan would be honored by the mayor and the provincial governor. The details of his adventure were entered into the official annals of the city and his story became the source of local legend for some time: "How the town fool saved the city".

The next day Santi found himself walking slowly next to his master down the main avenue of the city and toward the market. "Santi..." Don Fernando began, "This is a violent world we live in. You never know from which direction Death will come rushing out at you..."

He paused for a minute as he walked. Then he stopped and looked at Santi. "Boy, I am an old man, my speed and agility are in the past. I need a strong spirited youngster like you to look out for me in my old age. I am going to teach you the art of handling a sword." the words rang inside Santi's head like the tolling of a church bell.

"Master, you are going to teach me how to fight with a sword like yours?" he asked, his face lighting up with overwhelming joy. "Yes, boy, you will become my bodyguard. I believe you shall make a very good one too." The old man winked and smiled. Then he strode smartly down the sloping street with Santi following happily behind.

Later that afternoon Don Fernando took Santi up to his personal chamber. He opened a dresser and withdrew a sword in its scabbard. He also pulled out a box. He handed the sword to Santi, then he opened the box and showed Santi a gleaming set of matchlock pistols.

"These shall be yours. I will teach you how to use them all."

Santi began taking lessons the very next week. His fencing teacher was Don Fernando himself with some help from Don Alonzo, the young captain of the local militia. Between the two men they imparted upon

Santi a style and grace that could not have been accessible to him under any other circumstances. He proved an able and versatile student.

The next few years turned out to be a time of profound transformation for Santi. As he became more adept at the deadly art in which he was being instructed he became more and more aware of the value of life. Every thrust, every parry carried with it the potential for death. He began to stay up nights pondering the startling reality of the power that Don Fernando was placing in his hands. He had never wielded such power. After all, it was the power of life and death! This preoccupation began to change his attitudes. He appreciated things in a different way. His relationship with his loved ones became more intense, more passionate. He was much slower to anger. His ability to hate mellowed into a stark realization of what such a powerful emotion could turn into if backed by the deadly skills he was quickly mastering.

Time flew by very quickly. By the early part of the year 1685, Santi had attained such proficiency with the foil that Don Fernando was able to claim: "Santi is easily one of the best fencers in the city!"

As he became more skilled, he grew more thoughtful, quieter still.

"What's wrong with him?" Luis whispered into Adriana's ear as she sat hemming a skirt one Saturday afternoon in late March.

"Oh, he's been like this for months. Sometimes he just stands there for hours staring out at the street."

Santi stood at the window. His mind was far away. He took no notice of their hushed comments. Luis walked briskly across the room and approached the immobile figure at the window.

"Hey, master swordsman, conquering knight, are you still in this world with us?"

Santi jumped, startled at the sudden intrusion into his reverie. He turned and smiled at his cousin. "Oh, Luis, forgive me... I fear I haven't been very good company. Here you finally find the time to spend the holiday with us and I am behaving like a ghost."

"Well, At least you recognize your error..." Laughed Luis good naturally. "Now, let's go for a walk and have a little man-to man talk..." He turned and winked at Adriana. "You don't mind do you honey? I'm just stealing him for a little bit."

"No, I don't mind at all..." Adriana answered beaming her heart-winning smile at the two young men. "Maybe you can wake him up a little." Santi smiled and nodded as Luis prodded him out the door.

Stevedores, their glistening dark skin rippling with tired muscles, shouldered huge loads of tobacco headed for Havana, and contraband rum and molasses headed out to the world market, and carried them along wooden gangplanks unto the waiting sailing vessels lined up in the harbor.

Luis and Santi walked along the waterfront quietly.

"You know, my cousin..." Santi finally said breaking the silence. "The priest down at the church tells us that God is merciful, and who am I to doubt the compassion of the Almighty? And yet, my cousin, I look around at the world we live in and I see so much injustice and pain. Those men there, I used to be one of them. Look at them. Their backs hurt, their muscles ache. At night they have little strength left even to love their wives!"

Luis smiled wryly.

"And yet, not twenty steps away fat men bedecked in the richest of finery stand and watch them at their toil."

Santi waved his hands at a group of wealthy merchants who stood near the docks overseeing the loading of their cargo.

"Santi, don't point at those men like that! They will know you are talking about them. Do you want a beating?" Luis whispered anxiously.

"Yes, yes, of course, we must not irritate our betters..." Santi slowly shook his head slowly looking down at the ground. "How merciful is a God that makes some men poor and unfortunate, who suffer all their lives without any hope and finally die in misery." Luis looked at Santi and exclaimed. "Do you realize that you are uttering blasphemy, Santi? Do you realize that your words are sinful?"

Santi closed his mouth. He kept silent for some time as they proceeded on their way.

Luis continued: "Santi, don't you understand that we come to this world to suffer, but if we are good we have the hope of eternal life after we die? After all, don't you remember what we have been told in church; we must shoulder the shameful legacy of our ancestor, Adam, the first sinner. We, as mortal men are cursed with his sin and must, as the Bible says, live from the sweat of our brow."

Santi stopped and again pointed in the direction of the wealthy merchants. "Those are mortal men also. They are also descendants of Adam, but I don't see any sweat on their brow. The black slaves holding parasols over their heads, shielding them from the sun are keeping them at a comfortable temperature, no sweat there!"

Luis reached quickly up and grabbed Santi's arms turning him and rushing him off. "Please, cousin, I beg you, don't point at those men anymore!" He looked nervously over his shoulder at the merchants as he hustled Santi away.

"I've been having dreams, Luis; disturbing dreams. I think I might be going crazy." Santi continued after a while. "I think God has already started punishing me. My mind is all twisted into knots. I don't know what's happening to me."

Luis looked at him and answered. "Maybe you are being tormented by demons from hell. I have heard of this kind of thing, it makes good men turn away from God."

"Maybe that's it." Santi agreed. And yet, deep in his heart he felt it was something much more complicated.

"Tell me your disturbing dreams, Santi." Luis requested placing his hands on his cousin's shoulder.

"Well..." Santi began thoughtfully. "I keep seeing an image of a beast, a hideous creature like a big shark-faced man. He seems to know me. He taunts me. And what's more frightening I feel I know him!"

"Yea just as I thought!" affirmed Luis triumphantly. "You are being possessed by a demon! All you need is a good cleansing and purging by a strong healer. That will chase this demon out of you." Santi looked at his cousin and nodded. "Maybe you're right, Luis. Maybe all I need is the services of a curandero, a peasant healer."

Luis and Santi walked back to the house in silence. On the following day Santi walked his cousin to the edge of town and waved him off on his way back to El Caney. Then he walked up to the small church where he heard mass every Sunday and confessed to a Spanish priest.

He walked home after serving a long penance and promising to carry out a heavy restitution imposed on him by the cleric. Deep down inside he knew he would never do it. His faith was faltering seriously and every nightmare-ridden night separated him one more step from the God he had believed in all his life. He trudged home morosely and retired.

He was still thinking disturbing thoughts three days later.

"I think there's gonna be a war here!" exclaimed Don Isidro, the healer as he pulled some herbs from his bag. "The local governor and landowners have been at odds with the big men in Havana for year over the illegal trade in Santiago, and all the smuggling that goes on here. If all this comes to blows I fear for young men like you who will likely be forced to fight!"

Santi watched in silence as the old man laid all sorts of ritual objects out upon a white cotton cloth that he had spread on the floor. Adriana sat and watched also from a corner of the room, next to her chair a pile of fabric awaiting cutting and sowing.

Santi no longer felt young. He was only twentyfour but his preoccupations and nightmares had aged his soul.

"What are you talking about, Don Isidro?" He asked the old man.

"It's these politicians, 'Lord So-and-so' demands that 'Duke This-n-that' relinquish command. 'Don Something-or-other' threatens 'Sir Something-Else' with an armed attack, and everybody's asking the king to arrest everybody else. It's all getting out of hand.

I know. My brother is a servant for one of the big fellows down at city hall. He keeps me informed on everything that is going on."

Santi was aware of some of the details pertaining to the local politics. His master, Don Fernando often hobnobbed with influential politicians. He often overheard their political conversations but never paid too much attention. His mind was usually distracted by his own personal problems.

Don Isidro finished setting up the things he had taken out of his bag. As he rose to his feet Santi recalled Doña Isabel and her words to him on the day that she read the sacred bones back in Banes.

Don Isidro approached the young man and said. "You say that you are tormented by dreams of a demon?"

Santi nodded "yes". "But it's more than that." He added. "I am always possessed by a sense of intense urgency, a feeling that I have something that I must accomplish. I feel like someone is out there somewhere expecting me to take some action, but I never know what that action is."

Santi looked away toward the window. A tear rolled down his cheek. "I am frustrated and filled with remorse and guilt..." He continued. "Every time I see the fellows working their backs raw down on the docks I ask myself what did I do to deserve being liberated from that horror? Why am I no longer one of them?"

Adriana listening quietly from the corner lowered her eyes sadly.

"Who makes these decisions: Who lives? Who dies? Who deserves to live in comfort? Who deserves to live in pain? Who is to be born a white master? Who is to be born a black slave, or a poor Indian peasant, or a rich city dweller, or a humble country farmer?

I often see a woman in my dreams. She is an Indian. She wears the old-fashioned white gowns that our women ancestors used to wear years ago when the Spaniards first began to force them to wear clothes. I feel this woman is related to me. But I can't tell who she is."

Santi turned to face the old man. "You see, it is very complicated. There are many questions I can not answer. Can you answer them for me? If these questions are not answered soon I fear I will go mad!"

Santi's large brown eyes gazed up pleadingly at the healer. Don Isidro stood motionless staring at him for a minute. Then he came over and sat down next to him.

"Son..." The old man began. "You don't need a cleansing...or a healing, or an exorcism, or any of that. What you need is a teacher."

Santi looked into the old man's greying eyes. "What do you mean, Don Isidro...a teacher?"

"Yes, son..." The healer continued. "You have a gift." Immediately Doña Isabel returned to Santi's thoughts. She had also told him that he had some sort of mysterious gift.

"No!" Santi screamed rising to his feet. "I don't need any teacher. I don't have any damned gift! I'm tired of all this pagan mumbo jumbo! What I need is a drink. That's what I need."

Don Isidro rose to his feet and Adriana covered her mouth with a gasp.

"I know what you're going through, my son..." Don Isidro called after Santi as he strode across the room to a cupboard.

"No you don't" Santi yelled reaching into the cupboard and retrieving a bottle of strong aguardiente molasses liquor. "No you don't..." He repeated. "No one knows what I'm going through. No one can see my own personal demons, no one feels my fear, my anxiety, not you, not her, not Luis, not even God himself, if he even exists!"

With that he uncorked the bottle and pulled a long anguished draught of liquor. Then bringing the bottle away from his lips he continued.

"Go, old man, Take all your things. Put them back in your bag and leave. I don't need you anymore. This will be my healing now!" He raised the bottle high.

Adriana covered her face and ran into the other room sobbing.

"Where are you going?" Santi called after her. "What's the matter, don't you like my medicine?" He took another drink.

"Santi, please don't..." The old man pleaded taking a step toward him.

"Stop, old man." Santi hissed at him. "Don't push me." He placed his hand threateningly on the hilt of the sword that hung at his side. The old man lowered his eyes sadly.

"Santi..." He said quietly. "Your destiny is inevitable. You will fight it, you will try to avoid it but it will catch up to you sooner of later. And when it does. You will have no choice but to embrace it."

Santi glared at the old healer and said. "Isidro, you are pushing your luck. Leave now while you're still in one piece!"

Don Isidro walked back across the room and began to gather up his things. Meanwhile, Santi finished the bottle. He rummaged through the cupboard for another.

When Don Isidro left, Santi stood at the door looking out after him. His heart hurt so badly that he was tempted to run the sharp blade of his sword through it himself to stop the pain.

He finished the second bottle and hurled it violently into the night. Then he staggered back in and sank unconscious into Adriana's cot.

The loud crowing of a rooster in the patio next door exploded in Santi's head like a cannon blast. He blinked his eyes open and was instantly overwhelmed by the painful brightness of the sunlight streaming in through the window. The rooster crowed again and Santi winced and groaned. He rose painfully.

"I'm going to kill and cook that cursed rooster!" he muttered holding his aching head and stumbling toward a basin of water that sat upon a small table by the window. He squinted and rubbed his eyes standing before the basin, and then he splashed water on his face. He reached up for a rag that usually hung from a peg by the basin but it was not there.

He looked around the room. "Where's the wash rag?" He croaked. Then he realized he was alone.

"Adriana..." He called going into the other room. "Adriana..." He gasped terrified emerging quickly from the empty bedroom and back into the living room. "Adriana! Adriana!" He screamed running out into the street.

People came out of their houses to look at him as he ran through the dusty avenues of the waterfront screaming her name at the top of his lungs. "Adrianaaaaaaa..." He called cupping his hands around his mouth. "Adrianaaaaa. Where are you? Adrianaaaaa..." He screamed over and over again until he was exhausted. He sank to the ground upon his knees and bent himself down low holding his head in his hands and burying his face into the dust. "Adriana, Adriana...please don't leave me..." He whimpered softly. "Please don't leave me...you're all I have left." He began to sob uncontrollably into the dust, his tears forming brown patches of mud on his face. "Adriana, please don't leave me..." He sobbed again gasping for breath. "Don't leave me...don't leave me... don't leave me..."

When people realized that the person curled up in the middle of the street like a madman was armed with a sword they shut their doors and bolted them tight. They peeped fearfully through their windows at him as he sobbed into the dust.

Then Santi felt the soft touch of a feminine hand upon his shoulder. He raised his face out of the dust, his eyes shut tight. Leaning his face to the side he rubbed his cheek on her arm. "Forgive me..." He whispered still sobbing. "I behaved like a cretin! I don't deserve you."

Then he opened his eyes and looked up into her face. Adriana took him by the hand and pulled him up. He rose and stood beside her.

"Let's go home." She said simply.

Adriana led Santi back to their little shack. He entered first and headed straight back toward his room, his head hanging in shame.

He reached the door into his chamber and extended his hand to part the heavy canvas curtain that acted as a door separating the two rooms. For years they had shared the same roof, Santi strictly respecting the girl's honor by sleeping in a different room.

"Santi..."

He stopped but didn't turn around, his hand frozen upon the half-parted curtain.

"Santi..." He heard her again, her voice mellow and husky. He turned to face her. Adriana stood by the window facing him. They stared at each other intently for what seemed an eternity. Santi could see the soft swells of the young woman's breast rising and falling rapidly as a single trickle of perspiration rolled down from her neck and disappeared into the hem of her neckline.

Adriana reached up slowly and drew the curtain of the window. Then she undid the knot of her scarf and dipped it into the wash basin that sat on the table next to her. She walked slowly across the room toward Santi.

He let go of the door partition curtain and turned to face her. She reached him and began to wipe the black streaks of dirt from his face, her sweet scent heavy on his nostrils. She wiped every grain of mud from his face. Then she transferred the wet scarf from his face to hers. With the corner of the scarf that still remained clean she began to wipe her own forehead, then her cheek, then she ran the wet scarf slowly down her neck.

Santi followed the progress of her slender hand as she moved the scarf down unto her breasts. Her head inclined backward slightly and she closed her eyes, then she squeezed the scarf tight. Cool trickles of water spread over the smooth tanned skin of her bosom. Santi leaned forward ever so slowly and pressed a gentle kiss on the moist skin.

Adriana dropped her scarf on the floor and placed her arms around Santi's neck. They sank slowly unto her cot just as the big bell in the cathedral began to toll the noon hour.

2. MOUNTAIN MAGIC

I awoke at 3:00 on the morning of August 18, 1982 to the sound of a distant dog barking. I crawled out of the tent and stretched. The trip was nearly over. We were very close to our destination. I began to think of Leni, my wife. In just a few days I would be back in her arms. I missed her.

In 1982 we were just six years into our marriage. In the last six years she had become ever so much more to me than just my wife. She was my friend, my partner in every crazy escapade I would think up. She was then, and is still to this day, even now after 39 years of marriage, fun to talk to, fun to be around and a confidant whose advice I often seek and usually pulls me through some tight spots.

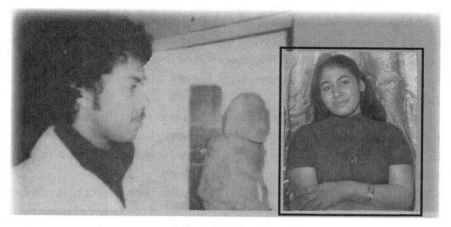

Miguel and Leni 1975

Leni also became a vital link between my cultural heritage and me.

Leni had played an influential role in the process through which I learned many of the folk traditions of Eastern Cuba. Her father, the son of Puerto Rican immigrants to Cuba, had grown up on a coffee farm near Maffo, in the mountainous countryside of the Sierra Maestra range. Growing up in the rural regions he had absorbed an enormous body of Cuban traditional lore, much of which was derived from the original Indian culture of times past, from the hunting and cooking of the wild Cuban goundhog, the jutia, to the proper time of the season for the agriculture of yuca. His Spanish was laced with hundreds of arcane Taino words which remain in common use among the peasants of the eastern mountains where he grew up. Her mother steeped in the folk tradition, had imparted upon her certain skills for spiritual cleansing and purifying. One of these ancient healing maneuvers, the "santiguo" bore an uncanny resemblance to a description given by the fifteen century Spanish chronicler Ramon Pane of an Indian ritual that he witnesses in the 1490's. When Leni taught it to me she grabbed my arms and tugged on them firmly, pulling and shaking them vigorously as if yanking something unclean from them. She turned me around, first in one direction then in the other. She spoke to me of something called "sobar", a procedure via which negative energies are rubbed out of the person by the vigorous rubbing of the surface of the body all in one direction from the head down to the feet. These things she had learned from her mother.

Although she was born in Cuba, my wife had been taken out of the country at a very early age. She was only five when her family moved to a predominately Puerto Rican neighborhood of Brooklyn, New York. There she grew up among the tenements of the big city, surrounded by the culture and tradition of the Barrio.

She had always felt very comfortable among the Puerto Ricans of Bedford Stuyveson and Spanish Harlem and perhaps even more so than the middle class Cubans who emigrated into New York after the victory of the 1959 Cuban Revolution.

She was very proud of her Cuban culture. But the aspect of that culture that she cherished was the simple rural tradition of her father's experience, not the competitive, aggressiveness that she saw in some of the urbanized Havanans that she met in the United States.

Sitting with her father, Don Israel, I learned the mentality of our Cuban farmers who lived in the countryside around Santiago and in the river valleys of the Sierra Maestra. When I was a child I used to travel through those rural areas I saw their palm-leaf-thatched shacks and their centuries-old farming techniques. Now, with Leni's dad I learned of their day-to-day concerns, their joys, their beliefs and their character. My experiences with Don Israel complemented much of what I had learned from my own father. Born of peasant guajiro stock, my father had absorbed the flavor of the countryside. Later his tenure as a newly graduated teacher among the peasants of rural Nuevo Mundo near Santiago, also brought him very close to the ways of the people.

Miguel and Leni 1998

I was thinking of Leni as I sat in the dark tent and took a swig of water from my canteen. I often thought of her whenever we were separated. I would feel the same sense of longing several years later when I visited Puerto Rico without her. The suddenness of my uncle's death right after our big Harmonic Convergence celebration did not allow us to make the proper preparations for the whole family to travel, so I had to go alone.

And so on that occasion also I found myself missing her and wishing for her company.

It was on that, my first visit to Puerto Rico, that I found myself thinking about Leni's Boricua ancestors as I maneuvered the vinyl-wrapped steering wheel of the rented Chevy. A strong air-conditioning unit in the car chilled the interior of the vehicle to a bearable level while I drove through the haze of the noonday tropical heat.

I negotiated the killer switchback turns of the narrow Puerto Rican country roads with the greatest of care, always apprehensive that some local "Mario Andretti" might appear suddenly around the next curve at 60 miles per hour. I had already had several hair-raising near misses and was in no mood to take any chances.

I was filled with a kind of heaviness. I had cherished the little silver medal that I had acquired from Eddie's girlfriend for over a year now. I had worn it on August 17,1987 and it had transformed my experience at Harmonic Convergence. I sensed a deep vacuum in my soul now after having buried it, and yet I felt no regret. Eddie's words had been clear. He had requested me to take the beautiful little object to what he called "the Indian village," near his hometown of Utuado.

"You will know what to do with it when you get there." He had said. And I did! As I knelt there before the central stone in the middle of the ancient circle of boulders I knew that I had to bury the little medal under the annatto tree. I didn't know why, but I got a clear message to do it. There was no doubt about it. I had to do it!

I turned on the car radio as I maneuvered around another petrifying mountain curve. The welcome strains of a traditional Puerto Rican "seis chorreao" tune lifted some of the heaviness from my insides.

The fine traditional Puerto Rican music could always be counted upon to provide me with inspiration for new songs, songs that would eventually form part of the repertoire of a salsa music band "Guaracha" which I would form a couple of years in the future. As it turned out, by the end of the 1980's and the beginning of the 1990's once our band had started to become known in the city, our lively dance music would gain a certain amount of popularity in Pittsburgh, and much of our repertoire would be composed of music based on Cuban and Puerto Rican traditional rhythms much like the one playing on the radio at that moment.

I was headed back to Utuado. I had an appointment to keep. Earlier that day as I sat in the modest living room of Eddie's Utuado relatives a curious old woman had knocked at the door. Eddie's mother rose from the table where we were all sitting. She walked to the door and spoke to the old woman in hushed tones. I could not make out the content of the conversation over the voices of those who were sitting about me at the table. When the old woman left, Eddie's mother returned to her chair and lifted a cup of coffee with milk to her lips, nodded toward the departing visitor.

"That old lady is Doña Celina. She is a medium, espiritista…a seer." Said Doña Amalia, Eddie's mom. "She wants to talk to you when you come back from Caguana."

My visit at the home of Eddie's mom that morning had actually not been a very pleasant one. The main topic of conversation during my brief stay there before setting out for Caguana was, of course, his recent incarceration in Pennyslvania. I knew that it would be incredibly difficult for his mother to visit him from Puerto Rico so her mood was, for the most, part deeply depressed. Nevertheless she managed somehow to set aside her sadness to give me good directions to the Caguana archeological site and to make sure that I knew about her friend's interest in talking to me after my visit there.

Now I drove back from the magical old mountain shrine of the Taino native spirit, Ata-Bei. As I drove I burned with curiosity at what the old woman wanted with me. I still vibrated with the intense magic of the sacred boulder that I had touched while I was inside the mystic uterine hoop of stones of the holy site, the conversation with my dead grandmother's spirit. And so, even as I drove now, enjoying the beautiful Puerto Rican music, my mind was actually focused on what I had just experienced. We believe that the old Taino settlement had been built and dedicated to Ata-bei's Love Spirit manifestation. We call this entity "Kaguana" the compassionate, creative, maternal patroness of affection.

Near the old archeological site I had discovered a little shop owned by a local artist who specialized in Indian crafts. His name is Miguel Guzman. His store was filled with plaster cast replicas of the most famous Taino carvings. I had entered the shop before starting back to Utuado. In the store I met this artist. He turned out to be one of the most remarkable men I had ever encountered. We talked for hours. Then he surprised me by giving me a beautiful replica of one of those three-pointed Taino Indian spirit statues that represents Ioka Hu, the Spirit of life. He called it the "Mountain Cemi", and pointed out the similarity between the shape of the conical figurine and the mountain that fronts the Caguana site. Now the figurine lay next to me on the front passenger seat of the car as I inched my way back to the little town to keep my appointment with Doña Celina. The sculpture of the "Mountain Cemi" was something of a consolation for the loss of Eddie's little medal, since this plaster statue represented the spirit of Light and Life. Eddie's silver talisman was a spiritual metaphor for this solar spirit, so I lost one solar spirit and then immediately gained another. It was as if I had traded one effigy of the sacred spirit for an equally powerful one.

Miguel Guzman is an artist that expresses his
Taino heritage in paintings and sculptures

Miguel Guzman called the sculpture "MOUNTAIN
CEMI" because it resembled the mountain that is
visible from the sacred site of Caguana

Miguel Guzman gave me a plaster replica of the Mountain Semi

My trip back to the home of Eddie's folks felt long and tortuous, but finally I arrived in front of their little whitewashed country house. Inside, Doña Celina was already there, waiting for me.

Eddie's mother still looked very depressed. She introduced the old woman to me and then walked away toward the kitchen. I knew she was sobbing. I felt sorry for her, and not a little angry at Eddie for putting such an obviously kind person through this type of hell.

Doña Celina nodded politely to me from where she sat at the sofa. Eddie's mother re-emerged with a pot of coffee and a platter of Puerto Rican "pastelito" pastries. She sat down next to her old friend with another cup of coffee. Doña Celina sipped her coffee in silence for a while. Eddie's mom just sobbed and wiped her eyes with a handkerchief. Then Doña Celina turned to me and said: "How long have you been working with the ancient traditions?" I assumed that maybe Eddy's mom had filled her in on my background as they waited for me.

"Oh, I've been celebrating Full Moon ceremony with my group since 1982." I answered.

She looked hard into my eyes. "How did you learn the traditions?"

I explained how I had encountered my guardian spirit during my vision quest, how I had been taught the lesson of the great giving beast. I told her of my journeys in the Spirit realm, my visions and dreams, and the enlightened teachings of my parents and Leni's parents and Don Federico, and the other elders from whom I had gotten my guidance and advice and education.

Doña Celina listened attentively. Then she leaned back in her chair and closed her eyes. I looked at her for a while. Then I looked up at Eddie's mother, Doña Amalia. She smiled sadly at me and nodded dabbing her eyes again with her moist handkerchief.

When I looked back at Doña Celina she had her eyes open and was staring at me.

"There is something missing in your life...." She told me.

I was totally puzzled by her remark.

"Uh...?" I grunted quizzically.

"You don't know it but there is an important message that has been kept hidden from you for several years. I have been chosen to reveal it to you."

I began to think the old woman was pulling my leg. Maybe she was trying to run some kind of a scam. But she had not mentioned money so I couldn't figure out what it could be.

"Close your eyes, now..." She commanded me. I went along with her game there because I was curious.

"You took a trip sometime back, right?"

At first I was confused by her words. "Yea, of course..." I said. "I had to take an airplane ride to get here from Pennsylvania..."

"No, no, no, silly not that trip...I mean a boat trip, a trip on the water."

I opened my eyes and stared at her in astonishment, my mouth dropped open. I had not told Doña Amalia anything about my canoe trip with Sven in 1982.

"Close your eyes again..." She said sternly, "You must concentrate!"

Again I closed my eyes.

"You took many days to complete your trip. During that time you dreamed. You dreamed every night of that time..."

I knew she was talking about my canoe ride with Sven.

"And you can't remember any of the dreams." She finished.

I sat there with my eyes closed in front of the old woman and realized she knew some pretty intimate aspects of my river journey that she had no business knowing.

I opened my eyes again and asked her, "How do you know all that?"

"Never mind that..." She answered. "Close your eyes, and don't open them anymore."

I closed my eyes again and listened for her next instruction. "I sense there is someone who wants to talk to you."

I kept my eyes closed tight and listened. "Now you must concentrate as hard as you can because I want you to visualize that person."

I didn't know quite what to do so I leaned back in my chair and relaxed. When I did that I began to see a figure in the darkness of my closed eyes. I concentrated on the hazy image, amazed. It was so blurry that I could not make out any more than a white blob with the general contour of a human being. Then the image began to sharpen, very slowly, ever so excruciatingly slowly! I struggled to bring the image into focus. I did.

I began to make out a woman, young and tanned, her black hair tumbling like a raven waterfall about her shoulders. She wore a white gown decorated with intricate patterns that had been methodically appliqued unto it in braided cording.

I studied the image intently. I realized I had seen her before, in my dreams on the river trip, yes, but also on another occasion. It was the day I went to the lake with Heaven Gazer. She was the girl who had appeared floating before me in the water the day I had my terrifying vision in Heaven Gazer's car. She had come between me and the dark threatening fog that was emitted by the malevolent naked shark-woman.

Now the young woman was back, standing before me in the darkness of my closed eyes. She smiled at me and began to speak:

"Do not be frightened, I am a spirit from your distant past." My heart began to pound with excitement.

"I come to you now because there is much I must tell you..." She continued, "First I have images I must share with you. I must share with you the Journey of the Five Suns."

With these words she began to fade into the darkness, then there was bright sunshine. The scene had changed to a dreamlike vision of a primordial landscape. I saw a distant band of primitive nomads moving across a broad cold tundra. The men carried spears as they walked wrapped in furs. They toted heavy sacks.

The women bore babies in slings strapped to their shoulders, or pulled little children along by the hand as they walked. Beyond them on the horizon dark storm clouds swirled threateningly over a forbidding glacier.

"This is the origin..." The young woman's voice floated above the scene.

"It is the beginning of the human story, small bands of hunters and collectors of wild plant foods."

Then the scene changed. I saw before me a dimly lit cave. In the flickering firelight a man ran his fingertips accros his bare chest, smearing them with the thick black vegetable-mineral and deer-fat paste that these people covered their bodies with during the insect season. They used this stuff to protect themselves from biting tundra black flies which literally swarmed during the mild-weather months and which could easily deprive any particular human being of practically pints of blood within minutes.

The wild caribou that these people hunted relieved themselves from the torment of the flies by travelling out into the colder regions of the tundra or taking long dips in cold water pools and rivers. But the people used their body paint, and that was what this man was removing from his chest at this moment as I watched.

Then he did something unexpected. He turned around and began to smear the black paste deftly over certain areas on the surface of the cave wall. The man had discovered that he could alter the appearance of certain random stains and marks that existed naturally on the rocky surface, marks that his highly imaginative mind noticed even as they were totally overlooked by others in the group. These random marks suggested images of familiar things to him, animals, people and objects. But the images were often incomplete. He felt compelled to complete them, and the black protective body lotion provided a convenient medium. He smeared the thick black paint over specific areas of the wall, accenting certain aspects of the naturally appearing stains, making them look more like the forms he originally saw in them. If a particular stain or rock discoloration suggested the head of a caribou, he completed the image of the animal and added the eyes and muzzle details to the face. Other members of the band watched and marvelled at what, to them, must have seemed like the most powerful magic, the emergence of a wondrous image from a collection of random marks. The first artist created something that had never existed before, and from a utilitarian item that had been created to protect people from biting flies he wrought a new and extraordinary means for the soul to communicate. From the available primitive technology he wrought something novel and wonderful.

I was witnessing the birth of Art, the medium of communication that humans all over the world learned to use to share elements of their spiritual experience that could never have been expressed before. By taking the existing common-place technology and ordinary behavior of the time and using it for a purpose other than what it had been intended those early humans created a revolution of the soul. With their fingers, they learned to pluck and twang strings of bows originally created to shoot arrows and kill game animals, transforming instruments of death into instruments of music. They modified patterns of common speech used to transmit ordinary conversation, and created beautifully crafted poetry that inspired the heart. They altered and stylized ordinary every-day body motions and transformed them into the beauty of dance and drama.

But I was also witnessing something else. Yes, I indeed was witnessing the first successful attempts by humans to accurately express and share the most intimate aspects of the human soul. And this could not be done previous to the invention of the Arts.

At the same time I was witnessing nothing short of the actual birth of spiritual expression itself. Only through this powerful new medium did humans first find an effective manner to experience the Divine as a group. Within the communal experience provided by the group participation in music, dance, drama, scupture, painting, poetry and the other arts, human beings were given the power to manifest themselves as trully spiritual beings.

Artists became the first spiritual guides, the first medicine men and women. This fact is most eloquently expressed in the image of a small group of Ice Age hunter-gatherers huddled around a fire in a cave. Impressive murals of expertly painted animals literally dance all around them upon the cave walls in the shifting flicker of the flames, moving to the rhythm of drums, rattles and vocal intonations, in unison with a masked medicine man and medicine woman who sport deer antlers on their heads and who, through expert dance moves, dramatize a fertility ritual as the congregation sways their bodies back and forth clapping their hands.

This was all happening at the beginning of the First Sun, of the Great Cycle of the Evolution of Human Consciousness, about 260 centuries ago. The First Sun lasted 5200 years and during those centuries the people developed the wonderful new medium to a magnificent degree. The images revealed to me by the specter continued to unfold there before me. I saw the development of Art as it went hand in hand with an increased spiritual apppreciation for the creative, propagating power of Mother Earth in collaboration with the energizing spirit of Father Sky, to support and nurture humanity. The fact of the importance of the Great Mother in these people's lives was expressed in the ancient art and was manifested in the production of sculptural images of spiritual females, sometimes in the shape or pregnant or matronly women, epitomized in a carving now popularly called "Venus of Willendorf". These objects reflected the devotion of those early people for the Great Mother of all.

And then I was allowed to witness the setting of the First Sun. The first period of 5200 years was finished.

And then I looked on as the Second Sun dawned, and the transpiring of another 5200 years took place. And the people continued to develop the medium, perfecting their painting, their sculpture, their dance and music, their singing, and drama, and placing these at the service of the community as they travelled through time and space, organized as tribes and hunter bands travelling over great expanses of territory with the ever-present backdrop of the Ice-Age glaciers always forming a vital element of their reality. Art, expressing images of sacred animals and occult messages of mysterious fertility themes, became the great healer, the accent in the life of each individual. Presented with infinite virtuosity on the walls of caves, in the medium of sculped clay and bone, and in the crafting of body adornments and jewelry, Art became the hallmark of the spiritual guide and the medicine men and women always in service of Mother Earth as well as Father Sky, in balance, and in the service of the community. The intimate effervescence of the aesthetic soul ruled supreme and dictated the minutest aspects of daily life.

And then, after the transpiring of approximately 10,400 years since the beginning of the Great Cycle, people saw the setting of the Second Sun and the rising of the Third Sun, a third period of 5,200 years. And then things began to change. During the mid portion of the Third Sun period the great ice sheets began to melt and receed. Huge expanses of territory previously covered in ice gradually became available to the people and the change in climate created opportunities that had not been available before. The people began to domesticate plants and animals in areas that had never been accessible before and under new climate conditions which were conducive to cultivation. The development and evolution of Art and mystical artistic tradition sustained the people spiritually throughout this new phase in their cultural evolution. By the end of the Third Sun, another 5200 years later, the people had firmly established a course via which the majority of the human species would become settled into permanent stationary villages and towns, and dependant on the cultivation of plants and the herding of animals. I saw the artist-magicians change and adapt to the new way of life. I saw the spiritual guides adopt new traditions and new forms to practice their vital techniques, and throughout all of this the spirit of the Great Mother was still venerated along with the spirit of Father Sky, and the people lived within the timeless equilibrium that their sacred art afforded to their lives.

The Third Sun set and the Fourth Sun rose and, as I watched, with the rise of the Fourth Sun began to rise also the origins of a great mental transformation which would impact humanity in extraordinary ways. Now the scholars call this period of time "The New Stone Age". The specter of my ancestor showed me images that illustrated that remarkable moment in the human story.

As the living things that these people were domesticating became common-place and household posessions, the mystery and mystic character of their being became blurred in the minds of some individuals. Certain people began to lose the sacred respect that they had always held for animals and plants and so to some, these became nothing more than mere property items. Familiarity bred contempt and so, for many people, the ancient mystery and magic seemed to leave them.

At the same time, the ease with which plant and food domestication allowed people to accumulate excess resources created an interest in further accumulation, and then excess accumulation and hoarding in an attempt to totally eliminate the possibility of famine or want. Excessive hoarding and accumulation of goods inevitably led to jealousy and greed, and the need to protect accumulated goods from those who would attempt to take them by force. People began transforming common-place utilitarian objects such as hoes and sickles into lances and swords, weapons to be used either in the stealing or for the protection of goods and land.

Those who succeeded in effectively stealing and/or protecting their surplus goods became extremely wealthy and powerful. This fact allowed them to also exert power over other people who needed what they possessed. Ruling hierarchies developed based on the ability to accumulate, protect and control resources, and the ability to pass these benefits from one generation to another. The mighty began to perceive themselves as naturally better and more worthy than those who were not as powerful. The leaders who were in control of the resources were transformed from guides and protectors into tyrants and oppressors. The sacred artists, the holy people, were hard-pressed to maintain the old tradition of equilibrium within the societies.

Then the strong leaders, who tended to be men, realized that a powerful, compassionate, nurturing female Mother deity was not useful to further their agenda. As the war-lords that they were, they needed strong male war-gods to define their spiritual experience, to lead them in battle and assist them in winning bloody turf-conflicts. They began a concerted program of purging the traditional spiritual system of as much of the Cosmic Mother's culture as they possibly could. I watched with interest as the specter showed me how these men invented new mythologies within which ancient maternal spirits were transformed into demons, and raised the male gods to the level of omnipotent divine creator patriarchs. The human female spiritual guides and medicine women were persecuted, murdered and, in many cases, exterminated. And the shrines to the Divine Mother were overthrown.

The strongmen and war-lords began to coerce the sacred artists into creating images and producing poetry, music and dance which glorified their male gods and their selfish, egotistical agenda. Many centuries later the ancient Mayaswould learn to identify this transition into tyranny as the rise of a splendidly regal mythical monarchic entity called "SEVEN MACAW".

The nature of sacred Art changed gradually during the Fourth Sun cycle. By the time that the Fourth Sun set, after another period of 5200 years, the whole character of Art had been transformed. For the vast majority of the human population on the Earth, every image, every song glorified the new order of things, the new gods, the new dictators.

For the majority of humanity the Great Mother in her ancient identity as the divine creative force had been severely demoted within the sacred pantheon and the status of women as a whole had been erroded dramatically. Art transitioned from a sacred medium of soul communication into base propaganda, officially sponsored commercials that advertised the way people ought to think, ought to eat, ought to buy, ought to worship, ought to live.

The reign of the legendary Seven Macaw was to be established firmly at the end of the Fourth Sun and he was to rule supreme during the entire length of the Fifth Sun. This was to be the last 5200 years of the Great Cycle, the sun that rose around the year 3114 B.C. and set in the year 2012. This is the Sun period in which I was born.

In the vision that was unfolding before me, during this tragic period of human history, this Fifth Sun, I witnessed the growth of great conquering empires ruled by a long line of dictatorial ego-maniacs, supported by lethal military systems, Asurbanipal, Xerses, Ramses, Caesar, Ghengis, Napoleon, Hitler. And behind the power of these single-minded despots stood rank after rank of media manipulators, artists whose task had been perverted and transformed from the creation of divine art to the production of crass propaganda promoting the tyrants and the war-gods of the tyrants, and the way of life that the tyrants required of those under their control. The images produced by these new artists were emblazoned upon the walls of the temples of the new war-gods. They replaced the sacred mystical images that had graced the walls of the ancient primordial caves. Eventually over the centuries the media manipulators would evolve, along with the progress of technology, into the masters of imagery like the ones in the Madison Avenue advertizement agencies. At the service of the modern-day political and commercial empires these contemporary-era magicians have the capacity to persuade thousands of people to support hypocritical politicians whose interests are completely at odds with their own and to spend millions of their hard-earned dollars to buy products that are harmful to their health in order to enrich multimillionaires that don't care whom they harm.

At the very beginning of the Fifth Sun, art suffered the ultimate transition into darkness. Until that time one of the most defining characteristics of Art as a sacred medium of communication for the human soul was that, after an artist had produced a work of art, others were left with the option to interpret the art through their own personal filters, each person understanding the art in his or her own way with the help of ancient traditional culture and tradition.

But that was just too ambiguous for the great lords of negativity who were rising to rule the vast majority of humankind. In their minds they could not allow any equivocation to exist in regard to the message they wished to convey to their subjects. Common people could not be allowed to interpret the message in their on way. These rulers assigned to their artist collaborators the most perverted task of their sad history of tasks. They were to take the propagada images which they had already created and they were to modify them and craft from these images a set of symbols that could represent specific sounds of the spoken word. That way, actual words could be represented and thus the lords could literally "speak" to their subjects via visual symbols. By doing this, they birthed a new medium of communication, one which would not leave anything to the imagination, a message with no ambiguity. This was to be a message that would express the will of the monarchs, word-by-word, literally. The message was invariably "How great I am", "What marvelous things I have accomplished with the assistance and protection of my war-god", 'this is how you, my subjects should live and think", and "This is how you, my subjects, are to render tribute to me".

And so the imaginative artists of the Fith Sun era invented writing and became the first scribes. And the new art was named "hieroglyphics" (the chronicles of the priviledged ones). We now recognize this as the beginning of creating a written record of events known as "history". But given the fact that this "history" was almost invariably manipulated to reflect the assumed greatness of those men who comissioned its recording, it has come to be known in the English language by the famous play of words "History". History, it is said, is always written by the victors. The magicians of the Fifth Sun period, with their power of propaganda, became experts at convincing the people to believe almost anything their masters wanted them to believe.

The Fifth Sun period of human consciousness evolution which began roughly 5200 years ago with the invention of writing and the firm establishment of Seven Macaw on his lofty perch atop the CosmicTree was to be the last period of the great 260-century cycle that started way back in the Ice Age with the florescence of Art. The new art magicians of the Fifth Sun period eventually evolved into the modern Madison Avenue advertising geniuses who can sell practically anything their masters order them to sell to the masses. Some now have assigned a new nickname to these magician advertizing men, these "ad men" of Madison Avenue. They call them the "Mad Men".

At that point in my vision the spectral woman exclaimed:
"The wise elders of the Maya civilization came to certain profound realizations that implied these facts that I am showing you, via their powerful medicine dreams and the articulation of their sacred calendars, and they shared them with our Taino ancestors who were their close geographic neighbors. Their sacred studies alerted them to the arrival of a time at the end of the Fifth Sun period when humanity would experience a moment of opportunity. This moment was predicted to manifest around the year 2012, the precise end-point of the Fifth Sun, and also the end-point of the huge 260-century, five-sun cycle. This is when the story of the human consciosness would circle around and would arrive at a point very similar to what it had been back at the beginning of that great cycle in the Ice Age." As I realized earlier, this point was indeed the conclusion of the fifth and final 5200-year period, the setting of the Fifth Sun. It was also scheduled to mark the beginning of a whole new five-Sun cycle with the initiation of a whole new First Sun, just like back in the Ice-Age. And just like back at the beginning of that previous First Sun, humans would again have to use the common-place available technology at their disposal

and completely circumvent the "Mad Men" to invent a whole new Art for the expression of the human spirit, a People's Art, for the sake of People.

As I watched spell-bound and absorbed all of these revelations that were being unfolded before me I came to realizations of my own, based on things that I had learned about Maya traditional thinking from my father back in the 1960's. That introduction into the mystical thought of the ancient Meso Americans, followed later by more in-depth study of this ancient wisdom from actual Maya elders from Mexico and Guatemala, eventually, over the years, confirmed the accuracy of the messages that I received from the spectral woman dressed in white up there in Doña Amalia's living room that afternoon, high in the central mountains of Boriken.

As I sat there on the couch across from Doña Celina, I also began to realize how relevant this message was to my own personal story. The demonic shark-faced entity who was haunting my life, who was dogging the steps of my family line since all the way back in the times of Caoba and Sagua and Cobo, this entity of discord that was so closely identified with resentment, greed, jealousy, bitterness, vengefulness, and above all, intolerance. This manifestation of the energy of Seven Macaw, was not always an enemy that would attack from the outside. It had roots in the distant past of the human experience and in fact it lives deep in the heart of every human. That is why he had warned that there was no way that he could be fully exorcized. So I asked myself. Is it even possible to defeat my enemy? Could I ever trully win?

The prophecy of Guaricheanao spoke of a special child who was born of the ancient Shell Lady, Ata Bei, the Cosmic Matriarch of my ancestors. This child was a manifestation of Ioka Hu, the lord of Life and Energy, who was also the spirit of hope. Yes, Hope, He was the Hope Child. During the five centuries of anticipation from the arrival of Columbus in the Caribbean to the year 1992 this Hope Child was manifested in the little infant at the hip of the female icon that was left to the Indians of Cueiba by the Spanish conquistador, Ojeda on that fateful day in the early 1500's.

Then the specter began to speak to me again:

"The Hope Child bears the potential for reconciliation; between peoples, between men and women, between people and animals, between humanity and the sacred Earth Mother upon which you live, and ultimately between each human being and his or her own soul. The Hope Child holds

286

the key to the ultimate victory that you seem to feel is so inaccessible right now.

The time draws close. It is the time of the Shift of Ages. New attitudes and new perceptions have been incubating for decades, hidden, subtle, unnoticeable, and are now ready to hatch, to blossom and come to fruition. The YEAR ONE of the new era, 2012 will soon be here. It is the time for paradigm shift, the time for transition. That transition is happening on a macroscopic global level as humans all over the world again begin to use the available technology and common-place usages of the every-day in new and unexpected ways, just like they did back in the Ice Age.

From those elements of practical life they are forging a new medium of communication for the soul, a new Art. This will again be a "PEOPLE'S ART", no longer the art of the Mad Men, at the service of the lords of negativity who have controlled the majority of us since the beginning of the Fifth Sun. With this new "PEOPLE'S ART" they will re-enact the great drama of the rising of the First Sun.

The end of the Fifth Sun is indeed the end of the Great Cycle, the end of the reign of Seven Macaw. And it is now time for a new First Sun, a new Great Cycle, and a new 260 centuries. The technology of the new millenium is providing humanity with a brand new cave wall upon which they will paint their new dreams and aspirations, to provide the back-drop in front of which they can sing their new songs, dance their new dances and recite their new poetry."

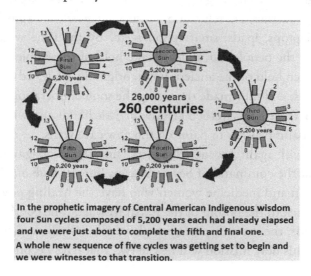

In the prophetic imagery of Central American Indigenous wisdom four Sun cycles composed of 5,200 years each had already elapsed and we were just about to complete the fifth and final one.
A whole new sequence of five cycles was getting set to begin and we were witnesses to that transition.

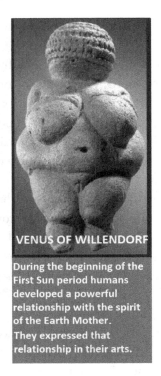

VENUS OF WILLENDORF

During the beginning of the First Sun period humans developed a powerful relationship with the spirit of the Earth Mother. They expressed that relationship in their arts.

Now, as I sit here writing all this, all these years later, I think of this time that we are all living. I think how excited we were when we celebrated the birth of the new First Sun on December 21st 2012. I know that she was refering to the technological media which had originally been created to enslave us further, via television, radio, and later the explosion of the computer, laptops, ipads, smart phones etc. By the time we celebrated the new Sun the people did, indeed, take hold of these objects like they had once taken hold of the ancient bows, originally designed for shooting killing arrows, and they made them sing the song of liberation. They were now holding these items in their creative artistic hands and wielding them like virtual paint brushes to paint on the new cave walls.

"There will again be sacred artists, not the propaganda-crafting Mad Men at the command of Seven Macaw, but the true magicians, the medicine men and medicine women who have the healing power to lead the people back to the bosom of the Earth Mother." She continued. "And in their hands, the most important tools which will allow them to move forward on this holy mission will be the two that have become evident to you several times in your personal experience, the sharp vigorous sword of determination and the compassionate, productive sea-shell of creativity.

These are the only weapons that you will need against your enemy. Just as the primogenitress, with her steadfast sea-cliff will, filled herself with determination and gave birth to the First, Second, Third, Fourth and Fifth Sun, so you and your fellow humans must give birth to this new era of Hope. You must also fill yourself with determination and creativity to conclude the twenty-four generation prophecy.

When the sacred clay statue of Ata Bey imaged as a pregnant woman disappeared from the altar in the Indian village of Cueiba 500 years ago the people were promised an interim symbol that would represent that same mother with her child already out of her womb and at her hip. And that new image came to them in the form of the little statue up in that chapel in El Cobre. Now, after 500 years, that child has come of age and has mainfested himself to you in the form of the plaster statue you have brought back from Caguana. He is the great Hope Child, the Majestic Spirit of Reconciliation, who was born in my time, and has finally come of age now, in your time. He is the great gift of the Earth Mother to your people and to all humanity. You must herald him in and enthrone him in his rightful position as master of history. He is the ultimate manifestation of Ioka-Hu, sitting on the passenger seat of your rented vehicle outside this house even as we speak. It is the primordial statue of the mountain cemi."

I remembered at that moment the little sculpture that Miguel Guzman had given me at his store earlier that day. She was right, of course. The carving was indeed sitting on the passenger seat of the rented Chevy parked outside.

The vision of the young woman then began to move. She stooped and picked up a stone from the ground, "Now I shall form the sacred circle." She said.

She took four large stones and placed them at the positions of the four directions, the South, the West, the North, and the East. Then she began to connect these four large stones with a circular line of smaller stones. She created a circumference that encompassed the four larger ones around the hoop of the smaller ones. As she picked up each stone she counted it. Having already laid down the original four stones she only needed twenty-four more to complete the circle of twenty-eight stones. This circle symbolizes the number of days in the fertility period of the moon, the period of days that manifests itself both in the cosmic womb of Ata bei, the Earth Mother and in the human wombs of earthly women. She counted each stone and called it a "Generation". "You are generation number one..." She exclaimed as she picked up the first stone. "You are generation number two..." her sweet voice declared as she picked up the second stone. "And you are generation number three...and you, number four, and you are number five." She continued counting the stones until her circle was completed.

Then she looked up at me as she stood in the middle of the sacred hoop she had created. "I am the spirit of your ancestor. I represent the beginning of the twenty-four-generation phase, the begining of the last 500 years of the Fifth Sun. You represent its end. You must take up the shell and the sword that has been passed down from hand to hand to your time.

In 1992 the 500-year period initiated by Columbus will end, and with it, his legacy shall cease to be relevant. A new legacy will arise. Your people will experience a rebirth and the guamo shall again be heard in the mountain announcing the sacred areyto. Then the 20-year count-down to the great Shift of Ages shall begin. It will last from 1992 to 2012, a Maya "katun", a sacred period of twenty years which will culminate in the gradual initiation of the new First Sun. After that, in the initial years of the new First Sun, the years 2013, 2014, 2015 and so on, the work of the warriors will begin, to struggle out of the old paradigm and into the new one. It will not be an easy task. During this period the forces of Seven Macaw will put up a fight. It will be a brutal struggle between the backward looking forces of negativity and convention that wish to keep humanity imprisoned in the Fifth Sun paradigm and the forces of progressive forward movement that wish to lead humanity toward a new paradigm which will create a new First Sun, placing the power of the magic back in the hands of the people.

I heard her words and a great emotional stirring of my soul brought tears to my eyes. I resolved at that moment to bring together the wisdom that had been imparted to me by my teachers and by the great human visionaries whose messages are a guiding light for the 20-year journey that lay ahead. I resolved to learn from the experience of Harmonic Convergence. Whole shifts in global mentality must be completed. Hot spots of old antiquated, obsolete, non-conciliatory attitudes and behavior, and colonized mindsets must be stamped out. This is all to be done as we assist the Earth in emerging from the last blazing gasps of a generations-old forest fire. The destructive fire has consumed enough vital human energy and creativity. It is time to put it out once and for all!

There is an arsonist in our midst, an enemy who wishes to re-ignite the forest. He is a deadly enemy, a reflection of Seven Macaw himself. We must be courageous enough to do battle with an enemy that can manifest within ourselves. This great enemy is a product of our own weaknesses. It is a manifestation of our own self-destructive tendencies. It is a construct made up of the basest of our inclinations.

She read my thoughts and added: "You must learn the powerful mountain magic of Hope, and chant the Hope-Child to power, dance him awake. Arouse him with the sacred colors of the magic art. Invoke him with the sacred poetry. Empower him through the mystical drama."

Then the bright specter raised her hands slowly and made a majestic gesture in the air. Immediately I began to recall the series of dreams I had experienced on my canoe trip. Astonished, I watched Caoba and Sagua as they made good their escape from the hacienda. I recognized Caoba and realized that she was the young woman whose specter now stood before me. As she stood there, the events depicted in my 1982 Allegheny River dreams unfolded all around her.

I witnessed the birth of her son Cobo, Cobo's life-long obsession with the little statue of the Virgin, his descent from the remote mountains that had sheltered his childhood and his move to my native city of Santiago when it was nothing but a small colonial town. I watched him grieve the death of his violated daughter. I contemplated the raising up of his grandson and Cobo's eventual arrival at an advanced old age. I saw him finally find the object of his life-long obsession, the little statue. I watched him set her on a wooden platform and place her in the storm-agitated waters of Nipe Bay. I witnessed his death, the maturation of his grandson and the birth of his grandson's daughter, Elena. I shared her terror as a result of the awful pirate attack. I watched her fall in love with the irreverent black fishmonger. I watched them move to Banes where she gave birth to Santi. I watched Santi grow up to become the manservant of the rich merchant, Don Fernando, and transform into one of the ablest swordsmen in the city. I watched the gut-wrenching spiritual turmoil that this newfound skill created in his soul. I witnessed with interest the culmination of his relationship with the young seamstress, Adriana. Ultimately, I watched them recite their wedding vows before Father Ricardo Molina.

3. LOSS

Father Molina used a frilly white handkerchief that he had produced from his big sleeve to mop up the large beads of sweat forming upon his forehead as he stood in the noon heat in his long, hot, black cassock and starched surplice. Santi looked over at Adriana. She radiated with joy in a beautiful lace veil that she had made herself. Her simple peasant dress shone white in the rays of sunshine cascading in through the window of the little parish church. Santi stood patiently, his broad-brimmed hat clutched tightly in his hands as the old priest read incomprehensible streams of Latin from a book of Roman Catholic liturgy. Finally the moment came for the priest to pronounce the young couple "husband and wife". His heart beat rapidly when he accepted his new responsibility as Adriana's husband.

The noisy marriage procession drew curious neighbors out of their houses along the streets that led from the church to Santi and Adriana's home. Musicians hired by Doña Leonor played multi-stringed mandolas, a brass trump and a drum as loudly as they could while they marched ahead of the newlyweds. The little procession of friends and relatives walked behind them, a disorganized mob chattering and laughing among themselves all the way to the house.

There was cheap aguardiente liquor, and plenty of fresh food at Santi and Adriana's little house as the celebration spread across the whole blocked-off and garishly decorated street. Relatives and other guests sat in wooden chairs along the length of an interminable, improvised table that had been set up at the edge of the curb, and reached from one cross-steet corner to the other, occupying the whole block. And later as the sun began to set behind the western mountains, the guests filed on home in two's and three's while Doña Leonor and several other helpful women cleaned up the huge mess, until Santi and Adriana were left alone and ready for their wedding night.

"Is your mind really made up about this move, Santi?" Adriana asked turning over to face him in the bed his uncle had made and given them as a wedding present.

Santi raised his head and rested it on his hand, his elbow sinking into the pile of cloth he was using for a pillow. "You can find new customers among the wealthy ranchers and plantation owners of the countryside." He smiled at her. "I'll help you deliver the finished clothing in our new buckboard."

Adriana smiled back. "Well, we'll see what destiny has in store for us, I guess."

That summer, the newlyweds packed their meager belongings unto their buckboard, snapped the whip over the head of a new mule called Grano De Oro, and moved up into the region of Gran Piedra Mountain not far from the city. Up in the mountainous region of the Sierra Maestra range there lived an old curandero, a folk healer and ritual practitioner who knew the old traditions of the local Indians.

Santi had arranged with this man, a cantankerous fellow called Don Manuel, to teach him. Santi would apprentice under him for several months every year. He planned to receive the instructions during the holiday season when he was free from his responsibilities to Don Fernando in Santiago.

By now he was Don Fernando's favorite servant. The old man treated him like a member of the family. He continued taking fencing lessons regularly. And that is why he found himself waiting one afternoon in the old man's courtyard.

Santi sat down on a stool at the corner of the broad courtyard. A young black slave carefully watered each hanging plant along the plastered, whitewashed walls. Santi looked up at the clouds gathering above. He started to think that the fencing lesson might not last too long today.

"It looks like rain, doesn't it?" remarked Don Alonzo as he approached him. Santi sprang to his feet and bowed from the waist at the young nobleman.

"No, go ahead and rest, I know you've been working hard today on your thrusts and parries." Alonzo sat on a stool next to Santi and motioned him to sit back down. Behind Alonzo another man walked up. It was his man servant, a young full-blood Indian named Alberto. Alberto carried two cups of a delicious root cider.

"Refresh yourself with these..." Alonzo said taking the cups from Alberto's hands and handing one to Santi. Santi drank the cider looking up at the young Indian who stood impassively behind his master, his arms crossed upon his chest. Alonzo noticed Santi's interest in his servant.

"This is Alberto..." He said motioning up toward the Indian. "I hired him in Las Indieras, the central mountains of Puerto Rico when I was serving there as commander of His Majesty's forces."

Alberto bowed slightly. "You never met him before because I have been loaning him out to my cousin when he goes hunting. Alberto here is an excellent woodsman and tracker." Santi smiled up at the young Indian. Alberto smiled back. Then the fencing lesson began.

Alonzo started to bring Alberto with him regularly whenever he came to Don Fernando's house to give Santi his fencing lessons. Santi and Alberto became close friends. When Don Alonzo and Don Fernando would withdraw to talk politics among themselves Alberto and Santi would remain in the courtyard sharing experiences of country life. It was obvious that Alberto missed his Puerto Rican peasant home. He often spoke of his parents and his sisters back in the mountains near the site of the old Indian settlement of Otoao. A small rural community had sprung up in that region of Puerto Rico which now carried the name "Utuado."

On his days off, Alberto took to visiting Santi's remote homestead near Grand Piedra Mountain. There, the two of them often went on long hunting expeditions bringing back wild ducks and jutias for Santi's table and as a gift for Santi's grouchy old spiritual mentor, Don Manuel.

When Adriana gave birth to a son, Alberto stood as godfather for the newborn.

"I have never tasted a jutia more deliciously prepared than this," exclaimed Alberto looking up at Don Manuel. The old man ignored him completely and continued gnawing on the bone in his hands with the few remaining teeth he possessed. Santi smiled and shook his head.

"Isn't this a wonderful meal?" Alberto insisted looking over at Santi. "Yes, yes, of course...Don Manuel is almost as good a cook as he is a healer." Santi remarked bringing a cup of cider to his lips.

Old Don Manuel grunted and rose from his seat. He picked up his own plate and then proceeded to snatch both Santi's and Alberto's dishes.

"I guess we're finished." Commented Alberto sarcastically, watching his half-eaten meal disappear into a large earthenware vessel that Don Manuel used to collect composting materials. The old man returned to the small table into which they were all crowded.

"How long's he staying this time?" He asked Santi abruptly. "Oh, just today. He will head back for the city tomorrow." Santi answered.

The old man grunted, then said nothing.

"I thank you very much for this meal that you prepared for us, Don Manuel. Santi's wife has not been home for a few days and I was beginning to tire of his lousy cooking." Alberto looked over at his friend with a mischievous smile. Santi leaned toward him and smacked him on the head with his hat.

"If you don't like my cooking don't come to visit." He laughed. "I can't help the fact that Adriana is not home. My cousin Luis took her and the baby back to the city to visit a sick friend in our old neighborhood. She should be back here on the mountain by the time we get home." "You boys better watch your red hides..." the old man grunted bluntly. "There is trouble afoot." The two young men's faces became serious. They stared at Don Manuel in puzzlement. "Slave hunters have been operating in this area taking Indians against the law."

For years certain slave hunters had supplemented their legal trade in recaptured black runaways by rounding up whole families of Indian peasants and selling them to the English in Jamaica. The North American English had long pointed an accusing finger at the Central and South American Spanish for the brutality with which colonization had been carried out in the Spanish territories with large Indian populations. And yet, now, long after Spanish rulers had outlawed the traffic in Indian slaves, the English continued to buy, sell and trade in Indians. Many Indians from the southern colonies of North America had paid for resisting English colonization by being shipped en-mass to the plantations of the British West Indies. Here, far from their temperate northern homelands these Cherokees, Creeks, and other North American natives, wrenched from their country, died of tropical diseases in wretched conditions. For their part the Spanish slave-hunters here in Cuba found it very profitable to clandestinely kidnap Cuban Indians and sell them to the English. Some of the local authorities even turned a blind eye to the illegal trade and eccepted bribes from the slavers in return for keeping them immune from Spanish law.

Santi shivered as the memory of his experience with slave hunters came flooding back into his mind like a nightmare. He would never forget the horrific drama that had played itself out in the little river valley that day, and his terror as he watched it all from his hiding place inside the hut of the unfortunate black couple.

"We better leave now..." Santi exclaimed rising from his stool. Alberto walked over to the wall and took his hat off the hook. He returned with his hat in his hands.

"Don Manuel, I want to thank you again for the meal you have provided us today."

Don Manuel rose to his feet and looked hard at the young man. Then he looked past him at Santi. "Your enemy is at hand, the ancient shark-faced foe of the Hope Child shall challenge you soon. His weapons are powerful; you must summon up extraordinary magic. But you can defeat him. I have faith in you."

Then something happened to the old man's face that Santi had never seen before. He smiled! It was a brief furtive smile, but it was a smile nonetheless.

Santi sensed that something important was about to happen. He threw himself nervously at the old man and embraced him tightly.

It was late afternoon and the two young men had been walking for about an hour. They walked in deadly silence, an ominous feeling of dread hanging over both of them. Then they saw him. It was Luis coming up the road to meet them.

Santi recognized him at once. Luis stumbled and tripped as he ran toward them. Santi's heart sank. He accelerated and rushed to his cousin. Luis fell into his arms, exhausted, gasping. There was a shallow but bloody gash on Luis' forehead, his clothes were torn and he bore bruises on his arms and legs. "They took them Santi, they took your family!" Tears rolled down Luis's cheeks. "The slave hunters took them..." Luis fainted in Santi's arms.

Santi threw his head back and let out an agonized howl. His voice reverberated in the valley and echoed on the nearby mountains.

4. CONFRONTATION

The darkness of the night closed in on Santi as he sat alone by the campfire that Alberto had started before retiring to sleep. He looked over at the two sleeping men on the other side of the fire. Then he buried his face in his hands and began to cry. It wasn't the first time he cried today. He had been weeping off and on for hours since Alberto and Luis had fallen asleep.

Why was this happening to him? What had he done? What sin had he committed that he should deserve his wife and his son to be torn from him like this? Where was the justice of Jesus now? Where was the mercy of Jesus now? What other cheek did he have left to turn?

He looked over again at his two companions sleeping peacefully not far from where he sat. He understood why Luis committed himself to helping him find and recover his family; after all, Adriana and her child were family. But Alberto's willingness to risk his life for him touched him profoundly. Alberto wasn't even Cuban. This wasn't his fight.

He rose to his feet and brought his hands up in front of his face. "I have strong hands..." He whispered. "What good are my strong hands now, I can't even help my own family!"

Then he reached down to his hip where his sword would normally hang when he was on duty for his employer, but the weapon was not there. He had left it back in the city in his quarters at Don Fernando's mansion. He was unarmed, defenseless.

Santi let both his hands hang useless at his sides. His shoulders drooped, his head low with shame, guilt and a hopeless realization that he may never be with his family again.

Just as his despair was reaching its bottom low he heard a sharp sibilant hiss in a thick stand of trees at the edge of the forest. It was a kind of "PSSSSST" people make when they are trying to attract your attention. Santi peered into the darkness of the jungle but was not able to make out who was in there. He looked over at Luis and Alberto but they were fast asleep.

"PSSSSST!" There it was again! louder and more insistent than before. Santi stepped forward approaching the dark mass of foliage before him. "Who's there?." He spoke up finally. There was no answer. Then "PSSSSSST" again. Santi jumped. He fidgeted nervously. "Who's there, I say?" He exclaimed in a loud voice.

But the only response he got was "PSSSSSST".

Santi looked over at his sleeping companions again. Alberto shifted a little but did not wake up. Luis snored on, oblivious of Santi's loud call. "PSSSSSST" Santi turned quickly and stared at the trees. His anger flared. He took another step forward, and then after a brief pause, he strode resolutely toward the jungle.

He entered the darkness of the forest where the light of the moon did not reach. In the murky blackness he groped about as he stumbled onward searching for he-knew-not-whom.

"PSSSSST" The sound was louder and closer.

"Who's in here?" He said. "Show yourself, don't torment me, who are you?" But the only answer he got was "PSSSSST"

This time the sound came from a spot not far away. Santi was able to pinpoint the location in the dark, and began making his way toward it. He stumbled and tripped as he struggled to close in on the source of the calls. "Who's there...?" He called out again reaching out blindly in front of him with his hands.

Then he struck the boulder, "Thump!" Santi fell, his feet lying on the large rock over which he had just tripped.

He rose to his feet and began to brush off the dead leaves and soil that clung to his clothing. "PSSSSSSSST!"

Santi practically jumped out of his skin. He turned and stared at the rock. Eventually his eyes grew more accustomed to the minimal moonlight which managed to filter in through the canopy overhead and illuminated the surface of the boulder. There on top of the boulder sat a small lizard, one of those ubiquitous little green reptiles the Indians called "chipojos" which haunt the night with their high-pitched hiss.

Santi felt like a fool. He stared at the little reptile for a long time, then he broke out laughing. The little animal scurried off and disappeared into the night.

Then something caught his eye on the surface of the boulder. He rose to his feet and leaned over the big rock. Something seemed to be purposely scratched on the top surface of the rock.

It was an old inscription and the grooves that made up the markings were filled in with moss. Santi used his finger tips to scratch out the soil and moss encrusted into the lines.

It took him about five minutes to clear out all the unwanted material from the marks. Then he stood back a bit and studied the design which the dim light allowed him to see.

It was a perfect little replica of the drawing he had seen many years earlier in his dream. That dream was the one he had experienced that strange magical night when he had stayed over at his grandmother's house while she was still alive. It was the dream where he had flown over the mystical jungle landscape like a hawk and had discovered the beautiful Indian woman standing in the clearing and looking up at him from the ground. It was the dream where he had spotted the mysterious pattern scratched into the dust at the woman's feet, the line pattern shaped in the form of a great bird with its wings outspread.

Santi stooped over the rock and studied the pattern more closely. The coincidence was remarkable. This little drawing was identical to the one in his dream!

Then Santi began to feel a mysterious tingle in the back of his neck. He looked around at the stone from all sides. There were no more designs. Then he suddenly got a strange idea. "What is under this rock?" He asked himself. He began to push on the boulder with all his might. He propped his feet on a nearby tree-trunk and pushed till the stone budged, then he pushed even harder.

Santi managed to move the stone enough to look underneath. He blinked and tried to focus on the bare spot of ground he had just uncovered. There was definitely something under there. He got down on all fours and brought his eyes close to the spot. He touched it. It was wood! There was some sort of wooden container buried under the rock.

He scratched around the buried object trying to loosen what was obviously the lid of a large wooden chest that had been sunk into the earth leaving only the top surface above ground. When he had succeeded in removing most of the soil from around the top of the box he used a smaller rock and tapped the top exposed portion of the box forcefully all around its perimeter, loosening it even further. The chest was obviously not locked. Santi did not attempt to dig out the whole box. He simply grabbed the latch and pulled up attempting to open the buried object and get at its contents while essentially leaving it still buried. At first the lid would not open but the young man pulled with all his strength and the lid lifted up with a loud squeal.

Santi peered anxiously into the box trying not to anticipate what he would find. There was something within, a large worm-eaten canvas bundle. Santi reached into the box and drew out the tatttered bundle. He laid it carefully on the forest floor and began to unwrap it.

Inside the bundle Santi found the most beautiful conch shell he had ever seen in his life. Even in the dim light the thing gleamed white. Next to the shell, he found, marvelously preserved in its gilt scabbard, a fine old Toledo sword from the previous century.

Santi rose to his feet holding the two objects in his hands. They were the same two objects he had seen in his dream so long ago, the two objects that had been held up to him by the young woman in the dream. Now here they were in real life! In his hands!

"I told you we would meet again in the woods my son..."

Doña Isabel's voice rang out from every corner of the forest, just as clearly and recognizable as it had the day she had read his destiny in the shell divination back in Banes all those years earlier.

Santi turned slowly still holding the sword and the shell in his hands. There, next to a large tree-trunk stood the old woman looking just as she had on the day Santi had saved her granddaughter's life.

The specter of the old black sorceress spoke:

"There is your inheritance from your ancestors, Santi, the shell of creative ingenuity and compassion, the sword of determination, and the element of technological progress that you can mold to shape the sacred art that must be placed at the service of the people. This is all you need to fight your enemy. But beware, for your enemy is not the white man that has kidnapped your family. That is not your real enemy. Your enemy is a spirit and that spirit can and will do his very best to defeat you in ways more final and far-reaching than the white man can ever conceive!"

The old woman then raised her right hand, and suddenly to her right there stood a young Indian man. Instinctively Santi knew the man's spirit that stood there was Cobo the grandfather of his grandfather, the man buried under the grave of his own grandfather back in Santiago, the mountain brujo he had heard so much about.

Then the old woman raised her left hand, and there stood Caoba, the young woman from his dream, Cobo's mother. Instantly, he knew these things had been hers a long time ago. She smiled at him. I recognized her also as I watched the unique drama unfold before me. She was the woman who had stood between me and the threatening dark entity in my vision during the car ride in Heaven Gazer's auto.

Slowly the vision disappeared and Santi was left all alone in the forest.

The young man emerged from the thick foliage carrying his newfound treasures. He wrapped them carefully with his baggage and prepared to go to sleep. As he crawled into his blanket he made plans for the following day. Luis would return to the city in the morning and go to his quarters at Don Fernando's mansion to fetch the match-lock pistols that the old Spaniard had taught him to use. Tomorrow evening they would track down and rescue his family.

Santi went to sleep.

5. AMBUSH

The sound of buzzing mosquitoes filled the air as five weary travelers paused to have a drink at the river's edge. The two mules that accompanied them also stepped forward and drank of the clear mountain water.

Two men waded into the cool water shedding their shirts on the riverbank. Three women walked upriver to a spot where thick foliage afforded them a little privacy. Here they pulled off their homespun cotton dressed and immersed themselves into the refreshing flow of the mountain stream.

The forest stillness was suddenly shattered by the loud report of musket. As Mateo looked up it seemed to him as if a large crimson flower suddenly blossomed upon his brother's chest. Then he saw the boy slump limply into the water. Still not quite certain of what was happening, the lad stared in stunned paralysis as the other young man's body began to slowly drift downstream. Behind it a dark cloud of blood stained the water and surrounded him in red. Then the forest exploded all around him with a cacophony of dog growls, the screams of women and the terrified braying of mules. He saw two large mastiffs burst from the undergrowth at the water's edge and splash into the river after him. The mules dashed off downstream.

When the young man finally came to his senses he spun around in the water and waded away out of the reach of the two huge dogs. From the corner of his eye he caught a glimpse of a bare-chested dark skinned man dressed in dirty canvas breeches, leather boots and a red bandanna tied about his neck. He emerged from the distant upstream brush holding a spear and shoving the three women before him. He had not allowed them to dress. They stumbled pitifully along trying to cover their nudity as best they could with their bare hands.

A simmering rage rose slowly in the boy's breasts when he saw his sister and cousins in their humiliation. Then he looked helplessly at the two big dogs splashing around the water's edge barking and snarling at him.

Eventually a tall rangy Spaniard appeared from downstream leading the jittery mules. As he splashed up along the river's edge he cooed gently to the animals in an attempt to quiet them. He looked in the direction of his shirtless companion.

"What have we got, Rolando?" The man demanded approaching his slave.

"Three squaws here, master...and a buck out there in the water." The black man answered pointing to Mateo.

The stubbly-faced Galician approached the three girls. They cowered away from him as he looked them up and down.

"These three certainly make a handsome set, Rolando, but we are not going to be able to pass them off as runaways. They look too Indian. We will have to set them aside with that other one we caught yesterday." He looked out at Mateo in the water and smiled. "These are all fine specimens. When we complete the delivery of the blacks we've got tied up back at the camp to their hacienda masters, we will take these Indians to Big Jack in Santiago. He's very discreet and we will not run any risk of getting in trouble with the authorities for trafficking in Indians. He'll sell them to the English up in the Bahamas. He'll get a good price for these ones."

The Spaniard whistled at his dogs. They immediately returned to his side. Then he called out to Mateo who was still standing in the water. "Come on in lad, I won't hurt you if you behave!" He shouldered his musket and petted his dogs. Suddenly one of the women let out an anguished cry when she spotted the corpse floating in the water. She was still sobbing uncontrollably when Mateo reached her side, his own throat developing a disconsolate knot. "Why are you hunting us? We are not escaped black slaves. We are free Indians. It's against the law to hunt us!" Mateo screamed up at the Spaniard. The Galician pulled his horse up to a full stop and turned to look down at Mateo. He glared down at him for a second and then exclaimed: "Did you hear what I said a minute ago, boy? I said, I won't hurt you if you behave. That means shut up and do as you're told. One more word from you and I will slice your head off right here." Mateo lowered his head and allowed himself to be led to his captive relatives. The group moved away from the bloody scene and back to the Galician's camp about half a mile upstream.

At the camp a young brown-haired boy stood guard with a musket in his hands over two black men and an Indian woman with her baby. He waved excitedly at the riders returning with their valuable human booty. Jose, the Galician rode into camp at the head of the sad little procession. He sat astride his vigorous white charger. Close behind him, his slave rode one of the mules they had taken from Mateo. He led the other mule which carried one of the new captives and some of their baggage. The rest walked along behind them, their hands tied.

The Spanish boy abandoned his post and ran to the arriving riders. He left the dejected prisoners squatting on the ground, their feet shackled and chained to a tree. He talked excitedly to the tall Galician:

"How many did you catch this time, Papa? Did they give you any trouble? Did you have to shoot any of them?" The Galician smiled as he hobbled his mount.

"Actually I did have to shoot one of the beggars this time." He exclaimed tussling his son's hair.

"That's all right, though. The one we brought back will bring us a fine price. And just you look at those girls back there. A set of pretty squaws like that is worth a fortune in the Jamaican slave blocks. Kinda makes you want to give them a little pop yourself, doesn't it boy?" The boy's face turned a crimson color. He looked down and fidgeted with his gun. Jose laughed and strode across the camp. He reached for a large bag and withdrew from it a set of iron ankle shackles. With Rolando's help he dragged their new captives toward the ones he already had there and throwing them on the ground he shackled all of them. Then he chained them to the tree with the others.

As night fell Jose and his son sat on the horizontal log of a fallen tree-trunk. All around them the darkness was alive with the trilling call of crickets and tree frogs.

"Never forget that you are superior to these animals, my son, Indians and Blacks both..." The Spaniard spoke in calm steady tones as he focused on the flutter of the campfire's flames. "The Almighty made us white for a reason, to denote the purity and sacredness of our origins. We are the descendants of a great race of peoples. These dark creatures were created to serve us, to provide us with a means for our prosperity.

Be strong. Don't allow yourself to fall into the great error that plagues our people in these colonies. There is a terrible mongrelization taking place throughout the Spanish possessions. Spanish men marry Indian and black women regularly, legitimizing their mongrel offsprings, making an abomination of our colonial populations."

The young boy looked up into his father's face drinking in the full measure of the poison that issued from the Galician's lips.

"Now go get some sleep. Sleep on the words that I have spoken." the boy rose and walked toward his bedroll.

"Boy..." The Galician called after his son. The boy stopped, spun around and looked back at his father. "Boy...I forget...How old are you now?"

The young boy looked at the man and answered, "I'm twelve years old papa, twelve."

"Yes, yes...that's right, twelve. You're getting to be a big boy, aren't you? Yes, a big boy..." He turned around and wrapped himself into his own bedroll. "Twelve..." he mumbled one last time before yawning himself to sleep.

The young boy wrapped himself in his roll and also went to sleep as the black slave Rolando began to snore in his hammock close to the prisoners.

Adriana shivered in the darkness. She wrapped her shawl tightly around the sleeping baby. The child had finally fallen asleep after a long horrifying day of forced marching and privation. There was no pity in her captors. She had finally come to realize that to the Galician, she was simply a piece of merchandise.

She looked over at the dark silhouettes of the two black men sleeping not far from them. This was all they knew, inhumane bondage, the lash, the inability to control their own destiny. No wonder they had escaped and now they had been recaptured. She wondered at their fate. What would be their punishment for running away? and what about her precious little boy? Several times she had heard the cold-hearted Galician speak of Big Jack, the Englishman from Jamaica.

Jamaica seemed like another world to her. She would be so far from her home, from her beloved Santi. Again her eyes welled with tears and she began to sob. Next to her, one of the three young girls who had been brought in that afternoon stirred at the sound of her sobbing.

The first slight stirring in the bushes beyond the Galician's sleeping area was barely noticeable. She was so full of grief that she paid little attention to it. But the second flurry of movement aroused her curiosity. Then as she strained her eyes into the dense darkness she caught glimpse of something light in color move quickly through the undergrowth. She pressed the sleeping child tight to her bosom, her heart beating wildly.

The Galician's slave stirred in his hammock. Then, he quietly slipped out of it and walked over to the dying embers of the campfire. He squatted over it for a minute scratching his back. Eventually he stood and laid a few new sticks in the coals bringing the flames back to life. He blew on it for a moment and then stumbled over to the little group of captives.

"Any of you need to shit or piss?" He growled roughly. Mateo raised his hand. The slave reached for the ring of keys at his waist and their jangle caused the Galician to raise his head and glance over at them briefly. Then he settled himself back to sleep. The slave detached Mateo's chains from the tree hissing: "If you try any funny business I'll kill you myself." The two mastiffs lay curled together nearby. One of them raised its massive head and looked at the slave as he helped Mateo up and unhooked him from the tree. The slave led the shackled young man into the forest and a few minutes later they returned. He quickly secured him back to the tree and then returned to his hammock. The dog laid his head back down and dozed.

Santi, hiding in the bush, squatted in the darkness, frozen in his spot. He watched the black man swing himself back to sleep in his hammock.

He looked up across the camp at the little group of captives with chains attached to their ankles illuminated by the light of the newly revived fire.

He spotted Adriana. She held the baby tightly to her breast, her eyes wide, staring in his direction. She was staring right at him but he knew she could not see him in the dark. She seemed so close and yet he could not touch her or speak to her, or let her know it was he hiding in the forest looking in at her.

He heard Alberto moving into position around the right side of the camp. And although he could not hear or see him, he knew Luis had taken up his position on the other side.

Suddenly all hell broke loose. First one dog, then the other jumped to his feet and began to bark wildly into the darkness, alerted to the presence of the three night-time stalkers by their acute sense of hearing and smell. The Galician jumped out of his bedroll reaching for his musket. Santi drew his sword and emerged from the bushes into the light of the campfire. Next to him lay the young brown-haired boy, his head foggy with sleep rubbing his eyes in confusion.

Santi saw the black slave jump out of his hammock and reach for his spear. On the other side of the perimeter Alberto and Luis emerged from the forest behind the Galician. Each man was armed with one of the match-lock pistols that Don Fernando had given Santi years before.

The next series of events happened so quickly that Adriana could barely keep up. First she saw the black slave dash madly in the direction of the two barking dogs, who strained at their leashes.

Santi threw himself behind the running slave but did not reach him in time. As the man loosened the ropes that bound the two wildly barking mastiffs, a bullet ripped through his chest killing him instantly.

Luis shoved the gun into his belt after he fired its one bullet and drew a sharp machete. He watched the Galician's slave slump to the ground, dead, as the two dogs pulled themselves loose and came bounding at him and Alberto. Alberto fired his pistol at the charging dogs but missed. A horrible shriek of pain rang out in the dark as one dog clamped its jaws on his leg. The other animal lunged at Luis. He parried this attack with the flat of his machete dazing the animal. In the meantime, Santi ran back toward the bushes. He dove into the undergrowth barely dodging a musket ball from the Galician's gun. The tall white man cursed and threw the gun to the ground. Then he drew his sword. He stood there for a minute listening at the fierce battle being waged toward his left between his dogs and the other two Indians. His eyes scanned the dark forest for a sign of Santi.

The brown-haired boy ran over to his father's side and pulled a dagger from its scabbard at his waist. "Courage lad..." His father whispered. "Remember we are better than these animals." Santi burst out of the jungle and dashed straight at Jose. The Galician parried his lunge easily, pushing his son behind him.

Santi squared off at the slave-hunter. The Galician stared at him in a half crouch, his sword at the ready. "May the man who placed that fine weapon in your filthy hand and taught you how to use it burn in hell for the rest of eternity." the Galician hissed. The two men crossed swords and began a nimble death dance. Jose attacked Santi with three vicious swipes as he moved forward quickly. Adriana gasped, holding her screaming baby to her breast. Beside her the other captives struggled to free themselves from their chains, their eyes riveted on the sword fight.

Santi dodged the attack and counterattacked with a fierce lunge. The Spaniard sidestepped it and brought his sword down on Santi's with such strength that he almost knocked it out of his hand. Santi recovered from the blow and stepped back. Just as he did Jose moved forward with lightning speed and swiped at his right leg. The sharp blade tip ripped through cloth and flesh. Santi winced and fell to one knee parrying Jose's follow-up lunges.

The young half-breed Indian sprang quickly back to his feet gritting his teeth against the pain in his leg. He saw a smile crawl across the Spaniard's cruel face.

"I'm going to kill you little-by-little, one cut at a time till I have cut all the white out of you, you mestizo mongrel." Jose laughed. Another scream rang out from the edge of the clearing as one of the dogs managed to sink his teeth into Alberto's leg again. Alberto now had a knife in his hand and stabbed the dog savagely. The animal yelped in pain and then whined loudly as Alberto perforated his back and sides with deep stab wounds.

The big dog faltered. Alberto dragged himself back away from it as quickly as he could, his leg bleeding profusely. The dog finally dropped to the ground gasping weakly. Not far to the right the other dog snarled at Luis, then moved in quickly. Luis tripped and fell backwards. The dog was upon him in seconds. The animal aimed at Luis' throat but the man dodged the attack and its teeth sank into his shoulder. A hoarse guttural cry escaped Luis' mouth. He lifted his free hand wielding the machete up in the air and brought it down on the dog's hindquarters. The dog screamed like a human being and let loose of the boy's shoulder. He limped back away from Luis, a deep gash on his left flank. Luis gripped his mauled shoulder with his machete-wielding hand for a minute and took several deep breaths. Then he threw himself at the snarling animal and finished him off with four whacks of the machete. He sank exhausted. He never had been a strong man and the ordeal of the last few days finally caught up with him. He fainted again right there next to the dead dog.

Santi had received two more deep sword-cuts, one on his left arm and the other one on his wounded leg just above the first. His white breeches and the sleeve of his cotton cloth shirt were stained with growing swatches of red. The men wheeled slowly trying to achieve the position of advantage, their blades flashing in the light of the fire.

Then Santi lunged again at his adversary. The point of his sword sank into Jose's shoulder and the Galician tripped backward. Santi stepped away quickly. The Spaniard fell back toward the spot where the captives crouched. He came crashing down on Adriana's lap.

The girl screamed and swept her baby out of the way just in time. Next to her, one of the other women reached over for the infant. Adriana looked into the stranger's kind face for a second, then she handed her the screaming child.

Adriana turned back to the stunned, wounded man lying across her lap. She reached over and picked up a stone. She held it over the man's head for a minute, then brought it down as hard as she could. The man saw the blow coming and shifted out of the way. The stone came crashing down on his collarbone, bruising it but not breaking it. "Aaaaaw!" cried out the Galician as the blunt pain of the blow spread over his whole torso. He turned swiftly and aimed a vicious backhand at the young woman's face. Before she was struck, Adriana caught a quick movement behind her husband. She watched as the young brown-haired boy, seeing his father fall, lunged at Santi with his knife. Just then she felt the violence of Jose's blow on her face. The world went dark and she blacked out.

I snapped out of my trance. The visions had disappeared. As hard as I tried I could conjure up no more memory of my emotional dream. I opened my eyes in frustration and cursed loudly in Spanish. Then I realized where I was and buried my face in my hands. "I'm sorry…I can't remember…" I groaned in despair. You have actually performed a miracle here! You have managed to make me remember almost all of the dreams that I had on the downriver canoe journey that I took back in 1982. I have no idea how you did it, but you did it. But in spite of that miracle I am still very frustrated. I still can't remember the final culmination of the dream sequence. I can't remember the end! I know I dreamed it. I know I did. But it's just not coming back to me now! I'm sorry, it's just so frustrating."

I felt that it was vital that I recover the memory of the dream's conclusion now even though several years had passed since I first dreamed it, but it escaped me. Doña Celina leaned over and placed her hand on my shoulder. "When did you have the final dream, honey?" She asked, a sweet kindness pervading her voice.

"It was the last night of my trip. We were only about a mile from Pittsburgh." I answered.

"Never mind, son, don't burn out your head trying to remember it now. This memory will come back to you in due time when you are ready for it. Now drink a cup of coffee and rest a bit."

I realized again that the old lady had accomplished nothing short of a miracle, that in spite of the fact that the end of the story still eluded me, I had, in fact recovered most of my canoe journey nights. I took her hands and told her. "Doña Celina, you are a very gifted person, and a great teacher. I want to thank you from the bottom of my heart for helping me remember my dreams. They mean a very great deal to me and it has been horribly frustrating not being able to remember them these past few years."

"It was nothing, my son, this is what I do…" she answered.

"Beware of that last dream. It will come when you least expect it."

I thanked Doña Celina and then I left the home of Eddie's mother never to return again. As I drove back down from the mountains to my recently widowed aunt's house in Arecibo I suffered with the anguish of my memory lapse. I struggled to conjure up the vital conclusion of the dream but it stubbornly eluded me.

Three years later in 1990 on a warm summer Saturday evening, I sat up late into night at my desk back in Pittsburgh. Hunched over my electric Yamaha keyboard and my notebook, I was putting the finishing touches to a fast-paced merengue song. The clipping rhythm of the new tune danced in my head as I strove for the most appropriate lyrics. By this time I had already formed my salsa band and it was beginning to attract a great deal of attention in the city. We typically performed covers of popular salsa and merengue songs but from time to time I would write an original piece for our repertoire.

Leni approached me from behind and threw her arms about my neck as I sat there. "How's the new song coming?" She murmured in my ear.

"Oh it's slow..." I answered. I became vaguely aware of the musky aroma from her perfume. I turned in my swivel chair and embraced her as she stood over me, my arms around her hips, my head on her abdomen. The memories of my canoe trip dreams were flashing about in my head like snapshots.

"Let's go up to the room. It's late." She said. I rose and clicked off the lights in my office. We climbed up the steps leading to our bedroom like two newlyweds on their first night. The light of the street lamp outside streamed in through our bedroom window shining in silver highlights on the copper-colored skin of Leni's shoulder.

I thought briefly of what it would be like if someone were to (heaven forbid) kidnap her, or my young son sleeping in the room next door, as had happened to Santi in my dream. The thought made me shudder, a cold chill rising up my back. I pushed the insane thought out of my mind and looked down at her face. She gazed up at me from her pillow, her lips parted breathing rapidly. Our kiss was like a prayer. No, our kiss WAS a prayer, a prayer of passion dedicated to the Lady of Kaguana, the Taino female spirit of love.

Throughout the night the sound of a thousand crickets sparkled in the dark like flashing stars blinking on and off. The rhythm of their primal chant gave us a song to dance to. We danced the ancient ritual dance of making, the dance of the love magic.

"There are important things happening..." I said hours later to Leni as we lay side by side on the bed.

By then she had slipped on a nightgown. She turned over and asked: "What do you mean, baby?"

"I mean Harmonic Convergence was nothing compared to what is in store for the world..." I continued. "I sense that the great Earth changes that the ancient Mayas had predicted will not come in the form of catastrophic cataclysms of nature like many are expecting. NO, it's going to be different. It feels to me like great things are going to take place. And they could be good."

I sensed more than saw Leni's smile in the darkness. She kissed me. We drifted off to sleep.

CHAPTER X

CYCLES OF COMPLETION

1. THIRTY YEARS OF CANEY CIRCLE

Sven and I awoke at around 8:00 in the morning on Wednesday August 18, 1982. As we launched the canoe near our Freeport area campsite we began to grasp the realization that we were only a day away from our destination. The ceremonies that revealed themselves to me on the rainy night stayed with me all morning long. I reviewed the details of each ritual carefully even as we again found ourselves gliding down the middle of the stream. The Shark Ceremony in particular had made a striking impression on me and would become an important ritual element of Caney Circle tradition on a permanent basis. As I look back now almost forty years later the power of that ceremony remains constant. And so in the summer of the year 2012 I stood surrounded by a large group of modern-day Tainos on the wide grassy lawn of Boardman Park located in the city of Youngstown Ohio. It was a warm June afternoon. The bright heat of the summer sun caused a thin trickle of perspiration to make its way down my cheek from under the headband of my white cotton cloth ceremonial feathered cap. We had just completed the Shark Dance just as I had dreamed it all those years ago during my down-river canoe journey.

Not far from where I was on that day an intelligent, intense man stood wearing a striking Taino headress of bright blue parrot feathers. I looked at him wearing his gold chief's guanin medallion on his chest and realized that I was looking at the future of my people. The ceremony had been organized collaboratively between the Caney Circle through our Ohio behike, Dr. Rose AnaO Quiñones and the United Confederation of Taino People, a tribal entity also represented in Ohio by Dr. Quiñones. This Solstice ceremony was the culmination of decades of evolution and growth of our spiritual community. At a specific point during our ceremony the young chief delivered an address to the assembled group. His talk was filled with hope and optimism. It was just the kind of energy that our ancestors traditionally expected from a leader, and now it was here among us again. The chief that attended our gathering that afternoon has come to represent true leadership in the Taino Resurgence movement. His name is Roberto Mukaro Borrero. The way in which we as a people had arrived at this level in our evolution was a story of its own.

Bibi AnaO
The representative of the United Confederation of Taino People in the Youngstown Ohio area became an initiated behike of the Caney Circle very early in the twentyfirst century. Her name is Dr Rose AnaO Quinones.

MUKARO

The charismatic director of the United Confederation of Taino People emerged as one of the most relevant leaders of the Resurgence Movement

KASIKE GUAMA MUKARO AGUEYBANA

In the years since my 1982 Allegheny River pilgrimage the twentieth-century descendants of the ancient Tainos, natives of the Caribbean islands such as myself, had experienced an extraordinary awakening that had materialized after 500 years of dormancy. By 1992, The year when much of the rest of the world was celebrating the quincentenial anniversary of Columbus' arrival in the Americas, small groups of modern-day Tainos had begun to band together into communities and organizations determined to make a defiant statement of survival in a world that considered us "extinct".

Eventually during the twenty years between 1992 and 2012 this new movement flowered and grew develping into what we began to call the "Taino Resurgence". Every day of that twenty years, more and more Puerto Ricans, Cubans, Jamaicans, Dominicans, Hatians and other folks from the rest of the Caribbean islands self-identified as Taino and began to call their homelands by their ancient Indigenous names. People of the island now popularly callled "Puerto Rico", specially, flooded into the movement in larger numbers as it grew both on the island and in the mainland diaspora of the United States, particularly in New York City. Now these people began to refer to their homeland again by its legitinate ancient name, "Boriken", and discarded the colonial word "Puerto Rico".

At first the drama of the nascent movement played itself out locally in the geographic communities where it had been born, especially the city of New York, with its surrounding suburbs, and also the various regions of the island of Boriken. The early years of the Taino Resurgence movement coincided with a pretty heady historical period, both in the International arena and in my own life. The first thing that happened soon after my 1987 visit to Caguana and my extraordinary meeting with Dona Celina, was that the great Soviet behemoth, that great unwieldy parody of Karl Marx's lofty idealistic dream fell apart and crumbled like a house of cards.

The world that had come to take for granted a bizarre global Cold War arms race and military balance of power between two supernations, the United States and the Russian Soviet Union. This perilous military balance of power was known popularly as "Mutual Assured Destruction" (MAD). The insane yet generally accepted premise of this global understanding was that, armed as they both were with apocalyptic nuclear weapons each one of these two opposing global superpowers could deter the other from starting a third world war simply because of the knowledge that any such war would end in the immediate destruction of both nations in a global thermonuclear cataclysm.

But by the end of the 1980's suddenly and unexpectedly this world found itself with only one side of the equation. The world was left in shock as people all around the globe watched on their television sets the unexpected dismantling of the Berlin Wall and the eventual fall of the Communist Party in Russia. The surviving side headed by the United States, persistantly calling itself the "Free World", finally got over the shock of the event and began to claim victory. "We won the Cold War!" was the joyous cry heard all over the western world during the early years of the1990's decade. Meanwhile, the various nation-states, pieces of the crumbled adversary rearranged themselves into new geographical patterns and either started on hope-filled paths into the future, or sank into bloody quagmires of ethno-religious warfare. Unfortunately these new conflicts began to dim the glow of the new perceived end of the Cold War. In the Balkans men of Eastern Orthodox faith killed their Catholic neighbors and Catholics killed their Eastern Orthodox neighbors, and they both targeted Muslims. In the Middle East, long simmering anger and animosity spawned by decades of injustice began to evolve into a new and energetic aspiration for final vindication. In some cases this aspiration manifested in a unique and virulent wave of nationalistic and religious extremism.

In the meantime, sinister new trends began to crop up in the United States. Freed from the "Us-versus-Them" anxiety of the Cold War some Americans began casting about them, looking for a new enemy to replace the old. Many extreme right wing racist fanatics began to cast a jaundiced eye on the now popular social programs that seek to assist people of color to reach a life of equal opportunities in a nation with a long history of inequality and injustice. Unhappy with the way contemporary U.S. government seemed to assist underpriviledged people of color to begin the long trek to economic parity these people began to see that government itself as the new enemy. Their hatred was fueled by the great strides that ethnic minorities had made here in this country in recent decades.

A whole new philosophy of Hate sprang up in small nuclei all over the country inspired by bigotted literature such as a book called "The Turner Diaries" by the author William Luther Pierce. This book raged against the US government, a government that supposedly sided with colored people and against whites. The new philosophy advocated violence.

At first this violence found its manifestation in horrific but isolated incidents, a shooting here, a dragging there, and the emergence of a new breed of hoodlums who called themselves "skinheads". Usually the victims of the violence were African-Americans, Hispanics, Orientals or Jews. The racists coined a new term to identify anyone they did not recognize as "white". They called us "mud races".

As the last decade of the century began, the violence took on new proportions. Throughout the 1990's, well-armed and well-organized congregations of these new bigots banded together, vocally and publicly inspiring a whole new generation of Hate and openly defying the United States government, which at that time was being led by what they considered to be the left-leaning, liberal government of Democratic president Bill Clinton. The government, for its part, often handled the instances of extreme provocation by these new elements of American society with extraordinary clumsiness, making matters that much worse.

Ironically in this era of anti-government sentiment among the extreme racist element of society, some police officers and other members of law enforcement became the brave and often-times heroic bulwark against the destructiveness of the fanatical right. Historically until that time, governmental law-enforcement systems had been viewed generally by genuinely oppressed people as a tool of the forces of oppression. And in many cases that well-justified perception continued to persist. But things were evolving and changing dramatically all across the board. Now, incresingly, the police were seen by the fanatical extreme Right as the protectors of the "mud races" and were often the targets of their attacks. In fact, the cases of police brutality against people of color continued fairly steady throughout that decade in spite of this perception in the minds of the extreme racist fringe.

Inevitably, more violence followed, on a grander scale. The whole thing culminated one terrible day in the month of April. A monstrous home-made bomb exploded in Kansas City, Missouri. In the bloody carnage that ensued, many men women and several pre-school children were indiscriminately killed. The incident destroyed much of that town's Federal building and awakening the people of this country to the seriousness and commitment of its own fanatic terrorist fringe. Later in the decade of the 1990's the new extremist movement discovered the Internet. Hundreds of web sites saturated in pure hate began to reach thousands of young minds in the quiet privacy of their homes. Soon, an increasing number of the killers were actually children...So many slaves!

All this was happening at the same time that the Taino Resurgence was taking flight. As the hate groups of the 1990's proliferated in the United States the Taino organizations coalesced and turned into true communities. During this time of momentous Earth changes our Caney spiritual circle continued to evolve. Subsidiary groups formed in New York, Philadelphia and Puerto Rico. Our medicine men and women tried as best they could to keep pace with the manic course that history was taking. We knew that the Twenty-four Generation prophecy was playing itself out. It became more evident that the world was in need of an accurate explanation for the direction that human lives were taking.

We knew that the traditions of the ancient Taino hold the kernel of hope. These people whose land became the touch point of the great final ultimate act in a 260-century drama, would hold out to the world the core of truth that offers capability for individual and communal redemption to all people, no matter what faith or philosophy they follow. And this wisdom was being held out to them all for free, without having to pay for it with money. In harmony with the core beliefs of Love and compassion from practically all the great spiritual traditions of the world this profound nature-path was destined to be reborn. It remained underground for five hundred years just to resurface at the pre-appointed time.

At the very beginning of this eventful period, late in the afternoon of May 26, 1991, on the eve of the fifth hundredth anniversary of Columbus' trip, I sat on the northern rim of a magnificent circle of people. At this point it had been four years since we had celebrated Harmonic Convergence right there at this same Singing Winds site of Pittsburgh's Council of Three Rivers American Indian Center. As chairperson of the board of directors of the Indian center and leader of our Caney spiritual circle I welcomed the honored representatives of the newly organized Taino Native American Association of New York city. These leaders of a reborn people, a people who had been pronounced "extinct" by anthropologists and historians now sat all around me in ritual regalia. I blew four long blasts on the conch shell as one of the Taino leaders, a woman called Naniki, sprinkled shredded tobacco on a fine old Taino tribal sculpture she had brought with her from New York. All around us in the circle men, women and children of all colors and nationalities sat and chanted the sacred songs which had been revealed to us in powerful medicine visions. As predicted in the ancient prophecy the strong voice of the guamo, the conch-shell horn of Taino tradition was calling out the message of reconciliation among the nations. In the middle of the circle, covered in shredded tobacco sat the 500-year-old stone-carved image of the mountain cemi that Bibi Naniki had brought with her. This stone statue was the original, the very model from which had been copied the plaster replica I had acquired from Miguel Guzman at Caguana, in Puerto Rico back in 1987. Now it sat enthroned in its place of honor and the sea-shell horn was heralding the dawning of this Hope-Child's new era. The culmination of that great 1991 ceremony was when one of the

New York Tainos, Domingo Turey, rose from his place and taught us all a song that had been inspired in him so that we could dance the "Guaitiao Dance", the dance of friendship, of family. The "Guaitiao Dance" is part of an ancient ceremony designed by our Taino ancestors to make relatives out of strangers. When two people who are not related sense that the divine forces mean for them both to belong to the same family and clan, this ceremony is performed. And so, at that moment, when Turey led us in that dance, the people who took part in our Full Moon Ceremony there at Pittsburgh's Indian center all became part of the same great human clan.

The mountain cemi that Bibi Naniki had brought to Pittsburgh lay on a bed of tobacco upon the grass during our ceremony.

That momentous Pittsburg Full Moon Ceremony gathering in 1991 had constituted my first concrete experience with the nascent Taino Resurgence Movement. Soon after that meeting, I established sustained contact with the members of the leadership of New York Taino groups. Several of these individuals requested training and initiation of behike status in the Caney Circle tradition and were granted that status. Two of those people still hold that title within the circle. Their names are Domingo Turey Hernandez and Edgar Konuk Rodriguez.

The work of the Caney Circle within the Taino community continued to evolve slowly during the decade of the 1990's while the storms of intolerance and conflict buffeted the world around us. In 1993, just as the racist skinhead movement gained momentum, I led the first Caney Circle ceremony at the sacred ancient ceremonial site of Caguana in the central mountain region of Boriken. On that day we organized a ritual tribute to Ata Bei within the same 600-year-old circular hoop of small upright stones where I had experienced my remarkable dialog with the spirit of my grandmother back in 1987, where I had buried Eddy's silver medal under the annato tree. Upon that ocasion we were joined there by Bibi Naniki again. She, once more, brought the magnificent three-pointed stone statue of the Hope Child, the Mountain Semi that remained in her care. We were joined as well by my long-time friend Spider from Pittsburgh. I was also accompanied at that event by my own family, my wife Leni and my teen-aged son Cha.

My son Miguel BanoManigua Sague. affectionaly known as "Cha" visits the Lady of Caguana

That 1993 ceremony in Caguana marked an extraordinary milestone in the history of our Caney Circle. On that day, after the ceremony within the stone circle we all got up and walked over to the main ceremonial plaza of the site, a huge rectangular enclosure lined with massive flat boulders. We went there to honor the big stone slab which bears the frog-legged image of Ata Bei in the position of birthing. This large chest-tall stone slab stands erect in the company of a whole row of other standing stones along one of the borders of the main ritual field. As we all stood there before the sacred petroglyph a lone hawk circled above us just like the hawk that circled over Sven and me when we crossed the state line from New York State into Pennsylvania in 1982. The circling flight of that hawk was a blessing that confirmed the importance of that moment.

Later in the decade of the 1990's I was fated to meet a fascinating man. It happened after I was invited by the museum called "Museo Del Barrio" in New York City to attend the opening ceremonies of a weeks-long exhibit of ancient Taino artifacts as part of the launching of a beautiful new book whose publication the museum was sponsoring. The museum paid my travel to and lodging in the city so I trekked to New York from Pittsburgh that weekend to attend the event and was confronted with the amazing growth of the Taino Resurgence movement there.

Many people who self-identified as Tainos were present, representing a growing number of organizations and communities. Among them was a Cuban-American man called Jose Barreiro, originally from the region of Camaguey. Jose Barreiro is a scholar, a professor who at that time was teaching at Cornell University in upstate New York. Having lived in the area for a long time and being roughly the same age as I was, it turned out that Barreiro and I had moved pretty much in some of the same circles for years without actually meeting. He had served for quite some time as editor of the prestigious Native American publication INDIAN COUNTRY TODAY. And back in the1970's he also had been closely associated with the Indian movement publication that was issued on the Mohawk reservation, AKWESASNE NOTES. It is very likely that when I was shaking hands with the young Mohawk woman on that unforgettable summer day after working on the maize fields to feed the rebels camped out at Genienke, Barreiro may have been somewhere near-by.

Now, in the 1990's Jose was busy creating the conditions via which the world would be introduced to the traditions of Cuba's contemporary Taino Indians. He travelled to the island and while there contacted local Cuban scholars such as the anthropologist Alejandro Hartmann of Baracoa, who were researching the survival of Tainos there. When everything had been said and done Barreiro ended up rediscovering the Indian community of Caridad De Los Indios, in the extreme eastern end of the country not far away from where I spent my childhood and its current leader, Don Panchito, a true modern-day kasike (chief). It turned out that these people were closely related to the Indios of El Caney where my own family had connections.

Barreiro put Don Panchito and his community on the global Indigenous map. He wrote articles about that community for INDIAN COUNTRY TODAY and a number of other publications. His influence in the North American Indian establishment even made it possible to persuade the New York Heye Foundation Museum of the American Indian to release a set of human remains that had been collected back in the beginning of the 1900's, by an American archeologist called Mark Harrington in behalf of the millionaire Indian artifact collector, George Gustaf Heye. The Native bones had been taken out of Cuba and brought to the United States to be housed in Haye's museum up in Washigton Heights, New York City, the same museum where I spent so many hours in the 1960's. As a result of his efforts, Jose eventually succeeded and experienced the unique honor of personally conveying the bones back to Cuba for ceremonial burial by Don Panchito and his community.

Working closely with Cuban anthropologist Alejandro Hartmann, Jose was able to organize a pilgrimage of several Native people from the United States, including a number of people from the U.S. Taino Resurgence to Cuba in the late 1990's. And so the members of Don Panchito's community had an opportunity to meet their counterparts from Puerto Rico and other parts of the Caribbean, as well as some North American Indians. I corresponded sporadically with Barreiro over the years after our meeting at the Museo Del Barrio. Our paths would cross from time to time and throughout all this I watched the progress of his work closely. Eventually The Heye Foundation collection was acquired by the Smithsonian museum and a brand new building was constructed in

Washington DC to house it called the "National Museum of the American Indian". Not long after that, Jose retired from his job at Cornell. He ended up moving to D. C. and becoming a permanent staff member of the National Museum of the American Indian there. Since that time Jose Hatuey Barreiro has become one of the most respected leaders of our Taino Resurcence Movement.

Dr Jose Barreiro

While all this was taking place my venture into the world of entertainment was panning out. My salsa band, Guaracha had prospered during the late eighties and early nineties. Soon my business venture, "Sagué Presents" branched out to include all sorts of colorful ethnic presentations which were very much in demand in Pittsburgh. I managed to secure two steady weekly performances with a number of monthly and annual gigs included. Along with that the rest of my time was filled up with private bookings and song- writing.

And so, it was fall, 1994, when I found myself at a weekend gig. The Cozumel Mexican restaurant and nightclub in the Shadyside neighborhood was particularly full that Saturday night. I struggled across the dance floor through the gyrating mass of young men and women. Gerardo, the restaurant owner, had just slipped a new CD into the house sound system and the throbbing rhythm of Gloria Estefan's "Ayer" sent waves of magic across the whole room.

I reached the bar. I was in a hurry. I had to order my drink past the clamor of the crowded bar and hope that Gerry the bartender would hear me before I had to return to the stage with my band for the next set.

"Hola Amigo!" Josh's friendly tone was a dead give-away. I knew who was talking to me before I turned to see.

"Hi Josh!" I answered waving my hand frantically at Gerry the bartender as he swept past. Gerry was very busy. I almost felt guilty trying to cut in front of all those other customers who had already ordered. But if I waited for him to serve them all I would never get my drink in time.

"It's tough to get a drink eh!" Josh exclaimed easing up beside me past the press of people around the bar.

"Yea Josh..." I answered. "During my last break I had to leave the restaurant and go to one of the other bars on Walnut Street to get my drink!"

Josh laughed. "Well, you will have our usual tequila at the end of the night, won't you?"

Josh had begun a kind of tradition. Every Saturday at the end of the night as people reluctantly filed out of the club he would snatch me from my tasks of clearing the stage of speakers, microphones and yards of quarter-inch cords, and he would drag me to the bar for a shot of tequila. We drank it the Mexican way with the slice of lemon and the salt.

"Oh of course..." I screamed over the din of Gloria Stefan's classic Salsa. "You know I would never miss that!" Josh smiled and walked away to find some pretty American girl that he could dazzle with his boyish Latin charm.

The night had gone well. We had made good money that evening so I insisted on buying the two tequilas. No matter how hard I try, the strong Mexican drinks always make me screw up my face. As usual Josh smiled. It was that open, innocent smile that all these Aztec-faced Mexican boys have.

"There sure are a lot of you fellows here tonight." I commented to him as I recovered from the drink.

"Yea..." He answered, "And there'll be more." He winked at me and ordered two more tequilas.

He was right. In the last three years there had been a sudden influx of Mexicans into the city of Pittsburgh which I was at a loss to understand.

There had never been a large Latino population in this city, and if one should develop I was expecting it to be composed of Puerto Ricans like that of the other Pennsylvania cities of Philadelphia, Harrisburg, Lancaster and Erie. But that was not to be. By 1994 it was obvious that if Pittsburgh was going to develop a Barrio it was going to be inhabited mostly by Mexicans.

"Hola Josh…" A youthful voice rang out behind me I turned to look into the eyes of a dark-skinned full-blood Indian from Mexico's interior. "Hello Pablo." Josh returned his greeting. The boy sat next to him and leaned toward me.

"You make beautiful music." He exclaimed.

"Thank you, I'm glad you enjoyed it. Did you dance?" The boy looked down shyly. "Maybe next time."

Most of these young Mexican men came more for the tequila, the music and the girls than for any love of dancing, but it was almost impossible to snag up any girls without moving your feet. Most of them broke down and made valiant attempts at the fast-moving, syncopated Cuban rhythms which were so different from their traditional Mexican corrido two-step rythms.

"I was feeling so lonely for almost a year now…" Pablo commented in Spanish, his laid back Mexican drawl slightly slurred by the effects of the tequila. He pulled out a crinkled picture of a pretty native girl.

"This is my girlfriend. I told her in my last letter that she didn't have to wait for me. It's taking me too long to make all the money I wanted to make. I told her she could get another boyfriend. But she told me she wanted only me."

As he said the last word of his sentence he made a gesture with his hand and the treasured snapshot fell to the floor. I jumped down off my stool and picked it up tenderly.

"Here amigo, take care of this picture; this girl sounds like a wonderful woman. Maybe she will be your wife some day."

Pablo smiled taking the picture from my hand and returned it to his shirt pocket.

"Now let me buy you both another Tequila before you go home." I said signaling to Gerry who was wiping off the bar as people continued to file out of the club into the night.

Hundreds of Mexicans had been pouring into the tri-state area of Pennsylvania, Ohio and West Virginia. Many had arrived alone, shipped in by local restauranteurs for the low-paying menial tasks of their establishments. In some cases the lonely homesick youngsters, fleeing the poverty and drug cartel violence in their own country ended up in crowded substandard housing provided by the restaurant owners themselves.

Fearful of all authorities, they usually had no access to medical care and did not qualify for welfare or low-income housing. They were at the mercy of those who were exploiting them.

7. SLAVES

Throughout the decade of the 1990's I stayed in touch with the Mexicans of Pittsburgh as well as the Puerto Ricans and Mariel Cubans of Erie, but one encounter in the fall of 1995 came as an unexpected surprise.

That October I was destined to meet Eddie again, but I did not know it. The meeting took place far from Pittsburgh at a Guaracha band performance. My long-time friendship with the young Puerto Rican was the furthest thing on my mind that October afternoon. And when I saw him I didn't even recognize him.

Eddie had changed dramatically. Yes, of course he was eight years older. But there was something else, something intangible that was so terribly different about this young man.

"Que pasa?" He greeted me as I wrapped my guitar cord. I was at a loss to figure out who he was, plus I was distracted and preoccupied with the lackluster performance I had just delivered. My performance was devoid of spirit that night, and that was because I was severely de-spirited myself. I was depressed and pessimistic. My head was filled with the horror of the new mass exodus of Cubans occurring that summer and fall in the Florida Straits.

On the floor beside me lay a recent issue of the Pittsburgh Post Gazette. On the front page photo two women and a young girl screamed desperately to be rescued from a flimsy boat drifting on the shark-infested waters off Florida. It was the Mariel boat-lift happening all over again. The accompanying copy of the newspaper remarked curtly "U.S. Rejects Cuban envoy's call at U.N. to lift embargo." Nearby the other members of my band also gathered their belongings together in preparation for our departure from the prison.

"Hey Miguel, wuzzup?" I looked up surprised. Now, the voice was familiar but I still could not recognize the face. The man stood before me in his prison garb.

"Who are you?" I asked a little annoyed at the interruption into my private reverie. The constant sight of men in prison uniforms was becoming a bit depressing. We had just concluded the fifth in a series of performances for the inmates of practically every state-run correctional facility in the state of Pennsylvania. The contract called for a two-week tour of the whole state, stopping at each one of the prisons, sometimes doing two prisons in one day. Our audiences were mostly Puerto Rican, with quite a few Cuban Mariel immigrants and a smattering of Mexicans and Mexican-American "Chicanos." I was tired that evening, and eager to return to my motel room.

"Don't you remember me, Miguel? I still have to thank you for the favor you did for me years ago."

Suddenly I realized whom I was talking to. "Eddie!" I exclaimed. "Eddie, its you man! I forgot you were here!"

"Oh yea, Miguel, I'm here. There ain't much chance of me getting outta here for a while. They keep shooting me down at parole hearings. It's that Zero Tolerance thing they got for drug trafficking offenders. You know, it works a lot tougher on blacks and Puerto Ricans than on anybody else."

Several other men in prison inmate uniforms had gathered around us, curious of our conversation. The guards watched us intently from a few paces away. "How's your mom?" I asked. "Not too good" He responded. She had a heart attack about a year after you visited her in Utuado. She ain't been the same since." This news depressed me even more than I was already.

"We got a lot of Cubans here, Miguel..." Eddie remarked looking around at the small circle of men. "Most of these guys come over in rickety, leaky boats back in 1980 just like Mario and Tony."

I looked at the young faces and involuntarily shook my head. What a waste of human potential!

"You see all these guys here...?" Spoke up an older fellow with a Cuban accent.

"This is nothing. Wait just a little while; we're gonna have another Mariel!" I instinctively looked down at the pitiful scene on the front page of the newspaper. I knew he was wrong. The U.S. president during this crisis, Clinton, was being careful not to repeat the mistakes of his 1980 predecessor. Now, 13 years later the Coast Guard was not picking up the exiles on the high seas and automatically bringing them to Miami as they had done during the Mariel phenomenon. This time the unfortunate boat and raft people were being shuttled right back to Cuba, to the U.S. naval base of Guantanamo. There they were festering in crowded temporary camps awaiting their fate while the U.S. and Cuban authorities hammered out the conditions of their repatriation. I began to reflect on the convoluted historical chain of events that had led Cuba from the decisive revolutionary victory over the Batista dictatorship in 1959 to the present low-ebb point, crippled by an unjust American embargo and the collapse of the Soviet state. Of course, I knew that in the late eighties and early nineties the fragile economy of Cuba had received a near-mortal blow when its most important benefactor, the Soviet Union, fell apart and disintegrated. Widespread shortages of fuel, basic household goods, food and medicine were creating a volatile environment throughout the country. I visited Cuba in 1994 and saw first-hand the difficulties that were being experienced there as a result of these conditions. A stubborn adherence to its thirty-year-old economic embargo by the U.S. singled out Cuba as the only surviving socialist state which the Americans still treated as a Cold War enemy, beside North Korea. China, a Communist state with which the United States had fought a deadly conflict during the 1950's was now a major trading ally. Even Viet Nam, a country with which the US had been at war barely a decade and a half earlier was now being eyed for diplomatic and economic ties by the U.S. government. But Cuba remained in the United State's hit list.

Thousands of Cubans had already made the desperate ninety-mile sea crossing in flimsy boats and rafts. They faced, not only the treacherous waters of the Florida Straits, but also the severe sanctions imposed by the Cuban government on anybody trying to leave illegally.

These sanctions had always been criticized by the U.S. as dictatorial, a tyrannical suppression of Cuban peoples desire to immigrate to a "Free Country". But now all this had changed. Suddenly this summer, Castro did the unexpected (again). He lifted all restrictions on emmigration. The Florida Straits were, once more, flooded with thousands of "balseros" (raft people) just like the 1980 Mariel Boat Lift. The U.S. was at a loss. Now that the Cuban government was no longer doing what it had been accused of doing for such a long time, the president actually sought negotiation to persuade Castro to re-instate his old emmigration restrictions. By Cold War logic it was as if he were negotiating with the East Germans to have them rebuild their Berlin Wall. It was the world turned up-side-down!

In the meantime, the U.S. stubbornly held fast to the economic embargo which made the crisis in Cuba that much more unbearable and gave so many Cubans the incentive to leave.

"The Americans are tightening the embargo on Cuba with the Helms-Burton Act..." A young inmate commented, "They say it's supposed to persuade Castro to correct human rights violations."

I looked at him and shook my head. He smiled and shrugged his shoulders in a kind of "Go Figure!" attitude. As I quickly picked up the rest of my equipment I wondered at the Irony of U.S. foreign policy gone awry. That was the last time I saw Eddie.

8. ELIAN

Not too long after the Guaracha prison tour, in 1998, the United States became embroiled in one of the most dramatic events of the decade's Cuban immigration saga. A young Cuban woman set out to sea from Havana with her boyfriend and her young child in what was at that point a familiar desperate attempt to cross the Florida Straights to the US. They rode a frail craft that quickly sank, drowning her and her boyfriend. The child, a boy called Elian Gonzalez, survived the ordeal. He was rescued by fishermen off the Florida coast and eventually he was put in the care of paternal relatives who happened to live in Miami. Elian became an overnight media celebrity in the United States. His miraculous rescue and the political overtones of his case put him firmly in the front pages and newscasts for weeks. The father in Cuba, a man who had been estranged from Elian's mother, but who still claimed parental rights to the boy, complained that the mother had made the attempt to take his son to the U.S. without his permission. This created an extraordinary international situation which put the U.S. president Bill Clinton in an incredibly awkward position. Once Elian was living in the Miami Cuban home he became a symbol of exile Cuban-American resistance against the Castro government. The extreme political Right in the United States embraced the efforts of the Miami relatives to keep Elian at all costs, and rejected any suggestion that the boy be returned to his father in Cuba. But two court decisions in Florida agreed that the boy belonged with his dad. Elian became a political football used to promote ideology. The Cuban-American family in Miami refused to give him up. Finally the Clinton government felt forced to send an armed raid into the Miami home, take the boy by force, and return him to Cuba, where he was hailed as a heroic returned hostage. Fortunately nobody was hurt during the action, but it was a very close call. These events of 1998 were inevitable and anyone with any sort of insight could have forseen them, even back then at the time that I stood in that prison auditorium surrounded by young inmates.

I was leaving the prison performance area when I spied a young Puerto Rican convict. His legs were shackled together. He shuffled awkwardly as he was led to some unknown destination. Images from my river journey dreams came floating back into my consciousness. They were images of the victims of Jose-the-Galician's slave-hunting forays. Those victims were slaves in chains and shackles. Was this young Puerto Rican man any less a slave? Was he not simply an inheritor of a five hundred-year-old legacy of colonial slavery? It was his colonized mind that had led him to the life of crime which had ended there at Huntingdon Prison. He was still a slave.

I thought of slaves, all kind of slaves. I thought of Josh and his Mexican buddies drinking tequila at Cozumel restaurant trying to forget their homesickness. I thought of the bitterness of the work of the illegal migrant, risking his life at the border crossing, attempting to escape his own private hell of increasing drug-cartel violence and poverty and trying to make it in a new country where many held a deep contempt for everything he was and everything he stood for. I also thought of my fellow Cubans venturing out upon the merciless stretch of ocean between their homeland and Florida. They were also slaves, hostages to hostile international politics that helped motivate them to seek the elusive American Dream. I thought of victims of a biased and prejudicial criminal system in the U.S. which seems to target the poor and disenfranchised, making slaves out of them. I thought of slaves to homelessness and poverty right here in the city where I now live. Finally I thought of Eddie, a slave to his own blurred, confused, colonized outlook on life, a vision of reality born of tough childhood experiences and misguided aspirations...so many slaves!

Then I thought of my own outlooks, my own attitude. Was I perhaps also a slave? I knew that deep down inside I carried deep wounds created by the intolerance of the society in which I had come of age. I recognized a hidden resentment towards those who reminded me of those early vulnerable years when I was recently arrived in the United States. I had not grown up in poverty like Eddie. But the color of my skin had allowed me a glimpse of the world in which kids like Eddie had grown up. And I was not immune to the racial bullying that Eddie had also known as a youth. Did those taunts and abuse when I was a teenager shackle me to a way of thinking from which I could not free myself? Was it difficult for me to separate the color of my skin from my outlook on life, to see a white man without automatically stereotyping in my mind what was in his heart? Was I, in spite of all my efforts, not much better than Eddie, crippled in my own way by my own set of prejudices and intolerance? Was I, in the final analysis no less enslaved by my own bias than the boys who had taunted me when I was young?

Barrio Warriors

Urban Conquistador

A couple of years after the 1998 prison tour I was invited to offer a Taino prayer at the closing ceremony of the global summit of the United Religions Initiative. It was 2001. The event was a world-class three-day phenomenon of ethnic and religious reconciliation which brought together religious people from all over the world. It felt like the beginnings of the Earth-remaking process that the ancient Mayas seemed to predict. Was I up to this challenge? Did I really belong in this brave new movement? Was I really free of my own personal demons of intolerance?

9. PROGRESS

Even as I worked, year after year in the 1990's, to promote the goals of the Caney Circle, I also became more and more deeply involved in the day-to-day nurturing of our family business, the musical endeavor I had now called "Sague Presents Entertainment Agency". By the middle of the decade I had quit my job in the private school and decided to dedicate myself exclusively to the entertainment agency. From a financial perspective, the business grew slowly, but it attracted a lot of public attention in the Pittsburgh area. We got to the point where we could field practically any type of Native, Indigenous or Tropical cultural presentation anywhere in the city. We competed with local Hawaiian hula groups. We provided

Philippine Tinikling dance troupes and traditional dance ensembles that represented the culture of India to the annual East Asian Festival. We presented my signature Latin salsa dance band, Guaracha, at every major city public event such as the Three Rivers Art Festival and the New Years Eve First Night extravaganza, and an Afro-Cuban traditional drum group for the African-American organization's annual shows. If I were a better businessman we probably would have done quite well, but as it turned out, I only barely managed to keep us breaking even most of the decade.

Guaracha Latin Dance Band during the 1990's

Then in 1998, just before we launched our Fall prison tour, our band was given the opportunity to make one of the most memorable statements in its history. We were able to organize a joint tour with one of Cuba's most important ethnic music icons, a singer called Lazaro Ros. This man had a resume that had impressed some of the biggest stars of Latin music all over the world, even in the United States, and on the evening that I met him while on a visit 1994 to Havana he was just freshly returned from an U.S. tour with non other than one of my musical heroes, Carlos Santana.

Wikipedia now describes his accomplishments in this way:

> "He received international acclaim with the Conjunto Folklorico Nacional de Cuba (National Folkloric Ensemble of Cuba) which allowed him to travel to France,

Spain and the United States. He also worked at the Cuban Institute of Ethnology and Folklore. He is recognized as the founder of Afro-Cuban Rock (music) due to his work with the (musical band) Sintesis and their album, Ancestros (Ancenstors)."

In October of 1998, on the first day of the tour, I stood on the stage of the Bellefield Annex Auditorium in front of hundreds of excited Pittsburghers, backed by my full 16-piece salsa band "Guaracha" and began singing an original song, "Semillas", that I had dedicated to the Afro-Cuban deity of Love and Compassion, Ochun, and to her synchretic Santeria Christian manifestation, the Virgin of Charity of El Cobre.

On a pre-determined cue near the beginning of the tune with the trumpets, trombones and saxophones of my band blaring, Lazaro stepped out of the shadows and into the stage spot light provoking thunderous applause. He began the familiar chant to Ochun "Ide were were nita Ochun, Ide were were nita ya" to the rhythm of three bata drums played by famed Cuban percussionist Carlos Aldama, whom we happened to snag temporarily from his California tour, accompanied by two accomplished young Newyorican percussionists from the South Bronx. Standing there with Ros and Aldama, I was litterally sandwiched between the very best Afro-Cuban talent of the time. Xiomara, an incredibly talented dancer from the Cuban-American community of West New York, New Jersey came whirling out of the opposite corner of the stage dressed in yellow and waving a fan in her hand. She interpreted the song with her body and painted images on the stage like virtuoso painters do it on canvas.

At that moment, the very act of breathing the same air as the human icons beside me, watching that amazing dancer, and listening to the beautiful rhythmic melody dedicated to the Seashell Lady had an electrifying effect on me. It brought back memories of the discussion that Sven and I had shared back there on the river about Ochun and her power of compassion.

I knew that it was a trully magical moment not only for myself but also for everyone in that auditorium. Bringing Lazaro to Pttsburgh so that my fellow Pittsburghers could participate in the ritual ceremony that he and that dancer from New Jersey were performing on that stage was actually part of the prophetic reality that I had become such a part of. We were all dancing around the new tribal sacred cave fire at that moment, like the dancer, we were all painting sacred images on the new cave wall. And the most significant element of that moment was that, although the cultural tradition being manifested on that stage was derived from a synchretic mixture of African, Spanish and Taino heritage, the experience was being shared by a crowd whos ancestry was from all over the world. The experience at that moment was truly global. The gathering in that particular sacred cave that night was the gathering of a global tribe.

I knew at that moment that we were part of a larger phenomenon, a world-wide phenomenon. Powerful magicians all over the world, disguised as commercial entertainment stars were turning the world of the Fifth Sun Mad Men upside down. Famous Salsa musicians such as Juan Luis Guerra of the Dominican Republic, emotionally and successfully appealed to the conscience of his huge international audidence with expressive socially conscious anthems such as the merengues "Mangos Bajitos", "Rompiendo Fuentes", and the block buster "Ojala Que Llueva Café". Then he broke ground by releasing his evocative and wildly successful melody "Naboria Daca, Mayanimacana", in the ancient Taino language.

Other iconoclasts of the Latin music industry had steadily contributed during much of the twentieth century to the gradual errosion of Seven Macaw's grip on humanity. The Argentinian Atahualpa Yupanqui, the Chilean Victor Jara sang moving anthems shining a bright light on the misery of life of the poor landless rural Indian peasant or the oppressed factory worker in South America. The Panamenian Ruben Blades touched thousands of lives with his emotional appeals for downtrodden urban Latinos to take back the power over their own lives.

This, of course mirrored similar trends in other parts of the world where other artists were using the influence and power granted them by a reluctant industry to spread the message of Hope and Empowerment. The Jamaican Reggae star Bob Marley reached into the conscience of an increasingly receptive world with his message of liberation. Right here in the United States artists such as the Fugees, featuring superstars such as Lauren Hill and Wyclef Jean took the hip hop genre to a new level of social responsibility. It was, and still is, a true revolution, and it is still going on today.

During my 10-year career as a professional musician my work in this arena afforded me the opportunity to meet several of these modern-day magicians. On one ocasion as my band performed at the Pittsburgh nightclub The Rosebud, I was approached on the stage by the famous Brazilian luminary Milton Nascimento, whose compositions inspired justice and reform idealists in Brazil and all over the world. Nascimento happened to be in the city on tour, appearing at another venue and decided to come in and listen to some salsa after his performance. On another night at the Rosebud, the whole upper deck of the club was taken over by performers accompanying famous Cuban trumpetist and former band-member of the Havana Latin fusion band, Irakere, Arturo Sandoval. Naturally the members of my band were desperate, waiting for the set to end so they could climb up the steps and meet the famous trumpetist.

On another opportunity the Manchester Craftsmans' Guild of Pittsburgh hired my band and my Cuban cabaret act to perform for another former Irakere superstar, Paquito D'Rivera as he and his United Nations Orquestra musicians took their lunch break during their Pittsburgh performance. It was a pretty exciting time in my life. I was constantly in the company of the modern-day artists who were actually medicine men and women.

Our Lazaro Ros tour was an artistic success and the indisputable climax of my musical career. There are still references to that tour posted on the internet. But financially, it was one of the worst disasters that Sague Presents Entertainment Agency ever experienced. It was one of the main reasons I accepted a position as Spanish teacher in the Pittsburgh Public School district later that year, and returned permanently to the profession of elementary school educator. Eventually I switched over to teaching elementary school Art which is what I did for the rest of my teaching career.

Our entertainment company continued to limp along financially for a few more years under my direction, and then when most of the fiscal damage that I was responsible for had been repaired I handed it over to my son, who has managed it quite capably ever since, signing lucrative ocean cruise contracts and even accomplishing what I never succeeded in doing.

In 2013 he landed his first major arts grant, guaranteeing the resurgence of an even more vibrant Guaracha Latin Dance Band.

10. A STONE WITH A MESSAGE

Early on the afternoon of Wednesday August 18, 1982, as Sven and I progressed down the last day of our journey I noted a large turtle siting upon a boulder on the river bank. The boulder served as a sturdy base upon which that turtle could stand and stare at us as we floated past. It made me think of the power of the timeless stone-beings to sustain and support. They are the foundation of the Earth Mother who some Indigenous people believe to be supported on the back of a cosmic turtle, and they are the firm base upon which we all stand, like that turtle on the bank. It brought back memories of our encounter with Indian God Rock and its ancient markings. The cryptic images scratched upon the surface of Indian God Rock were a magical incantation which formed the basis, the foundation upon which sacred ceremonies were performed there on the river. Many years later at the end of the eventful decade of the 1990's I would again come face to face with the ability of stones to deliver a powerful message.

The year was 1998 and the stone in question was a large hunk of sandstone which sits in the middle of East Commons Park in the neighborhood of Pittsburgh called "North Side". Its task is to bear the weight of an old cannon in front of a historical monument. This monument consists of a stone statue depicting a Civil War soldier standing behind the cannon. It is dedicated to the brave fighting men of an artillery unit called "Hampton's Battery".

Pittsburgh Captain Robert B. Hampton started recruiting his independent light artillery unit in 1861 right here in the city. The unit was mustered into service in October of that year. The young men from Western Pennsylvania for whom this monument was erected handled the cannons for the Union Army at the bloody battle of Antietam. The war they fought and died in changed forever the character of their country. As a result of that war the well-entrenched and time-honored American institution of slavery, an institution which had created much of the agricultural wealth of this country, came to an abrupt and ignominious end.

Sure enough the monument was dedicated to men who had handled cannons in the 1860's during the Civil War, but curiously the cannon which now sits heavily on that long-suffering piece of sandstone in front of the statue, is not one of those guns. This particular piece of artillery is from a different war, a war fought more than thirty years later in 1898. I met that stone and the cannon which has ridden it all this time in January of 1998, exactly one hundred years after the gun saw its last war-time action. On that evening I was taking a rare break from my non-stop efforts organizing the Lazaro Ros tour that would eventually take place later that year.

It wasn't very cold that night, and the jacket I was wearing was beginning to make me sweat. "Why don't you take that thing off..." said Alan as he polished off the last drop of his Heinekin and set the glass down on the table.

"God! You're right. I don't know why I even wore this thing tonight; it's so warm out." I responded shedding the heavy down parka. "What do you think this weird weather is all about? Is it Global Warming or El Niño?"

"Aw, I don't believe in any of that shit..." Alan laughed. "It's just warm out, that's all, It's just warm out...All that Global Warming, El Nanny stuff is for the birds. I've been living too long 'n seen too much to believe in that mumbo jumbo! All's I believe in is God, the Bible and Jazz, in that order."

I had just met Alan. He had been sitting at the far end of the bar when I walked into the popular Pittsburgh nightspot called "The Balcony". The place was packed, as usual. There were no tables open and so both he and I had been forced to sit at the bar and wait for a table to get freed up. I had earlier spent a little time across the street at the Cozumel Mexican restaurant to check out an out-of-town Latin band that was performing that evening but got bored of listening to one merengue after another. I like merengues, but I was also expecting to hear a little salsa. I need to hear some salsa every now and then! I wasn't getting what I wanted at Cozumel at that moment. I knew the popular Balcony Big Band was playing that night and was eager to enjoy the great sound they put out. I had left the Mexican club and crossed the street.

As I entered the Balcony, I waved at George, the Balcony Big Band's conga drum player, an old friend of mine who at that time often substituted for one of my percussionists in my own band, Guaracha. I sat down at the bar and ordered a Bloody Mary. I heard a snicker next to me. When

I turned I saw an older black man sitting on the adjoining stool smiling at me.

"What the hell kinda drink is that?" He asked with a mischievous chuckle. I was caught off balance by his question.

"I like tomato juice..." I answered, almost apologetically. "I like Jazz...!" he answered with a smile and took a swig of his beer.

It was a strange way to start off a friendship, but we hit it off and remained together for the rest of the night. Eventually we were able to make it to a table.

"I recognized you when you walked in..." he commented. I remembered your face from that article come out in the papers back 'round New Years. The papers said a lotta nice stuff 'bout your band. I like all that Latin rhythm m'self. That feller over there with the tom-toms, he play with a Latin Jazz band. I like their sound."

He was referring to George who at that time also performed with Pittsburgh's talented Latin Jazz ensemble, Salsamba.

"I thought they be playing jazz here tonight, but they ain't!" He continued as he waved at the waitress for another beer. "Don't you like this big band music?" I asked.

"Yea, it's all right, but it ain't Jazz. I listened to this shit long enough when it was new, and when I was new. Now that I'm old it just sounds like the same old crap"

The waitress approached us, but Alan got up suddenly and put on his coat. "I'm going to the North Side to James Street Tavern. They always got jazz playing there. Ya coming?" He winked at me tossing a five dollar tip on the table.

"Yea, what the heck; I'll tag along." I answered and put my coat back on.

We descended the steps and walked out unto Walnut Street. I cranked up my van and followed Alan's black '88 jaguar up and down the hilly streets of the city, across the 40'th street bridge over the Allegheny river, and up to James street in the North Side. We parked our vehicles and met in front of the entrance to the James Street Tavern. But just as we were going to enter the club, Alan stopped and turned to look at me.

"What's that on your cap?"

I looked at him puzzled. Then I took off my cap and looked at it. "Oh...This is my Cuba hat." I said smiling at him. It's a cap I acquired at a Latin shop in Cleveland which has the Cuban flag and the word CUBA embroidered into the front over the visor.

"Right!" He said. "I can tell you sumt'n 'bout that too, if you wanna hear it."

Now he really had my attention. "What do you mean?" I queried him.

"C'mon, let's go for a little walk...I'll tell ya 'bout my grandaddy." Alan let the door to the club shut and started walking down the street.

"Hey don't you want to go in and listen to Jazz?" I called after him standing puzzled on the sidewalk as he walked away.

"C'mon, c'mon... let's take a walk, I wanna show you sumt'n."

Again I followed Alan, this time on foot.

"I grew up 'cross the river up in the Hill district. At that time you stayed in your own neighborhood, not like 'tis now. But, sometimes me 'n my grandaddy use'ta come up here. 'N ya know what? somehow we never got into no trouble...lucky I guess!

My folks were orig'nally from Massachusetts. My grandaddy lived in Boston for a long time. That wuz way back in the 1800's. Back then, he joined the 54th Regiment Massachusetts Volunteer Infantry colored Army unit and fought in the Civil War when he wuz only 16 years old!

Anyway, he survived that mess, but he talked a lot about it when we wuz kids. He said it was a terrible war!

Later, when the U.S. went to war with Spain he tried to join up again but they didn't let him. I never wuz able to figger out whether it wuz because he wuz colored or that they thought he wuz just too old by then. Musta been forty! But anyway, He felt he just had to go!

He said he wanted to go overseas. At that time the US army wuz fight'n over in your country, in Cuba."

I realized that Al was talking about the Spanish-American war of 1898 which was fought mainly in Cuba and the Philippines. "Well that old boy he wuz still single back then. Din't have no wife'r nutt'in. He found hisself a way to go down there. He got hisself hired by some Boston newspaper to be a kinda "go-fer" for their reporters. The reporters bought him a ticket on a boat from Key West and they followed that army right over to Cuba. So the way he told it, He ended up taking care of them reporters in their hotel suite, running errands fer them tidying up after they mess and generally keeping them in food and rum as long as they stayed down there in some little town name o' S'tigo or Sattigo, or some damned thing like that...I cain't pr'nounce it."

I stopped walking and exclaimed. "Your grandfather was in Santiago? That's my city! That's where I was born!"

"See...I figgered when I seen ya, I needed t' talk t'ya. Aint that the darndest thing!" He laughed. "Wait till ya hear th' rest." Alan had stopped walking when I stopped, but now he turned around and began to move down the street again.

"My grandaddy always used to talk about Teddy Roosevelt'n San Juan Hill 'n how he got to see him in person. Roosevelt eventually became the president of the United States years later ya know. 'N my gramps used to say that when all the shoot'n wuz over they had this big surrender thing, like a big-ass ceremony, in the middle, of that little town where the Spanish gave up to the Americans and the Americans got to keep Cuba, right?"

"Yea that's true..." I answered. "At the end of the Spanish American war the Americans took over my country for a few years, then, later Cuba was granted independence."

"OK..." He answered. "I don't know nutt'n 'bout that other stuff...I just know what my old grandaddy used to tell us. When the Americans won they took over. 'N he always remembered that there wuz a whole bunch'a Cuban fighters around. 'lotta them wuz, blacks, just as dark as he wuz. 'N they had been fight'n them Spanish for a long time, and a lotta them had died. 'N don't ya know non a'them wuz allowed up there for that big surrender ceremony on account'a the Spanish general didn't want to surrender to a buncha coloreds, and he set that as a condition of his surrender. So all them black Cuban rebel troops wuz forced by the Americans to stay outside'a town while the lily-white Spanish general handed his sword over to the lily-white American general. Grandaddy always used to make me laugh cuz he said the American general wuz the biggest man He'd ever seen. He said that ol' boy look like a blimp, he was so fat!"

"Your grandfather saw all that?" I asked as we crossed the street and walked unto the grass of East Commons Park.

"Yup..." He answered. "And something else... When he got back to the U.S. he got married and moved to Pittsburgh to work in the steel mill. Well he found sumt'n right here in this park."

Alan stopped in front of the old Civil War monument. I looked at it in puzzlement. It looked like dozens of other historical monuments around town. "What's this?" I asked.

"My grandaddy used ta tell me that when he wuz down there in Cuba he saw the Americans load up cargo ships with all kind'a stuff they took from th' Spanish cuz the Spanish had lost th' war, 'n all. He used ta bring me up here to the North Side...'twas called 'Old Allegheny' back then. He used ta show me this here cannon, cuz it's been sitt'n right here all this time. He used ta say 'Ally...' That's what he called me, Ally.

'Ally...' he said. 'You look real hard at that thar cannon. That thar cannon ate up a lotta them poor colored Cubans down there. Them folks fought real hard to make they country free just like Washington an' them did here in the USA. But you know what? When they time came we shut the poor bastards right outta they own victory celebration, like we had done it all ou'selves.

'N them niggers down there had to just swallow they pride and go home wit' they tails tucked up between they hind legs.' That's what my old grandaddy told me right here, in fronta this ol' statue, and knowing what I know now I believe everything he said".

I leaned over and stared hard at the cannon sitting on top of its stone pedestal. I saw that there were words inscribed on the side of the stone.

"yea... you look real hard. 'n read it, read it. My grandaddy said he actually saw when this here gun was hoisted up unto one of them ships. Me 'n my daddy we believed everything he told us. but momma wuz from South Carolina. She always thought he wuz crazy. When she an' daddy split up I never got to see my ol' grandaddy that much anymore. That wuz too bad cuz I loved that ol' coot!"

I strained to read the dim weather-worn words inscribed on the side of the stone. "THIS CANNON PRESENTED BY THE UNITED STATES GOVERNMENT TO ALLEGHENY JUNE 29 1899 CAPTURED FROM THE SPANISH AT SANTIAGO CUBA BY THE AMERICANS UNDER COMMAND OF GENERAL WM C. SHAFTER JULY 17, 1898 ".

HAMPTON BATTERY MONUMENT

This cannon presented by the United States government to Allegheny June 29 1899 captured from the Spanish at Santiago Cuba by the Americans under Gen. Wm C. Shafter, July 17, 1898

A STONE WITH A MESSAGE

Alan told me he was 68 years old. We didn't exchange telephone numbers or addresses that night, we just went our separate ways. I may meet him again someday, but not at the Balcony; the popular club closed down that same year, 1998. I don't really frequent James Street Tavern, so it's very possible that I might never see Alan again. But I'll never forget him, or his story of the cannon sitting atop that hunk of sandstone in the middle of East Commons Park in the North Side of Pittsburgh.

I think now about the cryptic markings on Indian God Rock sitting out there on the bank of the Allegheny River and the petroglyphs carved by ancient Tainos in the cave of Patana that I visited as a child in the company of my family in the 1950's and I wonder about the invisible spiritual connection that bound together the two different folk who had executed those two works of shamanic art. And was there any connection between those two rocks and the much more modern rock with its own unique message, a story reflecting an act of injustice that awaited reconciliation, etched into its surface sitting right there in Pittsburgh's East Commons Park?

11. The 2000's

The progress was steady all day on Wednesday August 18. We had made good time that afternoon and managed to cover more distance than we had expected to cover. We decided to take a break at around 4:00. We sat quietly on the river bank eating jerked beef and trail mix, and we watched the broad expanse of the Allegheny as it rolled slowly past us taking twigs, leaves and branches down to Pittsburgh ahead of us. As I sat there staring into the water I made plans to find a pay telephone soon and call home to inform Leni that we would be arriving the following day. I wanted her to be waiting for me at Point State Park on the confluence of Pittsburgh's three rivers.

I was not aware of it but as I sat on that riverbank looking at the slow flow of the river a musician right here in the United States was releasing a song called "1999". The musician is called Prince. His song has been described as "apocalyptic but upbeat". The fact is that Prince's song with its line which would eventually become iconic, "party like it's 1999", was making an allusion to a theme that would become widespread all over the world, that the transition from the twentieth century into the tentyfirst might be apocalyptic. Prince's song suggested that we spend this moment of the "Last Days" partying, but his message masked a deeper angst that was slowly creeping into the global awareness and also being expounded in a lot of literature. This theme maintained that as the1990's wound down toward the beginning of the year 2000 there was going to be some sort of world-ending event. Alternatively some people began to expound an even more absurd notion. That was the idea that the real apocalypse was scheduled for December 21st 2012, the date that ancient Mayas had predicted as the end of the Fifth Sun Period and the beginning of the new Great Cycle.

The fact is that as the slow river of time flowed past the decade of the 1990's things did indeed look cataclysmic. The horrible ethnic war raged in the Balkans region of Europe where people were exterminating each other over differences in religion, ethnic affiliation and regional politics. And right here in the United States Timothy McVeigh detonated his monstrous home-made bomb in Kansas City killing little pre-school children who were the same age as the babies that Leni and I had cared for in our daycare back in the 1980's. At around the end of the decade the racist skinheads discovered the internet and went global. Religious fundamentalists in the Middle East, chafing under the weight of many years of injustice quietly plotted vengeance.

But the fact is that even as these negative events were unfolding other events were taking place also and these events were about a determined and optimistic human species who refused to accept the victory of the spirit of negativity. At around the same time that the racist skinheads discovered the internet, the modern-day Tainos also discovered the internet at the end of the 1990's. New Taino groups arose and grew, and then fragmented into yet newer Taino groups. And each group evolved and matured in its own way.

This process was a real miracle within which hundreds of modern-day Tainos who had begun to coalesce into organized groups back in 1992 gradually found their voice and their identity, one by one. At the end of the 1990's, by discovering the public presence on the internet of more and more vibrant and active Taino organizations the movement picked up speed. Groups of modern-day people who identified as Tainos found the opportunity to organize get-togethers and to meet and surround themselves with other people who also identified as Tainos. Increasingly larger and larger gatherings materialized and the movement blossomed.

On the world stage the decade of the 1990's ended anticlimactically in regard to the pessimistic expectations of some. Complete dependance on computers for the most intimate aspects of business and society made the possibility of a globally widespread computer glitch, a source of great concern at the beginning of the new century. However the anxiety that this apocalyptic so-called "millennium bug" created proved to be exaggerated.

The real threat to humanity showed itself the following year. It was not a computer anomaly after all. Instead, this catastrophe was entirely man-made.

On September 11 of 2001 the world came face to face with the ultimate manifestation of ethnic and religious intolerance and bitter rage. The events of September 11 were inspired by the eternally persistent Spirit of Discord who has been dogging the steps of our species for 5200 years since the rising of the Fifth Sun. Zealous young men of one major world religion mounted a murderous assault on civilian citizens of a nation they perceived to be mortal enemies of their faith. These men boarded four different airliners at different airports in the eastern United States. They violently overpowered the helpless stewardesses, mercilessly knifing some of them to death in cold blood in front of horrified passagers. Then they proceeded to invade the cockpits, kill the pilots and crash one of the jets into the United States main U.S. military headquarters, the Pentagon. They also crashed two other planes into the most prominent sky-scrapers in New York City, the twin towers of the World Trade Center. In the spectacular aftermath of the attack the lives of over 2000 human beings were snuffed out in one day.

I was walking toward my classroom early in the morning at the beginning of the school day at Pittsburgh's Rooney Middle School when all this mayhem took place. By that time, I had given up management of Sague Presents Entertainment, handed control of the performance arts company to my son Cha, and returned to teaching full-time. As I was walking up the hallway to my classroom that fateful morning I was actually very happy. I was lost in thought about a recent gathering that I had helped organize in New York City that summer. I had collaborated in the organizing of a meeting of the leaders of several of the prominent Taino Resurgence groups that had cropped up in New York during the previous decade. I had collaborated on this project with a Taino woman who had requested to be trained as a behike of the Caney Circle, and who now felt a sense of urgency about the disunity in our nascent Taino communities. Discord had arisen in the movement and created deep rifts among the leaders. The gathering had been only partially successful, but I had come away with a great deal of optimism.

Now as I walked calmly up the hallway I felt a smile dawn upon my face. Suddenly, without warning the physical education teacher appeared breathlessly out of nowhere. "New York City is being bombed!" she managed to gasp at me as she ran past.

It took at least two or three hours for the facts to become clear among the teachers at Rooney Middle. By that time any attempt at teaching had become unrealistic as one parent after another showed up at the door of the school and demanded their child. One of the highjacked airplanes had been purposely crashed in Summerset that day, not far from Pittsburgh. We felt like the whole nation was under attack, not just New York. And, of course, in a way, we were right.

The rationalization of those who masterminded the attack in the name of God was as ancient as the Fifth Sun itself. It has been used for millennia by warring members of every major religious faith. Throughout all that time the supposed religious leaders in collusion with political leaders controlled by the spirit of discord, have told us "God is on our side. The enemy is against the laws of God. They must die so we can live". This line of intolerant thinking has more recently been considered antiquated and obsolete by much of humankind. But it still can strike a powerful chord when expounded by manipulators of religious media to create a murderous level of fanatic zeal that can prove extremely destructive.

One of the most notable features of that tragedy was the fact that for all intents and purposes the focal heroes of the day were the New York City fire fighters who bravely entered the two doomed buidings to attempt to extiguish the original fires that were set by the plane crashes, and also, the New York City police officers who just as bravely helped hundreds of people get out of the way of danger both in the buildings and outside in the streets. They all selflessly assisted total strangers of all colors, races, religions and life stations. Many of these people died during the catastrophe. They were "Giving Beasts" in the tradition of the Black Ribs image I had dreamed during my vision quest, giving until there was no more to give. They were all shooting stars who decided to shine in a particular dark moment of history.

And so the mechanized, technological West had arrogantly looked outward toward the flashy, high tech cyber-threat of the "millennium bug" as its most dangerous challenge in the new century, when in fact, the real threat turned out to be much more human, much more visceral, much more ancient, much more persistent, and much more fanatical. So many slaves!

12. TAINOS ON THE INTERNET

Around the year 2003 I began to interact with a Taino Resurgence organization that began to manifest itself as one of the most distinct entities to emerge in the late 1990's and early 2000's. This organization is the the United Confederation of Taino People which had been founded in the mid 1990's. Guided by its charismatic and energetic director, a young Boriken Taino living in the New York area called Roberto Mukaro Borrero, the UCTP rose to prominence at this time as a result of its policy of enthusiastically reaching out to Tainos and other Caribbean people all over the islands and the diaspora. This organization also gained valuable recognition for modern-day Tainos in the international Indigenous community by establishing a powerful presence in the United Nations. Ultimately Mukaro came to hold the distinguished position of chairperson of the Non Governmental Organization Comitee on the International Decade of the World's Indigenous People, closely associated with the UN Permanent Forum on Indigenous People, a move which significantly raised the visibility of Tainos on the world stage. From a very early point in the history of the UCTP I recognized its potential for unifying and consolidating the Taino Resurgence movement. I could tell that the steadfast determination of its director and the clear goals that were articulated in its publicly promoted statements of policy made this the Taino organization most likely to achieve those goals. The Caney Circle that I guided began to co-operate more and more closely with the UCTP. Roberto and I began to see each other more and more as true friends.

In those days my son had taken complete control of the business I had created in the early 1990's, Sague Presents Entertainment. By the year 2006 he had negotiated a couple of contracts with the University of Pittsburgh's Semester At Sea program for a two week cruise on which our band Guaracha would perform on board for the passengers. It was during one of the ocean cruises on which my son had booked us that a kind of explosive critical mass finally reached full manifestation in my relationship with the Taino Resurgence. It was Winter Solstice season of 2006, a time when most of the Christian world is celebrating Christmas. I had taken a few extra days leave during my December holiday vacations from school so that I could perform with Guaracha band on our two-week ocean-liner cruise along the whole Pacific coast of Mexico down the shores of Central America and through the Panama Canal into the Caribbean Sea. My son was firmly in control of the whole enterprise so all I had to do during the entire cruise was perform for a few hours a night, and spend the rest of my time enjoying such marine natural attractions as humpback whales breaching off the coast of the Baja penninsula and flying fish scooting just above the surface of the water alongside the ship's bow off the coast of Guatemala. And that does not include the wonders of the Maya market in Puerto Quetzal, the ancient pre-Maya ruins of El Baul, magnificent waterfalls and traditional Carib Indian tribal dances on the Caribbean island of Dominica, a personal guided tour of the sacred Taino ceremonial center of Tibes near Ponce, Boriken led by my friend, the Boriken Taino UCTP leader, Bibi Joanna Aya Soto Aviles, and a visit to a gorgeous secluded beach in Jamaica where I performed ceremony in the company of Native Jamaicans.

I could not possibly imagine what in the world could go wrong under those circumstances. But never underestimate the power of mischief in the hands of the great spiritual enemy that had been dogging the steps of humanity for 5200 years. Since the year 1999 when I bought my first personal computer I had made a point of learning to navigate the internet. At first it seemed a weird and irrational place to me and I tried my best to become acquainted with its unfamiliar ins and outs. Eventually I became more adept in the intricacies of this medium and realized quickly how important it could become in the process of providing the new artist-medicine people their new cave wall. The internet was immediate, and a person could potentially reach the whole world community via this medium in real time. It was the closest that modern humans could come to the immediacy of the ancient communal prehistoric Ice-Age cave council fire on the scale of the global human tribe. And what was most important, it was almost completely accessible to the common man and woman. It was not exclusively controlled by the enemy like traditional media such as television, radio, and a great deal of published print material had been for decades. The Mad Men did not control the Internet.

As the years of 1999 and 2000 progressed I became computer literate enough to open a website for the Caney Indigenous Spiritual Circle, and a little later I established a Yahoo Group forum which I made available to the world community in general, but especially to my own Taino people. In this forum I began to post material related to the work of our circle and I began to share the ancient wisdom of our people without revealing the deeper more private matters that are traditionally shared only in person and out of the public eye. Others began to share there also and wonderful dialogs ensued.

Unfortunatelly, by the beginning of the year 2000 there had arisen a great deal of antagonism and competitive bitterness among the new Resurgence-era Taino communities and leaders. Some of the dialogs on the internet at times became heated. My response to the antagonism and the discordant discourse that was growing on the internet was not to take sides and attempt complete neutrality. For the most part this earned me the trust of the majority of those who were sharing their opinions on the forum page. But sometimes this stance became difficult because any statement on my part aknowledging the authenticity of one group or someone in one group, would earn me the suspicion of the members of the opposite group. There was such polarization that I could not make a positive statement online about someone without immediately being challenged on the point by that person's adversaries. Nevertheless, my attitude of neutrality was the right path at that point, since the agression was raw and most participants in the movement were in no mood for reconciliation.

This state of affairs continued from the year 2000, right through the horrific trauma of September 11, 2001, a tragedy which affected many New York Tainos profoundly, and then later, up through 2005. During that time I busied myself attempting to cement incresingly stronger bonds of trust between the Caney Circle and the various leaders of the Taino resurgence movement, as well as the members of each Taino community, most of whom identified their group by the Taino word "yukayeke" which is used as a generic term for "village".

As early as 2001, both before and after the 9/11 event, I began travelling to New York City and Philadelphia to perform ceremony with my Taino people and their supporters there, as well as to support the work of the behikes of our community who were keeping our Caney circle traditions alive in those two cities. By this time I began to realize that the ceremonies of the Caney Circle and the sacred songs of our tradition were beginning to take hold among many Tainos and even non-Tainos in those two cities. It was part of the great resurgence movement that the people were slowly recovering something precious that had been lost long ago.

My friend Bibi Margarita Noguera in the town of Jayuya, Boriken began to contact me as early as 2002 to co-ordinate my participation in an annual event that the crafts collective she belonged to was planning to sponsor in the central mountains of the island. Eventually the Caney Circle became a fixture in that yearly event as Tainos consistantly gathered to celebrate the sacred White Cemi, the Hope Child of unity and reconciliation.

Margarita Noguera The Jayuya Gathering

The author

Besides participating as spiritual guide and teacher during the yearly gatherings in Jayuya, we established a cycle of ceremonies around the United States. There were Caney Circle Full Moon ceremonies with Arawaks in Texas, with Cuban Tainos in upstate New York, and with Boriken Tainos in Youngstown, Ohio. There were Caney Circle Winter Solstice ceremonies with Tainos from all the islands in Miami, Florida, and Summer Solstice ceremonies back in Ohio. I also was invited to officiate spiritual ceremonies at various communal yukayeke areitos in New York City.

Back in Pittsburgh we continued the co-operative labor with other individuals who were inspired like us to work toward the accomplishment of the promise that we all as humans had inherited from the ancient prophecies. The sacred work was getting done and my Taino people along with many others with whom we came in touch all benefitted from it. And most of this work was organized on the internet, and inspired by the work we were doing on the internet.

But things began to take a distinctly different tack on the internet in 2006. A new member began posting in the Caney Yahoo group. At first her posts were relatively innocuous. She mostly shared under the Taino name Bano-Sheiti, which means "Black Bird". At around the same time we began to see posts by a man identifying himself as Ama-Waribo which means "River Warrior".

As I mentioned earlier, Bano-Sheiti normally posted positive statements regarding Taino tradition and general Indigenous tradition as a whole. She also demonstrated an advanced knowledge of Afro-Caribbean spiritual tradition and often interpolated the two traditions as if there really was not much difference between the two, or that one was some how an outgrowth of the other. Her posts, although sometimes a little unconventional in their content, tended to be thought-provoking and exhibited intelligence and an informed perspective. However, on occasion she would suddenly post an unexpected remark that gave the impression of extraordinary anger and violence of emotion in response to specific comments by myself or others. On one occasion she responded with such vitriol to a remark posted by an old friend of mine, Spider, who now lived in north-western New York State that Spider stopped posting altogether.

The anger and animosity increasingly exhibited by Bano-Sheiti was scary enough for some people that whole groups of the original subscribers in the online forum either unsubscribed or simply stopped paricipating completely. In other words, Bano-Sheiti was driving away our friends.

At first I and others attempted to reason with her. And sometimes she would respond with what appeared to be sincere remorse and contrition, and promises to adjust the tenor of her speech. But these were only temporary.

As this drama unfolded the man who identified himself as Ama-Waribo also began to post. His messages always carried a tone of sage wisdom and advice, and at first, also humility and consideration. He also expressed himself in a manner that indicated that he was a Taino. His remarks did not suggest any particular connection with Bano-Sheiti but there was a similarity in his words to hers and the spiritual concepts that he brought to the dialog were very similar also, with many references to Afro-Caribbean tradition, and the ever-present suggestion that the relationship between the spiritual path of the ancient Taino Indigenous people and the spiritual path of the African ancestors was really one and the same, and that adopting one was just as important as adopting the other.

It is common knowledge that modern Taino spirituality owes much to the synchretic tradition of Afro-Cuban Santeria. African slaves were brought to the Caribbean to work the tobacco and sugar fields and to mine the rich ore deposits of the islands. These people brought their powerful culture with them. And that culture flourished in the slave quarters of the plantations and free black neighborhoods of the towns.

That culture combined the teachings of the Catholic religion which they were forced to adopt by their Spanish masters, with the traditional African ways that they brought with them. That is the reason the synchretic culture is called "Santeria", because it includes the veneration of Catholic saints (santos) as representations of the traditional African gods.

The Santeria culture not only added many elements of Christian tradition to its usage but it also borrowed heavily from the tradition of the Tainos who at that time were still practicing some of their spiritual ways in the mountains and fields of the islands.

Over the course of centuries, as many of the main Taino traditions died slowly, drowned by the forces of religious persecution of the Spanish, some of these ways continued to live on in the practices of Santeria, and therefore we modern Tainos now have inherited many of those Taino traditions by gratefully taking them back out of the Afro-Caribbean Santeria context and re-instating them as a force of their own in our own Indigenoua life-path.

These facts are very evident in most of us Tainos of the Resurgence era. But Ama-Waribo and Bano-Sheiti seemed to be promoting something quite different in their online forum messages of the early 2000's. Their message seemed to suggest that the African element was part and parcel of the original Taino way from the very beginning and that there really was no valid separation between the two. This is inacuarate. Of course, because their attitude tended to be very Afro-centric and anti-caucasian, they totally ignored the very prevalent Spanish White European Christian element of Santeria in their argument, and their reaction was negative and dismissive if that element was ever brought up or suggested by anyone in the forum. In addition to all this, the messages posted by Bano Sheiti and Ama-Waribo tended to be extremely divisive promoting a bizarre theory that all white or light-skinned people were descended from an ethnic group who were fundamentally dieased and inherently inferior to people with darker skin.

They were both obviously practicing this uniquely racist form of Santeria and other Afro-Caribbean traditions that not only purged the European Christian elements from the practice but actually condemned all people who were not people of color. And they seemed to believe that this was the spiritual tradition of our Taino ancestors. It added a confusing twist to our efforts at re-constituting our ancient Indigenous ways and drove some Resurgence movement Tainos from the conversation.

Eventually Bano-Sheiti revealed the fact that she was a student of Ama-Waribo, and claimed that he was actually a respected Taino elder and teacher in his own right. Of course there were very few of us in the forum by that time to whom this revelation and claim was a surprise.

Many participants in the forum who lived in the New York Taino community scratched their heads wondering who these two anonymous people could be. Although they, at first, were careful not to reveal their place of residence, in their posts, they appeared to be cognizant of the history of the New York Taino Resurgence process.

While all of this was happening, the old feuds and grudges that had always existed among the groups of the Tainos continued to fester, and from time to time these antagonisms would boil over and make themselves evident in the form of back-and-forth snide remarks or outright offensive verbal attacks and arguments in our forum and in other Taino forums that began to spring up all over the internet.

That was the way things were in December of 2006 when I boarded the cruise ship along with my son Cha, and the other members of our salsa band in Cabo San Lucas, Mexico. The excitement among the musicians was palpable since none of us had ever performed on an ocean cruise ship, and the journey itself seemed to most of us the stuff of dreams. How could you beat getting paid to spend two weeks cruising the Pacific coast and the Caribbean?

The cruise proved to be everything we expected and much more. How cool is it to be doing what you love to do every evening, making great music in the company of outstandingly talented performers, eating and drinking way too much, while the ship plowed its way south from port to port. And in the daytime we visited each one of those ports, discovering and awakening amidst the beauty and culture of Central America and the Antilles?

In the evenings after each performance I attempted to log on at the shipboard computer station and check on our online forum to monitor the progress of the discussions. This proved to be a very difficult mission. On many occasions the whole internet service aboard the ship simply crashed and stayed offline for hours. This problem was compounded by the fact that the internet service was extremely expensive and I had to slow down on my online time just to stay solvent.

It seems to me now that this vulnerable moment in the history of the Caney Circle online forum, when it was difficult for me to moderate the daily exchanges in the conversation, provided Bano-Sheiti and Ama-Waribo, and ultimately the ancient spirit of discord and intolerance who controlled them, with the opportunity to make the move they had intended to make all along.

One day during the cruise when I had been off-line for a few days Ama-Waribo posted a long message containing a list of questions, specifically directed at behikes, the spiritual leaders of the Taino community. I now believe that this was a kind of test directed mostly at me and the Caney Circle, since at that time there were very few behikes on the internet besides those who belonged to the Caney Circle. The questions were designed to provoke answers that could then be attacked and could make it easy to question the legitimacy of the whole Caney Circle community and our work.

I totally missed the message at first because, by the time I was able to return to the internet, a lot of other messages had already been posted. Most of the subscribers who did see Ama-Waribo's post seemed to realize the real intent of his questions and avoided them altogether. Others attempted to respond and, of course, fell into his trap. His responses were calm but pointed, and always tainted with the flavor of a judgemental elder's lecture. Nobody likes to be lectured to, especially online by a faceless character operating from behind the guise of a nom-de-plume, and who has not demonstrated the courtesy to properly reveal his real identity.

Although Ama-Waribo's actions during my absence were annoying to some and disruptive to the community as a whole, his calm and sage online demeanor and the wise elder tone with which he delivered his statements engratiated him to some of the Tainos on the web, who were easily swayed by his rhetoric. Eventually Ama-Waribo began to win a small following. By the time I realized what was happening in the group it was almost too late. A lot had already transpired and Ama-Waribo had even posted a follow-up message subtly questioning the integrity of the behikes who had not responded to his challenge.

Finally I was able to catch up with the thread and began to post a series of individually issued responses to his many questions.

This turned out to be a discouraging excersize because as I attempted to address each one of his many original questions, restrained as I was, by the limitations of my poor internet access on the ship, he promptly began to counter my responses, as quickly as I posted them, even before I was finished with the slow painfully tedious process of answering all the queries in his original list. It was a classic trap. I was hesitant to go after these new statements until I had completed the task of answering all of the questions in the original list. So I ignored the new comments while I continued with my original list of answers.

In the meantime while I was tediously plodding along this course he continued to post in quick succession, bringing up a whole slew of new arguments which I could not address right away, attempting to make it look like I was avoiding his statements and questions altogether.

This experience taught me some valuable lessons about internet interaction, and made me a much wiser internet resident.

It's important to understand that I had not joined the World Wide Web to entertain nonsense antagonism from faceless agitators who seemed simply to be motivated by jealousy and the hope to acquire a following at the expense of the work that we had been carrying out for the past twenty years. It was extremely disconcerting that the community that we had nurtured all these years since my canoe trip of 1982 now had to be distracted by this senseless digression.

Some of us did research on them in 2006. It turned out Ama-Waribo was, in fact, a former member of one of the 1990's New York Taino communities. He had left the city and moved to a rural region of West Virginia for mysterious reasons. I was informed about this by a friend in the city who had known him back in 1993 when Ama-Waribo, under a different name, had participated in Caney Circle ceremonies guided by Caney Circle behikes working in the New York City area.

Months after the 2006 ocean cruise I had an opportunity to drive to West Virginia and visit him at his home during a brief truce in what eventually developed into a contentious relationship. I visited him even after the trouble he had caused during the time that I was trapped on that cruise ship practically without internet access because I was always attempting to come to terms and reconcile with individuals with whom I had problems. I drove several hours to West Virginia and I met him in person at his residence. When I arrived there I was surprised to discover that Bano-Sheiti was actually his wife, or unmarried life-partner (I never was able to find out which), that they had a beautiful little daughter together, and most surprising, that Bano-Sheiti looked to be, for all intents and purposes, a white Anglo-American woman! As hard as I tried, I could not discern the faintest hint of any black or Indigenous ethnic physical feature evident in her. She was not a light-complected black woman or even a white Hispanic or Taino. She just was very obviously Anglo white!

It took me a little while to get over that particular detail since she had demonstrated such disdain for the Caucasian race as a whole, even denying in one particularly virulent online post that white people had any kind of ancestral spiritual root at all, and that they had stolen any spirituality they now possessed from dark skinned people. These words resonated in my head now as I looked into her very white face.

One remarkable thing that I discovered in West Virginia was that Ama-Waribo's alliance with Bano-Sheiti had turned out to be a very profitable one for him. Somehow she had managed to help him procure a prodigious tract of land. I think I remember now that she seemed to imply that they had somehow aquired it for free or through some sort of grant, or something like that. They had organized it and also his personal spiritual projects asa non-profit entity under the formal title of the "Caribbean Tribal Society". It never was made very clear to anyone who the actual members of the Caribbean Tribal Society were, beside Ama-Waribo and Bano-Sheiti.

Ama-Waribo and Bano-Sheiti had been very busy at the Caribbean Tribal Society grounds in West Virginia. They erected whole batey ceremonial fields, surrounded by huge upright stone slabs which they had specially trucked in. The bateyes looked very much like the 500-year-old ones that are found at Caguana in the mountains of Boriken. They had erected huts that looked just like the ancient bohio dwellings of the Tainos. And they had dedicated a great deal of time and care to the meticulous tending of agricultural fields which fulfilled their goal of becoming as independent as possible of commercial processed food. It was all actually quite admirable if it were not for the toxic divisive rhetoric that accompanied it.

Accompanying all of theTaino Indigenous symbolism up there on the grounds of the Caribbean Tribal Society there was also a great deal of African spiritual symbolism all over the place in keeping with their belief that the one went hand-in hand with the other, that somehow, the one could not exist without the other. I left their compound very impressed with the work they had completed there but not long after I returned home and continued following their rhetoric online it became obvious to me that their intentions were not to be trusted. Essentially the trouble stemmed from the fact that Bano-Sheiti and Ama-Waribo were not capable of countenancing any variance or disagreement with their very narrow bigoted perspective.

If anybody disagreed with their extreme, intolerant rants they immediately resorted to personal attacks and insults that ranged from name-calling to ridicule to acusations of their target not being "Taino enough".

Bano-Sheiti was an extremely intelligent and capable individual, and in the long run turned out to be a formidable oponent. It became evident to my wife Leni at first and then slowly to me as their online attacks became more and more persistent and effective that it was she and not he that was the true brain behind their campaign to discredit everything that we had worked for.

During my visit in West Virginia before the really vicious attacks began, Ama-Waribo confessed to me that he was practically illiterate and could not read or write very well. Now, knowing that fact, I wondered how in the world he had managed to post the intricately articulate material that had caused so much trouble in our forum. Then I realized that his speech and the clumsy reasoning patterns that he utilized when he spoke in person did not match the sophistication and verbal dexterity that he exhibited online. However they did match the speech and reasoning patterns of Bano-Sheiti. It slowly dawned on me that it was not he but Bano-Sheiti who posted under his non-de-plume. She was speaking for herself and also for him, cleverly assuming a sage, wise male teacher persona whenever she posted under his name.

Not long after my visit to West Virginia they resumed their disruptive work. Reluctantly I began to edit the content of the forum, purging out the most offensive material since they had recruited allies who became very disrespectful and so vulgar in their talk that we lost more subscribers, not to mention the fact that at that point the statements posted by these people in Caney Circle group were severely streching the limits of the Yahoo Groups terms of service for offensive speech.

When the content that Ama-Waribo, Bano-Sheiti and their allies posted ceased to be available on the Caney Circle forum I, of course, was accused of censorship. A new forum appeared in the Yahoo Groups under the management of what was obviously a fake female identity who claimed to be a very young Taino woman called "Taina Voice". Of course Taina Voice's posts exhibited the same speech patterns and logic of Bano-Sheiti and she was also critical of the Caney Circle in general and myself in particular. Nevertheless, she accepted me when I applied for subscription in her new forum.

The new forum was called "Taino Free Speech" and it became pretty obvious to everyone right away, that it was created simply to establish a platform for the unfettered exposition of their corrosive views and continued attacks on the Caney Indigenous Spiritual Circle.

In this new forum Ama-Waribo's attacks became even more virulent and pointed. Ultimately he publicly confirmed that he had participated in Caney Circle ceremonies while he lived in New York back in the1990's. Now he claimed that he had been fooled by them. He claimed that now he knew the truth that the Caney Circle was a fake entity, and that Miguel Sague was also a fake. He made it clear that his mission was to expose all of us so other Tainos would not be fooled like he had been.

There were people who actually began to believe these lies. As a result of the un-ending attacks from those two faceless voices from the internet, for the first time in the history of our work, we actually began to hear fellow Tainos express doubts as to the sincerity of the work of the Caney Circle.

Later on, as the attacks of Ama-Waribo and Bano-Sheiti became more strident they managed to recruit more and more allies, Tainos who bought into their venom. Unfortunately they managed to skilfully exploit the already existing divisons and on-going feuds in the Taino communities to create from that place of anonymity of their computer keyboards, even more discord and more divison. It was a serious blow to the progress of our work of reconciliation.

This contentious period was the low point in the on-going "Taino Wars" in general, and the indisputable nadir of the twenty-odd years of labor that the Caney Circle had dedicated to the ancient tradition of theTaino. It was not a good time. In spite of all this I continued to remain scrupulously careful not to burn any bridges among the Taino community, even in regard to individuals who appeared to support the opinions of Ama-Waribo and Bano-Sheiti. That was not easy to do. It hurt deeply to see people with whom I had cultivated friendship and trust for years, actually agree with some of the filth that was emanating from Taino Free Speech forum about us.

But I remained steadfast. I continued to swallow my pride and even more importantly, my anger. I continued to treat all these people as the relatives that they were, and I even maintained my subscription in Taino

Free Speech forum in force. In fact, I occasionally posted messages there whenever there was something important concerning the Caney Circle that I needed to publicize, an up-coming scheduled ceremony or a blog concerning Taino or Maya culture. Often these posts were received with scorn, ridicule and disrespect. I almost never responded to those disrespectful responses. I simply waited for the next opportunity to post another important piece of information and then I posted it.

The years of 2006 and 2007 ran their course and we at the Caney Circle continued our work of bringing the ancient tradition of our ancestors to as many Tainos as we could reach, and also to any non-Tainos who showed interest in this path. During that time, one of the daughters of my sister Rosa and her Canadian Cree Indian husband Melvin John, now a young lady, participated in the annual Gathering Of Nations Pow Wow in Arizona. The whole family had taken after their pow wow-dancing dad. As a family, Melvin, Rosa and their four children had excelled marvelously in Native events all over the world, from traditional affairs on Canadian rural reserves and Toronto gatherings, to the annual Miccosukee Indian festival in Florida, and also from South America to New Zealand. The globe-trodding John family had made an international name for themselves as performers in their family ensemble "Kehewin Native Dance Theater".

The Kehewin Native Dance group is the world-renown performance arts and educational ensemble founded by the author's sister Rosa, her husband the Cree pow wow star from Alberta, Canada, Melvin John and their family.

Now Violet, the talented fancy-shawl dancer of the family had entered the Miss Indian World competition at the Gathering of Nations pow wow in Arizona, and she won! A huge surge of pride swept the world-wide Taino community when this striking young member of our tribe, a tribe that had been written off as "extinct", was recognized publicly by tribal name at the prestigious Native American event, on the day of her official coronation, and her victory was publicized globally on the internet.

Violet spent that whole year touring reservations and urban Indian communities. As part of her year-long itinerary she visited the Taino community in New York City and I, her uncle, was honored to act as spiritual guide in the ceremonies accompanying the official receptions organized there by the two biggest Taino organizations in town. In the midst of theTaino Wars, this was a beautiful breath of fresh air that allowed us a moment to take a break from the discord and feel proud to be Tainos.

The vitriol manipulated by Ama-Waribo and Bano-Sheiti continued unabated throughout the year 2007 and right into 2008. Then things began to turn against them. It had always been true in my experience with the demonic spirit of discord and hate that has dogged my steps and the steps of my people since the very beginning of the period of the Twenty-Four Generations, that he often uses ambitious individuals with confused motives such as Ama-Waribo to do his destructive work, and then when he is done with them, he casts them aside like trash. The ultimate debacle for Ama-Waribo and Bano-Sheiti began when they started allowing Tainos to actually come to West Virginia to visit them. It is easy to disguise your association with the demon of discord when you are hiding behind a computer screen, but in the truth-revealing glare of the sun, Ama-Waribo and Bano-Sheiti began to lose their on-line luster. One after another, the members of the Taino community travelled there and began to see with their own eyes and hear with their own ears the reality that motivated the rhetoric they read on the internet. It repulsed them. The word spread like wildfire in the Taino community and the West Virginia couple began losing followers at a dramatic rate.

As I followed the process online, I began to notice growing rifts in the alliances that Ama-Waribo and his wife had crafted. These rifts grew and manifested in extremely ugly exchanges on the Taino Free Speech forum. Eventually Ama-Waribo and Bano-Sheiti were contending with serious criticizm of their own, and hurling insults back at other individuals and organizations beside us. This, of course, relieved some of the pressure on us, and demonstrated to theTaino community that just about anyone could suddenly become the target of the West Virginia couple's venom.

Then one afternoon I received an unexpected phone call from Tim Hernandez, a member of the governing body of one of the larger New York Taino yukayeke communities. "Hey Miguel how've you been?" Tim exclaimed opening the conversation with his usual jovial tone. I was glad to hear from Tim. He was one of theTainos with whom I had established a warm relationship. I knew that he had recently visited the West Virginia couple, and I was curious as to what his impression was of the things that were taking place there.

Tim had come away dissapointed. "I like all of the bateyes and the land there is impressive, but the only thing that Ama-Waribo wanted to do while I was there was speak evil of you and your work" he continued. "I got tired of all the bad-mouthing. Anyway, what happened later was the straw that broke the camel's back. Ama-Waribo took me to an out-building and showed me a weird altar-looking thing. On that altar there was some kind of large iron cauldron and inside that pot there was a human skeleton with a bunch of sticks..."

I knew what Tim was talking about because Ama-Waribo had shown me the same altar when I visited him. It was his "nganga", a special kind of ritual set-up that invariably includes real human bones. This kind of altar is the normal arrangement maintained by practitioners of an Afro-Cuban spiritual tradition called "Palo". Tim's description did not surprise me because I was superficially familiar with certain aspects of Palo. For him it was all kind of new, since Palo is still relatively unknown among many people of Boricua (Puerto Rican) ancestry. It was obvious that Ama-Waribo had learned his ceremonial tradition from a Cuban or from someone who had acquired it from a Cuban source.

"I know what you're talking about, brother..." I responded "I also saw that nganga when I visited them." But he continued urgently. "Yea, Miguel but there's something else!" I paused to listen and he went on, his voice assuming a tone of alarm. "I looked real hard at that skeleton and I saw that Ama-Waribo had a photo of you in its mouth." This news sent a chill up my spine. "What?" I asked nervously. "Yea buddy...Hes got a photo of you in that thing's mouth. Looked like some kind spell or witchcraft, or black magic, or something",

Tim must have noticed a longer-than-usual pause in my conversation. "Hey…Are you still there on the line?" he asked. "Yea brother…yea, hey, thanks for the heads-up. I'm glad I got friends like you." This was all I could come back with. I spent the rest of that week busying myself with the work of creating protective spiritual shields around my family and myself to defend us against whatever Ama-Waribo might have been sending at us. Unfortunatelly the December holidays caught up with me and I had to leave the protection spells go until I could finish them when I returned from Florida in January.

My son Cha and I flew south to Miami to celebrate Winter Solstice Ceremony among the group of Cuban, Kiskeyan (Dominican) and Boricua Tainos, and other friends that had gotten into the habit of gathering with us every year at Women's Park in the western region of the city. Women's Park is a city-administered park which had been established a few blocks from my father's home in Miami. It was named in honor of prominent women in the history of the Miami community. It had become the perfect meeting place for our group as we observed the Caney Circle Shark Dance in the familiar tropical warmth of South Florida.

While Cha and I went to Miami, my wife Leni had taken a Greyhound bus to New York City, and then had ridden a mass transit passenger van through the Lincoln tunnel to the city of West New York in Bergen County, New Jersey, to visit her folks there. It was a rather unfortunate fact about the winter holidays, that we could not spend them together since we both felt a need to be near our respective parents at that time of the year.

Winter Solstice Ceremony that year was a real pleasure, surrounded by our tribal brothers and sisters, and by other wonderful people whom we had welcomed into our sacred circle. As usual the ceremony culminated with one of the male participants shooting the ritual arrow into a palm-leaf effigy of kahaya the shark. Something odd happened when the arrow penetrated the effigy. At that moment my mind was suddenly filled with a short but painfully loud and shrill screech that forced me to rip off the conch-shell mask that I was wearing and grip my forehead tight with my right hand for a brief instant.

The episode was so brief that none of the participants noticed my painful reaction. I myself did not know what it was, and looked around to see if perhaps one of the children that were present at the time had screamed. At first I was alarmed by the unusual occurrence but I ignored it. My concern disappeared gradually in the warmth and camaraderie of the after-ceremony meal, warm Boricua arroz con gandules and pasteles deliciously prepared by our dear friend Bibi Mildred Karaira, as well as other goodies brought in by other women and men of our people gathered there.

When I returned home to my father's house after the food sharing, I called Leni long-distance in New Jersey and excitedly shared with her how beautifully things had worked out that afternoon at Women's Park. She shared with me how things were going at her parent's home in the cold North-East.

At the end of the conversation she confirmed that she would be travelling back to Pittsburgh before me as usual. As an employee of the Pittsburgh Public School District, my winter holiday vacations were invariably longer than hers. I was off a period of days that streched between Christmas and New Years. She only got Christmas day off at the daycare center where she was employed.

The rest of that evening proceeded without incident and finally I stayed up to watch TV while my dad and other members of the family who, like me, had converged on Miami to celebrate the holidays with my parents retired to sleep. I had shoved a DVD into my dad's player. It was a recording of an old episode of the television series "Law and Order SVU". The theme of this particular episode focused on the subject of Afro-Caribbean spiritual tradition as practiced in New York, and the possibility of a ritual human sacrifice murder.

As I tried to follow the thread of the show's story I realized that I was very drowsy. I drifted in and out of consciousness and I repeatedly nodded off to sleep. The voices of the actors playing cops, interrogating an actor impersonating a Santeria priest seemed distant and shallow. Sometimes I was watching the TV screen and sometimes I was seeing things that my mind projected into the room with me. Then slowly the image of a nganga kettle seemed to materialize before me out of nowhere, floating right in front of me, the elaborately arrayed sticks and feathers and goat's horn protruding from the top of the iron pot, the hollow-eyed human skull at the top of the arrangement, stained and smeared with unfathonble dark, grimy substances. Then my attention was directed to the mouth of the skull. I saw it. The gaping mouth of the skeletal head contained a small photo that lay there as if trapped in the toothy grin of the macabre object. I began to perspire. I began to tremble. Then the thing began to grow and approach me, as if some invisible force was carrying the whole elaborate arrangement toward me. There was nothing I could do to keep the terrifying thing from getting progressively closer. I could not move. I felt paralyzed, just like in the experience on the little man-made beach with Heaven Gazer years before. My breathing became labored and I felt like I was asphyxiating. I tried with every bit of my will to move my arms, to bring them up so I could ward off the dark stained bony face that was getting closer and closer to me. But my arms were as if dead.

The skull atop the nganga was so close to my face that it was easy to see the thing in its mouth. It was a photo, a photo of me! Then I heard that screech again, like the one I had heard during the Shark Dance that afternoon. But, if it had been startling in the brightness of the afternoon sun, now it was terrifying in the deep darkness of night. It was thin, and high-pitched, and piercing. And the teeth of the nganga skull were now right in front of my face, and the photo of me in its mouth. The teeth were no longer human teeth, sharp and jagged, and the screech now more of a snicker, a villanous giggle. The skull was no longer a human skull. It was the diabolically threatening skull of a huge shark with sharp serrated teeth, and the photo slightly ripped and torn hanging, pierced, impaled on one of the teeth. The threatening giggle began to fade.

Then I was suddenly able to move. My eyes snapped open. I was bathed in sweat, breathing spastically. I could hear the street-slang synical tone of voice of Law and Order's Detective Munch as he dutifully investigated the murder of a young child whose decapitated body was found in a public city park, surrounded by ritualistic objects that hinted at a human sacrifice. I sat there for about five minutes staring at the TV screen but I did not see anything there. I was not paying any attention to the show. My mind was rivetted on the mental image of that skull with my photo in its mouth.

A few days after the New Year celebrations I sat in my dad's Miami living room, my suitcase already packed in preparation for my departure the next day. The phone rang and Vicky, my mother's caretaker answered it. Mom had been stricken by Alzheimers years earlier and by now she had been reduced to a shadow of her former energetic, lively self. She required 24-hour care that Papi could no longer give her personally at his advanced age. The Nicaraguan woman who took care of mom called me to the phone. "The call is for you." She said in Spanish.

I brought the receiver to my ear and immediately it was accosted by the excited voice of Debra, a family friend we have that lives in Illinois. Calling long-distance from her home in Chicago, she sounded out-of breath as she gasped: "It's Leni...she had an automobile accident. She's been taken to the hospital!" I caught my breath and bit my lip hard. "What?" That was all I finally managed to mutter. Debra responded: "I called her to gab about her visit in New Jersey because I knew she was back home in Pittsburgh now, and when she answered she told me she was lying in the street surrounded by emergency responders! She told me she would talk to me later, and hung up!"

There was very little that could come out of my mouth at that moment except "How?" But Debra added: "I don't know. She said she was OK but I didn't believe her. I called Moises and informed him. I think he's with her now." "Alright, thank you Debra...let me call and find out what's going on. I'll talk to you later" I finally answered.

I tried to call Leni's cellular phone but no one answered. I assumed she was on her way to the hospital emergency department. I was frantic. Then I thought of calling our tenant, Moises, a friend who at that time was staying in a little annex house that stands on our property separate from the main house. I was finally able to get through to his cellular phone. He informed me that Leni had been struck by a car while crossing a street on her way home from the neighborhood bus stop. He explained to me that he had rushed out of his house and hurried up the street right after Debra called him and found Leni streched out in the middle of the road surrounded by ambulance workers. Then he rode the ambulance to the hospital with her. She had several fractures in her left leg.

Only people, who have gone through the trauma of receiving the news that a loved one has been involved in an accident and has been injured, can understand the feeling of anguish and helplessness. The most acute aspect of that helplessness was the terrible distance that separated me from my wife at that minute. I have never been that far away during an emergency like this since the episode with Cha's severe skin rash when I was on the canoe trip over twenty years earlier. I was revisited by the same guilt and insecurity now, that I had experienced on that day on the the waters of the Allegheny. I returned on the next flight home.

Leni's recovery was slow and painful. Her injuries required the insertion of metal pins in the thigh bone and knee of her left leg, and months of physical therapy. A great deal of her misery was brought about by the simple reality of being forced to lie on her back without being able to move freely for that long. Leni is a very active woman and lying on her back is not in her nature.

One Saturday afternoon I sat at the local Eat'n Park family restaurant down the street from where Leni was being put through her paces by the therapist on duty at the PT office on the second floor of the Penn Hills Shopping center complex. I nursed a root beer float, and as I chewed absentmindedly on the cherry, I suddenly recalled the words of Tim Hernandez on the day after he returned from his visit to Ama-Waribo's house in West Virginia. "Yea buddy…Hes got a photo of you in that thing's mouth. Looked like some kind spell or witchcraft or something" I stiffened in my seat as I thought of that miserable jealous creature up there in West Virginia, huddled in his delusionary world, spouting hate from behind his computer keyboard, and hurling vile curses at my home, curses which might actually have harmed my wife instead of me. It was just a little more than I could handle. Wild imaginings of revenge began to rush through my mind, and my heart hardened to a degree that even frightened me. A dark angry mood descended on me and I pushed the drink away with such force on the table that I almost spilled it.

I got up and paid my check. Then I left and began to walk along the sidewalk on Frankstown road. I walked and walked, trying desperately to work out of my system the violent feelings of white hot anger, vengefulness and vindictiveness that were taking hold of me. I don't have any idea how long I walked on that sidewalk. Suddenly I stopped and looked around me and realized that I had walked almost two miles away from the PT office. Leni would be finished in about ten minutes. I breathed a deep sigh and closed my eyes, standing there alone on the sidewalk of the deserted suburban road. I summoned the image of my guardian spirit, the cricket, and my animal guide, the red tail hawk. I saw the beautiful streamlined figure gliding in the darkness of my closed eyes. I heard the thin crystal clear song of my insect guardian. My heart stopped racing. The heat in my face cooled and I thought I heard the sweet calm voice of my grandmother. Then I turned around and began walking back.

It took almost half an hour for the hired car to arrive. I gave Leni an extra snug hug as I held her, helping her struggle into the seat of the automobile with her crutches. She looked up at me and smiled, and at that point I knew that everything was going to be alright. I was calmer when I returned to the internet. I watched as things plummeted for the man and woman who had hoped to destroy our beautiful community. Everyone appeared to turn their backs on the disruptive couple in West Virginia. They gradually retreated from the public eye and refused to post anything in the various forums where the rest of us were still enthusiastically sharing.

After a while most of us had switched over to the new Ning networks and the Yahoo groups were largely abandoned by the Taino. Ama Waribo started a Google blog site which for the first few years was dedicated mostly to maligning the Caney Circle in general and me in particular. The blog never won more than a pathetic handful of three or four followers. By the time that the bulk of the online Tainos had switched over to the new up-and-coming Facebook social network at the end of 2009 hardly anyone even remembered Ama-Waribo and Bano-Sheiti. They ceased to exist in the general consciousness of the Taino Resurgence.

I needed a powerful cleasing and healing experience after the worst of the "Taino Wars" and that healing experience was manifested during a magical visit to the city of Washington D.C. in 2008. It turned out that during that visit I was destined to stand before the actual Taino clay representation of the ancestral Earth Mother, the legitimate artistic representation of the Mother Spirit from the era of the First Sun, who had now returned back here among the people with her son after a 500-year-long absence to usher in a new First Sun. This reunion of the ancient icon and her people took place during that Washington DC visit.

A woman called Grandmother Vanessa Inaru, who is a prominent leader of our contemporary Taino Resurgence, invited me to join a small group of modern-dayTainos to visit the newly built National Museum of the American Indian in Washington D.C. in April of 2008. The museum now houses one of the largest collections of American Indigenous artifacts in the world; a collection that at one time had been located in New York City at the Heye Foundation Museum of the American Indian in the Manhattan neighborhood of Washington Heights.

My aunt Adela had moved into that New York neighborhood in the early 1960's when she arrived in the United States from Cuba and I had grown up knowing that there was this magnificent place that I could easily walk to from her house anytime I visited her. Back in those days, the museum was always a place of infinite wonder to me during the 40 years that I repeatedly visited it because, in addition to the huge collection of beautiful artifacts from hundreds of other Indian tribes that were held there, it contained a treasure trove of artifacts of my own people, the Taino. For me it had always been a sacred honor to stand there before the display windows of those ancient relics and commune with them with only a thin pane of glass between us. Now, in 2008, as I stood here in the lobby of the special annex where the new museum in D.C. currently holds the artifacts that are not on regular display, it began to dawn on me that something extraordinary was about to occur.

Our little group was led back to a great hall lined with enormous racks of storage shelves. These shelves were filled with an inconceivable wealth of ancient Taino stone, clay, bone, wood, ivory and shell artifacts. We were escorted up and down the isles of racks by museum employees who pushed a couple of wheeled multi-shelved carts. We were told as we strolled up and down these isles that we were free to choose any number of the artifacts that we wanted to perform ceremony with and they would pull them out of the storage shelves and place them on the carts. So we selected a large number of the most precious objects of our ancestors originating in a number of Caribbean islands, including Cuba, Kiskeya and Boriken. Then we were led to a special private chamber, reserved only for Native people. That room was equipped with a round, shallow, sand-filled pit dug into the paved floor, which could accommodate a small ceremonial fire if necessary.

The museum employees carefully unloaded all of the artifacts off the carts and unto special stands all around the room. It was a little overwhelming for me. I never dreamed that I would ever be allowed to actually touch and hold those beautiful objects that I had revered from the other side of those glass panels at the old Heye Foundation museum in New York for so many years.

For me the most exciting point of that whole experience was the moment when I picked up a rare and beautiful representation of the Cosmic Matriarch, Ata Bei, sculpted in the form of a clay pot. I stood there holding that magnificent object and I began to choke up. My eyes began to well up. It was extremely difficult to hide my tears of emotion from my friends there with me. I just knew that this statue was identical to the one that had been housed within the home of the medicine woman Guaricheanao in the village of Cueiba back in 1510. I knew that it was a clay icon just like this one that had miraculous disappeared way back then to make way for the El Cobre statue. I knew that the return now, of this particular object to Taino hands for sacred ceremony, represented the end of one era, the beginning of another. The Shell Lady, now, like her son, the male Hope Child mountain cemi that had graced our 1993 ceremony in Caguana, had indeed returned in her original form, and at that magic moment, to her original people. We no longer needed the yellow-dressed Catholic Spanish virgin of El Cobre. We no longer had to hide behind the synchretic mixture of European and African tradition. Now, free to honor our mother in her original Indigenous form, there she was in our hands!

I gazed down at the serene face of the 500-year-old little clay pregnant matriarch in my hands, with her globular belly. I thought of my musings of maternity labor contractions and the birth of the Fifth Sun that I had experienced as I paddled down the Allegheny River with Sven in 1982. I stared at the holy thing in my hands and marvelled at how closely this little sculpture resembles the rotund, equally pregnant, 20,000-year-old Ice Age representation of the self-same Earth Mother. That older icon, the "Willendorf Venus", was crafted in stone by primordial hunter-gatherers during the First Sun period of the Ice Age, perhaps to represent the divine pregnancy that produced the birth of that First Sun itself. The two sacred artists who crafted those two masterpieces, the Willendorf Venus and the Taino clay Mother statue, were separated in time by dozens of millenia, and yet their hearts shared the very same space, the very same energy.

When I held the little statue I knew that a powerful symbolic image of the Cosmic Matriarch had returned to the people.

13. BROTHERLY LOVE

The city of Philadelphia, Pennsylvania was founded by a man called William Penn in the 17th century. The name means "City of Brotherly Love". Penn gave it that name in honor of the religion that he followed The Society of Friends (The Quakers).

In September of 2008 I stood on a corner of North Fifth Street in the city of Philadelphia, looking out on a beautiful scene of celebration and cultural pride. On that day I was participating in that year's observance of the Feria Del Barrio street fair, a glorious outdoor celebration of Latino traditions sponsored annually in the heart of the predominantly Puerto Rican neighborhood of North Philly by the cultural center called "Taller Puertorriqueño", a place that I had visited on a number of ocasions over the years since the mid 1990's.

I had driven from Pittsburgh all the way to New York City where I had picked up my friend, Kasike Roberto Mucaro Borrero and his family. We had all driven back to Philadelphia to take part in the street event. We were joined there by Chris Sibaboinael, a Boricua friend of mine who was originally from this same North Philly Boricua neighborhood, but who had recently moved to New Jersey. Chris had driven in from Jersey and joined us at the event. I had known Chris since the mid-1990's when he was a member of the Philadelphia branch of the Caney Circle. He was an initiated behike of the Caney.

On that occasion in 2008, we were included in the scheduled agenda of the event's performances to represent Taino culture. Mucaro brought a hand-crafted Taino mayohuacan log drum on stage. First he delivered an inspiring talk that introduced the audience to the reality of the current Taino Resurgence movement. His talk explained the nature of the organization of which he was the director, the United Confederation of Taino People and its mission of bringing the truth of contemporary Taino culture to as many Tainos as possible in the world-wide Taino diaspora.

After he finished his presentation Mucaro picked up the log drum and he and I collaborated in a number of Taino songs that were so lively and engaging that we got the majority of the crowd dancing in the street. In keeping with the original purpose of song and singing in general, as it was formulated almost 260 centuries earlier, these beautiful musical expressions of the reawakened Taino indigenity accomplished what People's Art was originally meant to do. It reached into the soul of those people and took them to a place they had never been before. It transformed them.

After the performance, Mucaro and I returned to the display table that we had left in the care of his wife Jossy, his son, and my friend Chris, while we took the stage. Upon our arrival at the table we found Jossy playing with his two beautiful girls, and Chris explaining the display to a young Boricua couple. At the table we had spread out a tasteful educational presentation of ancient Taino culture which included traditional Taino and Arawakan objects such as a cibucan or mapeetee used for processing yuca into cassava. There were also a collection of replicas of the ancient Taino statues that represent the important divine personalities in the Taino pantheon.

On that table was my beautiful plaster replica of the mountain cemi, the stone statue that represents Ioka Hu, the Lord of Life, as the great Hope Child, grown to full maturity. I looked at that statue and remembered that my friend Margarita, the co-ordinator of the annual August Jornadas in Boriken had begun to call this image "The White Cemi".

Caney Circle Taino cultural exhibit at Philadelphia's FERIA DEL BARRIO Puerto Rican neighborhood festival

I sat in my chair next to the table gazing in silence at the crowd that strolled non-challantly past our display, occasionally pausing to snap a photo of the colorful objects. As I sat there my mind wandered. I was taken back to the first time I had been introduced to a replica image of the White Cemi in 1989 just before I drove back to the home of Eddy's mother in Utuado from Caguana. It was that plaster replica that had been given to me by Miguel Guzman in his mountain craft shop next to the ancient ancestral site. I thought of all that had been revealed to me by Doña Celina later that day in the living room of Doña Amalia's humble mountain home, the sacred nature of this cemi as the manifestation of the primordial prophetic promise, the ultimate fundamental significance of my canoe-trip dreams.

I also thought of the day in 1991 when I actually found myself in the presence of the original statue, the heavy stone relic that had been brought to Pittsburgh by Bibi Naniki. She brought it to us when she came there with other prominent members of the early Taino Resurgence movement to join us of the Caney Circle in celebration of Full Moon Ceremony. I thought of the awesome energy that emanated from that holy stone three-pointed object lying there in the center of our ceremonial circle covered in shredded tobacco. In a way, that stone statue represented some of the same ideals that had inspired the name of the city of Philadelphia, "Brotherly Love". I remembered how it had once been explained to me by my teacher, Federico, that the ancient Tainos had a ceremony called "guaitiao" (the making of relatives) via which a stranger could be converted into a brother through a celebration of Love; "brotherly love". The three-pointed stone cemi sculpture of the Hope Child was the physical manifestation of the guaitiao, the physical manifestation of the ceremony to make relatives. It was a symbol of the capacity for humans of different background to find ways to beging seeing each other as members of the same family.

14. A CONCH SHELL

On a beautiful Saturday afternoon, April 24, 2010, five days after my fifty-ninth birthday, I sat next to Leni at a table in the Neuyorican Poets Café in New York City. As we sipped our drinks a beautiful young Bronx-born Taino rap celebrity called Caridad De La Luz "La Bruja" stood on the stage with a microphone held up to her mouth. With the skill of an experienced emcee, and a toss of her long black hair crowned by a gorgeous feather headband, she declared the official opening of the second annual "Taino Awards Ceremony".

I had received a special invitation to the event from the organizers, two Taino women, one called Bohike Warixi and another Bohike Marie Maweyaru Crooke. The event had been created to honor people who were recognized in the global Taino community as having made a significant contribution to our Resurgence.

Watching La Bruja's expert management of the stage that day was a spiritual experience in itself. The fact is that this artist personifies the very essence of the World-Age Shift prophecy. She is an artist magician in the tradition of Juan Luis Guerra, Lauryn Hill and Wyclef Jean. The social consciousness of her poetic message and the esthetic excellence of her performance do justice to the name by which she is known, "La Bruja" a term that she herself defines as "La Curandera" (The Healer). This makes her a direct inheritor of the tradition of the first ancient artists who began to sing, dance and express their healing poetry over 260 centuries ago at the beginning of the First Sun. Here is how her online bio describes this magician:

> "Caridad De La Luz is a Bronx-born Performer known as La Bruja, considered one of America's leading spoken word artists. She is a renaissance woman that has performed internationally as well as in respected venues such as The Apollo, The Museum of Natural History, and the famed Nuyorican Poets Café where she began her career. NY Times called her "a Juggernaut" after the 2009 run of her musical Boogie Rican Blvd. where she played 7 different characters and wrote the musical score alongside famed Afro-Rican Jazz artist William Cepeda. Her acting career has taken her from the stage to film, she has appeared in several movies including Bamboozled, Down to the Bone, El Vacilon and Gun Hill Road, which features the title track 'Nuyorico' and four more of La Bruja's songs. Her unique music has crossed over

internationally with her debut album "Brujalicious" and her latest release "For Witch It Stands" both available on iTunes. She is featured on Prince Royce's new album Phase II and Bobby Sanabria's upcoming album Multiverse. Best known for her captivating performance on Russell Simmons' HBO Def Poetry Jam, she is the Founder of the Latinas 4 Life spoken word movement, a board member of Voices UnBroken and works with youth throughout the country teaching the benefits of self-expression and art for positive change."

As I sat in that chair next to Leni, dressed in my white ritual cotton regalia, wearing my parrot feather penacho on my head, I realized how far things had progressed. The place was packed. There were representatives from every one of the prominent Taino organizations, no exceptions. There were few hints of the old emnities. The room practically vibrated with good will and general love among people who at one time had been figuratively at each other's throats. It was as if the Hope Child Mountain Semi was hovering over the gathering as La Bruja spoke on the stage.

Among the other honorees were my friend Chief Roberto Mucaro Borrero, and several other leaders who were working tirelessly in behalf of the Resuergence Movement. I really felt like I was in very good company.

Later in the ceremony I was called to the stage. As I stood there I was honored by the two women. I was handed a lovely large conch shell guamo with a special inscription, and a paper document that recognized me as a behike that had made valuable contributions to the cause of the Taino re-birth. It made me think of the guamo sea shell horn in the hand of the sacred ancestral woman of my visions.

There is no way that I can explain how humbled, honored and grateful I was when the room exploded in applause. After I was awarded the honor, I stood in the middle of the stage and sang the sacred song to Ata Bei that we sing at every Full Moon Ceremony in the Caney Circle, and practically everybody in the audience sang along. They all knew the words.

After that day there was an almost unstoppable positive improvement in the way Tainos continued to interact, both in person and on the internet. That progress continues unabated to the present time. This progress is still taking place in spite of continuous challenges posed by jealousy, arrogance and recurring manifestations of animosity and especially intolerance. These challenges now present themselves primarily in occasional eruptions of conflict within the medium of the internet, and yet they no longer dominate the Taino dialog as they did in 2006. Now that dialog is increasingly an experience of sharing, of teaching, of learning, and reconciliation. Although the ancient enemy is still very much alive and active in our online interactions those of us who recognize his presence are mounting a vigorous and oftentimes successful counterattack.

Like a curandera healer of souls, the rap artist CARIDAD "LA BRUJA" DE LA CRUZ weaves a vocal tapestry of sacred timeless medicine.

15. GUATEMALA AND MIAMI CIRCLE

Throughout the decades of the 1990's and the 2000's, while we worked hard to promote the tradition of our ancestors and the sacred message of our spirituality in the hearts of contemporary Tainos and others who respected our ways, I had also carried out a great deal of work in the Pittsburgh area and on the internet, promoting the truth about the message that the ancient Maya had shared with my ancestors. During that time I augmented the knowledge that I had acquired on the subject from early teachers like my father and my 1970's college Yucatec Maya friend, Hernando.

The information about Jose Arguelles that I received from my friends in New Mexico during the late1980's and early 1990's was extremely helpful since these people were actually working with Arguelles at the time.

Then an extremely perceptive independent scholar called John Major Jenkins, revolutionized the public perception of the ancient Maya calendar when he published a book called "Maya Cosmogenesis 2012". I was so impressed with this publication that I began to interact with this man and we became long-distance friends. Above everything else, I was struck with the fact that in spite of the growing perception of apocalyptic images which were expanding rapidly in the popular psyche of the time, Jenkins promoted a refreshingly sane attitude of hope and understanding in association with his view of Maya prophecy.

Then in the mid 2000's I met and worked in co-operation with the chief of the Guatemalan council of Maya elders, Don Alejandro Cirilo Perez Ox Laj during his visit in Pittsburgh. Most of his message on that occasion coincided perfectly with what had been taught to me by previous teachers and confirmed also what my friend John Major Jenkins had to say.

After that my work with the Maya calendar intensified. At that same time I began working in co-operation with a group of people in my area of western Pennsylvania who identified themselves as "Peaceburghers". These enlightened individuals include a particularly articulate woman called Vikki Hanchin, who, to this day, provides an amazing amount of leadership and guidance to the local movement, allowing for the dissemination and propagation of the positive and constructive message of hope that the genuine Maya Shift of Ages prophecy trully represents. It was through Vikki's efforts that Don Alejandro was able to visit Pittsburgh.

One of Vikki's most important contributions to the advancement of the Maya traditional wisdom in Pittsburgh was her succesful effort to bring the world-recognized Maya wise woman Grandmother Flordemayo to Pittsburgh on two different ocasions during the decade of the 2000's. Vikki continued to organize and advocate and also to produce important articles and publications that illustrate the significance of the resurgence of the sacred femenine during this era of transition, culminating in her 2012 publication of her book "The Seer and the Sayer".

By 2009 I had met and befriended a Guatemalan Kiche Maya man called Antonio. Antonio had recently moved to Pittsburgh. He brought with him a wealth of wisdom about the ancient Maya Calendar and its relevance to the Taino experience. He had acquired this wisdom from his father, a wise Maya elder who had shared these teachings with him during the tragic era of the Guatemalan Civil War in the 1980's. Antonio was just a few years older than my son Cha and I offered to help him with his work of sharing the wisdom of his elders here in the United States. I helped him open a new website dedicated to the interrelationship of the Taino culture and the Maya culture called "Maya-Taino Prophecy Initiative". The new project operates under the auspices of the Caney Circle and created a platform for Antonio to share the teachings that were becoming so relevant just two years before the epochal 2012 Shift date and beyond.

Antonio and I began a schedule of lectures and presentations all over the eastern United States, appearing on college campuses, metaphysical establishments, and Mind, Body and Spirit festivals, even appearing on the same stage as, and in collaboration with John Major Jenkins.

Antonio's message was simple and to the point. The 2012 End-Of-The-World scenario that was being bandied about by alarmists all over the media at that time had absolutely nothing to do with the true Maya Calendar reality. In that respect our message was identical to that of the author Jenkins. Our message also educated people as to the meaning of the Five World Ages or "Suns". Antonio shared the teachings he had learned from his father and from other Kiche Maya elders about what Seven Macaw really was, and how we humans of this era had the opportunity to defeat him just like the sacred twins of the ancient Maya holy narrative had defeated him in legendary times.

Throughout most of the years 2009, 2010 and 2011 I assisted in getting the authentic message of the Maya 2012 prophecy to as many people as possible in co-operation with legitimate Kiche Maya teacher Antonio Aj Ik.

My work with Antonio culminated in the summer of 2011 when we co-ordinated with Antonio's father, Don Telesforo, and with prominent archeological scholar, Ed Barnhart to organize a group tour of sacred Maya sites in Guatemala. Our tour was a beautiful exploration of the true heart of Maya contemporary tradition. It was carried out among the hallowed ruins of the civilization that was attacked and conquered by the Spanish in the 1500's and 1600's. The descendants of that civilization had survived over 400 years of colonization, only to rise again triumphant in the twentieth century as some of the most globally recognized Indigenous seers.

Accompanied by Don Telesforo and other elders of the Kiche Maya community of the Indigenous highlands, we travelled with a contingent of twenty North Americans from almost all walks of life and from many parts of the United States, to some of the most significant sacred sites of Guatemala. We climbed the ancient pyramids of Antonio's ancestors offering ceremony at each site.

Traditional Kiche Maya teacher ANTONIO AJ IK

Antonio travelled all over the US sharing the true message of the Maya 2012 prophecy

By the following year the Caney Circle was ready for the ceremonial celebration of the great World Shift of Ages that Antonio's ancestors predicted. This was no less than the conclusion of the Fifth Sun period, and the beginning of the new First Sun period, the opening of a brand new cycle of 260 centuries, the opening of a brand new five-sun sequence. We were there to stand as ritual midwives at the birth of the next great era, the birth of a new Sun.

We gathered on December 21st 2012, on the day after we had already celebrated Taino Winter Solstice. We gathered to celebrate the Shift of Ages. Our gathering was scheduled at an ancient ceremonial site created by the ancient Tekesta Indians of South Florida over 500 years ago. These people are believed by us to be ethnically related to our Taino ancestors. The site is called "Miami Circle". It is located near the spot where the Biscayne River empties its waters into the Atlantic Ocean. It consists of a curious circle of holes excavated into the living bedrock under the thin layer of top-soil right there in the middle of what is now Miami's busy metropolitan center. The holes undoubtedly served as sockets for the erection of support poles holding up a large round ceremonial structure.

The circle was discovered back at the beginning of the new 21st century when many people were worrying about the "Millenium Bug" computer threat. Construction workers excavating the foundations of a new high-rise building found the large perfectly circular pattern of holes in the rocky ground. A decade-long battle ensued between the urban developers and passionate conservationists who insisted that the archeological site needed to be preserved. The conservationists won. By 2010 the city of Miami built a beautiful park around the ancient sacred site and all hopes of a high-rise evaporated. I have shared ceremony with my Florida Taino relatives there on a number of occasions. One important member of the Taino Resurgence who has shared ceremony many times with us in Miami is the powerful warrior woman Tai Pelli. She became the UCTP representative in Orlando and has also represented the interests of Tainos in international forums associated with the work of the United Nations. It is enegetic and capable women like Tai who keep the movement on track in spite of our internal issues.

Central Florida is blessed with one of the most energetic promoters of contemporary Taino culture in this era, a woman known to us all as Tai Pelli. She is the local representative of the United Confederation of Taino People in her area.

TheTaino Resurgence

From the Boricua Barrio of Philadelphia to the mountains of Boriken the Resurgence blossomed

There in that holy place, surrounded by Tainos who had travelled there from all over Florida and North America, and by other friends, and also surrounded by relatives from other tribes and nations of humanity who felt called to celebrate with us, I had the opportunity to share the wonderful, optimistic message of Antonio's Maya people with my fellow Tainos and with all people of the world. We prayed. We sang. We danced as our Taino ancestors danced the dance of Guaitiao. We celebrated the great efforts of a determined primogenotress bearing down on the cyclic waves of heavy labor, and we shared the joy of the outcome of that mighty effort, the birth of the new Sun.

Over the years the Caney Circle reached out to people of Taino ancetry all over the North American and Caribbean diaspora. At the same time we strove to open the doors of love, brotherhood and sisterhood to people of all races

The Caney Circle maintains a guanara sweatlodge for kansi ceremomies at the Circle's Verona, Pennsylvania teaching center where Miguel lives

At the end of the ceremony I sat quietly while the others around me chatted cordially and shared the wonderful food brought by some of them for our customary after-ceremony meal. I became lost in concentration as I looked out on Biscayne Bay. I though of slaves, all the slaves who still exist in the world and could not share in the joy we here were experiencing. I thought of the physical slaves who must work against their will under dehumanizing conditions all over the world, from illegally smuggled foreign house-servants in California subburbs to sweatshop workers toiling under degrading conditions in Latin American free-trade zones, manufacturing designer tennis shoes for the wealthy. I also thought of the spiritual slaves who labor under the weight of the chains of the great ancient enemy, the demon of the colonized mind, the demon of hoplessness, frustration and discord that humanity needs to defeat during this wonderful new era. I thought of Eddie rotting away in the concrete, steel and razor-wire confines of Huntindon State Correctional Facility back in Pennsylvania. I though of that evening when I had the opportunity to see him again one last time after our performance in the prison. Also, my mind drifted to the thought of his son growing up in the world of drugs and violence of Broadhead Manor in the West End of Pittsburgh.

Broadhead Manor no longer existed now. As I sat there on the bench of Miami Circle Park and listened to the sounds of my friends socializing with each other over the Boricua food, I attempted to do the math to figure out what the age of Eddie's son would be at that point. The little boy had to be over twenty years old by now. I remembered that the old housing projects had been bulldozed over a decade ago. The city had attempted to elliminate the blight of that sad neighborhood by destroying the buildings. I smiled a wry smile to myself as I considered the ridiculousness of that solution. If Eddie's family stayed in the West End after the demolition of Broadhead Manor, I knew they would have moved into some other substandard housing nearby. And I knew that their lives had not been improved by the elimination of the concrete and brick buildings where they had lived all those years ago. Buildings don't create the restraints and limitations manipulated by the demon of turmoil and despair. His chains exist in our own hearts, attached, like a parasite, deep within the human soul. That is where we must battle him.

I sit here now recalling all of these events of the past thirtytwo years and weighing the positive aspects against the negative aspects of that history. I can't help but be struck by the extraordinary wonder of it all. Yes, the plight of Eddie's son growing up amidst the spiritual emptiness of his environment was tragic, and there were indeed many slaves, a slavery created by humanity's inhumanity. And yet, it was amazing how far we humans had come in spite of all that.

Much of the misery that humanity is responsible for upon this planet of ours has come about as a result of the predatory systems of oppression and subjugation that were established approximately 5200 years ago at the beginning of the Fifth Sun. Those systems not only oppressed people's bodies but enslaved their minds in such a way that the damage has lasted centuries after the actual physical oppression subsided and is inherited from one generation to another like a genetic disease. Those systems also not only oppressed human beings, but also the majority of the other creatures with whom we share the earth, animals and plants. When humanity largely lost the sense of mystery and magic associated with Life and living things, when these became nothing but subjects to be subjugated, harvested, used and perceived as resources, it set the stage for the degradation of all life on earth, even our own.

And now, almost at the eleventh hour, exactly as the prophecy foretold, at the end of the Fifth Sun, it is as if humanity has gradually begun to awaken to the folly of those systems. There is a palpable sense of urgency and awareness that did not exist even as recently as sixtyfour years ago. This is a world radically different in attitude than the one I that was born into in 1951. In the 1950's and 1960's when I was a child the idea of multinational agreements officially endorsed by world governments to protect the environment would have been unthinkable, laughable. And yet they exist now. Even if at this early point in their evolution these official proclamations in behalf of the health of the Earth still don't have the broad positive effect that we wish they did, the very fact that they exist at all is miraculous. When I was a baby the attitude toward women in most countries was that of scorn and condescention. Now, even the most chauvinistic societies of the world at least attempt to present an image of respect toward women under the global pressure of changing attitudes around the world.

When I arrived with my family in the United States in 1961 thousands of people of one race living in this country were forbidden to sit in the same section of a public lunch counter and drink from the same water fountain as people of another race. This was taken for granted and no one ever dreamed at that time that there would ever be a time when that state of affairs would not exist. But now it doesn't exist and there are millions of people who live in this country today who take this new different way of life for granted because they have known nothing else.

The contemporary television program "Mad Men" purports to show how the 1950's Madison Avenue magicians crafted the images and messages that those in power wanted those without power to consume and internalize. And those without power had no power, largely because they had little access to knowledge, to information. Lacking knowledge, they lacked power because, as the old saying goes, "knowledge is power". Those without power did consume and they did internalize the images fed to them by the "Mad Men", images of happy children cheerfully consuming cereals containing unhealthily massive quantities of sugar and preservatives, images of contented subservient housewives who literally bubbled at the thought of an effective detergent that would clean the ring around their husband's shirt collar and please the "lord" of the household, images of submissive black "Step-And-Fetch-It" Pullman car porter types dutifully assisting successful white corporate executives up into a train, humiliating and grossly offensive images of distorted "Indians", bristling with garish multicolored feathers, who would scream and yelp garrulously either as they attacked and massacred heroic settlers, or as they inspired sport teams to victory.

This TV program reveals the behind-the-curtain story of those who were the experts at controlling the minds of the powerless masses with false images, and who had sole access to the media means for creating those false images. Most of the work that those "Mad Men" carried out was in behalf of almighty corporations, the new empires, with absolutely no sense of the human factor, the human dimension of what they were doing, who had no regard for the welfare of those to whom they aimed their toxic message or for the welfare of the world in which we all live. Anyone working for those empires of noxious consumerisn and absolute control back then was in conspiracy with them.

Now, in 2015 that paradigm has been turned upside down. In this new world, in which knowledge and information is rampant and expanding, as a result of technological advancements which have inadvertantly tilted the balance, the common person is no longer quite as powerless as he and she used to be back in the good old glory days of the 1950's "Mad Men". Increasingly, the average man or woman is so much better informed that it is quite a bit more difficult to sell him or her a message now simply based on the lies woven by those "Mad Men". Those who now hire magicians to craft their message must be more conscious of the fact that their target population will not simply follow blindly as they did in 1951, that their target audience are human beings, with knowledge, with feelings, with consciousness, with a will of their own. Increasingly, these people are no longer tools to be manipulated, or resources to be harvested. In other words, those in power are gradually being forced to treat the rest of us as thinking human beings, or else!

I am sitting here typing these words into my word processor and I am reminded of an experience that I had just a year ago. I participated in a professional enrichment seminar offered to the staff of my school. As part of our Saturday morning experience we were bussed to two local institutions in which technology and media are being utilized in novel and creative ways. The first was the Pittsburgh Children's Museum, the same place where Sven was considering employement when it first opened in 1983. It is a vastly different place now. In keeping with the original dream of its creators, the Pittsburgh Children's Museum is presently a world-class, extraordinary place where children can explore and re-create the world in which they live through the magic of play, using technology that is especially designed to be within their reach, and capable of being manipulated by them and adapted to their needs. As the children play, they learn, and give birth to their own dreams. In the words of the Children's Museum online promotional material: "Challenge your abilities and understand the world we live in at the Children's Museum. Our permanent exhibits are based on the philosophy of Play with Real Stuff". Squeegee the Clown would have approved!

The other half of our morning experience was to visit a place called MAYA Design. Inspired by the philosophy called "HUMAN CENTERED

DESIGN", the wide-eyed young artists and magicians who work here devote their time deconstructing the theme created by the 1950's "Mad Men". In the words of their promotional material: "At MAYA, we recognize the critical role that environment plays on fostering innovation"

One of the core concepts implemented at this amazing place is the idea of a circular meeting space. The room has curved walls that are completely covered with dry-arase whiteboard, upon which the creative people who are meeting there can explain to each other what they want to share right on the walls by doodling and sketching grafitti-style images with dry-erase markers, images that will express their most imaginative conceptualizations. They call this physically implemented principle of human space manipulation the "kiva" because they say that it was inspired by the traditional circular spiritual meeting spaces of the Pueblo Indigenous people of the U.S. SouthWest.

I understood immediately where this concept came from, a place in which there was no front and no back, an egalitarian place in which no one seemed more important than anyone else, a place where the walls of the enclosure came to life with the essence of what dwelled within the human individual, in which humans could again feel a sense of creative community and in which talent and ability were being used to support the new paradigm. It was a place in which the artist was indeed the magician, weaving his or her dream upon the "cave wall" and propelling the craft, the canoe upon which all of the participants were riding together, into an exciting future.

The MAYA Design representative who led us on our tour of the center explained that the most effective way to share an idea was to grab a pencil or a marker and sketch it, to visualize it graphically. I understood this concept because I have practiced it all my life. There is very little that I can explain to another person without using graphic images. When I was a child I was very intolerant of books with no pictures. I still am.

I was realistic about my perception of this vision. As I moved through the various areas of the MAYA Design space led by our young host, I understood that the only way that this place could stay in business was to convince corporations with a lot of money to hire them. In essence, their clients were the same clients who hired the "Mad Men" back in the 1950's.

And yet I could not help but image these innovative magicians as a kind of guerrilla infiltration force, who had somehow stealthily stormed the well-guarded battlements of the old establishment and, like the legendary hero twins of Maya sacred narrative lore, were defeating the corrupt Xibalban demonic mentality from the inside. I thought that changes in attitude could be forged from within as long as the magicians had gained a toehold within the system. I could not help but image that these magicians possessed the powerful magic blowguns that would eventually shoot Seven Macaw down from his lofty perch and help hand control of the world back to real people.

And so as I sat on the park bench in Miami Circle Park on December 21st, 2012 I reflected on the Indigenous structure that stood there in that spot near Biscayne Bay 500 years ago. Now, thinking back to that day I realize that, judging by the perfectly circular symetry in the pattern of post-holes sunk into the bedrock, it obviously followed the same exact design philosophy that was being promoted by the magicians of MAYA Design. I understand that, for all the glitz and sparkle of modern technology, the real answer to the deepest questions of our generation lie in the human-based ancestral wisdom that we can access from our own past. The wizards at MAYA know this. That is why they designed their "kiva" to mimic the essence of a primordial cave whose walls are covered with petroglyphs and pictographs. They went back to the roots of spiritual sharing and found the truth in the past.

In October of 2013, almost a full year after the Winter Solstice ceremony in Miami Circle, Eddie and his son were again brought back to my consciousness. I had not thought of Eddie or his son since the previous December. Then on that chilly Wednesday morning in the end of October of 2013, I arrived at the bus stop to wait to ride into the city on my way to work.

The only other person waiting there at the bus stop with me on that chilly morning was a forty-something East Hills resident, an employee at one of the many downtown banks called Ada. She and I rode into work on the same bus every morning. Ada was always very talkative when we waited on the corner.

"Hey, I guess they're scribbling some pretty nasty grafitti on your cave wall these days" She opened the conversation as I walked up to the corner. "What do you mean?" I answered, setting down my knapsack. We had been engaged in a running debate for weeks over my theory of the use of technology by inspired contemporary spiritual artists. Every day we exchanged ideas as we stood there on that corner waiting for the bus.

"Didn't you tell me yesterday that the internet was some kinda magic cave wall where modern-day folks were going to re-enact the creation of "People's Art". Didn't you tell me that this was a re-enactment of the spiritual awakening that took place back in the Ice Age?"

I looked at her and answered. "Yea, I think it's happening already."

"Well how about that business in the West End yesterday?" She insisted.

I had no idea what she was talking about. "What business?" I asked. "That video that got posted on WorldStarHipHop.com yesterday...Didn't you hear about it?" "No, I didn't. Tell me about it." She looked straight at me to make sure I got the full impact of what she was going to share. "It happened up there in the West End and one of them kids got it all on video and uploaded it to WorldStar, or one of them sites... I can't remember which. They all the same to me, trash! Bad enough that you got police killing or hitting our young black men over the head and hauling them off to jail for no reason, but this crap, black kids beating each other stupid on camera and then posting it on the damned internet. It's just ignorant, that's all, just simple! That's why we African Americans can not get the respect we deserve".

I had heard of the internet sites where thousands of young people watch illicit videos taped surreptitiously in school yards and inner city streets. These videos reveal horrific scenes of young people battering each other, sometimes to death, and they are tremendously popular. Many of these videos go viral in a matter of days, sometimes in a matter of hours. They appeal to the very basest level of human depravity.

I was impatient. The bus was going to show up pretty soon and I wanted to know what she was talking about. "What did they upload?" I asked. "Did something bad get videotaped in the West End yesterday?"

"Yea, a bunch of girls ganging up on one other girl, beat the crap outta that poor kid. She was all tore up! And then they uploaded the video to one of those sickening sites. Cops're trying to figure out the identity of the perps now. The police is checking out the images on the tapes. There was even a grown woman in the video. Instead of stopping the fight, she joined in and stomped on that poor girl's face!"

"Wow!" I exclaimed. "Is the victim still alive?"

"Yea, she's still alive, but they got her in intensive care! and all those crazy kids watching it all online. And you said the internet is the answer to everything. I guess your cave wall's got some pretty nasty graffiti on it now. Don't you think?"

Instantly I thought of the old song lyrics that I had penned during the 1982 canoe trip on the Allegheny. I had called that song "Grafito" which is the Spanish word for "graffiti". I had been inspired to write that song by the violent exchange of words between a Puerto Rican and a Mexican scribbled on the partition wall of a toilet stall at the Port Authority Bus Terminal in New York City.

"That's not what I said!" I answered. "I didn't say that the internet is the answer to all the problems of humankind. I know we have a long way to go. The internet itself is not the answer. But it is one of the accessible tools where humans are now discovering potentials that were not originally expected. I told you, back in the Stone Age, some humans crafted deadly bows to shoot arrows that could kill. Other humans took those bows and turned them into musical instruments. I understand that there is immense potential for evil in this powerful new medium, the internet. But there is also immense potential for good. How do you think the dictatorial governments of the Arab Spring were toppled back in 2011? It was thousands of young people using facebook and twitter, inspiring each other, encouraging each other, by painting images of freedom on the cave wall of the cyber-community that could not be controlled by the tyrants, by the Mad Men. I disagree with you. You are looking at the empty half of the cup. I choose to see the half-full part." Then the bus arrived and she boarded to sit and chat with one of her girlfriends. That forced an end to our conversation.

In April of 2014 I went back to my own roots of spiritual sharing. Inspired by what I saw at MAYA I travelled again to the ancestral sites of my own people in Cuba and became immersed in the reality of the Taino vision. Like the visit to the Museum of the American Indian, this became a pilgrimage of learning. I had gone to Cuba in the company of my sister Rosa and her husband Melvin. We arrived at a place called Chorro De Maita. It is the site of a mass burial of Tainos that ocurred during the colonial era. The skeletons are now on display inside a museum space there. After offering tobacco and tabonuco smoke for those ancestors and reciting an earnest prayer that some day soon they will be liberated from that indignity and properly buried, we walked across the road to a beautiful full-size reconstructed Taino village. We walked all around among the palm-thatch covered huts and plaster statues depicting fifteenth century Taino every-day life. Then we entered the main structure. It is huge circular wooden structure, also thatched with palm fronds, representing the traditional chief's house of a typical Cuban Taino village. Standing there inside that building I knew that I was returning to the very beginning of my long journey. This is the Caney, the sacred temple within which ancient Tainos carried out their indoor ceremonies which had served as the inspiration for the name of the spiritual circle that I now lead. I looked around at the circular wall and imaged a similar building standing on the shore of Biscayne Bay in Miami where the archeological site of Miami Circle now stands and where I had led the great Shift of Ages ceremony back in December of 2012. As I stood there I looked out the entrance of the building and spotted a skilfully crafted scene right outside. It was an ensemble of statues depicting a traditional ceremonial areito dance. The Taino men and women, their faces painted and their heads adorned with parrot feathers, were depicted holding hands in a circle, dancing and singing, led by a medicine man with a rattle. As I looked out at that scene I heard the old melodies that I remember from my childhood days at my grandmother's house listening to the chants of the Cordon dancers next door.

On the day after our visit to Chorro De Maita we headed for the main center of the present-day Cordon dance tradition in Cuba, a place called Monte Oscuro in the Bayamo area. This is a place where human beings gather to invoke healing energies, energies of soothing reconciliation, the same energies embodied by the Mountain Cemi that Miguel Guzman gave me in the 1980's. Aside from my visit with relatives, that was the high-point of the whole 2014 Cuba pilgrimage for me. As I stood in the center of a large circle of men and women, singing and rythmically stomping their feet on the wooden floor of the palm-thatched hall where they now carry out their ceremonies, I continued to realize that these experiences were the ultimate full-circle return to the origins. Like the visit to Chorro de Maita the previous day, this circle of humans singing and dancing around Rosa and Melvin and me was the confirmation of over thirty years of journey and search. The wooden floor was the sacred symbolic floor upon which brotherhood and sisterhood are spawned. It was the same wooden floor that I had experienced way back when I helped out in the maize crop at Akwesasne. The song of the Cordon Dance was the message from spirit realm. It was the primordial melody of the ancient Ice Age cave right here in twentyfirst century Cuba. It was the ritual inside the old kiva that I needed to learn so that I could use it like the magicians of MAYA were using what they learned from the past to interpret the future. I knew that this was what it felt like to participate in the ceremonies of the ancestral caney of the Caribbean islands. It was also what it felt like to participate in the ceremonies of the ancestral circular structure at Biscayne Bay, Florida now called "Miami Circle". I knew that this was the only way that we humans could solve the problem of liberating an enslaved human species. The modern cave wall can be created from the tools provided by currently available technology but we must dig way down deep into the timeless ancestral reality to learn how to do it properly. I brought back to the people of the Resurgence Movement the lessons I learned there in Monte Oscuro. This is something many of us activists have been doing. In much the same spirit another fellow Taino light worker, my friend Jorge Baracutey Estevez has been visiting the remote sites of his own home island, Kiskeya (Dominican Republic). Jorge has been researching and learning the tradition called Golpe De Gamao. This tradition is a syncretic complex similar to the Cuban Cordon, in which ancient Taino folkways have been mixed with customs from other cultures. He brings this wisdom back to the people and also includes it in his responsibilities associated to his work as an employee of the National Museum of the American Indian in collaboration with Jose Barreiro. His work also strives to delve into the primordial wellspring to seek solutions to the modern challenge of the ancient demon.

Jorge Baracutei Estevez of Kiskeya
(Dominican Republic) is one of the leading
figures in the Resurgence Movement

In November of 2012, almost a month before the Miami end-of-cycle ceremonies I met a man and a woman that would eventually become very important in the work of reconciliation of the Caney Circle. I was invited on that occasion by the kasike of a Taino yukayeke community in Lancaster, Pennsyilvania to their autumn gathering. Amidst ritual ceremony and wonderful Boricua food I was introduced to Guatu Iri and his sister Erlinda Toa Kao. Over the next year I established a relationship of friendship and trust with these two people, communicating frequently with them both by phone and on the internet. Eventually both of them became formal trainees for the position of behike within the Caney Circle. Erlinda Toa Kao finished her training first and immediately assumed her responsibilities ministering to the Taino community of Lancaster. She began leading Caney Circle Full Moon Ceremonies there. I attended some of the original gatherings and was struck by the commitment and dedication that she demonstrated. Then her brother Guatu Iri became the kasike of his own yukayeke community called "Yukayeke Manicato". Eventually they managed to establish a cultural center in the heart of the city's Boricua neighborhood. Kasike Guatu Iri proved to be just as dedicated as his sister; taking very seriously the responsibility he had accepted as both a behike and a kasike. He sometimes alternated with his sister in the responsibility of leading the regular ceremonies and at the same time via his leadership the community center prospered. He managed to acquire genuine ancient Taino artifacts which now grace the community center's museum. The two-floor structure now serves as ceremonial center and social gathering site for the community and is beginning to attract the attention of Tainos all over the North American Diaspora.

In 2013 I was given the honor by Kasike Guatu Iri and Behike Erlinda Toa Kao to begin creating a mural depicting allegorical elements of our Taino tradition on the walls of the cultural center. I was thrilled. I began the work that same year and as of 2016 it is ongoing. I travel to Lancaster whenever I get the opportunity and add new touches to the acrylic painting.

In 2015 Jaimi Kaurix Rodriguez, another respected leader of the current Taino Resurgence Movement, invited me to contribute two of my oil paintings that feature Taino spiritual motifs for a wonderful art exhibition that he organized at the Passaic County Community College in Patterson, New Jersey. He called the exhibition "Native Visions" and managed to include in it a magnificent collection of some of the most evocative paintings by the most talented Taino artists of the Resurgence. As I stood there on the evening when I delivered my painting to Jaimi and looked around me at the powerful images hanging on those walls I could not help feeling like I was witnessing a true manifestation of the birth of the new First Sun cycle. I can't help thinking of the connections between the modern-day images of the Lancaster mural and the paintings hanging in the Patterson, New Jersey college lobby, and the ancient cave paintings of 260 centuries ago. Some of the pieces in the Lancaster mural and in the New Jersey exhibition feature the image of the pregnant Earth Mother spirit, Ata Bei. Of course, she is the same person represented in the Ice Age sculpture known as the Wilendorf Venus.

My mural in Lancaster and my painting hanging in the lobby of the Patterson, New Jersey college are a continuation of the work that was begun by the artist-magicians of that by-gone era and the interior of both, the Lancaster Yukayeke Manicato Taino Cultural Center where I am creating these mural images, and the New Jersey college lobby constitute another aspect of the new "cave wall" just like the Internet.

There are many people now in this era who are enslaved by the demonic spirit that haunts humanity relentlessly since the dawning of the Fifth Sun. These enslaved minds also have access to the same technological and media tools that have liberated many of today's new artist-creators, the same media tools that have allowed the creation of the new cave walls. Unfortunately these enslaved minds exist ensnared in the same web of confusion that controlled Eddie, Heaven Gazer, Jimmy and Waribo in my own personal life experiences. The effect of this enslavement can be spectacularly destructive. The demonic magic of this mind enslavement has inspired thousands of men and women to allow themselves to be guided by monstrous ideologies like the religious extremism that somehow can justify the cold-blooded murder of thousands of men, women and children by gunshot and decapitation, and the enslavement and trade of young women as sex slaves just because they do not share the same faith, all taking place now in a Middle East wracked by sectarian warfare. It is the very same demonic magic that allows a United States presidential candidate to rise meteorically in the popularity polls in 2015 by appealing to the basest instincts and hysterical fears of an alarmed populous, by suggesting the mass deportation of millions of immigrants and the prohibition of return of United States citizens traveling abroad based on their race and their religion. And the demon has convinced these people that their God actually condones this behavior.

One morning on a day early in the month of December 2015 I was listening to a discussion on the N.P.R radio Diane Rehm Show concerning the horrific terrorist attacks in Paris, France in November of that year. One of the commentators remarked that the brutal Middle Eastern terrorist organization now known as ISIS, who claimed credit for that event, had perfected the use of social network organizing which had been used so successfully by the Arab Spring demonstrators in Egypt. During the same program I heard a remark by one of the commentators that the Republican presidential candidate, Donald Trump was very successfully using the Twitter social networking tool to advance his extreme racist and prejudicial propaganda. I thought of my discussion with Ada. That night I had a dream that took me back to a very frightening place in my psyche. I found myself totally in the dark in my dream. I could see nothing. In the gloom I heard a familiar voice, a familiar snicker. "Do you really think that I can be defeated by Facebook and Twitter, you idiot!" I recognized his voice. I knew who he was. My stomach became queasy as I remembered the beating he had given me when I was much younger. He was that terrible spirit of discord who wishes to defeat humankind using our own personal failings against us. It is our own self-enslavement that constitutes his most powerful weapon against us. "Look shaman, think about it. The world is full of sad, bitter, enraged, disappointed people. Many of those people are veritable lethal time-bombs just waiting for some ass-hole to manipulate them all together and create some pretty impressive bangs. BANG!" The vice exploded in my ear suddenly. It made my brain hurt. "BANG!" he repeated. They use the internet also you dummy. You want the internet to save you. I am gonna use the internet to BURY YOU!" His words echoed the mentality presented by Ada back in 2013. I took a deep breath as I realized that this was a lucid dream. I could have ended it by opening my eyes. But I didn't. I fixed my gaze intently on the darkness before me and I manifested the familiar comforting image of my ancestress in her white cotton cloth gown holding the sword in one hand and the conch shell in the other. Then I answered. "You are much more knowledgable than Ada, you miserable creature. She misunderstood my words, but you know what I meant. It is not the new technology itself that holds the hope for humanity. It wasn't the Ice Age technology itself that created the miracle of the prehistoric awakeing that enlightened our Paleolithic ancestors. It was the extraordinary, unexpected, imaginative new uses that some creative humans found for that technology back then. It was the artist creating the

402

astounding and inspiring image of a spirit stag upon a cave wall using a substance, the body paint that had originally been created for the practical run-of-the-mill purpose of protecting the skin against insect bites. That was the use of the available technology in new, imaginative surprising ways. It was the budding musician who learned to play a song by twanging the string of a bow which had been created to kill. That was the use of the available technology in new and imaginative ways. Some practical men invented computers to aid in running business. Their original tools were confusingly imposing and never meant to be used by anyone but the annointed priests of the modern technology. Other men took that tool and changed it, simplified it, made it user-friendly, and placed it in the hands of common people. They took it and made it available to those who could then turn around and use it to storm the stronghold of the Mad Men. Yes it is true that this powerful tool is also in the hands of those who are slaves of their own colonized mentality, and they are very deadly and dangerous. But I have hope in humankind because humankind is now entering a powerful new era of rebirth. We are still just discovering all the creative, constructive ways of adapting the available technology to bring rhythm into our collective heartbeat and save our species. We have the power to defeat the forces of negativity that manipulate and inspire the slaves who populate retrograde human movements like ISIS, and I fully expect us to win. I fully expect us make the magic painted on the new cave walls to jump off those walls and aid in our recovery. I fully expect us to beat you!" He did not speak again that night.

16. INTOLERANCE

On the evening of Wednesday, August 18 1982 we camped just north of the city of Pittsburgh. We could clearly see the lights of the suburbs in the distance as we wrapped ourselves in our bedrolls inside our tent. We camped not far from the riverside property of the Verona Canoe Club. I lay in the dark wondering if I would again fall asleep and have strange dreams but that did not happen that night. Instead I rested confortably for about an hour before slipping into a calm dreamless sleep. As I lay there before I dozed off I thought of the experiences I had during this trip. In particular recalled the image of Chief Hatuei as he had looked when he appeared to me that night at our campsite next to Kinzua Dam. I thought the tragic death of Hatuei was an inevitable result of the mentality that controlled those Spanish men of the year 1511. An important factor that motivated them to kill him was their religion.

And yet religion is only the natural derivative of historic spiritual tradition. Many modern-day Indigenous people attempt to perceive a separation between religion and the traditional spiritual folkways of their Native cultures. All Religious thinking evolves from spiritual thinking. To imagine a sharp separating demarcation between religion and spirituality is simplistic.

One has to admit that the religion of the men who were conquering Hatuei's land had given them the authorization to take the actions that they took. It gave them an excuse. Their religious leader, the Pope, had issued official permission for them to forcibly subjugate the people that they met in the Americas. Their actions were raised to the level of sacred acts and, in a sense, actions which would normally be perceived by a sane mind as senseless and unconscionable were made acceptable and even ethical. This phenomenon is not rare or difficult to encounter. It has happened many times throughout the course of history. But it is a mistake to simply blame their religion for everything they did. The argument that the actions of those men were just the natural product of their era and their religion, and that anyone under the same circumstances would have behaved in the same way is not a valid one. The fact is that there were a number of people of the same country, upbringing and religion living at that time who vigorously objected the actions of those men. Among these was the monk Fray Bartolome De Las Casas who shared the same religion and nationality of the murderers of Hatuei but did not agree with his execution. So it is obvious that having been born in that era, of itself, did not make those men heartless. You could be of that era, of that nationality and have a heart.

The fact is that the most important reason Hatuei was burned at the stake by those men was because his rebellion represented a dangerous obstacle to the attainment of their goal of achieving complete control of the land, resources and inhabitants of the region they had recently discovered.

So religion was only an excuse and the Pope's authorization of these men's violence was used by them for their own purposes more than creating a true spiritual crusade. It is not religion itself that creates the evil of the Fifth Sun era. It is the manipulation of this powerful human experience which is the legacy of an extremely profound and ancient heritage of human behavior, a heritage of human behavior that, for better or worse is now hard-wired in the human psyche after thousands of years of consciousness evolution. Spirituality and its offspring, religion, are a fundamental element of the human experience. There is a reason why absolutely every human community on the earth practices some sort of spiritual tradition. Not withstanding the earnest and forceful objections of atheists all over the world, humans are born spiritual. It is part of what we are.

In the current Taino Resurgence Movement we are struggling with the meaning of what it really means to be a spiritual person in this era. Unfortunately (and inevitably) there is a very vociferous element of our movement that is still so ensnared by the deception of the demons of the Fifth Sun that they confuse typical intolerant prejudice for spiritual zeal. This is the oldest confusion of religious thinking. It is the conviction that since "I just know that my belief is the right one a different belief held by someone else MUST BE A LIE, and probably evil". Of course this is precisely the justification used by the Spanish conquistadores who murdered Hatuei. After all, they believed in the "one true God", and Hatuei was a pagan who believed in "false idols". There are now Tainos who confidently post outrageous indictments on current Facebook group pages which condemn the belief of fellow Tainos just because they don't believe the same way. Tainos who don't agree with their belief are condemned as "traitors" to their race and even seen as the "enemy".

Facebook now glows with the presence of Taino group pages where modern-day Tainos share important information about our resurgent culture. Individuals post informative material about obscure traditions still observed in remote regions of the Caribbean islands, traditions that hark back to an ancient Indigenous past and which almost vanished. These traditions now can again see the light of day and be adopted by the rest of the Tainos struggling to recover our past. On these Facebook group pages we discuss elements of our culture that were rubbed out by 500 years of oppression but that were originally recorded by colonial-era writers such as Ramon Pane. These discussions allow us to recover these lost traditions and again make them a relevant part of our twentyfirst century reality.

In the midst of this wonderful effervescence the ancient demon also rears his hoary head. In the waning weeks of the year 2015 I participated in a discussion in which a Taino woman complained about the way that Taino Christians are currently treated in these facebook pages. The fact is that there is an element in the internet Taino public that can not understand why a person now claiming Taino inheritance could also claim to be a Christian. They demand that anyone claiming to be Taino must also adopt and embrace ancient non-Chrsitian Taino spirituality. There is one particular influencial Taino leader who inceasantly hammers the page with posts that feature gruesome colonial-era wood-cut images of fifteenth-century Spanish Christian colonists chopping off the hands of Tainos who did not gather enough gold in the allotted time. He also consistently posts similar images of Spanish Christian colonial slave-hunters using huge ferocious dogs to track down escaped Taino slaves, feeding the children of those slaves alive to the dogs, burning Taino leaders alive in huge bonfires in groups of thirteen to celebrate the number of people in the gathering of Jesus and his twelve apostles. These posts are accurate representations of real history, but they are used by this particular individual to then point an accusing finger at any modern-day Taino who still chooses to be a Christian. It is the classic, time-proven technique used by every manipulator in history to inflame emotions and create enmity toward people who the manipulator perceives as the "enemy". These tactics are easy to use and very effective and are the most effective weapon in this modern day of the ancient enemy, the REAL enemy, who dwells within our own hearts, the enemy that has followed us as humans throughout the past 5,200 years. This enemy is the great divider, the one who creates the rifts between modern humans that can then be used to destroy us all. Fortunately, the overwhelming number of modern Tainos is not swayed by this type of divisive tactic and understands that our Chrisitian Taino brothers and sisters are fellow tribespeople. They are not the enemy. They represent the legacy of 500 years of colonialism and deserve to be respected for their choice of spirituality in an age when non-judgemental freedom of spiritual choice is extremely important. There is no doubt that even in this era of Hope this demon still has the capacity to ultimately win.

Intolerance is not a little thing. It can inspire the most horrific acts of history. If it is skillfully manipulated by the Mad Men it can move men and women to some of the most inhuman of actions. Intolerance is the most important weapon of the timeless demon, and this era that we are living right now, this dawning of the new First Sun, is our opportunity to defeat it. This is true whether one is a Taino, or the member of any other ethnic, or religious or spiritual group on this earth.

17. HOMECOMING

As I mentioned earlier, Ada's words at the bus-stop on that chilly October morning in 2013 again brought back thoughts of Eddie and his son to my mind after all these years. If the twenty-something boy had not somehow escaped the environment in which he had been raised, he might very well be one of the faces that show up in that sad video that Ada told me about, filmed in the West End, urging the brawling girls to greater violence. The bus-stop conversation took me back again to the last time I spoke to Eddie in 1998, while I gathered up my stuff at the end of our performance in the auditorium of the Huntindon State Correctional Facility. I was still thinking about him as Ada and I boarded the bus. Then, later, as I sat in my seat and watched the buildings of the city float past my bus window on my way to work, I was taken back to a key episode of my life that took place just a few days after that prison-auditorium encounter with Eddie.

It was still November 1998. We left Huntingdon, Pennsylvania and travelled east. We had completed almost half of the prison tour. The performance schedule now took us to Graterford State Correctional Facility, in the suburbs of Philadelphia. Since we were so close to Philly, I had made plans to visit Shadow, the leader of the Caney Circle there. I planned to stop in at her house after the performance.

My visit with Shadow was brief because I also wanted to drop in, for the first time in my life, at the Puerto Rican barrio of North Philadelphia. I wanted to visit the wonderful community organization located there, called "Taller Puertorriqueño" which I had heard about for years. Later, during the decade of the 2000's, I would repeatedly visit and become very well-acquainted with this place, and even offer presentations and workshops there. But back in 1997 I had not been there yet. This would be my first visit.

I rushed to North Philadelphia after my visit with Shadow Wolf, but in spite of my best efforts, I wasn't able to get there in time. When I arrived, the sun had already set and the place was deserted. I got out of my van and walked around the area of the community center in the fading light of dusk, with its murals and sculptures. There was no one around. It was getting dark and I felt an urgency to get back to my motel room. Nevertheless, my curiosity was getting the better of me. I kept walking around the block admiring the wonderful mural imagery that graces the buildings, hoping to find somebody that I could talk to about the center. That's when I heard the pattern of steps behind me.

I realized that as I moved down the street, the footsteps behind me were keeping pace with my progress. They stopped whenever I stopped to look around the deserted street, and started up again when I began to walk. I cursed my stupidity of having walked so far from my vehicle and pushed my hand into the pants pocket where I carried my jack knife. Whoever it was that was following me was between me and the "Salsamobile", my blue Dodge touring van. I was forced to continue moving farther and farther away from it.

Then I broke into a run hoping to circle the block and return to my vehicle from the other side. I heard the steps behind me quicken, then they also began to run. I realized then that I was being chased by more that one person and I did not stand a chance of outrunning them. I looked behind me as I panted breatlessly. It was two men. I could not make out their faces in the dark twilight shadows. I began a headlong run pounding the sidewalk hard with my tennis shoes. I looked back again, one of them was coming at me along the sidewalk. The other one ran down the middle of the empty street, lit by the glare of the street lights. I turned the corner and into a side street. Then I dodged in between parked cars and spotted a big ten-wheeler freight truck parked up ahead with some stacks of cardboard piled up on wooden palettes next to it on the sidewalk. There were a couple of cars double parked just behind the truck and two consecutive street lights had burned out overhead, casting this particular area of the street in very dense darkness. It presented an attactive place to hide for me in my desperation. The truck was parked right in front of a couple of businesses that were already closed for the night.

"He went behind the truck, Ricky...He is behind that truck!" I heard a youthful voice cry out as I dodged deep into the darkness next to the big vehicle.

"No, man! he kep' on going. He shot out behind that car up there, and kep'on straight up the street!" I heard an older voice respond excitedly.

"No Ricky, man, I'm telling ya, he went behind the fuckin' truck!" The younger voice insisted.

"You dumb little faggot! You go back there behind that goddam truck if you wanna. I'ma catch that mutherfucker by myself. You hear me you little cabroncito!"

I heard the older man's accelerated footsteps run past the opening between the truck and the car in front of it where I was hiding. Then I heard the heavy breathing of the younger one approaching right behind.

I scooted behind a big trash dumpster and squatted in the reeking darkness, heavy with the odor of rotten garbage and stale urine, panting and out of breath. I was peeking around the side of the dumpster as my pursuer cautiously came around the side of the truck. He was silhouetted against the bright background of the lit-up street a block away.

He couldn't see anything behind the truck. It was too dark. I could make out a small caliber revolver in his right hand, but I could tell it was trembling. He took a few steps in the darkness toward the dumpster and then stopped to listen. I could hear my own heart-beat pounding in my head. Then he turned and called out, "Ricky, I'm telling you he's in here, he's in here!" The last words were more of a whine than an assertion.

He stepped forward a couple of steps into the darkness and said: "You in here you maricón sonnovabitch?" He took a few more steps, shoving the gun up ahead of him nervously. He repeated: "Are you in here?"

I stayed very still, very quiet. My fear began to turn into anger, Why did I have to be subjected to all this? The silhouetted figure turned around, exposing the side of his face to me. The light from the street lamp in the corner illuminated his face. He was a light-skinned Hispanic youth, his Philadelphia Phillies cap turned around sideways, thug-style, on his head. He wore a large "Fila" brand sweatshirt equipped with a hood, above his baggy low slung jeans.

It was a white boy! Maybe he was mixed with Anglo-American or maybe he was just a pure-blood descendant of the Spanish. But now, to me, he was just a young light-skinned ghetto junkie trying to get his next fix at my expense!

I began to simmer with rage. All the years of repressing my pent-up frustrations, all the years of cultivating a carefully constructed aura of progressive, socio-ethnic tolerance fell from around me like a discarded cape. All that was left was raw resentment. It was as if this young kid of white Spanish ancestry represented all the insult and hurt I had nursed since my adolescence. I thought of the white cops that roughed up Al Chee during my college years. I thought of the white vice principal who called me a "spic" in highschool. I thought of the white boys who tormented and bullied me in elementary school, who made me feel low and worthless. All those memories were now focused on that white-skinned kid.

"Look at that little white motherfucker, playing ghetto gangbanger on my time!" I thought, as my fingers fidgeted with the knife in my pocket.

"I ought to fix it so his drug-addict, welfare mamma'll find him right here in the street, bleeding."

My movements began to take on a life of their own. I was changing, transforming, right there as I crouched behind that garbage dumpster. I looked at the light-skinned boy. He lowered his right hand, the hand with the gun.

"His fucking Castillian ancestors probably chased mine all over the countryside back in the bad-old slave days. His great great great great gandaddy probably tried to sell my great great great great grandaddy to Big Jack to work in the Jamaican sugar cane fields."

The more I thought about it the more irrational I became. Suddenly just because of this light-skinned kid, all the sociopolitical issues of the world which irritated me were resolving themselves quite simply in clean unambiguous racial terms. "It's no-good Castillian-descendants like this guy who are helping to keep my people starving!" I began to perceive anyone with light skin as responsible for those who were dying in the shark-infested Florida Straits.

Then I began to think about brutality directed toward people of color in Pittsburgh, in Philadelphia, in New York, in Los Angeles, in the world! I thought of the white skinheads. I thought of the little pre-school victims of the racist Oklahoma City bomber. I thought of my paranoia that some day my teen-aged son might be picked on by some biased policeman like the two who had stopped Al Chee and me on the street that night when we were walking back to our college dorms in 1972.

My personal problems also became simple black and white issues. At that moment they were responsible for everything that was going wrong in my life, even my financial problems, my debts, everything! I felt like blaming these people for everything. Hell, it was <u>all</u> their fault!

My irrational anger was working itself to a frenzy. All of a sudden the young boy's light skin became the target of all my pent-up emotions, even my feelings of dispair about Eddie, in Huntingdon prison, and Eddie's young son in a prison of his own creation on the streets of the West End.

Suddenly I exploded from behind the garbage dumpster. Just as the boy turned to see me I struck him hard on the face with my fist. He fell backward. The gun went clattering loudly across the hard concrete and slid under the wooden pallet next to the truck piled high with a mountain of carefully strapped corrugated cardboard. With one motion I pulled out and opened the jack knife, and I leapt upon my fallen adversary. My knee landed on his groin and he grunted in excruciating pain. He was breathless and still groaning when I pressed the sharp blade of the knife to his throat.

"You're gonna die you little motherfucker. You've mugged your last victim!" I growled at him.

"No, no dude...Don't kill me. Oh God don't kill me...!" The boy cried out crazy with fear and pain. The more he pleaded the angrier I became. I jammed my knee into his groin a second time harder than before. Again he grunted loudly and screwed up his face in a terrible grimace. His hands went up instinctively and grabbed my sweater. But he didn't dare pull hard or struggle for fear that I was going to cut him. I kept the sharp blade pressed to his throat.

"Oh God mister pleeeeese let me go...please don't hurt me any more!" He whined, his steel grey eyes welling up with tears of pain.

"You were gonna be a big tough guy today, eh?" I laughed hysterically. "Right? You were gonna be the big tough white guy? You were gonna hurt me. What were you gonna do with that pop-gun, eh? Were you coming up to say hello, eh? eh? You little white sonnovabitch. Were you coming up to say hello?"

"I may be a dumb Cuban, I may not be all street-smart and ghetto like you with your thug cap turned sideways on your head, but I'm not stupid. I'm not your victim today!".

I felt giddy with power, and a hunger, such a ravenous hunger for revenge as I had never felt before.

I felt I had no control over my actions. There was a terrible compulsion within me. It pushed at the hand with the knife it made me visualize a neat red line along the contour of the boy's pale throat. I wanted to see that line. I wanted to see what it would look like, how would he react when I slit his throat?

The street was filled with my laughter. I could hear my laughter reverberating from the brick walls of the buildings around me. The laughter echoed inside my head. It vibrated inside my heart. I really could feel it in my heart! It was weird! I looked at the helpless boy beneath me. My laughter rose to a terrible crescendo.

The boy's braided gold chain, the bright red ruby pendant, slipped from his neck and dropped to the ground beneath him as I gripped his frilly collar tight. The ruffles on his rich handsome satin shirt-sleeves quivered as he felt the razor-keen edge at the tip of the blade against his throat. "Free them..." I yelled at the Galician.

At first the Spaniard rose slowly to one knee, terrified, riveted to the spot, staring at me helplessly as I held my sword to his son's neck. It had been easy to catch that kid. I heard his footsteps behind me as he rushed at me with his dagger drawn. I dodged, turned, snatched and twisted his arm violently with a quick jerk.

My long hours of fencing lessons under Don Fernando had paid off. The boy had cried out in pain just as his father, the Galician, struck Adriana senseless. Now I glared at the slave-hunter, his son under my blade. He glared back at me, fuming, but helpless... I HAD HIM!

"Free them!" I screamed, spittle frothing from my mouth. "Or, by heaven I will slit your son's throat from ear to ear and enjoy it!" I could see Adriana's unconscious form sprawled out behind him. He rose slowly, very slowly, rubbing his painful shoulder where Adriana had struck him with the rock before he knocked her unconscious.

"Don't harm him!" He said quietly as he reached for the key ring lying on the ground next to the corpse of his African slave. The black man had dropped it when he was shot. "Don't harm my son. I will do what you ask." He repeated.

"That's right you will do as I ask..." I echoed "You will do as I ask, Spaniard, WHITE MAN! I am the master now. You are the slave now. You will do as I ask, as I order...as I command, Spaniard, as I command!" The boy shivered violently beneath me. Jose kept his eyes fixed on me as he brought the keys up from his waist. He worked at Adriana's shackles first. She was still unconscious. As he worked, the jingle of his keys mixed with the loud dissonance of my baby's cries pouring out of the little one where he lay curled up in the arms of the Indian girl to my right.

The shackles fell from Adriana's limp ankle. Then he moved over to the three Indian girls. When he loosened their bonds they crawled up carrying the baby to Adriana, who was still lying there uncoscious, and began to gently revive her. Still staring at me the Spaniard now moved on to the young Indian boy. The minute he approached Mateo, the Indian boy threw himself angrily at the Spaniard and began to pummel him with his fists. The Spaniard fell back.

"Stop, stop, stop, stop...!" I screamed, the sword quivering in my hands. "Stop...curse you, or I'll get up from here and cut you with this blade!" Mateo ceased his attack and crumpled into a little fetal ball.

The Galician hauled himself up on one elbow and wiped the blood trickling from the corner of his bruised lip. He shook his head a couple of times, then he rose to loose Mateo's ankle.

"Now, the blacks..!" I pointed to the three Africans chained to the next tree. The three men chattered to each other in Yoruba as they watched the goings on.

"What are they to you? They are just a bunch of niggers. Let me take them back to their masters."

"NOW THE BLACKS...!" I repeated, screaming. I shook the terrified boy till he whimpered. The Galician freed the African escapees. The three men scampered to their feet. One of them ran into the forest and returned with Luis, uncoscious, in his arms. Another emerged with Alberto limping at his side. The third picked up the dead slave's spear and ran back to my side, the spear pointed at the Spaniard.

413

"I will give you gold if you let us go." Jose exclaimed. The African approached him, brandishing the spear threateningly at his chest.

"You will return to your wife a rich man!" He said pointing at his saddlebag on the other side of the clearing.

"That's my wife on the ground behind you, you animal!" I roared.

He paused and turned to look down at the fallen woman surrounded by the three girls still trying to revive her. Then he turned again to look at me.

"Very well…I understand your anger, but if you are a Christian, you will let us go for the love of Jesus." He exclaimed pleadingly. "Don't hurt my son.…"

I AM NOT A CHRISTIAN!" I screamed. I shook the boy again more violently than before. At that moment Adriana groaned. I looked past the Spaniard at my wife as she came back to life. The sound of the baby crying filled my ears. Adriana rose to a sitting position and rubbed her head. An ugly purple bruise swelled near her lip. She looked around and finally spotted me, squinting to bring my image into focus.

"What are you doing?" She exclaimed in a soft voice. She began to rise. She stumbled. When she stumbled, Jose started to move toward her but the African pushed him back unto his knees with the spear.

"What are you doing Santi?" Adriana asked again and made another attempt at rising to her feet. She finally stood on wobbly legs and took a couple of steps toward me.

"He is only a boy, Santi!" I stared into her big shiny brown eyes. Then I looked at the wretched creature in my grasp. Suddenly he was human. Suddenly I was no longer filled with rage and aggression. It drained out of me. I let go of the young boy. He scrambled to his feet and ran to his father. When he did that the Galician reached quickly into the folds of his jacket. He produced a long wicked-looking dagger, at the same time, pushing himself quickly up to a crouching position, sweeping away the spear pointed at his chest with his left hand, and throwing himself at me. I fell back, startled. The African holding the spear moved as swiftly as lightning. In an instant Jose lay transfixed, face-up upon the ground, his eyes wide. Blood oozed where the thick staff of the spear protruded from his chest. He coughed and blood sprayed from his mouth. He gurgled quietly.

The boy screamed and threw himself on the dying man. Jose quivered for an instant, then lay very still. I rose to my feet. The din of the baby's insistent cry blended with the cries of the young brown-haired boy.

I stood for a moment looking at the pitiful scene. The boy stroked his father's face repeating the word "Papa, papa, papa...!" I felt confused. One side of my consciousness still screamed for revenge, but every sob of the young boy twisted my stomach tighter. The cry of the baby pierced me like an arrow. The cry of the baby blended with that of the young white boy. The cry of my dark-skinned baby <u>was</u> the cry of the young white boy. They were the same cry. The cry of the young boy was akso my cry. A tight, bitter knot squeezed my entrails and turned my guts inside out.

I began to sob. I wept for the innocent boy who was as much a victim of his father's evil as my own baby was.

As I wept I looked around me and realized for the first time that I was living a bizarre waking dream, a kind of hallucination. I realized that at that particular moment I was no longer in the side street in North Philadelphia. I had somehow been transformed into Santi, transported to another place. I had become the "Santi" of my 1982 dream voyage. And yet for some curious reason it was not a strange feeling I did not find it unusual that I was no longer Miguel of 1997, but instead, a seventeenth century half-breed on a mission to save his family. My tears continued to flow but not only for myself, or Adriana, or the unfortunate boy who had just lost his father. I wept for other boys, boys like Elian Gonzalez, who lost his mother, boys who at that very moment found themselves floating in their flimsy rafts among hungry sharks in the Florida Straits. I wept for Eddy's boy, growing up without a father in the drug-infested squalor of what had once been Broadhead Manor, cheering at brawling school girls for the amusement of internet voyeurs. I wept for the young men struggling to send a little money home to their families in Mexico from the pittance they earned working in the restaurants of Pittsburgh. I wept for poor Arab boys and girls living the hell of refugee camps in the Middle East, growing up bitter and enraged, blinded by the slavery of their own colonized mind. I wept for boys forcibly recruited to fight in ethnic wars of west and central Africa. I wept for all the boys and girls lost in the darkness, who suffer all over the world. And I wept for the boy lying on the urine-infected concrete beneath me, a boy who had hoped to rob me of a few bucks, probably to feed his crack habit. I was weeping for all the boys and girls of the world who still groan under the weight of the enslavement of the Fifth Sun demon.

I had not wept in a long time. Now, I wept. As the tears rolled down my cheeks, I saw a flash of light before me, a large bright spot glowing before me. Suddenly my vision was filled with an image of a huge bird. Its wings beat majestically and thousands of crickets chirped as it rose into a bright sunlit sky, flashing its ruddy tail feathers in the solar glare.

I fell back on my haunches. The hand holding the knife fell to the side, freeing the light-skinned kid in the Fila hoodie. The great bird winged away into the bright spot. Then all was darkness and night again there next to the parked truck. I sat and watched as the boy picked up his Phillies cap and crawled slowly along the sidewalk away from me. He stared at me with terror in his grey eyes, his face flushed. When he felt he was at a safe distance he jumped up and ran down the street as fast as his legs could carry him. "You crazy muthafuckah, man! You crazy-ass Cuban muthafuckah!" He screamed as he ran away.

I knelt there, still dazed, still confused. The smell of danger filled my nostrils, but I could not move. I looked around me slowly trying to come to terms with my surroundings. I picked up the jackknife looked at it in my hand for a minute. Then I folded it and returned it to my pocket. I walked over to the pile of cardboard. It sat heavily on its wooden pallette. I stooped down and reached beneath it, searching for the little revolver. I couldn't find it. The cardboard pile on that palette was huge and heavy. I could not hope to move it very far. Only a fork lift could budge that thing. So I continued to search by pushing my hands under the palette as far as they would go.

Just when I was going to give up I touched something. I lowered my body down as close as I could to the ground and I grabbed at it and yanked at it. It did not feel like a gun. I grew curious. I pushed and reached as best I could till I had a good grasp on the object. Then I pulled. At first, slowly then more easily the object came out of hiding.

Eventually I stood by the pile of cardboard with an old ornamental sword in my hand. It was a cheap replica. It was a plain, quite inexpensive piece of wall decoration made of base metal that someone had cast off and forgotten. But to me, it was Caoba's sword brought to my hand in the darkness of the North Philadelphia barrio. Did a light-complected boy, who had inspired pure hate in my heart, unwittingly make a gift to me with a symbolic contemporary representation of Caoba's sword on a frightening November evening of 1997? And, for that matter, would two Taino women of the Resurgence Movement make a gift to me with Caoba's conch shell thirteen years later at the 2010 celebration of theTaino Awards event, while a young, modern-day magical, rap-artist, Guabonito-like, bruja, curandera looked on? Only Yaya, the Great Spirit knows the answers to these questions for certain.

I walked with the sword into the light of the street lamp and held it in the air. Near the hilt was an engraving of the word "Toledo". In the distance I heard the faint rhythmic strains of an urban Afro-Latin Santeria cadence. The beautiful sound of the distant drums was wafted to me over the city streets by a cool Autumn breeze. Woven into the intricate patterns of the drum beat I could make out the words of a chant dedicated to Ochun, the Yoruba Goddess of Love and Comppassion: "Ide were were nita Ochun, Ide were were nita yamme..." As I stood there the distant music began to change, to morph. It began to blend, and then slowly evolve into another cadence. This rhythm was the sound of a hollow log drum, the deep booming voice of a large Taino maiohuakan drum. The chant changed also. Now the words were no longer in the Yoruba language of Africa but in the original Taino language of my own native Caribbean island. The tune reminded me of the Cordon-dance melodies that I had heard wafting through the walls of my grandmother's house from next door in the1950's, the same melody that would dramatically surround me at the ceremony under the palm-thatched roof in Monte Oscuro during my 2014 pilgrimage to Cuba. As the chant rose in pitch and the drum-beat gained momentum, I heard the unmistakable sound of a guamo, a conch-shell trumpet booming in the distance, I stood there with the sword in my hand, and I listened to it...

And I listened to it...

On the afternoon of Thursday August 19, 1982 Sven and I arrived at he confluence of the Allegheny and Monongahela rivers in Pittsburgh. The triangle formed by these two rivers as they flow together at an angle into the Ohio River is locally known as "The Point". There is a beautiful tree-lined, public green space that covers the triangle of land created there at that spot. The park is called, appropriately enough, "Point State Park". That was the end of our journey. We had arrived at our destination. We were home!

Behind me lay over two hundred miles and almost two full weeks of river adventure. Before me lay decades of momentous life decisions and unimagined spiritual challenges, the resurgence of my Taino people, and, with the help of Yaya the Great Spirit, the resurgence of all humankind.

On the left bank of the river, standing on the rim of the Point State Park, my young bride, Leni, stood waiting with our three-year-old son, Cha. I rose from the woven-cane seat and knelt upright in the canoe as we approached the river's edge, and I blew four triumphant blasts from a conch shell guamo that I had carried all the way down the river. In my water-proof knapsack at the bottom of the canoe lay the finished version of my new song, "Grafito".

Printed in the United States
By Bookmasters